Globalization and Social Change

Globalization and Social Change challenges conventional thinking regarding the inevitability of globalization. Rather than seeing globalization as "the end station of capitalism," it presents the development of this phenomenon as a disruptive and conflicting process. It considers the capacity of the state as the agent behind the implementation of the neoliberal project and discusses the potential for resistance and alternatives to globalization.

This volume's excellent panel of international contributors examines the question of globalization from many angles, providing a fresh perspective on this influential movement. Rather than the exclusive interaction of economic actors on the world scene, globalization is perceived as the socio-economic strategies and policies which prioritize market forces at the expense of social sectors and social cohesion. Subjects addressed include the dynamics of labor; the effects of globalization in India, South Korea, and Thailand; regional polarization as the result of global capitalist integration; and the interaction of Western and non-Western knowledge traditions. The book also considers Gramscian, regulation theory, culturalist, and Marxist approaches to globalization.

This thought-provoking volume is essential reading for all those interested in the development of and the potential alternatives to globalization. It is of particular value for students of politics, international political economy, and development studies.

Johannes Dragsbaek Schmidt is Research Fellow in Social Science and International Development and **Jacques Hersh** is Professor of Development Studies and International Relations, both at the Research Center on Development and International Relations, Aalborg University, Denmark. Their previous joint publications include *Social Change in Southeast Asia* (co-edited with N. Fold) and *The Aftermath of "Real Existing Socialism" in Eastern Europe*.

Routledge advances in international political economy

Globalization and Social Change

Edited by
**Johannes Dragsbaek Schmidt
and Jacques Hersh**

London and New York

First published 2000
by Routledge
11 New Fetter Lane, London EC4P 4EE

Simultaneously published in the USA and Canada
by Routledge
29 West 35th Street, New York, NY 10001

Reprinted 2002

Routledge is an imprint of the Taylor & Francis Group

Typeset by The Running Head Limited, Cambridge
Printed and bound in Great Britain by
Biddles Short Run Books Ltd, Kings Lynn

British Library Cataloguing in Publication Data
A catalogue record for this book is available from the British Library

Library of Congress Cataloging in Publication Data
Globalization and social change / edited by Johannes Dragsbaek Schmidt and Jacques Hersh.
    p.   cm.
  Includes bibliographical references and index.
  1. International economic integration. 2. Globalization. 3. Social change. I. Schmidt,
Johannes Dragsbaek, 1960– . II. Hersh, Jacques.
  HF1418.5.G58174 2000
  303.44—dc21   00–036773

ISBN 0–415–24171–5

Contents

Figures and tables

Figures

Tables

Contributors

Samir Amin, Research Institute, Third World Forum, Dakar, Senegal, West Africa.

Amiya Kumar Bagchi, Center for Studies in Social Sciences, Calcutta, India.

Martijn van Beek, Department of Ethnography and Social Anthropology, Aarhus University, Denmark.

Manfred Bienefeld, School of Public Administration, Carleton University, Canada.

Ellen Brun, Research Center on Development and International Relations, Aalborg University, Denmark.

Barry K. Gills, Politics Department, University of Newcastle, United Kingdom.

David Harvey, Department of Geography and Environmental Engineering, The Johns Hopkins University, Baltimore, United States.

Jacques Hersh, Research Center on Development and International Relations, Aalborg University, Denmark.

Joachim Hirsch, Johann Wolfgang Goethe-University, Frankfurt am Main, Germany.

Andrew Jamison, Department of Development and Planning, Aalborg University, Denmark.

Mark Juergensmeyer, Global and International Studies at the University of California, Santa Barbara, United States.

Philip McMichael, Department of Rural Sociology, Cornell University, United States.

Anne Showstack Sassoon, School of Social Science, Kingston University, London, United Kingdom.

Johannes Dragsbaek Schmidt, Research Center on Development and International Relations, Aalborg University, Denmark.

Kwang-Yeong Shin, Department of Sociology, Hallym University, South Korea.

Preface

The contributions to this volume are the combined result of an International Conference and a number of seminars and workshops organized by the Research Center on Development and International Relations (DIR), Aalborg University, Denmark, on the theme of Globalization and Social Change. The following topics were addressed: (1) Globalization and social change: the intellectual problem; (2) Critical perspectives on politics; (3) International political economy: crisis and transformation in East Asia; (4) Disharmony and potential conflicts in the post Cold War era; and (5) Resistance and alternatives to globalization. This book is similarly divided into five sections.

In their introductory chapter, the editors of this volume subject the globalization phenomenon and its accompanying avatar, neoliberalism, to a critical political reading. In the course of putting present-day capitalism in its historical context, they touch upon the controversy within the Marxian perspective, namely whether the global system is "simply" the manifestation of capitalism by other means or whether the transformation brought about by technological change has basically altered the *modus operandi* of capitalism.

Looking at the logic for resistance to the societal model offered by the dominant ideological and political framework, which has been generalized on the world scale, the projection is made that the hope of going back to the "golden age" of capitalism is based on an unrealistic conceptualization of the Keynesian welfare state. This era of political intervention in market mechanisms saved capitalism from self-destructing. Anti-systemic movements have therefore to look beyond the alternative of defensive counter-movements and must offer a fundamental rupture from the status quo while maintaining the struggle for preservation of the interests of the underprivileged.

In Part I, David Harvey takes a critical position to the Marxian approach with regard to the geographical dynamics of capital accumulation and class struggle. He views globalization as involving three major shifts: (1) financial deregulation, (2) financial revolution, and (3) reduction of the costs of moving commodities and people. This raises the issue of "What's to be done?" in the new context. What are the types of organizations and politics needed to take up the challenge that is posed by the new situation?

Samir Amin treats the concept of regional polarization as the outcome of the global integration into the capitalist system. This evolution leads to "global disorder," arising from a triple failure: (1) new forms of political and social organization—i.e. beyond the nation-state—have not evolved as demanded by the new requirement of the global system of production; (2) new economic and political relationships reconciling the rise of competitive peripheral zones in Asia and Latin America with the pursuit of global growth have not emerged; and (3) the African periphery, which is not engaged in competitive industrialization, has been marginalized. These global failures are behind the problems found in the European context (particularly with the incorporation of Eastern European states).

Manfred Bienefeld follows up on the issue of development in the Third World. Three main conclusions are offered: (1) Globalization was a general attack on the quality of peoples' lives through the 1980s despite the fact that some groups and a few countries, mainly in Asia, were able to protect themselves. (2) The neoliberal policies of the period have intensified this general trend by exposing weak, divided, and often heavily indebted societies more intensively to competitive pressures emanating from an unstable and deeply contradictory global economy while simultaneously undermining their capacity to manage the resulting challenge in a nationally coherent and effective manner. (3) The proposed solution must involve the creation of political entities that are both cohesive and powerful enough to manage the centrifugal forces of unregulated markets and the risks of global interdependence.

In Part II, Anne Showstack Sassoon discusses the tendency to underestimate the complexity of globalization and to formulate valid questions as to the possibilities and limits imposed by the international level on political intervention. The author notes that the value of bringing Gramsci's framework into the analysis of globalization is that his contribution established concepts and methods which are of relevance in conceptualizing the present historical moment. The guideline for progressive politics is to make use of the results of political science but also to understand that effective reality is never a given but depends on what has been built. Both methodologically and especially politically, it is of importance to avoid considering globalization as a self-fulfilling prophecy in which space for progressive politics is foreclosed.

The chapter by Andrew Jamison examines the interactions of Western science and non-Western knowledge traditions. The relationship has been ambivalent to the extent that during the nineteenth and twentieth centuries, Western science spread around the world either as part of the imposition of colonial rule or as part of the development of modern scientific and educational institutions. During this process, non-Western knowledge traditions were banished in some places while they continued to exist in others, even though receiving little if any support from government or imperial authorities. After independence, two approaches could be observed: a traditionalist trend to revive the pre-colonial past in a more or less unadulterated form, and an integrative tendency seeking to combine elements of indigenous traditions in one or another developmental framework.

All liberation struggles in the Third World experienced tensions between the two approaches, which are still present in most developing countries. At issue is the question of what is the most appropriate way to develop "non-Western" ways of doing science.

Joachim Hirsch offers a frame of reference for the applicability of regulation theory to a general analysis of the international-nation-state-systems, their inter-relations and their transformations. The discussion refers to how changing patterns of dominance and dependency within the "world order" can be analyzed. A shift in political priorities has been decisive for the failure of the regulatory models based primarily on the Keynesian welfare state; the so-called "security state" seems to be superseded by a new type of capitalist state, the "national competitive state." This is a type of state which concentrates on the mobilization of productive forces in order to face international competition while setting aside the former politics of materially based social and political integration. It is the victory of doctrines of neoliberalism which provided the ideological basis for this transformation.

In Part III, the focus of attention is on the evolution of the domestic socio-economic and political contexts of (East) Asian capitalist development as related to the global political economy. Amiya Kumar Bagchi discusses the complexities of globalization as a process and as a policy stance. Globalization is seen as implying increasing integration with implications for economic management. The characteristic aspects of the process, such as the growth of trade, growth of foreign direct investments (FDIs), patterns of labor movement, and GDP growth in South Asia in relation to the East and Southeast Asian experiences, are given attention. Bagchi stresses that India is no newcomer to external influences and impact. From independence until the 1980s, India implemented a type of pro-tective governed market economy. Consequently, planning of resource utiliza-tion was implemented while the power and socially damaging behavior of foreign capital and monopolies was curbed through regulation of the private and public sectors, the allocation of investment and finance as well as control of foreign funds. The policies behind the promotion of globalization were officially adopted in 1991. The different aspects of the process show the relationship between internal decision-making—catering to internal interests—and external economic influences such as the IMF. Bagchi criticizes the adoption of neoliberalism by confronting these economic policies with classical economic theories.

Kwang-Yeong Shin discusses the effects of globalization on the politics of South Korea in a comparative perspective. As the author shows, the responses to global change differ from country to country. In East Asia, contrary to a widely held opinion, globalization hampered the emergence of democracy in the 1980s and 1990s by undermining the strength of the labor unions and democratic social forces. In the case of the Korean political transition, the author notes that under the impact of globalization, capital replaces the authoritarian state in initiating anti-labor propaganda and controlling democratization. Thus, the capital logic of competition and accumulation has become hegemonic with the help of the developmental state even after the democratic transition. The analysis draws out some of the issues behind the financial and economic crisis which touched South Korea in the summer of 1997. What we are seeing is a weakening of the state and a strengthening of capital, which after the crisis will include a greater degree of foreign capital.

Johannes Dragsbaek Schmidt focuses on the paradox whereby the official discourse in Thailand presents itself as supportive of a small public sector, an open economy, and the blessings of the market, while on the other hand major popular pressures are entering the political arena with demands for welfare provision and social security. The weakening of authoritarianism translates into a "soft" restructuring of the "Thai-style" strong developmental state into a more welfare-oriented political entity giving priority to a more redistributive public sector. The chapter discusses the social welfare debate from a structuralist political economy perspective by first focusing on the Asian–Western controversy on the question of entitlements. The chapter also considers existing independent impacts of states on social welfare policies in Thailand and lastly explores the class nexus between labor rights and labor market regulations.

In Part IV, potential intersocietal conflicts are examined from a geo-political and geo-economic angle as well as from a civilizational approach. Philip McMichael argues that globalization is a political project pursued by a global managerial elite, with contradictory features and ultimately an unrealizable ideal as it is both socially and environmentally unsustainable. Globalization targets the nation-state and its policies of social regulation which have fettered profitability. The two principal constraints on profitability have been the wage relation and the system of capital control associated with the Bretton Woods regime. With the rise of global productive capacity together with a global money market, these restrictions came under severe attack. This leads McMichael to focus on the reality of capital as a social relation, which implies that the restructuring of capital cannot but have a parallel impact on labor; secondly, if globalization is seen as an institutional phenomenon it has to be realized that it is transforming the conditions of governance. As labor rights are diminished by the political project of globalization, there is an increasing gap between governance of the market and governance of the population.

In his chapter on conflictual trends in the international setting, Jacques Hersh discusses the apparent paradox that exists in the capitalist globalization of the world and the eruption of conflicts and contradictions on many levels. The notion of "Clash of Civilizations" is critically discussed and the author offers an understanding based on international political economy, thus countering the culturalist interpretation of contradictions and conflicts. These are seen as principally a function of the inequalities and polarization created under globalization which accentuates dormant contradictions. The insecurity and instability which results from this state of affairs are thus related to the division of the world between "haves" and "have-nots" which is untenable because of increased tensions, especially as new players emerge who will challenge the position and wealth of the Western world. The attempt to create a New World Order under such circumstances is more than problematical.

The chapter by Mark Juergensmeyer proceeds to discuss the global issues of social and political unrest from a "culturalist" perspective. In his view, civilizations do exist, but to a great extent the disorders in the world are caused less by their clashes than by widespread dissatisfaction with them all. The alternative outcomes will be either global cultural anarchy or global cultural consensus in a new worldwide civilization, or both at the same time. In the emerging world society, the question is not whether Modernism will triumph but whether any civilization will survive at all. Four options for world order are suggested: (1) Fortress Modernica; (2) the North vs. the South; (3) regionalism—global Balkanization; and (4) global civilization. Even though the last option is to be preferred, we are reminded that this might not be a formula for peace, as throughout history some of the most vicious wars have taken place within civilizations.

Following along the line of refusing the imposed determinism of TINA, Barry Gills analyzes the elements required for a politicization of the globalization debate. The terms of the discussion have to be changed and its intellectual and political direction altered. The understanding and mere critique of transnational neoliberalism have to be transgressed by focusing on the theorization of the "politics of resistance" and the analysis of the configuration of social forces upon which state power ultimately rests. The counter-attack against neoliberal ideas of globalization and their advocates should concentrate on political aspects, as opposed to the more "technicist" and definitional arguments. The author proposes that the term "globalization" be redefined as "neoliberal economics" in order to bring out its meaning. The revalidation of progressive alternatives to neoliberal globalization must begin by putting people back into the analysis as actors and agents in the processes of social change and historical evolution.

In his contribution, Martijn van Beek takes aim at the sensitive dichotomy between the anti-development discourse found in some circles in especially advanced countries and the people's expectations and wishes at the local level in a Third World country. When looking more closely at social movements, questions arise as to the goals of "the people" who are being mobilized or represented and more specifically about the convergence between activists' ideas and popular ideas. The crucial problem is less with the diagnosis of why movements, resistance, or responses emanate from "civil society," but whether they represent resistances and if so to what? The empirical study of Ladakhis' expectations questions the over-idealizing of social movements in the context of an anti-developmental paradigm. The author warns against easy generalizations and emphasizes the need to come to grips with the voices expressing pro-developmental sentiments and not silencing them or considering them as expressions of false consciousness.

In the last contribution, Ellen Brun explores the possibility of developing a radical alternative to the capitalist mode of functioning, especially in advanced industrialized countries. In her view, the challenges of the socio-economic and ecological crises related to the globalization of capitalism make new thinking imperative. A central element behind the needed transformation is the concept of a "citizen wage" which is discussed by including the difficulties and possibilities of eventual implementation. This would require a radical departure from what has been known as the Welfare State, which has shown a tendency to be patriarchal and patronizing in the disbursing and administration of entitlements. In a society where a subsistence-based "citizen wage" guarantees material security independent of the labor market and the state, the "Welfare Society" with a more genuine sense of welfare and security could emerge. This type of new thinking represents a challenge to both the traditional labor movement as well as to market forces, and Ellen Brun calls for the adoption of a political platform which could incorporate these demands in the coming social struggles in Europe.

Acknowledgements

We are grateful to the editors of *Rethinking Marxism* and Guilford Press for giving us permission to publish a slightly revised version of David Harvey's contribution in this volume. This project has received generous funding from a number of sources. Here we would especially like to thank the Research Funding Committee of the Department of Development and Planning and the Chancellor of Aalborg University. Furthermore, the following Danish institutions have provided invaluable financial assistance: Research Council on Development Research, the Social Science Research Council, and the Center for Peace and Conflict Research. In addition, the Asia Research Center, Murdoch University, Western Australia supported financially one of the contributions.

We would also like to acknowledge the moral and intellectual contributions from a number of colleagues and friends at the Research Center on Development and International Relations, and a very special thanks goes to both Ellen Nyrup and Jytte Kongstad for their help in organizing the conference, to He He and Peter Trillingsgaard for their work in preparing parts of the manuscript. Last but not least, we want to express our warm gratitude to Marianne Hoegsbro for her patience with us and tireless effort in finalizing the manuscript. A final comment is in order: the comments and analyses we present in our introductory chapter do not necessarily reflect the opinions of those mentioned above, nor those of the contributors or the funding agencies who provided support. The responsibility for that chapter rests entirely with us.

Introduction

Globalization or the coming-of-age of capitalism

Johannes Dragsbaek Schmidt and Jacques Hersh

Since the demise of Soviet-type socialism, a debate has been going on concerning the scope and nature of globalization. This can be understood as the expression of concern about the evolution of the capitalist world system now that there apparently does not seem to be any viable alternative.

The intention of this introductory essay is not to review the various interpretations of globalization, but to present a three-fold perspective of the problematique: (1) a critique of the neoliberal rhetoric; (2) a critical review of revised versions of neo-Keynesian policy recommendations; and (3) a political reading of the "highest" stage of capitalism, i.e. globalization.

The contributors to this volume all take a critical stance in their analysis of globalization and its accompanying neoliberal policy complex. Implicitly or explicitly, their common concern is to discuss the system-created social consequences and the need for resistance and for alternatives. In this respect, dissidents of globalization face a dilemma: on the one hand identifying sources of resistance and offering support to the politics of opposition, while on the other hand realizing the context and limitations of everyday struggles imposed by the socio-economic system which sets the criteria and options of resistance. Implicitly this creates an essential distinction between antisystemic alternatives and defensive resistance struggles. This is a predicament with which most authors are familiar. Although unable to offer clear-cut conclusions and guidelines, this is a discussion whose time has come and we as editors feel that the diversity of the analyses in this volume represents a positive contribution to the conceptualization of globalization and the counter-movements and tendencies.

Situating capitalism "sans frontières"

In contrast to the fate of "real existing socialism," the dynamic of capitalism has reached a point of maturity which makes understanding both the strength and limitations of this mode of production necessary. As discussed above, this should not be considered exclusively as an academic exercise. The endeavor of visualizing the future of the world by taking stock of the present can hardly remain neutral and value-free. As pointed out years ago neutrality in the social sciences is neither possible nor worthwhile (Myrdal 1968: 39ff.). This does not mean that social sciences have no usefulness. Rather, what is at issue is the choice of priorities and methods employed in the analysis. In this respect, since capitalism has been in existence for centuries, a historical approach, not exclusively as a tool of analysis but as a mode of thought seems appropriate in trying to conceptualize the evolution of the world. This cannot but have epistemological consequences because, as Robert Cox points out, "history is a form of knowledge which combines past, present and future; it is a particular way of thinking about the human situation in its entirety" (Cox 1999: 394). From this point of view, it may be argued that although other domains of social sciences can make positive contributions to the understanding of human activities, their relevance should be judged in the light of their contribution toward a holistic comprehension; in the last instance this is facilitated by history as a form of knowledge. In other words, there is a need for transcending the inherited nineteenth-century distinction between the different institutionalized social sciences which expressed itself in separate disciplines: economics for the study of the markets, political science for the study of the state, and sociology for the study of civil society. These separations no longer make intellectual sense (Wallerstein 1999: 400).

With such a frame of reference in mind it is somewhat puzzling to observe the degree of commotion the concept of "globalization" has released. This buzzword has become "a label that is presently in vogue to account for peoples, activities, norms, ideas, goods, services, and currencies that are decreasingly confined to a particular geographic space and its local and established practices" (Rosenau 1997: 360).

This state of affairs, however, cannot be entirely ascribed to present-day capitalism. What the world is experiencing is the outcome of the historical evolution of a globalizing social system and mode of production which from the very beginning organized the world spatially and geographically as well as compressing time and space (see David Harvey, ch. 1 this volume). In this connection, if there is one thing which history shows it is that the development of capitalism from the very outset depended on establishing contact and relations with extra-European regions of the world. Awareness of the importance of this element was acknowledged by both Adam Smith and Karl Marx from different perspectives. According to their conceptualization of capitalism, the system would not have evolved as it has without an international division of labor made possible by access to external markets and raw materials. In relation to the problematique of globalization, a rereading of the *Communist Manifesto* reveals a high degree of prescience in the description of the dynamics of the capitalist social system and its constant striving to revolutionize its environment:

> Modern industry has established the world-market, for which the discovery of America paved the way. This market has given an immense development to commerce, to navigation, to communication by land. This development has, in its turn, reacted on the extension of industry; and in proportion as industry, commerce, navigation, railways extended, in the same propor-

tion the bourgeoisie developed, increased its capital, and pushed into the background every class handed down from the Middle Ages.

(Marx and Engels [1848] 1958: 35)

Regardless of the realization of the dynamics behind capitalist development that could be identified at the time, there is a wide range of controversies surrounding present-day capitalism and the prospects for its evolution. One suggestion within the Marxian tradition identifies globalization as the latest epochal shift of capitalism. This approach is predetermined on a periodizing of historical capitalism into four distinct phases: (1) the age of discovery and conquest characterized as the epoch of mercantilism and primitive accumulation; (2) the birth of industrial capitalism, the rise of the bourgeoisie and the establishment of the nation-state; this was the age of revolution, capital, and empire as analyzed by the historian Eric Hobsbawm; (3) the emergence of corporate (monopoly) capitalism and the financial industrial corporation, inter-imperialist conflicts resulting in World War I, followed by the Bolshevik Revolution as an attempt to create an alternative socialist system and mode of production; (4) the current epoch of capitalism (globalization), characterized technologically by the "information age" (microchip and the computer) and politically by the demise of socialism as a societal system (Burbach and Robinson 1999: 11).

It is especially around the interpretation of the present phase of capitalism that disagreement has become quite heated among social scientists of Marxist orientation. The argument revolves basically around two positions. The first sees globalization as the continuation of capitalism by other means—in other words seeing the basic dynamics and mode of functioning of capitalism as not having fundamentally changed. The second position argues that the transformation brought about by technological changes has altered the mode of functioning of capitalism as well as the forms of struggle which the new technology offers (Sivanandan and Wood 1997: 19–32).

The politics of globalization

Although not wishing to participate in the specificities of this debate concerning the divergent views on the present phase of global capitalism, the point that needs to be stressed is that economic and technological influences also played a determining role during the previous epochs of capitalism, but that in the last instance the epochal shifts were nevertheless principally the expression of political processes. This is quite evident as far as the creation of the world economy and international division of labor is concerned. But this was also the case in the establishment of national market economies which required, as Karl Polanyi showed, large-scale political initiatives. On the one hand, there was the tearing down of old institutions and arrangements that had previously regulated local and regional markets. Rules and customs which impeded the movement of labor, goods, services, capital and—not least—prevented the commodification of land had to be removed. On the other hand, the state came to displace, through political means, the pre-capitalist arrangements with new institutional mechanisms of control: bodies of property, contract, labor, corporate laws, and regulations on competition. According to this interpretation, the construction of national market economies rather than industrialization was the determining element in the process (Polanyi [1944] 1957). However, it is necessary to keep in mind that there were differences in the way the European nation-states developed as well as in the vitality of national capitalist formations. In a discussion on the rise of capitalism and the nation-state, Ellen Meiksins Wood offers an interpretation based on certain assumptions which can be contrasted with the present apparent process of globalization. Some of the main presuppositions are:

> that capitalism was not simply the natural outcome of certain transhistorical processes like technological progress, urbanization, or the expansion of trade; that its emergence required more than the removal of obstacles to increased trade and growing markets or to the exercise of "bourgeois" rationality; that while certain European, or Western European, conditions, not least the insertion of Europe in a larger and non-European network of international trade, were necessary to its emergence, those same conditions produced diverse effects in various European, and even Western European, cases; and that the necessary conditions for the "spontaneous" or indigenous development of a capitalist system, with mutually reinforcing agricultural and industrial sectors, existed only in England.
>
> (Wood 1999: 3)

When considering the present-day globalization discussion, it is worthwhile to reflect upon whether there is an analogous process at work leading toward a breakdown of the structure of national market economies by forces trying to give priority to the global market economy with little consideration to the social costs such a transformation might bring about in the different entities. In other words, a sort of "Second Great Transformation" (Robinson 1995: 373) which this time would entail a shift from a world economy characterized by economic intercourse between different national market economies—each with its own regulatory and distributive arrangements—to a global market economy governed through a single set of rules and regulations. If this were the case, it would involve the transformation of the various "national social structures of accumulation"[1] which historically were determined by the socio-political processes in each country and their replacement by a uniform "global social structure of accumulation." It should be noted however that domestic economies in the past operated in the context of international arrangements. But in the present context the relationship would involve a greater subservience of the national to the international level. What kind of political processes does this perspective involve? Would the decoupling of the state from the national body politic and its devolution into a transmission belt for the institutionalization of globalization not have disturbing domestic social consequences in the various societies? Have the national foundations of capitalism been so weakened that contradictions between countries and classes have disappeared or are in the process of disappearing? There is little doubt that such an ideal-type projection is not yet around the corner, although it is forcefully promoted by neoliberal ideologues and proponents of the so-called "Washington Consensus."[2]

The neoliberal discourse on globalization is being propagated by what has been called a transnational elite with its base in the corporate world of business, international financial institutions, universities and research institutes, the media, etc. The case for globalization is presented as a process driven not by politics and people but predetermined in large measure by economic laws and technological innovations. In other words, outside the realm of politics. For good measure, the rhetoric of neoliberalism usually conveys a message of irreversibility. Consequently, the TINA syndrome ("There Is No Alternative") contributes to sentiments of insecurity and anxiety at the societal level as well as fatalism at the political level.

According to the neoliberal interpretation, one of the most significant assumptions is that "globalization" denotes a decrease of the importance of old preoccupations such as territoriality and the state. In this worldview the global market economy is projected to be one in which the distinct national economies are subsumed and reintegrated into the world system through market transactions and international processes of exchange as well as through the spread of the benefits of the technological revolution. This fits well with neoliberalism to the extent that the market is conceptualized as the dominant driving force of the world economy with the tacit implication that states need only adjust their macroeconomic strategies and policies to the demands of the market.

In fact, the similarity of policy-making in different countries does suggest that this is the area which seems to have been internalized by political elites. Following the so-called "economic counter-revolution," in which Keynesian economics was defeated and replaced by the monetarist and neoclassical paradigms in the 1970s, official international organizations and the political mainstream have been active in promoting variants of the same neoliberal recipe (Toye 1987). This can be grasped from the policy statements of the OECD and the WTO as well as from the conditionalities of the International Monetary Fund (IMF) and World Bank imposed on debt-ridden countries of the Third World and Eastern Europe or on the newly industrializing countries (NICs) of East Asia who experienced a financial crisis in 1997.[3]

As a consequence of neoliberalism as a strategy, we have seen the implementation of similar austerity policies by governments in OECD countries, shock therapy strategies in former state socialist economies, and structural adjustment programs (SAPs) in Third World countries. The paradox is that the recommendations are based on a one-size-fits-all model. Regardless of the level of development of the countries and the source of their difficulties, the recommended policy-measures show similarity: export-orientation, more market and less state social spending, free trade, deregulation, flexibility, privatization, and priority given to the fight against inflation in order to maintain price stability.

While these measures were encouraged (to use a mild expression!) through conditionalities, the question of full employment in industrialized societies lost its previous salience and was no longer the primary goal of policy-making. With regard to the Third World, the notion of development was replaced by the simplistic belief that the opening of the economy would bring about positive results and improvement in the economic situation. The modernization theory of growth has insidiously been replaced by the discourse of adjustment. There are no longer the same debates and discussions of economic strategies and social policies but instead prominence is given to the stabilization and the structural adjustment programs as determined by the IMF and the World Bank.

However, it should be recognized that states have not been innocent bystanders in this evolution. They were active participants in the reorganization of the national and international economic environment. From its source in the United States and Britain, the trend spread to Europe to be imposed on former socialist countries and on the Third World. Without the acceptance by Western governments of policies of deregulation, privatization, and liberalization of trade, multinationals and financial capital would not have acquired the hegemonic status and control of the world economy (Chesnais 1994: 23). In other words, politics played an important role in this evolution.

At the societal level, the "counter-revolution" in economic policies has altered the post-war social balance by reducing the bargaining power of labor under the guideline of tackling inflation. Deflationary macroeconomic policies during the 1980s and 1990s, together with changes in trade union laws and deregulation of the labor markets in the advanced industrialized countries contributed to shifting the social balance of forces in favor of capital, so discounting the gains made during the most productive era of capitalism. There is an ironic paradox in this evolution. The proponents of the neoliberal mantra and policy-making have claimed for themselves the role of saviors of the world from the forces of public ownership, bureaucracy, welfare states, and socialism. But as Eric Hobsbawm put it:

> In fact what they attacked was the reformed post-war capitalism which had produced the golden age that ended in the 1970s. They attacked the contradictions of the most successful phase of capitalism there has ever been, because even that generated its own crises; and they were themselves symptoms of these contradictions.
>
> (Hobsbawm 1991/1992: 18)

Keynesianism through a political prism

The architecture of the welfare state is of course being affected differently in various countries. Differences in the balance of social and political forces between proponents and opponents of the golden years affect the speed and scope of the dismantlement of the former social structure of accumulation. The fact that the logic behind this process appears to have been internalized by all countries allows a more sober evaluation of the Keynesian welfare state itself. The interesting aspect behind such a reconceptualization is that, in most cases, it has been political parties representing the working classes who traditionally were the agencies behind the implementation of social security, that have retreated to neoliberal positions to the extent that differences between, for example, a "Third Way" and a "Right Way" might not be self-evident. On the other hand, there is an argument to be made that instead of succumbing to the paralysis inflicted by the globalization process and the neoliberal discourse, the task of progressive political forces at the state level is to implement measures which improve the national economy's competitiveness and humanize the downsizing of the welfare system (see Anne Showstack Sassoon, ch. 4, this volume).

There is presently a tendency to take the era of the welfare state as the frame of reference for an ideal-type societal arrangement for highly developed capitalist formations. A certain nostalgia is expressed for the defense or return to the social market policies of that period. Without wishing to negate the positive social aspects of the "golden thirties," this position nevertheless demands a few comments.

Contrary to conventional wisdom, Keynesian macroeconomic strategies and policies which were implemented in the 1930s to stimulate industrial economies did not succeed in overcoming what had been the most threatening crisis to date faced by advanced capitalism. Historical evidence has shown that public spending and social welfare measures were not the major factors behind resolving the depression in the world's strongest economy. In fact, it was the mobilization related to the war effort in the early 1940s which put the United States back on the track of near full-employment (Baran and Sweezy 1966: 160–1). World War II, followed by the reconstruction of the war-torn societies in Europe and Japan, the Korean War, and military expenditures related to the Cold War with the Soviet Union did more than their share in contributing to the boom years which have been called the "golden age" of capitalism. In other words, left to its own devices the economic logic of capitalism leads to stagnation. This doesn't refute the fact that the Vietnam War, at a time of almost full employment, had the opposite effect—that is, of destabilizing the US economy and fueling the trend toward general inflation in the rest of the capitalist world.

The strong growth in the decades following World War II gave rise to optimism on all sides—even Richard Nixon declared himself to be Keynesian (Magdoff 1998: 3). The "new economics" was given credit for the prosperity of the period. However, the belief that capitalism had now found the mechanisms for self-generation was based on an assumption needing modification. As Harry Magdoff observed: "The notion of the 'Keynesian Welfare State' has tended to disguise the fact that what really turned the tide was not social welfare, Keynesian or otherwise, but war. In that sense the whole concept of Keynesianism can be mystification" (Magdoff 1998: 2).

This notwithstanding, the relatively well-functioning economies (especially those in Western Europe) permitted welfare policies, though not without the pressure of labor movements and social democratic parties. Elements behind the popular mobilization and willingness of the political and economic elites to accept the welfare state compromise were related to the historical memory of those populations whose frames of reference were the years of depression and war—as well as the existence of the socialist camp in Europe, which had given attention to social security during that time—although these societies were unable to match Western consumerism later on (Sklair 1991: ch. 8). Another contributing element in satisfying the demands of workers without challenging the social system and the maintenance of class differentiation was the tribute the colonial and post-colonial world paid through the unequal terms of trade (Emmanuel 1972).

Besides internal conditions, the international environment was also conducive to creating the conditions for the establishment of national structures of accumulation in the different industrialized countries of the Western world. There was a certain compatibility in the mutually reinforcing social, economic, and political institutions including domestic and international arrangements. Together with ideological and cultural components, this facilitated a successful regime of capital accumulation. The importance given to social institutions and conscious political intervention was able to alleviate the disruptive consequences of the international–national contradictions of pre-war capitalism.

In this context, Keynesian economic strategy was appropriate in creating a set-up which was beneficial not only to the working population but to productive capital as well. It cannot be stressed enough that during the Great Depression of the 1930s and World War II, as well as the difficult years of economic reconstruction in Europe, capitalism experienced its most serious challenge. Thus, under the impact of Keynesianism, a new lease on life was given to the system. This has led to the recognition that the post-war political project of social democracy actually saved capitalism. John Kenneth Galbraith (1997: 5) acknowledges this when he states that "the survival of the modern market system was in large measure, our accomplishment. It would not have so survived had it not been for the successful efforts of the social left . . . Let us not be so reticent: we are the custodian of a political tradition that saved classical capitalism from itself."

The fact that the labor–capital compromise could be implemented is a testimony of the viability of the system. In this regard it ought to be realized that the history of capitalism shows flexibility and that capacity for change and adaptability were essential features of the system (Braudel 1982: 433). Seen in this light, two different, although not mutually exclusive, readings of the Keynesian project can be made. One sees it as a tool of political and ideological compromises at a time when the survival of capitalism was at stake. With Keynesian economics, crisis-free capitalism was said to have been achieved! Another reading concerns the socio-economic dimension (i.e. the problematique of surplus absorption); by functioning as a demand primer, including social expenditures, Keynesian macroeconomics alleviated the tendency toward stagnation.

Furthermore it ought to be pointed out that the golden years were also characterized by the geo-politics and geo-economics of the US hegemonic system whose policies served to simultaneously reduce the problem of overproduction and overcapacity. As a consequence, this dominance was benevolent for Western

Europe and Japan. The bottom line was that the United States assumed a self-serving responsibility for the functioning of the capitalist world-system and in so doing allowed a certain amount of autonomy to its allies in giving them economic assistance in the first post-World War II period. It should however be noted that this benevolence was making a virtue out of necessity. The Cold War, as well as the balance of social forces in Europe during this period, dictated the strategy of the United States. The neutralization of anti-capitalist forces and promotion of pro-capitalist (and pro-American) political forces, especially in Western Europe,[4] encouraged the formation of historic blocs which made these countries more likely to adapt to the capitalist world economy under US hegemony. The "configuration of social forces upon which state power ultimately rests" permitted a certain internationalization of states (Cox 1987: 105–6). From having functioned as a buffer for the protection of domestic economies and societies, the state in the post-World War II era took the form of mediator between the constraints of the external level and accountability to internal social forces. In this process, according to Cox (1987: 254–5): "The centre of gravity shifted from national economies to the world economy, but states were recognised as having a responsibility to both."

Seen in the context of the systemic rivalry between the Soviet-dominated state socialist system and the US-dominated capitalist world, the social-democratic welfare state, by offering both security and consumerism, functioned as a window display for capitalism and weakened the ideological foundations of the proto-socialist discourse in the USSR and especially Eastern Europe as well as in Western Europe. In contrast, a similar function was fulfilled in Asia by the authoritarian capitalist development state which, with US acceptance and support, undermined so-called totalitarian self-centered socialism through the rapid industrialization of the NICs.

The return to capitalist normalcy

All in all, the trade-off between acceptance of the hegemonic system and the responsibility for the domestic welfare functioned rather well until the allies, following the reconstruction of their economies, became competitors to the United States who during these years had used a great deal of resources to make the world safe for capitalism. Within a relatively short time, a higher degree of competition entered the relationship between the industrialized countries, and the question of markets grew in importance as all economies tended to become export-oriented. In other words, regardless of the militarization of the international economy through defense expenditures, the hot wars on the Asian continent, foreign aid, and so on, the inherent problem of overproduction was returning. This is also nicely illustrated in the *Communist Manifesto*, the "epidemic of over-production" as an "absurdity" which is only conceivable under capitalism.[5]

The tendency toward increased competition at the same time as the introduction of expensive labor-saving technology with no corresponding increase in demand led to outlet problems. In addition, new producers with a cheaper production base were entering the world economy. The result has been a downturn in the growth rate of capitalist economies compared to that of the golden years. MIT economist Lester Thurow (1992: 17) wrote: "If one looks at the growth rate of the non-communist world, it slowed from 4.9 percent per year in the 1960s to 3.8 percent per year in the 1970s, and then again fell to 2.9 percent per year in the 1980s." According to World Bank statistics (2000: 184) the rate of annual growth of the GNP for 1990 to 1998 was 2.5 percent. There seems to have been an improvement since then. However, much of this growth was fueled by the buoyancy of the economy of the United States, which became the market of last resort. This cannot but be a temporary respite from the more general downward trend.

The trend toward slower growth made it difficult to sustain the historic compromise behind the welfare state as well as the employment levels of the golden years. In addition, the power relation between capital and labor had become potentially detrimental to the former. Related to this evolution had been the increase of the significance of financial capital and its delinking, relatively speaking, from the constraints of the real economy. During the years of high growth capitalism, there had been a much more balanced relationship between finance and production. In the Marxian scheme (M)oney was invested to buy labor, machinery, and raw materials to produce (C)ommodities which, when sold, yielded a greater amount of money (M^1). As this $M–C–M^1$ scheme didn't offer sufficient profitable investment opportunities in a situation of overproduction, the corporate world turned to financial ventures and speculation in order to bypass production and continue accumulation ($M–M^1$). The process, which started in the United States and spread later to other regions in the 1980s, was described in the following way by the editors of *The Monthly Review*: "Unable to find profitable productive investment opportunities in the face of excess capacity and flagging demand [the corporations] have been eager participants in the merger, takeover, and leveraged buyout frenzy that has swept the country in recent years, becoming in the process both lenders and borrowers on an enormous scale" (Magdoff and Sweezy 1987: 17). It was with this upsurge of finance capital that the offensive in all leading markets came about. The ideological discourse/rhetoric to back this up was one of favoring liberalization from government control, except, of course, when rescue operations for banks and other financial institutions were needed. A case in point has been the reaction to the various financial crises—from the Savings and Loans scandal in the United States to the Mexican default and last but not least the financial crisis in East Asia. But as noted by François Chesnais (1994), the process as well as the speed behind it could not have been the same without the active acquiescence of politicians and state bureaucracies.

The duality of resistance

Seen in the light of the above discussion, it is clear that twenty-first century capitalism—whether called globalization or not—will inherit a set of unresolved contradictions created by the dynamics of this socio-economic and political system. When put this way, the implication is that it might be more fruitful to consider globalization as the culmination of a process rather than as a rupture. It may be no more than capitalism by another name as the system has always been international. Although what can be observed is the universalization of capitalist production relations, consumption patterns and the delinking of financial capital from social and political control, the world is not being homogenized as polarization is simultaneously taking place.

Some of the contradictions affecting the future shape of social change consist of a series of determining traits and tendencies: (1) The stage of a fully integrated world economy under the governance of a supranational political and economic structure has still not been reached. This contributes to the continued existence of divergent societal tendencies. States still compete through what has been called *competitive austerity* in order to gain advantage in international trade and attract investment by keeping production costs down in the so-called race to the bottom (Albo 1994). (2) The globalization of competition leads to a double process of polarization (within countries as well as between countries). The UNDP reports confirm the evolution toward greater inequalities.[6] (3) The institutionalization of unevenness and inequality gives rise to criticism and countermovements. Some political forces belong to the extreme right which together with sections of organized labor are beginning to question the fallouts of participation in the world economy. This has been apparent in the United States as well as in Europe with the appearance of ultra-nationalist movements and political parties (these questions are discussed by Barry Gills, ch. 13, this volume).

Simultaneously, progressive social movements and organizations are becoming aware of the need for an internationalist agenda and networking against the dominant economic and social logic of neoliberalism as well as against the potential rightist reaction to globalization. Although the world has experienced a resurgence of labor militancy in Western Europe, America, and East Asia as well as the emergence of numerous social movements with specific objectives together with the large number of NGOs in Third World countries, these are still, as yet, nothing more than isolated initiatives far from what is understood in the strategic concept of "globalization-from-below" (Falk 1997).

An important point in the discussion of present-day globalization is to determine the extent of the viability of its future as well as the agencies for resistance and transformation. Within this analytical frame, it is worthwhile to conceptualize the conditions of crisis which seems to be affecting the social bodies in different societies. A significant conceptualization challenging different orthodoxies can be made on this question. It is manifest that most contemporary societies are in crisis, i.e. the workings and logic of the system cannot meet the expectations of the majority of the people. This notwithstanding, as Samir Amin has pointed out, this condition does not make for a crisis of capitalism—as the two are not incompatible because the logic of capitalism itself generates crisis. Consequently, opposing forces to capitalism have to come to realize that without political intervention, capital is able to manage the crisis it creates but cannot resolve. One could be tempted to add that capitalism lives on crisis as an aspect of "creative destruction." Under these conditions, the formulation and mobilization around an alternative becomes an important task: "To speak of the 'crisis of capitalism' . . . has no meaning until such time as the popular social forces opposed to the logic of capital have coherent and feasible counter-projects, as was the case in the anti-fascist post-war years" (Amin 1997: 96). However, as developed above, it is questionable whether the social democratic welfare state represented an anti-systemic alternative to capitalism, although this project was indeed related to the traditional confrontation between labor and capital. This raises a number of issues concerning strategies of class struggle which still have not been resolved. Often criticized for "ouvriérisme," Marx nevertheless showed awareness of a basic contradiction in the struggle of labor by pointing to the limits of the "guerrilla fights" of workers in their everyday conflict with capital in order to protect their living conditions; to him these struggles did not represent larger antisystemic strategy (Marx [1867/1887] 1958: 446).

Seen from the perspective of the problem-solving approach, it can be said that history has revealed the paradox of class struggle to the extent that the working class and its political parties have fought more against effects than causes. Implicitly expressing an awareness of the duality of the strategy (rarely acknowledged by opponents of neoliberalism), Wood formulates the dilemma as follows:

> Class struggle is a constant necessity to ward off the worst excesses of exploitation, and the working class has had a long and heroic history of achievements in that respect. Class struggle has, paradoxically, also been necessary to save capitalism from itself and its inherently destructive, even self-destructive, drives . . . A strategy limited to the objective of wringing concessions from capital, while it may be all that is possible in certain conditions, is in the long run self-defeating.
>
> (Wood 1998: 40)

The future of opposition

The circumstances which in the past allowed for "guerrilla" warfare against the system are changing and there is now a need to put an alternative discourse and practice on the agenda. The transformations taking place will, at the least, affect core countries and strengthen counter tendencies. Although the external expansion of capitalism historically represented an inherent aspect of the solution to internal social and economic contradictions, the present "universalization" of capitalism represents an important historical change. It is interesting to recall Cecil Rhodes who, in 1895, expressed the logic of British imperialism as a response to the demands of the working class for better conditions: "The empire, as I have always said, is a bread and butter question. If you want to avoid civil war, you must become imperialists" (cf. Lenin [1920] 1952: 514). The reason for reaching the conclusion that as a virtual universal system, capitalism no longer has the same scope to resolve internal difficulties in its favor by internationalizing them is that "it has become subject to those contradictions in historically unprecedented ways" (Wood 1998: 41). Consequently, the processes at work are bound to affect the future of neoliberal globalization and resistance. The case can be made that, being unable to sustain maximum profitability through economic growth, the system's mode of functioning relies more on redistribution of wealth and inequalities within domestic economies and between national economies through the supervision of the neoliberal state and international institutions and agreements. In developed industrialized societies this translates into a situation whereby patterns of labor are more insecure than warranted by an absolute decline in the need for living labor. Although there is in the debate on globalization a tendency claiming that production has become "dematerialized," the new technologies resulting in changes in the division of labor and the restructuring of economic activity do not signify the disappearance of industrial processes necessitating labor (Huws 1999).

A related element regarding the position of labor which likewise will have to be faced by universal capitalism in the next century concerns the question of how the global reserve army of workers will be absorbed. This is bound to create tensions as the world economy will have to make room for the integration of the economies of populous countries. The spreading of market-oriented production in South America, Indonesia, India, parts of China, as well as Southeast Asia will add about 1.2 billion workers to the worldwide labor pool over the next generation. With a much lower wage level than that existing in developed industrialized societies, this cannot but put a tremendous strain on the economic arrangements in advanced capitalist countries (Hoogvelt 1997: 240). This prospect poses a fundamental challenge to the assumption of the adjustment rhetoric which implicitly projects a generalization of the society of mass consumption for all market economies.

The concern about intra-working class competition has somewhat been ignored in the debates on globalization at the same time as the disappearance of the imperialist problematique. However, the future rivalry between societies for a place in the sun is implicitly taken up by hard core realism. One may agree or disagree with the culturalist argumentation behind the thesis on the "clash of civilizations," but Samuel Huntington does address the basic issue of future power and wealth sharing. Will the West be able to maintain its predominance and what will the means be? How will the other societies (the "Rest") react if forced to continue accepting an inferior status? (These questions are discussed in Part IV of this volume.)

Given the context of the contradictions facing the global social system, it seems utopian to believe in a return to the golden age of welfare capitalism. Consequently, it is difficult to share the optimism of the problem-solving approach concerning the possibility of transforming the defensive struggle into a strategy for a viable alternative. Overproduction is the basic tendency that will be accentuated as the wage-based system of capitalism has to confront the fact that labor-saving technologies create more wealth with less labor. In addition, because of overcapacity and competition from underpaid workers in Third World countries, conditions of full employment cannot be expected nor would it represent a desirable solution to the malfunctioning of advanced capitalist societies. This state of affairs poses a challenge to movements who see the struggle for full employment in developed industrialized societies as resistance to globalization. In other words, counter-movements are not by definition antisystemic movements. Awareness of this distinction is of importance in the discussion of resistance.

Opposition to globalization within the socialist perspective expresses itself "grosso modo" in two positions. The first is the attempt to negotiate the best possible deal within the world market; this is a social democratic variant of Keynesianism or what can be conceptualized as a reformist state-centered approach. The second is grounded on a more non-compromising resistance and rejection which is more socially and politically fundamentalist as well as ecologically motivated. This can be considered as a more people-centered approach. There is of course no Chinese Wall between the two types of opposition, as the viability of reformism as an option depends on the back-up of a strong radical social movement, while resistance and rejection still need to be translated into a political strategy.

Taking the environmental dimension into consideration, new alternative thinking is more necessary than ever. This is where critical theory, which rejects the assumption that the major mechanisms of the capitalist system are not subject to change, has a role to play. This implies that a methodological approach and strategy which relies both on problem-solving as well as on critical theory needs to be adopted by engaged "organic" intellectuals. However, given the need to understand globalization as well as the necessity for resistance gives precedence to the conceptualizations which critical theory offers. In the words of Robert W. Cox (1999: 393): "it also seems to me that in periods like our own, which I think is a period of important structural change, we need particularly the emphasis on critical theory, which directs our attention to the whole." Understanding the system's mode of functioning and the resulting potential chaos increases the urgency for new thinking in order to chart an antisystemic alternative. In other words, a project which would entail detaching the material conditions of people's existence from the logic of capitalism would represent "the most radical rupture with traditional ideas."[7] Perhaps the new thinking involved in the resistance to neoliberalism, whose policies encourage wealth creation outside the realm of production, can make the idea of such a break with the past realizable. What such a strategy involves is discussed in the final part of this book.

The rationale behind this collection of contributions by engaged social scientists is to problematize what the contributors consider to be the main element of globalization, i.e. the neoliberal discourse and strategy, which has been internalized by most, if not all, elites. Globalization is not seen as the exclusive interaction of economic actors on the world scene, but as the implementation of socio-economic policies which give priority to market forces at the expense of social sectors and groups such as labor, minorities, and the marginalized.

As the heuristic point of departure most contributors express a healthy dose of skepticism toward the discourse which sees neoliberal globalization as the "end station of capitalism." As such, the gist of many contributions in this volume underlines the notion of the state as a significant agency in promulgating neoliberalism (both as discourse and strategy) while simultaneously considering the state as a potential mediator in the possibility of the creation of a social market ("Sozialmarktwirtschaft"). Inspired by the notion of the "double movement" (Polanyi), this volume does not focus exclusively on the state but also considers social interactions between the economic, societal, political, and confrontational levels.

Bibliography

Albo, G. (1994) "'Competitive Austerity' and the Impasse of Capitalist Employment Policy," in *Socialist Register*, London: Merlin Press.

Amin, S. (1997) *Capitalism in the Age of Globalization—The Management of Contemporary Society*, London and New Jersey: Zed Books.

Baran, P. A. and Sweezy, P. M. (1966) *Monopoly Capital. An Essay on the American Economic Order*, New York and London: Monthly Review Press.

Braudel, F. (1982) *The Wheel of Commerce*, New York: Harper and Row.

Burbach, R. and Robinson, W. I. (1999) "The Fin de Siècle Debate: Globalization as Epochal Shift," *Science and Society* 63 (1), Spring.

Chesnais, F. (1994) *La mondialisation du capital*, Paris: Syros.

Cox, R. W. (1987) *Production, Power and World Order: Social Forces in the Making of History*, New York: Columbia University Press.

—— (1999) "The Millennium Symposium," *New Political Economy* 4 (3), November.

Emmanuel, A. (1972) *Unequal Exchange: A Study of the Imperialism of Trade*, New York: Monthly Review Press.

Falk, R. (1997) "Resisting 'Globalization-from-above' Through 'Globalization-from-below,'" *New Political Economy* (March).

Galbraith, J. K. (1997) "Preface," *New Political Economy* 2 (1), March.

Greider, W. (1997) *One World, Ready or Not. The Manic Logic of Global Capitalism*, New York: Simon and Schuster.

Human Development Report 1990–1999, New York: Oxford University Press.

Hobsbawm, E. (1991/1992) "We've Got Problems Too . . .," *Marxism Today* (December/January).

Hoogvelt, A. (1997) *Globalization and the Postcolonial World*, London: Macmillan.

Huws, U. (1999) "Material World: The Myth of the Weightless Economy," in *Socialist Register*, London: Merlin Press.

Julien, C. (1968) *L'Empire américain*, Paris: Editions Bernard Grasset.

Kotz, D. M., McDonough, T., and Reich, M. (eds) (1994) *Social Structures of Accumulation: The Political Economy of Growth and Crisis*, Cambridge: Cambridge University Press.

Lenin, V. I. ([1920] 1952) "Imperialism, the Highest Stage of Capitalism," in V. I. Lenin, *Selected Works in Two Volumes*, vol. 1, Moscow: Foreign Languages Publishing House.

Magdoff, H. (1998) "A Letter to a Contributor: The Same Old State," *Monthly Review* (January).

Magdoff, H. and Sweezy, P. M. (1987) *Stagnation and the Financial Explosion*, New York: Monthly Review Press.

Marx, K. ([1867/1887] 1958) "Wages, Price and Profit," in K. Marx and F. Engels, *Selected Works in Two Volumes*, vol. 1, Moscow: Foreign Languages Publishing House.

Marx, K. and Engels, F. ([1848] 1958) "Manifesto of the Communist Party," in K. Marx and F. Engels, *Selected Works in Two Volumes*, vol. 1, Moscow: Foreign Languages Publishing House.

Myrdal, G. (1968) *Objektivitetsproblemet i Samhällsforskningen*, Stockholm: Raben og Sjögren.

Polanyi, K. ([1944] 1957) *The Great Transformation—The Political and Economic Origins of Our Time*, Boston: Beacon.

Robinson, I. (1995) "Globalization and Democracy," *Dissent* (Summer).

Rosenau, J. A. (1997) "The Complexities and Contradictions of Globalization," *Current History* (November).

Sivanandan, A. and Wood, E. M. (1997) "Capitalism, Globalization, and Epochal Shifts: An Exchange," *Monthly Review* (February).

Sklair, L. (1991) *Sociology of the Global System*, London: Prentice Hall/Harvester Wheatsheaf.

Thurow, L. (1992) *Head to Head—The Coming Economic Battle Among Japan, Europe, and Latin America*, New York: William Morrow and Company Inc.

Toye, J. (1987) *The Dilemmas of Development. Reflections on the Counter-Revolution in Development Theory and Policy*, Oxford: Basil Blackwell.

Wallerstein, I. (1999) "The Millennium Symposium," *New Political Economy* 4 (3), November.

Wood, E. M. (1998) "Class Compacts, the Welfare State, and Epochal Shifts," *Monthly Review* (January).

—— (1999) "Unhappy Families: Global Capitalism in a World of Nation-States," *Monthly Review* (July/August).

World Bank (2000) *World Development Indicators*, Washington, D.C.

Part I

The intellectual challenge: discourse, ideology, and reality

1 Globalization in question

David Harvey

Since the early 1980s, "globalization" has become a key word for organizing our thoughts as to how the world works. How and why it moved to such a central position in our vocabulary is an interesting tale. I want here, however, to focus on the theoretical and political implications of the rise of such a mode of thought. To that end, I begin with two general sets of questions in order to highlight what appear to be important political changes in Western discourses (though not necessarily in realities), including that of much of the socialist movement.

1   Why is it that the word "globalization" has recently entered into our discourses in the way it has? Who put it there and why? And what significance is to be attached to the fact that even among many "progressives" and "leftists" in the advanced capitalist world, words like "imperialism," "colonialism," and "neocolonialism" have increasingly taken a back seat to "globalization" as a way to organize thoughts and to chart political possibilities?
2   How has the conception of globalization been used politically? Has adoption of the term signaled a confession of powerlessness on the part of national, regional, and local working-class movements? Has belief in the term operated as a powerful deterrent to localized and even national political action? Are local and national working-class movements such insignificant cogs in the vast infernal global machine of international capitalism that there is no room for political manoeuvre anywhere?

Viewed from this perspective, the term globalization and all its associated baggage exact a severe political price. But before we reject it or abandon it entirely, it is useful to take a good hard look at what it incorporates and what we can learn, theoretically and politically, from the brief history of its use.

Let me begin with a suggestion: That we view "globalization" as a *process* rather than as a political-economic condition that has recently come into being. To view it this way is not to presume that the process is constant; nor does it preclude saying that the process has, for example, entered into a radically new stage or worked itself out to a particular or even "final" state. But a process-based definition makes us concentrate on how globalization has occurred and is occurring.

Certainly from 1492 onwards, and even before, the globalization process of capitalism was well under way. And it has never ceased to be of profound importance to capitalism's dynamic. Globalization has, therefore, been integral to capitalist development since its very inception. It is important to understand why.

The accumulation of capital has always been a profoundly geographical and spatial affair. Without the possibilities inherent in geographical expansion, spatial reorganization, and uneven geographical development, capitalism would long ago have ceased to function as a political-economic system. This perpetual turning to what I call "a spatial fix" to capitalism's contradictions has created a global historical geography of capital accumulation whose character needs to be well understood.

Marx and Engels emphasized the point in the *Communist Manifesto*. Modern industry not only creates the world market, they wrote, but the need for a constantly expanding market "chases the bourgeoisie over the whole surface of the globe" so that it "must nestle everywhere, settle everywhere, establish connections everywhere." They continue:

> The bourgeoisie has through its exploitation of the world market given a cosmopolitan character to production and consumption in every country . . . All old established national industries have been destroyed or are daily being destroyed. They are dislodged by new industries, whose introduction becomes a life and death question for all civilized nations, by industries that no longer work up indigenous raw material, but raw material drawn from the remotest zones; industries whose products are consumed, not only at home, but in every quarter of the globe. In place of the old wants, satisfied by the production of the country, we find new wants, requiring for their satisfaction the products of distant lands and climes. In place of the old local and national seclusion and self-sufficiency, we have intercourse in every direction, universal interdependence of nations. And as in material, so also in intellectual production. The intellectual creations of individual nations become common property. National one-sidedness and narrow-mindedness become more and more impossible, and from the numerous national and local literatures, there arises a world literature.
>
> (Marx and Engels 1952: 72)

If this is not a compelling description of globalization, then it is hard to imagine what would be. And it was, of course, precisely by way of this analysis that Marx and Engels derived the global imperative "working men of all countries unite" as a necessary condition for an anti-capitalist and pro-socialist revolution.

Since Marx and Engels, a variety of accounts has been offered of how capitalism has structured its geography (such as Lenin's theory of imperialism, Luxemburg's positioning of imperialism as the savior of capitalist accumulation, and Mao's depiction of primary and secondary contradictions in class struggle). These have subsequently been supplemented by more synthetic accounts of accumulation on a world scale (Amin), the production of a capitalist world system (Wallerstein), the development of underdevelopment (Frank and Rodney), unequal exchange (Emmanuel), and dependency theory (Cardoso). As Marxist ideas and political practices have spread throughout the globe (in a parallel process of globalization of class struggle), so innumerable local/national accounts of resistance to the invasions, disruptions, and imperialist designs of capitalism have been generated. And a widespread but less visible group of thinkers and practitioners has paid much closer attention to local/regional differences and the role of urbanization as part of a process of uneven geographical development of capitalism (both of its productive forces and social relations) in space and the uneven geographical and social forms of anti-capitalist struggle.

The effect is tacitly to recognize that the grounding for class struggle is often specific to places and that the universalism to which socialism aspires has to be built by negotiation among different place-specific demands, concerns, and aspirations. As Raymond Williams (1989: 242) suggested, the grounding of socialist politics always lies in what he called a "militant particularism" embedded in "ways of life" and "structures of feeling" peculiar to place. By this he meant, in the first instance:

> The unique and extraordinary character of working-class self-organization . . . to connect particular struggles to a general struggle in one quite special way. It has set out, as a movement, to make real what is at first sight the extraordinary claim that the defence and advancement of certain particular *interests, properly brought together,* are in fact the general interest.
>
> (Williams 1989: 249; my emphasis)

The further implication, which many socialists may be loath to accept, is that:

> A new theory of socialism must now centrally involve *place.* Remember the argument was that the proletariat had no country, the factor which differentiated it from the property owning classes. But place has been shown to be a crucial element in the bonding process—more so perhaps for the working class than the capital-owning classes—by the explosion of the international economy and the destructive effects of deindustrialization upon old communities. When capital has moved on, the importance of place is more clearly revealed.
>
> (Williams 1989: 242)

It is not my intention to review the vast literature that deals with the spatial and geographical aspects of capitalist development and class struggle (even if such a task were feasible). But I do think it important to recognize a series of tensions and often uncomfortable compromises within the Marxist tradition over how to understand, theoretically and politically, the geographical dynamics of capital accumulation and class struggle. When, for example, Lenin and Luxembourg clashed on the national question, as the vast controversy on the possibility of socialism within one country (or even within one city) unfolded, as the Second International compromised with nationalism in World War I, and as the Comintern subsequently swayed back and forth on how to interpret its own internationalism, so the socialist/communist movement never managed to evolve, politically or theoretically, a proper or satisfactory understanding of the geographical dynamics of capital accumulation and the geopolitics of class struggle.

A careful scrutiny of the rhetoric in the *Communist Manifesto* indicates a key source of the dilemma. For while it is clear from the passages cited that the bourgeoisie's quest for class domination was (and is) a very geographical affair, the almost immediate reversion in the text to a purely temporal and diachronic account is very striking. It is hard, it seems, to be dialectical about space, leaving many Marxists in practice to follow Feuerbach in thinking that time is "the privileged category of the dialectician, because it excludes and subordinates where space tolerates and coordinates" (Ross 1988: 8). Even the term "historical materialism," I note, erases the significance of geography, and if I have struggled these last few years to try to implant the idea of "historical-geographical materialism" it is because the very shift in that terminology prepares us to look more flexibly and, I hope, more cogently at the class significance of processes like globalization and uneven geographical development. And if I am now struggling in my work (Harvey 1996) with how to be dialectical about spatiotemporality (and the fusion of those terms is itself, I believe, highly significant), then it is because I feel we need far better ways to understand if not resolve politically the underlying tension within Marxist accounts between what often degenerates into either a temporal teleology of class triumphalism (now largely negated by the equally teleological class triumphalism of the bourgeoisie declaring the end of history) or a seemingly incoherent and uncontrollable geographical fragmentation of class and other forms of social struggle in every nook and cranny of the capitalist world.

In practice, even diachronic class struggle accounts are for the most part territorially bounded without much concern being shown to justify the geographical divisions upon which such accounts are based. We then have innumerable accounts of the making of the English, Welsh, French, German, Italian, Catalan, South African, South Korean, and so on working classes, as if these are natural geographical entities. Attention focuses on class development within some circumscribed space which when scrutinized more closely, turns out to be a space within an international space of flows of capital, labor, information, and so on, in turn comprised of innumerable smaller spaces each with its own characteristics. When we look closely at the action described in Edward Thompson's classic account of *The Making of the English Working Class*, for example, it turns out to be a series of highly localized events often loosely conjoined in space. Foster may have rendered the differences somewhat too mechanical in his own account of *Class Struggle in the Industrial Revolution*, but it is, I think, undeniable that class structure, class consciousness, and class politics in Oldham, Northampton, and South Shields (read Colmar, Lille, and St. Etienne or Minneapolis, Mobile, and

Lowell) were quite differently constructed and worked out, making geographical difference within the nation-state rather more important than most would want to concede. This mode of thinking uncritically about supposedly "natural" geographical entities is now most familiarly perpetuated in neoMarxist accounts of capital (particularly those inspired by "regulation theory") that make it seem as if there are distinctive German, British, Japanese, American, Swedish, Singaporean, Brazilian, and so on versions of capitalism (sometimes broken down into more regionalized orderings, such as North versus South in Italy, Brazil, Britain . . . all in competition with each other within a global space economy.

So there is a clear line of tension within the Marxist tradition. On the one hand, we have spaceless and geographically undifferentiated accounts (mainly theoretical these days, though polemical and political versions can still be found) which understand capitalist development as a purely temporal process. Class struggle is primarily depicted as a matter of exploitation of one class by another and history is seen as an outcome of that struggle. On the other hand, we have geographical accounts in which class alliances (and this often includes a working class characterized by what Lenin condemned as a limiting trade-union consciousness) form within places to exploit class alliances in other places (with, perhaps, a *comprador* bourgeoisie as agent). The theoretical justification for viewing the exploitation of one class by another as homologous with the exploitation of one place by another has never been strong. And the assumption that struggles to liberate spaces (struggles for national liberation, for example) are progressive in the class-struggle sense and vice versa cannot stand up to very strong scrutiny. There are, in fact, numerous examples of each kind of struggle confounding the other. How, then, can we unconfound this problem?

One of the things that adoption of the term "globalization" now signals, I believe, is a profound geographical reorganization of capitalism, making many of the presumptions about the "natural" geographical units within which capitalism's historical trajectory develops less and less meaningful (if they ever were). We are therefore faced with a historic opportunity to seize the nettle of capitalism's geography, to see the production of space as a constitutive moment within (as opposed to something derivatively constructed by) the dynamics of capital accumulation and class struggle. In a sense, this is an opportunity for Marxism to emancipate itself from imprisonment within a hidden spatiality that has had the opaque power to dominate (and sometimes to confound) the logic of both our thinking and our politics. It also permits us to understand better exactly how class and inter-place struggles can confound each other and to confront the capacity of capitalism to constrain class struggle through a geographical divide and rule of that struggle. We are in a position, furthermore, to understand the spatio-temporal contradictions inherent in capitalism and, through that understanding, better position ourselves to exploit the weakest link and so explode the worst horrors of capitalism's penchant for violent though "creative" destruction.

How, then, can we dance to this agenda, both theoretically and politically? There are, of course, innumerable signs of a willingness to take on the theoretical implications of changing spatialities and reterritorializations. It was, I believe, one of the main virtues of Deleuze and Guattari's *Anti-Oedipus*, for example, to point out that the territorialization and reterritorialization of capitalism is an ongoing process. But here, as in many other accounts, the virtue of a respatialization of social thought has been bought at the cost of partial and sometimes radical breaks with Marxist formulations (both theoretical and political). In my own work, I have sought to show that there are ways to integrate spatialities into Marxist theory and practice without necessarily disrupting central propositions, though in the course of such an integration all sorts of modifications to both theory and practice do arise. So let me summarize some of the main features of this argument.

I begin with the simplest propositions I can find. There are dual tensions deeply embedded within any materialist accounting of the circulation process of capital. These periodically and inescapably erupt as powerful moments of historical-geographical contradiction.

First, capitalism is under the impulsion to accelerate turnover time, to speed up the circulation of capital and, consequently, to revolutionize the time horizons of development. But it can do so only through long-term investments (in, for example, the built environment as well as in elaborate and stable infrastructures for production, consumption, exchange, communication, and the like). A major stratagem of crisis avoidance, furthermore, lies in absorbing overaccumulated capital in long-term projects (the famous "public works" launched by the state in times of depression, for example) and this slows down the turnover time of capital. There is, consequently, an extraordinary array of contradictions that collect around the issue of the time-horizon within which different capitals function. Historically, and now is no exception, this tension has primarily been registered through the contradictions between money and finance capital (where turnover is now almost instantaneous), on the one hand, and merchant, manufacturing, agrarian, information, construction, service, and state capitals on the other. But contradictions can be found within factions (between currency and bond markets, for example, or between land developers and speculators). All sorts of mechanisms exist, of course, for coordinating among capital dynamics working on different temporal scales and rhythms. But uneven development of turnover times and temporalities, of the sort produced by the recent implosion of time-horizons in a very powerful financial sector, can create an unwelcome temporal compression that is deeply stressful to other factions of capital, including, of course, that embodied in the capitalist state. The time-horizon set by Wall Street simply cannot accommodate to the temporalities of social and ecological reproduction systems in a responsive way. And it goes without saying that the rapid turnover time set in financial markets is even more stressful for workers (their job security, their skills, etc.) and for the lifeworld of socio-ecological reproduction. This stress-point is one of the crucial features of political economy these last twenty years.

Second, capitalism is under the impulsion to eliminate all spatial barriers, to "annihilate space through time" as Marx puts it, but it can do so only through the production of a fixed space. Capitalism thereby produces a geographical landscape (of space relations, of territorial organization, and of systems of places linked in a "global" division of labor and of functions) appropriate to its own dynamic of accumulation at a particular moment of its history, only to have to destroy and rebuild that geographical landscape to accommodate accumulation at a later date. There are a number of distinct aspects to this process:

1   Reductions in the cost and time of movement over space have been a continuing focus of technological innovation. Turnpikes, canals, railroads, electric power, the automobile, air and jet transport have progressively liberated the movements of commodities and people from the constraints of the friction of distance. Parallel innovations in the postal system, the telegraph, the radio, telecommunications, and the worldwide web have now pushed the cost of transfer of information close to zero.

2   The building of fixed physical infrastructures to facilitate this movement as well as to support the activities of production, exchange, distribution, and consumption exercises a quite different force upon the geographical landscape. More and more capital is embedded in space as landed capital, as capital fixed in the land, creating a "second nature" and a geographically organized resource structure that more and more inhibits the trajectory of capitalist development. The idea of somehow dismantling the urban infrastructures of Tokyo-Yokohama or New York City overnight and starting all over again is simply ludicrous. The effect is to make the geographical landscape of capitalism more and more sclerotic with time, thus creating a major contradiction with the increasing liberty of movement. That tendency is made even more emphatic to the degree that the institutions of place become strongly articulated and loyalties to places (and their specific qualities) become a significant factor in political action.

3   The third element is the construction of territorial organization, primarily (though not solely) state powers to regulate money, law, politics and to monopolize the means of coercion and violence according to a sovereign territorial (and sometime extraterritorial) will. There are, of course, innumerable Marxist theories of the state, many of which engage in an unhealthy degree of abstraction from history and geography, making it seem as if states like Gabon and Liberia are on a par with the United States or Germany and failing to recognize that most of the state boundaries in the world were drawn between 1870 and 1925 (and a good half of those were drawn up arbitrarily by the British and French alone). Most states became independent only after 1945 and many of them have been in search of a nation ever since (but then this was as historically true of France and Mexico as it has recently been of Nigeria or Rwanda). So while it is true that the Treaty of Westphalia established for the first time the principle that independent sovereign states, each recognizing the others' autonomy and territorial integrity, should coexist in the capitalist world, the process of globalizing the territorial organization of the world according to that principle took several centuries to complete (accompanied by a good deal of violence). And

the processes that gave rise to that system can just as easily dissolve it, as some commentators are now arguing is indeed happening as supranational organizations (such as the European Union) and regional autonomy movements within nation-states do their work. In short, we have to understand the processes of state formation and dissolution in terms of the unstable processes of globalization/territorialization. We then see a process of territorialization, deterritorialization, and reterritorialization continuously at work throughout the historical geography of capitalism (this was one of the fundamental points that Deleuze and Guattari picked up on in *Anti-Oedipus*).

Armed with these concepts we can, I think, better understand the evolution of globalization as a process of production of uneven temporal and geographical development. And, as I shall hope to show, that shift of language can have some healthy political consequences, liberating us from the more oppressive and confining language of an omnipotent process of globalization.

Bearing that in mind, let me come back to what the term "globalization" might signify and why it has taken on a new allure and thereby become so important in recent times. Three major shifts stand out:

1   Financial deregulation began in the United States in the early 1970s as a forced response to the stagflation then occurring internally and to the breakdown of the Bretton Woods system of international trade and exchange (largely because of the uncontrolled growth of the Eurodollar market). I think it important to recognize that the wave of financial deregulation was less a deliberate strategy thought out by capital than a concession to realities (even if certain segments of capital stood to benefit far more than others). But Bretton Woods was a global system, so what really happened here was a shift from one global system (hierarchically organized and largely controlled politically by the United States) to another global system that was more decentralized and coordinated through the market, making the financial conditions of capitalism far more volatile and far more unstable. The rhetoric that accompanied this shift was deeply implicated in the promotion of the term "globalization" as a virtue. In my more cynical moments I find myself thinking that it was the financial press that conned us all (myself included) into believing in "globalization" as something new when it was nothing more than a promotional gimmick to make the best of a necessary adjustment in the system of international finance. I note, coincidentally, that the financial press has for some time now been much more emphatic about the regionalization going on in financial markets (the Japanese co-prosperity sphere, the NAFTA, and the European Union being the obvious power blocs) and that even many of the boosters of globalization in the capitalist press are warning that the "backlash" against globalization (mainly in the form of multiple populist nationalisms) are to be taken seriously and that globalization is in danger of becoming synonymous with "a brakeless train wreaking havoc" (Friedman 1996: A19).

2   The media and communications system and, above all, the so-called information revolution brought some significant changes to the organization
of production and consumption as well as to the definition of entirely new
wants and needs. The ultimate "dematerialization of space" in the communications field had its origins in the military apparatus but was immediately seized upon by financial institutions and multinational capital as a
means to coordinate their activities instantaneously over space. The effect
has been to form a so-called dematerialized cyberspace in which certain
kinds of important transactions (primarily financial and speculative) could
occur. But then we also came to watch revolutions and wars live on television. The space and time of media and communications imploded in a
world where the monopolization of media power has become more and
more of a problem (in spite of proclamations of libertarian democratization
via the internet).

The idea of an "information revolution" is powerfully present these days
and is often viewed as the dawning of a new era of globalization within
which the information society reigns supreme. It is easy to make too much
of this. The newness of it all impresses, but then the newness of the railroad
and the telegraph, the automobile, the radio, and the telephone in their day
impressed equally. These earlier examples are instructive since each in its
own way did change the way the world works, the ways in which production
and consumption could be organized, politics conducted, and the ways in
which social relations among people could become converted on an ever
widening scale into social relations among things. And it is clear that the
relations between working and living, within the workplace, in cultural forms,
are indeed changing very rapidly in response to information technology.
Interestingly, this is a key component in the right-wing political agenda in
the United States. The new technology, says Newt Gingrich (advised by
Alvin Toffler, whose right-wing utopianism rests entirely on the idea of a
"third-wave" information revolution) is inherently emancipatory, but in
order to liberate this emancipatory force from its political chains it is essential to pursue a political revolution to dismantle all of the institutions of
"second wave" industrial society-government regulation, the welfare state,
collective institutions of wage bargaining, and the like. That this is a vulgar
version of the Marxist argument that changes in productive forces drive
social relations and history should not be lost upon us. Nor should we ignore
the strong teleological tone to this right-wing rhetoric (perhaps best captured
in Margaret Thatcher's famous declaration that "there is no alternative").

3   The cost and time of moving commodities and people also ratcheted down-
wards in another of those shifts that have periodically occurred within the
history of capitalism. This liberated all sorts of activities from former spatial
constraints, permitting far more rapid adjustments in locations of production, consumption, populations, and the like. I suspect that when the history
of the globalization process comes to be written, this simple shift in the cost
of overcoming space will be seen as far more significant than the so-called

information revolution *per se* (though both are part and parcel of each other in practice).

These three shifts in the globalization process were accompanied by a number of other important features, perhaps best thought of as derivatives of the primary forces at work.

1   Production and organizational forms changed (particularly of multinational capital, though many small entrepreneurs also seized new opportunities), making abundant use of the reduced costs of commodity and information movement. Offshore production that began in the 1960s suddenly became much more general (it has now spread with a vengeance even to Japan). The geographical dispersal and fragmentation of production systems, divisions of labor, and specializations of tasks ensued, albeit often in the midst of an increasing centralization of corporate power through mergers, takeovers, or joint production agreements which transcended national boundaries. Corporations have more power to command space, making individual places much more vulnerable to their whims. The global television set, the global car, became an everyday aspect of political-economic life. The closing down of production in one place and the opening up of production somewhere else became a familiar story—some large-scale production operations have moved four or five times in the past twenty years.

2   The world wage-labor force more than doubled in less than twenty years. This occurred in part through rapid population growth but also through bringing in more and more of the world's population (particularly women) into the wage-labor force, in, for example, South Korea, Taiwan, and Africa, as well as ultimately in the ex-Soviet bloc and China. The global proletariat is now far larger than ever (which should, surely, put a steely glint of hope into every socialist's eye). But it has been radically feminized. It is also geographically dispersed, culturally heterogeneous, and therefore much harder to organize into a united movement.

3   Global population has also been on the move. The United States now has the highest proportion of foreign born in the country since the 1920s, and while there are all sorts of attempts to keep populations out, the flood of migratory movements seems impossible to stop. State boundaries are less porous for people and labor than they are for capital, but they are still porous enough. London, Paris, and Rome are far more immigrant cities than they used to be, making immigration a far more significant issue worldwide (including within the labor movement itself) than has ever been the case before (even Tokyo is caught up in the process). By the same token, organizing labor in the face of the considerable ethnic, racial, religious, and cultural diversity generated out of migratory movements also poses particular problems that the socialist movement has not often found easy to solve.

4   Urbanization ratcheted up into hyper-urbanization, particularly after 1950 with the pace of urbanization accelerating to create a major ecological,

political, economic, and social revolution in the spatial organization of the world's population. The proportion of an increasing global population living in cities has doubled in thirty years, and we now observe massive spatial concentrations of population on a scale hitherto regarded as inconceivable. Organizing class struggle in, say, Manchester or Chicago in the 1870s was a quite different proposition from organizing class struggle (or even developing the institutions of a representative democracy) in contemporary Sao Paulo, Cairo, Lagos, Shanghai, Bombay, and so on, with their populations reaching close to (or over) 20 million.

5   The territorialization of the world has changed not only because of the end of the Cold War. Perhaps most important has been the changing role of the state, which has lost some (though not all) traditional powers to control the mobility of capital (particularly finance and money capital). State operations have, consequently, been more strongly disciplined by money capital and finance than ever before. Structural adjustment and fiscal austerity have become the name of the game, and the state has to some degree been reduced to the role of finding ways to promote a favorable business climate. Even Japan is now suffering from rapid movement of production operations out from the home base to China and other cheaper labor zones in Southeast Asia. The "globalization thesis" here became a powerful ideological tool to beat upon socialists, welfare statists, nationalists, and so on. When the British Labour party was forced to succumb to IMF demands to enforce austerity, it became apparent that there were limits to the national autonomy of fiscal policy (a condition the French also had to acknowledge after 1981). Welfare for the poor has largely been replaced, therefore, by public subventions to capital (Mercedes-Benz received $US 1.25 billion of subventions in a package from the state of Alabama in order to persuade it to locate there).

Reterritorialization has not stopped at the nation-state. Global institutions of management of the economy, environment, and politics have proliferated as have regional blocs (like the NAFTA and the European Union) at a supranational scale, and strong processes of decentralization (sometimes through political movements—sometimes violently separatist—for regional autonomy or, as in the United States, through an increasing emphasis upon States' rights within the federal system) are also to be found. State formation is, furthermore, now seen as one key means to defend ethnic and cultural identities and environmental qualities in the face of time–space compression and global commodification. And it is also seen as the prime locus of that "backlash" against globalization that appeals to populist nationalism.

6   But while individual states lost some of their powers, what I call geopolitical democratization created new opportunities. It became harder for any core power to exercise discipline over others and easier for peripheral powers to insert themselves into the capitalist competitive game. Money power is a "leveller and cynic." But, as Marx observes, a powerful antinomy then arises: while qualitatively "money had no bounds to its efficacy," the quantitative

limits to money in the hands of individuals (and states) limits or augments their social power in important ways. Given deregulation of finance, for example, it was impossible to prevent Japan from exercising influence as a major financial power. States had to become much more concerned with their competitiveness (a subtheme of the globalization argument which has become very important). Competitive states could do well in global competition and this often meant that low-wage states with strong labor discipline did better than others. Labor control became, therefore, a vital ideological issue within the globalization argument, again pushing socialist arguments onto the defensive. Authoritarian, relatively homogeneous territories organized on corporatist principles—like Singapore, Hong Kong, and Taiwan— have done relatively well in an era when "free-market Stalinism" (for such it should be called) became much more the norm within the capitalist globalization process.

Two broad questions can be posed about these trends. While everyone will, I think, concede the quantitative changes that have occurred, what really needs to be debated is whether these quantitative changes are great enough and synergistic enough when taken together to put us in a qualitatively new era of capitalist development, demanding a radical revision of our theoretical concepts and our political apparatus (to say nothing of our aspirations). The idea that this is the case is signalled primarily by all the "posts" that we see around us (e.g. post-industrialism, post-modernism). So has there been a qualitative transformation wrought on the basis of these quantitative shifts? My own answer is a very qualified "yes" to that question, immediately accompanied by the assertion that there has not been any fundamental revolution in the mode of production and its associated social relations and that if there is any real qualitative trend it is toward the reassertion of early nineteenth-century capitalist values coupled with a twenty-first-century penchant for pulling everyone (and everything that can be exchanged) into the orbit of capital while rendering large segments of the world's population permanently redundant in relation to the basic dynamics of capital accumulation. This is where the powerful image, conceded and feared by international capital, of contemporary globalization as a "brakeless train wreaking havoc" comes into play.

If the argument for a limited qualitative shift has to be taken seriously, then the question is how to reformulate both theory and politics. And it is here that my proposed shift of language from "globalization" to "uneven spatio-temporal development" of capitalism has most to offer. For conditions of uneven geographical and temporal development offer abundant opportunities for political organizing and action at the same time as they pose particular difficulties. Understanding the difficulties is crucial to the formulation of an adequate politics.

The primary significance for the Left in all of these changes is that the relatively privileged position of the working classes in the advanced capitalist countries has been much reduced relative to conditions of labor in the rest of the world (this transition is most glaringly seen in the re-emergence of sweatshops as a fundamental form of industrial organization in New York and Los Angeles over the past twenty years). The secondary point is that conditions of life under advanced capitalism have felt the full brunt of the capitalist capacity for "creative destruction," making for extreme volatility of local, regional, and national economic prospects (this year's boom town becomes next year's depressed region). The neoliberal justification for all this is that the hidden hand of the market will work to the benefit of all, provided there is as little state interference (and they should add—though they usually don't—monopoly power) as possible. The effect is to make the violence and creative destruction of uneven geographical development (through, for example, geographical reorganization of production) just as widely felt in the traditional heartlands of capitalism as elsewhere, in the midst of an extraordinary technology of affluence and conspicuous consumption, which is instantaneously communicated worldwide as one potential set of aspirations. No wonder even the promoters of globalization have to take the condition of backlash seriously. As Klaus Schwab and Claude Smadja have recently written:

> Economic globalization has entered a critical phase. A mounting backlash against its effects, especially in the industrial democracies, is threatening a very disruptive impact on economic activity and social stability in many countries. The mood in these democracies is one of helplessness and anxiety, which helps explain the rise of a new brand of populist politicians. This can easily turn into revolt.
>
> (cited in Friedman 1996: A19)

The socialist movement has, of course, to configure how to make use of these revolutionary possibilities. It has to counter the trend toward multiple right-wing populist nationalisms, often edged with outright appeals to a localized fascism. It has to focus class struggle around the construction of a socially just and ecologically sensitive socialist society. To do this, however, the socialist movement has to come to terms with the extraordinarily powerful waves of uneven spatio-temporal development that make organizing so precarious and so difficult. But in exactly the same way that Marx saw the necessity that workers of all countries should unite to combat the globalization of the bourgeoisie, so the socialist movement has to find ways to be just as flexible over space in its theory and its political practice as the capitalist class has become.

There is, I believe, one useful way to begin to think of this. Ask first: Where is anti-capitalist struggle to be found? The answer is, I think, everywhere. There is not a region in the world where manifestations of anger and discontent with the capitalist system cannot be found, and in some places anti-capitalist movements are strongly rather than weakly implanted. Localized "militant particularisms" (and I deliberately return to Raymond Williams's phrase) are everywhere to be found, from the militia movement in the Michigan woods (much of it violently anti-capitalist and anti-corporate as well as racist and exclusionary) to the movements of Mexican, Indian, and Brazilian peasants militating against the NAFTA,

World Bank development projects, and the like. And there is plenty of class struggle at work even in the heartlands of capitalist accumulation (varying from the extraordinary outbursts of militancy in France in the fall of 1995 to the office-cleaners' strike in New York in early 1996). If we look carefully within the interstices of the uneven spatio-temporal development of capitalism, then we will find a veritable ferment of opposition. But this opposition, though militant, often remains particularized (sometimes extremely so) and always threatens to coalesce around exclusionary and populist-nationalist political movements. To say the opposition is anti-capitalist is not to say it is necessarily pro-socialist or that it can even get to the point of understanding that some alternative to capitalism is needed. This broad-based anti-capitalist movement lacks coherence and a concrete vision as to what an anti-capitalist alternative might look like. The movement also lacks direction: the moves of one element confound and sometimes check another, making it far too easy for capitalist class interests to exercise a divide-and-rule form of domination. It lacks, in short, an agreed-upon framework for understanding how different struggles might relate and how to shape a global anti-capitalist agenda.

One of the historical strengths of the Marxist movement has been its ongoing commitment to synthesize diverse struggles with divergent and multiple aims into a more universal anti-capitalist movement with a global aim. Let me now distil from the inspiration of that tradition a number of arguments that seem particularly applicable to the current conjuncture.

The work of synthesis has to be ongoing, since the fields and terrains of struggle are perpetually changing as the capitalist dynamic and global conditions change. The Marxist tradition has an immense contribution to make toward that work of synthesis, because it has pioneered the tools with which to find the commonality within multiplicities and differences and to identify primary/secondary/tertiary conditions of oppression and exploitation. I recall, here, Raymond Williams's phrase (1989: 249) as to how "the defense and advancement of certain particular interests, *properly brought together*, are in fact the general interest" and emphasize "properly brought together" as the core task to be addressed. This work needs to be renewed.

We need first to understand the production of uneven spatio-temporal development and the intense contradictions that now exist within that field not only for capitalist trajectories of development (entailing, as they do, a great deal of self-destruction, devaluation, and bankruptcy) but also for populations rendered increasingly vulnerable to the violence of down-sizing, unemployment, collapse of services, and degradation in living standards and in environmental qualities. We need to go beyond the particularities and emphasize the *pattern* and the systemic qualities of the damage being wrought. And that pattern is perhaps best captured by calculating the consequences of neoliberalism as it works through globalization.

We need, furthermore, to extend that analysis outwards to embrace a diverse array of issues. We need to show how issues like AIDS, global warming, local environmental degradation, the destruction of local cultural traditions are inherently class issues, and how building a community in class struggle can better alleviate the conditions of oppression across a broad spectrum of social action. This is not, I emphasize, a plea for pluralism but a plea that we seek to uncover the class content of a wide array of anti-capitalist concerns. This will encounter opposition from within the radical Left, for to insist upon a class formulation invites dismissal as pure sectarianism of the old-guard sort (to say nothing of being rejected as passé in academia). But "all for one and one for all" in anti-capitalist struggle continues to be a vital slogan for any effective political action, and that inevitably implies some sort of class politics.

This work of synthesis has, however, to re-root itself in the organic conditions of daily life. This does not entail abandoning the abstractions that Marx and the Marxists have bequeathed us, but it does mean revalidating and revaluing those abstractions through immersion in popular struggles, some of which may not appear on the surface to be proletarian in the sense traditionally given to that term. In this regard, Marxism has its own sclerotic tendencies to combat, its own embedded fixed capital of concepts, institutions, practices, and politics which can function on the one hand as an excellent resource and on the other as a dogmatic barrier to action. We need to discern what is useful and what is not in this fixed capital of our intellect and politics, and it would be surprising if there were not, from time to time, bitter argument over what to jettison and what to hold. Nevertheless, the discussion must be launched.

For example, the traditional Marxist categories with which I began—imperialism, colonialism, neocolonialism—appear far too simplistic to capture the intricacies of uneven spatio-temporal development. Perhaps they were always so, but the reterritorialization and respatialization of capitalism, particularly over the past thirty years, make such categories seem far too crude to express the geopolitical complexities within which class struggle must now unfold. While a term like "globalization" repeats that error in a disempowering way for socialist and anti-capitalist movements, we cannot recapture the political initiative by reversion to a rhetoric of imperialism and neocolonialism, however superior the political content of those latter terms might be. Here, too, I believe a shift to a conception of uneven spatio-temporal development (or, more simply, uneven geographical development) can be helpful in order both to appreciate the tasks to be surmounted and the politics of multiple militant particularism that need to be combined.

I take up, finally, just one other organizational point. The traditional method of Marxist intervention has been via an avant-garde political party. But difficulties have arisen from the superimposition of a single aim, a singular objective, a simple goal upon anti-capitalist movements that have a multiplicity of objectives. As many critics within the Marxist tradition have pointed out, the emancipatory thrust of Marxism here creates the danger of its own negation. It is therefore vital to understand that liberating humanity for its own development is to open up the production of difference, even to open up a terrain for contestation within and among differences, rather than to suppress them. This is something that the right wing sometimes argues for—though it rarely practices it, as its turn to fundamentalism indicates. But we should note the power of the argument. The production of real as opposed to commodified cultural divergence, for example, can be just as easily posed as an aim of anti-capitalist struggle. The aim to create a unified, homogeneous socialist person was never real and requires more careful articulation if it is to be useful. After all, capitalism has been a hegemonic force for the production of a relatively homogeneous capitalist person, and this reductionism of all beings and all cultural differences to a common commodified base has itself been the focus of massive anti-capitalistic sentiments. The socialist cause must, surely, be just as much about emancipation from that bland homogeneity as it is about the creation of some analogous condition. This is not, however, a plea for an unchecked relativism or unconstrained post-modern eclecticism but for a serious discussion of the relations between commonality/ difference, the particularity of the one and the universalism of the other. And it is at this point that socialism as an alternative vision of how society will work, social relations unfold, human potentialities be realized, itself becomes the focus of conceptual work.

We still badly need a socialist avant-garde. But we do not necessarily need an old style avant-garde party that imposes a singular goal. On the other hand, we cannot function either armed only with Derrida's fantasy of a "New International without status, without title and without name . . . without party, without country, without national community." This is, as Eagleton (1995: 37) remarks, "the ultimate poststructuralist fantasy: an opposition without anything as distastefully systemic or drably 'orthodox' as an opposition, a dissent beyond all formulable discourse, a promise which would betray itself in the act of fulfillment, a perpetual excited openness to the Messiah who had better not let us down by doing anything as determinate as coming." For Derrida, the move that makes this possible is to separate "dialectical materialism" from all tangible sense of historical-geographical conditions as well as from any rootedness in a tangible and organized politics. I here part company with that genre of relational dialectics that has become pure idealism and find myself writing *against* an emerging avant-gardist trend, grounded in dialectical and relational ways of thinking, producing what might be called "a new idealism" in which thought and discourse are believed to be all that matter in powering the historical geography of socio-ecological and political-economic change. We have to abandon that particular version of avant-gardism, now so trendy in the academy, in which immersion in the flows of thought and ideality is somehow imagined to be radical and revolutionary in itself.

We need not only to understand but also to create organizations, institutions, doctrines, programs, formalized structures, and the like. And these political activities must be firmly grounded in the concrete historical and geographical conditions under which human action unfolds. Between the traditional avant-gardism of communist parties and the idealized avant-gardism (what might be called the Specter of Derrida) there lies a terrain of political organization and struggle that desperately cries out for cultivation. That terrain is not empty of possibilities. There are several substantive movements that claim our attention.

Consider, for example, the January 30, 1996 call by the Zapatista Army for National Liberation for "A World Gathering Against Neoliberalism and for Humanity," a whole series of intercontinental congresses of those opposed to neoliberal capitalism through globalization. Their call points out how the power of money everywhere "humiliates dignities, insults honesties, and assassinates hopes. Renamed as Neoliberalism, the historic crime in the concentration of privileges, wealth, and impunities democratizes misery and hopelessness." The name "globalization" signifies, they suggest, the "modern war" of capital "which assassinates and forgets." Instead of humanity, this Neoliberalism "offers us stock market value indexes, instead of dignity it offers us globalization of misery, instead of hope it offers us emptiness, instead of life it offers us the international of terror." Against this international of terror, they conclude, "we must raise the international of hope." If only, they suggest, everyone touched by the violence of neoliberal globalization could come together politically, then the days of this "brakeless train wreaking havoc" would be numbered.

The work of synthesis and organizing anti-capitalist struggles on a variegated terrain of uneven geographical development must proceed apace. That is what avant-garde political organization should now be focusing upon. We have abundant work to do. Let's do it!

Bibliography

Amin, S. (1974) *Accumulation on a World Scale*, New York: Monthly Review Press.

Cardoso, F. and Faletto, E. (1979) *Dependency and Development in Latin America*, Berkeley: University of California Press.

Deleuze, G. and Guattari, F. (1984) *Anti-Oedipus: Capitalism and Schizophrenia*, New York: Viking Press.

Derrida, J. (1994) *Specters of Marx*, London: Routledge.

Eagleton, T. (1995) "Jacques Derrida: Specters of Marx," *Radical Philosophy* 73: 35–7.

Emmanuel, A. (1972) *Unequal Exchange: A Study of the Imperialism of Trade*, New York: Monthly Review Press.

Foster, J. (1974) *Class Struggle in the Industrial Revolution*, London: Routledge and Kegan Paul.

Frank, A. (1969) *Capitalism and Underdevelopment in Latin America*, New York: Monthly Review Press.

Friedman, T. (1996) "Revolt of the Wannabes," *New York Times* January 7, A19.

Harvey, D. (1996) *Justice, Nature and the Geography of Difference*, Oxford: Basil Blackwell.

Lenin, V. I. (1970) *Questions of National Policy and Proletarian Internationalism*, Moscow: Progress Publishers.

Luxemburg, R. (1976) *The National Question: Selected Writings*, New York: Monthly Review Press.

Mao, T.-T. (1968) *Four Essays on Philosophy*, Peking: Foreign Languages Press.

Marx, K. and Engels, F. (1952) *Manifesto of the Communist Party*, Moscow: Progress Publishers.

Rodney, W. (1981) *How Europe Underdeveloped Africa*, Washington DC: Howard University Press.

Ross, K. (1988) *The Emergence of Social Space: Rimbaud and the Paris Commune*, Basingstoke and London: Macmillan.

Thompson, E. P. (1968) *The Making of the English Working Class*, Harmondsworth, Middlesex: Penguin.

Wallerstein, I. (1974) *The Modern World System*, New York: Academic Press.

Williams, R. (1989) *Resources of Hope*, London: Verso.

Zapatista Army for National Liberation (1996) "A World Gathering Against Neoliberalism and for Humanity," *La Tomada*, January 30.

2 The future of global polarization

Samir Amin

History since Antiquity has been characterized by unequal development of regions. But it is only in the modern era that polarization has become the immanent by-product of the integration of the entire planet into the capitalist system.

Modern (capitalist) polarization has appeared in successive forms during the evolution of the capitalist mode of production:

1   The mercantilist form (1500–1800) before the Industrial Revolution, which was fashioned by the hegemony of merchant capital in the dominant Atlantic centers, and by the creation of the peripheral zones (the Americas) as a function of their total compliance with the logic of accumulation of merchant capital.

2   The so-called classical model, which grew out of the Industrial Revolution and henceforth defined the basic forms of capitalism. In contrast, the peripheries—progressively all of Asia (except for Japan) and Africa, which were added to Latin America—remained rural, non-industrialized, and as a result their participation in the world division of labor took place via agriculture and mineral production. This important characteristic of polarization was accompanied by a second equally important one: the crystallization of core industrial systems as national auto-centered systems which paralleled the construction of the national bourgeois states. Taken together, these two characteristics account for the dominant lines of the ideology of national liberation which was the response to the challenge of polarization: (1) the goal of industrialization as synonym for liberating progress and as a means of "catching up;" (2) the goal of constructing nation-states inspired by the models of those in the core. This is how modernization ideology was conceived. From the industrial revolution (after 1800) up to the end of World War II, the world-system was characterized by this classical form of polarization.

3   The post-war period (1945–90) witnessed the progressive erosion of the above two characteristics. It was a period of industrialization of the peripheries—unequal to be sure. It was the dominant factor in Asia and Latin

America, with the national liberation movement doing its best to accelerate the process within those peripheral states that had recently regained political autonomy. This period was simultaneously one of the progressive dismantling of autocentric national production systems and their recomposition as constitutive elements of an integrated world production system. This double erosion was the new manifestation of the deepening of globalization.

4   The accumulation of these transformations resulted in the collapse of the equilibria characteristic of the post-war world system. This evolution is not leading to a new world order characterized by new forms of polarization, but to "global disorder." The chaos which confronts us today comes from a triple failure of the system: (1) it has not developed new forms of political and social organization going beyond the nation-state—a new requirement of the globalized system of production; (2) it has not developed economic and political relationships capable of reconciling the rise of industrialization in the newly competitive peripheral zones of Asia and Latin America with the pursuit of global growth; and (3) it has not developed a relationship other than an exclusionary one with the African periphery which is not engaged in competitive industrialization. This chaos is visible in all regions of the world and in all facets of the political, social, and ideological crisis. It is at the origin of the difficulties in the construction of Europe and its inability to pursue market integration and establish parallel integrative political structures. It is the cause of the convulsions in all the peripheries in Eastern Europe, in the old semi-industrialized Third World, in the new marginalized Fourth World. Far from sustaining the progression of globalization, the current chaos reveals its extreme vulnerability.

5   The predominance of this chaos should not keep us from thinking about alternative scenarios for a "New World Order" even if there are many different possible future "world orders." What I am trying to do here is to call attention to questions which have been glossed over by the triumphalism of inevitable globalization at the same time as its precariousness is revealed.

The reader will no doubt have discovered that this analysis of world capitalism is not centered on the question of hegemonies. I do not subscribe to the successive hegemonies school of historiography. The concept of hegemony is often sterile and not scientific because it has been so loosely defined. It does not seem to me that it should be the center of the debate. I have, in contrast, developed the idea that hegemony is far from the rule; it is rather the exception. The rule being conflict among partners which puts an end to the hegemony. The hegemony of the United States, seemingly in effect today, perhaps by default, is as fragile and precarious as the globalization of the structures through which it operates.

In my opinion the debate should start with an in-depth discussion of the new features in the world-system which are produced by the erosion of the previous one. In my opinion there are two new elements:

1   The erosion of the autocentered nation-state and the subsequent disappearance of the link between the arena of reproduction and accumulation together with the weakening of political and social control which up to now had been defined precisely by the frontiers of this autocentered nation-state.
2   The erosion of the contrast of industrialized center/non-industrialized peripheral regions, and the emergence of new dimensions of polarization.

A country's position in the world pyramid is defined by its capacity to compete in the world market. Recognizing this truism does not in any way imply sharing the bourgeois economist's view that this position is achieved as the result of "rational" measures—the said rationality being measured by the standard of the so-called "objective laws of the market." On the contrary, I think that this competitivity is a complex product of many economic, political, and social factors. In this unequal fight the centers use what I call their "five monopolies." These monopolies challenge the totality of social theory. They are:

1   Technological monopoly. This requires huge expenditures that only a large and wealthy state can envisage. Without the support of the state, especially through military spending (something liberal discourse doesn't mention) most of these monopolies would not last.
2   Financial control of worldwide financial markets. These monopolies have an unprecedented efficacy thanks to the liberalization of the rules governing their establishment. Not so long ago the greater part of a nation's savings could circulate only within the arena—largely national—of the financial institutions. Today these savings are handled centrally by institutions whose operations are worldwide. We are talking of finance capital: capital's most globalized component. The logic of this globalization of finance could be called into question by a simple political decision to delink, even if limited to the domain of financial transfers. Moreover, I think that the rules governing the free movement of finance capital have broken down. This system had been based on the free floating of currencies on the market (according to the theory that money is a merchandise like any other) with the dollar serving de facto as a universal currency. Money as a merchandise theory is unscientific and the position of the dollar is only *faute de mieux*. A national currency cannot fulfil the functions of an international currency unless there is a surplus of exports in the "international currency" country thus underwriting structural adjustment in the other countries. This was the case of Great Britain in the late nineteenth century. This is not the case of the United States today, which finances its deficit by imposed borrowing. Nor is this the case for the competitors of the United States: Japan's surplus (that of Germany disappeared after reunification) is not sufficient to meet the financial needs occasioned by the structural adjustment of the others. Under these conditions financial globalization, far from being a "natural" process, is an

extremely fragile one. In the short run it leads only to permanent instability and not to the stability necessary for the efficient operation of the processes of adjustment.

3 Monopolies of access to the planet's natural resources. The dangers of the reckless exploitation of these resources are now planet-wide. Capitalism, based on short-term rationality, cannot overcome these dangers posed by this reckless behavior, and it therefore reinforces the monopolies of already developed countries. Their concern is simply not to let others be equally irresponsible.

4 Media and communication monopolies. These not only lead to uniformity of culture but also open up new means of political manipulation. The expansion of the modern media market is already one of the major components of the erosion of democratic practices in the West itself.

5 Finally, monopolies of weapons of mass destruction. Held in check by the post-war bipolarity, this monopoly is again, as in 1945, the sole domain of the United States. If "proliferation" risks getting out of control it is still the only way of fighting this unacceptable monopoly in the absence of democratic international control.

These five monopolies taken as a whole define the framework within which the law of globalized value operates. The law of value is the condensed expression of all these conditions, hardly the expression of objective "pure" economic rationality. The conditioning of all of these processes annuls the impact of industrialization in the peripheries, devalues their productive work, and overvalues the supposed value added to the activities of the new monopolies from which the centers profit. What results is a new—more unequal than ever before—hierarchy in the distribution of income on a world scale, subordinating the industries of the peripheries and reducing them to subcontracting. This is the new foundation of polarization, presaging its future forms.

In contrast to the dominant ideological discourse, I maintain that "globalization via the market" is a reactionary utopia. We must counter it by developing an alternative humanistic project of globalization consistent with a socialist perspective.

Implied in the realization of such a project is the construction of a global political system which is not in the service of a global market but one which defines its parameters, just as the nation-state historically represented the social framework of the national market and not its field of deployment. A global political system would thus have major responsibilities in each of the following four domains:

1 The organization of global disarmament at appropriate levels thus liberating humanity from the menace of nuclear and other holocausts.

2 The organization of access to the planet's resources in an equitable manner so that there would be less and less inequality. There should be a global decision-making process with a valuation (*tariffication*) of resources, which would make obligatory both waste reduction and the distribution of the

value and income from these resources. This could also be the beginning of a globalized fiscal system.

3   Negotiation of open, flexible economic relationships between the world's major regions which are unequally developed. This would reduce progressively the centers' technological and financial monopolies. This means of course the liquidation of the institutions presently running the global market (the so-called World Bank, the IMF, GATT, etc.) and the creation of other systems for managing the global economy.

4   Starting negotiation for a corresponding management of the global/national dialectic in the areas of communication, culture, and political policy. This implies the creation of political institutions which would represent social interests operating on a global scale, the beginning of a "world parliament" going beyond interstate mechanisms that exist presently.

It is more than evident that current trends are not going in the direction described above and that the humanist objectives are not dominant today. I would be surprised were it otherwise. The erosion of the old system of globalization is not able to prepare its own succession and can only lead to chaos. Dominant forces are developing their activities in the framework of these constraints, trying to manoeuvre for short-term gain and thereby aggravating the chaos. Their attempt to legitimate their choices by the stale ideology of the "self-regulating" market, by affirming that "there is no alternative," or by pure and simple cynicism, is not the solution but in fact part of the problem. The people's spontaneous responses to degradation are not necessarily more helpful. In a time of disarray, illusory solutions such as fundamentalism or chauvinism can be very politically mobilizing. It is up to the left—that is its historic mission—to formulate, in theory and in practice, a humanistic response to the challenge. In the absence of such an undertaking, and until it is formulated, regressive and criminal scenarios will be the most likely order of the day.

The difficulties confronting the European Union today are a good illustration of the impasse of "globalization by market mechanisms." In the first blush of enthusiasm over the European idea no one foresaw these difficulties. Yet they were perfectly predictable by people who never believed that the Common Market by itself could create Europe. We said that a project as ambitious as this one could not be accomplished without a left capable of making it socially and culturally progressive. If not, it would remain fragile and the least serious accident would be fatal. It was necessary therefore for the European lefts to make sure that each step of the integration was accompanied by a double series of measures: on the one hand, insuring that profits go to the workers thereby reinforcing their social power and their unity; and on the other, beginning the construction of a political system which will supersede the nation-state and which may prove to be the only unit that can effectively manage an enlarged market. This did not happen. The European project, in the hands of the right, was reduced to mercantilist proportions, and the left sooner or later offered its support without imposing any conditions. The result is what we see before us: the economic downturn has put the European partners in an adversarial position. They can only imagine solutions to their problems (notably unemployment) that are at the expense of others, and they don't even have effective tools for doing that. They are increasingly tempted by involutive pullbacks. Even the sincere efforts to avoid such action on the part of French and German politicians on the right and on the left have resulted only in incantation.

Little Europe (the EU) is experiencing problems at the same time as big Europe is giving a new meaning to the challenge. This is an opportunity for the left to rethink the European project as a whole and to begin the construction of a confederal political and economic big Europe that is anchored on the left by a reconstructed and united European labor force. They have missed this opportunity, and, on the contrary, have backed the forces of the right which were in a hurry to profit from the collapse of the Soviet Empire by substituting a wild capitalism. It is obvious that the "Latin-Americanization" of Eastern Europe can only weaken the chances of success for a European project anchored on the left, and that can only accentuate the disequilibrium among the Europe of the EU to the benefit of the only partner able to profit from this evolution: reunited Germany.

The crisis of the European project is one of the major challenges confronting the construction of the new globalization. But these involutive manifestations, these inadequate and tragic responses to the challenge of the construction of a renewed global system, are not found exclusively in Europe. They are seen throughout the former Third World, especially in regions marginalized by the collapse of the old world order (Sub-Saharan Africa and Arab-Islamic areas), and also in the new Third World of the East (as in the ex-USSR and ex-Yugoslavia), where we see autodestructive involutions rather than valid responses to the challenge.

Given this background, there are few realistic scenarios that can be proposed. I will examine several of them and show that they do not reply to the exigencies of the construction of an acceptable and stable world order. They therefore do not provide an exit from chaos.

The European question is at the center of theorizing about the future of globalization. With the breakdown of the European project and the threat of disintegration, forces faithful to the European idea could find it useful and possible to regroup at their "second best" position, that is, a German Europe. There is reason to believe that in this scenario the British ship would sail close to American shores, keeping its distance from "continental Europe." We have already started down this path and some have even legitimated this choice by giving priority to the "neutral management of money" (a technocratic concept based on ignorance of the political meaning of money management), and conferring it (where else?) to the Bundesbank! I do not believe that this caricature of the original European project can be truly stable, for neither Russia nor France will accept the erosion of their positions, which it implies.

To make matters worse, the preferential position of the United States is not challenged by the scenario of Germany's going it alone or of a German Europe.

Nor is it clear that there is anything in this project that could challenge America in any of the areas of the five monopolies discussed above. A German Europe would remain within the American orbit.

There is a second scenario—for lack of an alternative—a second edition of "American hegemony." There are many variations. The most likely one is a "sharing of the burden" associated with neoimperialist regionalization: hitching Latin America to the US wagon and Africa to the German-European one (with crumbs for France), but not the Gulf oil region and the "common market of the Middle East," which would remain the domain of the United States. The American presence is felt by the military occupation of the Gulf and indirectly by the alliance with Israel. And, one can say, by the symmetry of leaving southern Asia to Japanese expansion. But there is no equality implied in this division among the three centers discussed above: the United States retains its privileged position. Here too I do not believe that neoimperialist options of this type guarantee the stability of the system. They will be disputed here and there by revolts in Latin America, Asia, and Africa.

We should therefore focus our attention on Asia, which has been largely outside the Euro-American conflict. It has often been observed that Asia—from Japan to Communist China, to Korea, and to a lesser degree to certain countries of Southeast Asia (Singapore, Thailand, and Malaysia) and even India—has not been affected by crisis and these countries have registered successes in terms of growth and efficiency (measured by competitivity on the world market). One cannot quickly jump ahead and say that Asia will be the locus of the next hegemony. Asia, in this globalizing concept, is more than half the world's population! This population is divided among distinct states. In the place of a vague concept of hegemony one could substitute one of an Asia becoming the principal region of capitalist accumulation. It remains to be described in detail how this is occurring: the articulation between the different nations, and between them and the rest of the world. There are variants of the model. The easiest to imagine— the domination of Japanese imperialism in the region—is, in my opinion, the least plausible. Admirers of Japan's recent success too often underestimate Japan's vulnerability. It is because of this weakness that Japan remains tied to the United States. It does not seem likely that China, or even Korea, would accept being subordinated to Japan. Under these conditions the maintenance of an inter-Asian equilibrium would depend on forces external to the region and here again only the United States is a candidate for this role, which would prolong its primacy on the world scene.

Nonetheless it is highly probable that the positions of these Asian countries will be reinforced within the world-system. How will the United States react to this? All strategies of alliances will, in my opinion, revolve around this question. It goes almost without saying that the development of China threatens all global equilibria. And that is why the United States will feel threatened by its development. In my opinion the United States and China will be the major antagonists in a future conflict. What will Europe's attitude be? It is hard to tell today.

Current developments suggest different possible scenarios, none of which questions the cause of "North–South" polarization. The commanding logic of the capitalist system perpetuates the center/periphery polarization. Its modes of operation are ever renewed and will in the future be founded on the five monopolies around which I constructed my argument.

One could say that there is nothing new in this view because polarization is almost part of the natural order of things. I do not conclude on this note precisely because this is what has changed over the last five centuries: peoples peripheralized by capitalist world expansion, who seemed for a long time to accept their fate, are not accepting it any longer (and have not been for the past 50 years) and will refuse it more and more in the future. The positive aspect of the universalization which capitalism inaugurated—and which can't get beyond its present truncated version—is that the worm is in the fruit. The Russian and Chinese revolutions began the attempt to go beyond the system on the basis of the revolts of peripheral peoples—and this will be continued in new versions. The final explanation for the instability of the "world-system" is found here. Of course the conflicts that will occupy the forefront of the stage in the future will, as always, not all be of equal importance. I would intuitively give determining priority to future conflicts opposing the peoples of Asia and the dominant systems. This doesn't mean others won't participate in this generalized revolt against polarization, just as it does not mean that transformations and progress won't emanate from the very centers of the system. I have previously treated this aspect of the socialist transformation of the world. This does not exclude failures, dramatic ones when people resolutely refuse a universalist perspective (Amin 1993, 1994).

A humanistic response to the challenge of globalization inaugurated by capitalist expansion may be idealistic but it is not utopian. On the contrary, it is the only realistic project possible. Let us just begin to develop it and powerful social forces will rally to it from all regions of the world.

This is the way to renew the perspective of global socialism. In preparation, ideological and political forces must regroup in order to be capable of combating the five monopolies, which reproduce capitalism. This combat will create conditions for "mutual adjustment."

In this struggle we have to reconsider fundamental questions on the ideological cultural front: (1) the universal/particular dialectic; (2) the relationship between political democracy and social progress; (3) the dialectic of so-called economic efficiency (and the ways it is expressed: the "market") and values of equality and fraternity; and (4) the definition of a global socialist objective in the light of all the above.

On the political front we have to develop world organizational forms which are more authentically democratic so as to be capable of reshaping economic relations on the basis of less and less inequality. In this perspective it seems to me that high priority should be given to reorganize the global system on the basis of large regions which would group together scattered parts of the peripheries. This would be the place for the constitution of Latin American, Arab, African, and

Southeast Asian regions, alongside China and India (the only continental countries on our planet). I propose that this objective receives priority treatment in the new agenda of the "Non-Aligned Movement." The regional groupings do not exclude others such as Europe or the ex-USSR. The reason for this exigency is simple: it is only on this scale that one can effectively combat the five monopolies of our analysis. The construction in turn of a truly global economic and financial system becomes possible on this basis.

Of course the transformation of the world always begins with struggles at its base. For without the beginning of changes in ideological, political, and social systems on the level of their national bases, any discussion about globalization and polarization remains a dead letter.

Bibliography

Amin, S. (1992) *L'empire du chaos*, Paris: L'Harmattan.

—— (1993) *Itinéraire intellectuel*, Paris: L'Harmattan.

—— (1993) *L'ethnicité à l'assaut des nations*, Paris: L'Harmattan.

—— (1993) *Mondialisation et accumulation*, Paris: L'Harmattan.

—— (1993) *Empire of Chaos*, New York: Monthly Review Press.

—— (1994) *Re-reading the Post War Period*, New York: Monthly Review Press.

—— (forthcoming) *Le système monétaire international est caduc, par quoi le remplacer?*

—— (forthcoming) *La gauche occidentale vu du tiers monde*.

3 Globalization and social change

Drowning in the icy waters of commercial calculation

Manfred Bienefeld

This chapter will make three arguments. First, it will suggest that the present process of globalization involves a significant and ultimately destructive shift in the political and institutional context within which competitive market forces, and the logic of capital, find material expression. Second, it will argue that current trends are not sustainable and that they are in the process of generating explosive contradictions that will eventually undermine efficiency and the conditions for the continued accumulation of capital. And finally, it will contend that the only political response that can hope to harness and redirect these forces in a socially responsible and desirable manner is one that is rooted in societies with a sufficient sense of their common interest and identity to act coherently through a political process that has broad legitimacy and that is primarily concerned with protecting and promoting public welfare. One can think of these responses as versions of Polanyi's "double movement," or as socially rooted forms of class struggle.

This discussion leads to two ultimately unanswerable questions, namely: Are such political responses feasible at all? And, if so, are they likely to materialize in our lifetime? Such matters of political struggle are, of course, inherently uncertain, but I believe the basis for the claim that "all is lost" to be very weak. In fact I would argue that a dramatic political response to these developments is inevitable. Indeed, judging by the accelerating disintegration of societies and nation-states around the world, it has already begun. The question is only what form this reaction will take. And here I believe that our main task as intellectuals and as responsible, politically engaged citizens, is to counter the incessant claims that resistance is futile; to critically examine the claim that these processes enhance human welfare; to oppose all efforts to lock these policies in to international agreements that constrain democratic choices; and to continue to build and to articulate a vision of humane and superior alternatives.

The global logic of the market

The chapter begins with an obvious, indisputable point. Competitive market forces are amoral, unsentimental and enormously powerful. In arm's length markets, goods and services compete without reference to the social or human conditions of their production. In the process, they become commodities; socially disengaged use values. And, when their appearance and their performance characteristics (their "use values") are equivalent, the cheapest ones survive. The question of whether that low price was made possible by superior organization, by better technology or by the more intense exploitation of labor is of no concern to the market, unless people, acting through a political process, make it so.

The history of capitalism is a history of this struggle: the logic of the market, pitted against the efforts of societies and cultures to define, and to sustain, some ethically rooted, politically defined structures that can limit, and direct, the potentially overwhelming force of the competitive market. This struggle has been uneven across space and time, but over time there has been a powerful tendency to erode affective social networks and to create increasingly fragmented and instrumental societies. In this process, human beings gradually become "human capital;" mother earth turns into a privately owned factor of production; and knowledge and ideas are made into "private property"—for sale or hire to those with the ability to pay.

The new neoliberal lessons of history incredibly redefine the "golden age" as being the period of the gold standard, around the end of the nineteenth century, and make no reference to the turmoil of the 1920s when drawing the lessons of the 1930s. Moreover, they almost entirely disregard the demonstrated potential of unregulated markets to generate serious speculative instability, and to polarize and to destabilize societies. These fatal flaws are simply treated as minor blemishes that can be fixed by the even more radical liberalization of markets, and especially those for labor, pollution rights, and information (James 1996).

It is surely ironic that the protagonists of this brave new neoliberal worldview, who love to talk about the unprecedented novelty of today's technologically driven and irreversible process of globalization, should offer us the nineteenth century as their vision of the golden age, and try to pass off the utterly discredited economic theories of the 1920s as their "new" contribution to theory. Moreover, under these circumstances, it borders on the ridiculous that it is the left that is continually accused of being wedded to "old ideas;" especially when too many on the left have unwisely abandoned a lot of important "old ideas" that would have served them far better than the murky pronouncements of post-Fordism. But, unfortunately for the left, all of this matters less than it should, since it is not those with the most persuasive arguments who succeed in the real world, but those whose power is enhanced by the changes occurring in that world.

In this sense, there is no doubt that victory has gone to the right, for the time being. By the end of the 1980s the nationalist upsurge in the Third World had been well and truly beaten back, disciplined by debt and by an increasingly aggressive and single-minded international system, willing to enforce the logic of the market with a degree of militancy and arrogance that had not been seen since the days of nineteenth-century imperialism—their new "golden age." The "evil empire" has also been dismantled, and debt played a major role in that process as well. And the 1990s have witnessed an intensification of the attack on working people, even in the industrial world; an attack that began in earnest in the 1970s and was reinforced in the 1980s when escalating real interest rates allowed ballooning public sector debts to become a primary weapon in the assault on the welfare state and on gains made by the working class over the previous quarter century. A London-based financial analyst described this assault very effectively and very accurately in 1993 when he replied to a journalist's question by suggesting that it was important for people to understand that "global financial markets are on a religious crusade to roll back social democracy" (*Globe and Mail,* January 16, 1995).

And so they are. Nothing would be more foolish or naive than to think that these financial markets are not political because they are "simply concerned with rates of return." The truth is that those rates of return are closely linked, especially in the short run, with the demonstrated willingness of governments to put the interests of bond holders first. And that is an eminently political matter; and it is why financial markets often react quite disproportionately to any indication that a government may be wavering in its allegiance to the "sound economic policies" that they favor and demand, even though they will frequently acknowledge that those policies may not be in the long-term interests of a country or a society. Indeed, individual investment managers will often say that such larger questions are "none of their concern."[1]

So what has the victory of the neoliberals produced? Has it produced the stability, efficiency and prosperity that its advocates promised? Of course it has not. It has produced results that strongly confirm and corroborate the fears that had led the architects of the early Bretton Woods system to be so cautious and to design such strong safeguards against speculative flows of short-term capital; against the excessive volatility of interest and exchange rates; and against the excessive deregulation of markets, in general. Their fears that failure to do so would once again lead to explosive and dangerous contradictions in the world economy have been amply justified. Economic growth has once again come to be associated with sharp increases in income inequality, with rising economic insecurity, with a financial sector that is increasingly divorced from the real economy, and with speculative bubbles that inflated and collapsed with awesome regularity. The consequences for millions of people have been devastating. And in the process, the rights of working people and of citizens have come under sustained attack everywhere as the "icy waters of commercial calculation" rise inexorably, driven by voracious financial markets that constantly extend their dominion by assigning private property rights to ever more diverse aspects of life, from life forms, to ideas, to pollution rights.

The results are truly disturbing, especially when they are compared to the high hopes of the 1960s, or to the stridently confident predictions of the mainstream economists of that day. There is no leisure society; no four-day work week; no increase in economic, social or political security. Quite the opposite. Regular employment is increasingly treated as a luxury that we cannot afford. The social wage is being eroded everywhere, and the attack on public pensions has become a relentless, global campaign. In the United States, real wages are below their level of 1973; and an Index of Social Health, calculated by Fordham

University for many years on the basis of 16 variables (including unemployment, income inequality, food stamp coverage, child abuse, teen suicide, etc.), has fallen steadily and dramatically, from 73 in the 1970s (under Nixon/Ford), to 43 by the end of the second Reagan presidency, to 38 by the end of the first Clinton term (*The Nation*, November 11, 1996).

This attack on labor is not easing, as one might have expected if it had merely been imposing "short-term pain for long-term gain," as some had suggested. In fact, the attack is intensifying even though those long-term gains are proving resolutely elusive; and even though there is now significant evidence to show that these policies are often misguided and destructive.[2]

The truth is that the attack on labor was never primarily motivated by a desire for greater efficiency; much less by a desire to enhance global welfare. It was about income redistribution; about enhancing the returns to capital; about raising real interest rates to historically unprecedented levels; about underwriting, and validating, speculatively driven increases in stock and other asset prices. And the result was a powerful and pervasive downward pressure on real wages and on the conditions of labor in large parts of the developed and the developing world, even including Asia in the wake of the crisis of 1997.

This captures the essence of the present situation rather well, except for the glib claim that these changes "yield faster growth and higher living standards," which is wholly unsubstantiated and quite incompatible with the evidence. The truth is that the sluggish growth rates since the mid-1970s compare very unfavorably to those achieved during the previous quarter century; the world's fastest growing economies in Asia were generally statist and highly regulated throughout the 1970s and 1980s when they were the engines of the world economy; and the endemic increase in the insecurity of work was accompanied by stagnation and decline in real wages for most working people in that country. Indeed, this is presumably why the article ultimately falls back on the claim that these changes have to be accepted because they are inevitable, in that: "the damage done by economic uncertainty is real. But the clock cannot be turned back to the economy of the 1950s and 1960s" (Mandel 1996: 94).

But one is bound to ask why this "clock cannot be turned back"; or whether that conclusion is completely unrelated to the question of where this process is heading. What if this "damage done by economic uncertainty" were to continue to escalate? Would there not come a point at which the question would have to be addressed? Indeed, even among conservatives such simplistic conclusions have begun to be called into question for some time now. So, in 1994, *The Economist* expressed its grave concern about the explosive increase in income inequality that had accompanied the neoliberal revolution around the world, but especially in those industrial countries in which it had been espoused most enthusiastically.

> Income inequality in America and Britain are greater than at any time in the past fifty years. The social consequences of this change worry many . . . It is no coincidence that the biggest increases in income inequalities have occurred in economies such as those of America, Britain and New Zealand,

where free market economic policies have been pursued most zealously . . . In 1992 the top 20 percent of American households received 11 times as much income as the bottom 20 percent, up from a multiple of 7.5 in 1969 [in] . . . Britain too the gap between rich and poor has been widening . . . the Gini coefficient rose from 0.23 in 1977 to 0.34 in 1991, a bigger jump than in any other country.

(*The Economist* 1994: 19)

But even this does not capture the full extent of the social revolution that is occurring as the icy waters of commercial calculation rise inexorably higher. Not only is work becoming more stressful, insecure and demanding; not only are most peoples' wages and salaries stagnating or falling; not only are public services being systematically eroded; not only are the rich appropriating resources beyond all reason or understanding; but the power of this increasingly concentrated wealth is being extended ever further into every nook and cranny of our personal and social existence. In time, everything will be "for sale" and in a world of increasingly unequal incomes that will further sharpen the spur of poverty—and the desperation of the poor.

The moral dilemma that arises when an increasingly unequal society creates powerful lobby groups—and armies of faceless investors—who profit from the incarceration of people is easily ignored—or trivialized by saying that it merely required "adequate regulation." But the dilemma is real—and it goes to the heart of the question of how societies are to set effective limits to the logic of the market in an increasingly unequal, competitive and "global" world.

These developments are not desirable, not ethically defensible, not sustainable, and not efficient. They reflect a desperately unhealthy situation in which political power is being used to allow public wealth and income to be appropriated and concentrated on an unprecedented scale. And, left unchecked, they must, in time, trigger a political reaction that will either lead to a dramatic reversal, or to an uneasy peace, in which increasing levels of repression contain an ever more alienated mass of marginalized people.

These lessons have been learned before, most recently in the 1920s and 1930s, and it seems that we are destined to learn them again. The lessons are that markets are powerful and benign instruments for diffusing power and for allocating productive resources, so long as they are embedded in relatively stable, coherent societies capable of curbing their centrifugal tendencies, and their tendency toward "instability and fraud" (World Bank 1989a: 4) capable of setting ethically, socially and politically defined limits to the search for competitive advantage; capable of nurturing and protecting the social values and networks whose existence allows contracts to be enforced at reasonable cost; and capable of protecting the political process and the media from complete domination by wealth and economic power.

The quarter century after World War II brought us the "golden age" because the experience of the 1920s and 1930s had generated political forces that allowed markets to be so embedded. And the early Bretton Woods agreement, by providing for extensive capital controls, forced capital to have a nationality, and therefore to negotiate and deal with those political forces at the national level. The result was a remarkably sustained, stable, dynamic, and inclusive process of growth and development. Growth was rapid and sustained and its benefits were widely shared—in the form of rising real wages, improved working conditions and strengthened social services. Profits were high though rates of profit tended to decline over time, as they should in a society in which capital is becoming relatively abundant (Keynes 1933).

Moreover, these lessons of the golden age have been further confirmed by the results of the subsequent neoliberal revolution, which have been briefly described above. Having become effectively disembedded, markets have proven to be extremely divisive and unstable; income and wealth are rapidly polarizing; growth and investment levels remain low, stifled by uncertainty, the high cost of capital and the presence of enormous mountains of accumulated debt; and, for most people, the quality of life is being undermined by increasing instability and stress at work, stagnant or falling real wages and incomes, and the systematic erosion of their claims on society and their rights as citizens. And, as in the 1920s, these developments are fuelling a dangerous process of political disintegration as ethnic nationalisms fill the void left by the collapse of coherent states.[3]

Developing countries and transition economies: some victories, more broken dreams

If the neoliberal revolution is polarizing and destabilizing the industrial world, it should come as no surprise that it has exacted a high price in most of the rest of the world, with Sub-Saharan Africa (SSA) and the transition economies of the former Soviet bloc being the worst affected, though Latin America as a whole has also paid a high price. Asia, and especially East and Southeast Asia, has been the exception, having enjoyed rapid growth and development throughout the 1980s and early 1990s. However, the crisis that erupted in 1997 has called even its future into question.

Africa's predictable tragedy

For SSA, the years since the early 1970s have been particularly devastating, as weak and unbalanced economies were exposed to increasing competitive pressure and to demands for institutional change that often far exceeded their political, institutional and technological capacities. Unable to service their accumulated debts, or to persuade their creditors to ease those burdens significantly, they found themselves trapped in a world of endless austerity; a world that stifled growth and investment, destroyed the viability of past investments (especially in infrastructure), deepened social and political tensions and gradually eroded the social fabric. And, in an increasing number of cases, this process eventually passed the point of no return when societies face a catastrophic collapse into anarchic instability.

But such disastrous outcomes should not have come as a surprise. The risks of applying the simplistic formulations of neoliberal "mono economics"[4] to this fragile region, were evident even in 1981, when the World Bank's "Berg Report" first elevated them to the status of "official" policy. The claim was that SSA's problems were primarily due to misguided state policies which had prevented market forces from ensuring rational and efficient patterns of resource allocation; and that these problems could be solved by shifting power from states to markets and by opening the economies much more fully to competitive pressures from abroad. But such "text book advice"[5] lacked credibility under SSA's actual circumstances, as I had tried to explain in a 1983 review of the "Berg Report:"

> the document as a whole [is] fundamentally wrong in its analysis; self-serving in its implicit allocation of responsibility for current problems; misleading in its broad policy prescriptions; and totally unrealistic both with respect to the social and political implications of its "solutions" and with respect to its assumptions about real aid flows, price and market prospects for African exports and the robustness of Africa's struggling institutional structure.
>
> It is both arrogant and meaningless for the Bank to assert in that context that . . . the way forward lies through a greater concern with technical expertise and a greater reliance on the market. Such advice cannot be followed for any length of time under current circumstances because the social and political consequences . . . would be so dramatic that the policies would be devastated by the political whirlwinds which would be unleashed. As in the past these domestic political responses could then be blamed for the disasters which follow, rather than being seen as more or less direct consequences of the acceptance of the(se) externally designed policy prescriptions.
>
> (Bienefeld 1983: 18, 22)

By the late 1980s, it was becoming clear even to the Bank that SSA was not doing well. In fact, the region was clearly regressing even in purely economic terms. It has been recognized that per capita incomes fell by over a quarter between 1980 and 1988, and the World Bank's assessment was similarly bleak.

> In the twenty-two debt-distressed, Sub-Saharan African countries per capita consumption dropped by about 3.2 percent a year and investment by 2.6 percent a year between 1980 and 1986. The debt crisis of the 1980s thus dealt a double blow to the more vulnerable developing countries. Reductions in per capita income lowered economic welfare immediately, while large cuts in investment threatened the potential for future growth . . .
>
> Moreover despite these drastic retrenchments, the low income African countries saw both their debt/GDP and their debt service/export ratios increase steadily between 1982 and 1987, the former from 48 to 76 percent and the latter from 14 to 35 percent.
>
> (World Bank 1988: 30, 31)

Worse still, the region's future development prospects were being blighted by low investment rates and a rapidly deteriorating infrastructure. And there was little evidence to suggest that this pain was being endured for good reason. The World Bank itself was forced to conclude in 1988 that the "hoped-for switching and growth-augmenting effects of adjustment lending is (sic) not apparent in the low income AL [Adjustment Lending] countries." (World Bank 1988: 24). In short, even for those who firmly believed in the neoliberal policy regime, it was increasingly difficult to avoid the conclusion that these policies were not solving SSA's problems.

But true ideologues are not easily swayed by the evidence. They can always choose to believe that those apparent failures are the result of inadequate implementation, insufficient time or unfortunate and unpredictable "exogenous" developments. Or they can claim that the outcomes would have been even worse in the absence of "their" policies, which allows the policies to be declared a success, irrespective of the actual outcomes. And it is on these grounds that the advocates of neoliberal globalization have continued to defend their policy prescriptions for SSA, though not without expressing "deep concern" at the disappointing "early" results. And, although the Bank and the Fund have recently abandoned the claim that the "magic of the market"[6] could restore SSA's development prospects even if they were required to repay all debts in full, their belated acceptance of the need for significant debt relief[7] is actually being used to further intensify their promotion of the neoliberal policy regime, in that only countries that commit themselves totally, and more or less irrevocably, to those policies will be eligible for such debt relief.

The Bank's commitment to its orthodox policies has, therefore, remained broadly unchanged despite the persistence of disappointing results; results which led its chief economist to declare in 1988 that:

> We did not think that the human costs of these (adjustment) programs could be so great, and economic gains so slow in coming.
>
> (O'Brien 1988)

Elsewhere, that same evidence led the Bank to acknowledge that "a longer time perspective is required for broader institutional changes" like those implied by its structural adjustment policies (World Bank 1988: 24). But such magnanimous admissions of fallibility are not much comfort to those suffering the "short-term pain" and waiting, in vain, for the long-term gain.

Behind the scenes, in the second half of the 1980s the World Bank did become aware of the fact that time did not appear to be on its side in SSA. Although the counter-factual claim that things could have been even worse in the absence of its policies might have allowed it to defend those policies in academic circles, this claim did not travel well in the real world where the people and the policy-makers of Africa actually lived. Here the dominant facts were that, in most cases, these policies were not delivering what they had promised, or what they had set out to achieve. And, in more than a few cases, they were worsening economic imbalances, deepening social divisions, and increasing political tensions.[8]

Some response was clearly needed to restore the credibility of the orthodox policy package under these circumstances, and this became a central concern within the World Bank. Its response was very effectively described by Ramgopal Agarwala, the senior World Bank economist who was eventually chosen to lead the team that was created by the Bank in 1987 to resolve these growing uncertainties.

> During the second half of the 1980s . . . the Bank's management sensed donor fatigue setting in as a reaction to the continuing African woes and repeated calls for more assistance. The international community was in need of reassurance that efforts to help Africa were effective and that there was "light at the end of the tunnel." The view, in the Bank, however, was that this possibility could only be offered as a long-term project.
>
> Thus was born the idea of a long-term vision for Africa, and the Bank initiated a study to demonstrate that, despite some major problems in the short and medium term, Africa could have a reasonably optimistic long-term future if appropriate policies were followed and external assistance made available at the appropriate level. The staff team assembled for this study struggled desperately to find "the light at the end of the tunnel," especially as the prospects for rapid economic growth seemed unrealistic over the medium or long term.
>
> (Agarwala and Schwartz 1994: 3–4)

At the end of the day, the team concluded that the Bank's adjustment policies were basically misguided and inappropriate for SSA.

> As the participatory process . . . started some doubts about the efficacy of adjustment in Africa began to emerge . . . But, ultimately it was the accumulation of anomalies, the realization of just how deep the crisis was, and the possibility that an alternative paradigm could explain the situation better . . . that opened the minds of the report's team . . . after ten years of stabilization . . . it was becoming clear that "prices and markets could not deliver" without a solid domestic institutional base for governance and development management.
>
> (Agarwala and Schwartz 1994: 13, 16, 26)

Ultimately these conclusions were framed in far more general terms—and it is in this form that they speak most directly to the argument that is being developed in this chapter. The team's rejection of the orthodox policies was presented as a "paradigm shift" that was made necessary because there were now too many "anomalies" that the existing paradigm could not explain—or comprehend.[9] And, although a new paradigm would take some time to emerge, the need for one was now incontrovertible; and, according to the team, it was most likely to be built around the idea of "the social market."[10]

The crisis in Africa and Latin America, and more recently in the former Soviet Union and Eastern Europe, may in time lead to the emergence of a new paradigm (Kuhn 1970: 11, 12) or a synthesis between the Keynesian and neo-classical paradigms. Also the growing interest in the East Asian "miracle" will lead to further questioning of the existing paradigm and the search for an alternative paradigm is likely to continue.

Unfortunately, these strong conclusions were not clearly reflected in the report that the Bank ultimately produced (World Bank 1989b). Although that document did raise some critical questions regarding the orthodox policy prescriptions, and although it did cause some controversy by suggesting that there was an urgent need to rebuild SSA's rapidly deteriorating infrastructure and to reverse the process of social polarization, it also explicitly endorsed the Bank's basic policy stance on more than one occasion. While such discrepancies are not unusual for the Bank,[11] in this case it seems that they arose largely because the team chose to "pull its punches" for strategic reasons. This is how the former team leader described that process in a paper written some years after its appearance:

> Partly for bureaucratic reasons, the issues were not spelled out [as] fully in the report as they have been here. The unorthodox findings . . . could only be presented in a low-profile manner, more as an undertone than an open challenge. The intellectual "ocean liner" of a large international bureaucracy cannot be turned around overnight.
>
> (Wade 1994: 27)

The tragedy is that the ocean liner did not turn. The Bank's next report on SSA made few references to those critical conclusions, and simply argued that the region's experience was compatible with the Bank's orthodox policy prescriptions. It would seem therefore that ideology still overrides the evidence, and that the commitment to the neoliberal policy regime is driven largely by power and interests, not by evidence.

The Latin American "recovery:" short-term gain for long-term pain?

The Latin American story is rather different. Having suffered dramatic reversals in the 1980s, its economies did generally recover some ground in the 1990s and this has led them to be widely hailed as great success stories in certain quarters. But their "success" has been very uneven—and remains extremely precarious. It is most apparent if one looks at foreign capital flows and the growing financial sectors; but it is not at all apparent when one looks at wages, poverty, and living conditions for the great majority of Latin Americans. But because the 1980s were so difficult, because Latin American societies have long been notoriously polarized and because significant minorities have managed to benefit substantially from the neoliberal policy regime in every country, these policies have a much stronger base of support within Latin America itself. These are, in other words, "home grown" policies to a much greater degree, although the international institutions do provide powerful backing and reinforcement.

On balance the evidence from this continent lends further support to the claim that the neoliberal policy regime is deeply divisive, endemically unstable, and ultimately unsustainable. And although that experience also shows that under certain circumstances these policies can have a positive impact for a time, they will not promote the emergence of politically stable, socially integrated, prosperous societies in which the quality of people's lives can be expected to improve steadily over time. In the longer run, they can only promise a future of endemic instability, extreme inequality, pervasive social conflict, steady environmental degradation and uneven growth.

Chile is, of course, the Latin American "success story" that is most widely touted and there is some basis for this positive response. It has grown relatively rapidly; it has been relatively stable for more than ten years; and it has dealt relatively effectively with its social problems. But the lesson of Chile is not therefore that neoliberal policies work automatically. These policies only function "positively" in a society that has a strong administrative infrastructure, a political balance of forces that requires it to pay some attention to social welfare issues,[12] a willingness to exercise control over foreign capital movements,[13] and a resource base and infrastructure that were very attractive to international capital at the time. But it is important to understand that most of these preconditions were the legacy of earlier policy regimes, and that the neoliberal regime itself actually tends to undermine those same conditions. It tends to impair administrative structures, undermine morale in the public service, foster tension and mistrust in communities, put less priority on infrastructure, privilege the interests of capital and impair a national society's capacity to control capital vis-à-vis the national interest.

In the rest of Latin America, only Costa Rica had similarly positive preconditions for a neoliberal policy regime. For the others, the disastrous 1980s have been followed by a roller-coaster ride in the 1990s, as massive quantities of speculative capital have once again flooded into the key countries of the continent, creating the illusion of prosperity while buying up resources, utilities, financial institutions, industries, politicians, policies. Meanwhile the underlying social and political tensions have continued to rise in most places, as the income inequality has grown, as informal sectors have grown explosively, as work has been casualized, as economic and social insecurity have increased, and as wages have lagged far behind other incomes (and often behind the cost of living). A recent ILO press release summarized the developments in this continent very effectively.[14] The statement cited a new ILO report which acknowledged that "reforms and modernization [had] succeeded in taming rampant inflation and prompted a return to growth," but then went on to warn that the social impact of these gains was giving rise to growing concern because the jobless rate of Latin American and Caribbean economies rose steadily in the 1990s and job insecurity increased as the modern sector of the economy virtually ceased to generate employment. The bottom line, says the ILO report, is that:

Economic growth and price stability have not produced a significant improvement of the employment situation or of wages . . . the burden of adjustment has been heavily borne by the work force. The modernization of the economy is coming about as a result of casualisation of labour relations, often with disastrous social consequences for workers. Workers' buying power fell dramatically during the past decade, dropping to 27 percent below what a salary bought in 1980 for minimum wage earners. The purchasing power of minimum wages fared much worse . . . the present minimum wage in Latin America stands 27 percent lower than at the beginning of the 1980s.

(ILO 1999: 1–4)

Of course, as always, one can argue that these "costs" represent short-term pain for long-term gain. Thus, Mr. Somalia, the ILO's Director General, in presenting the above report went out of his way to endorse the basic orthodox policy stance, referring to Latin America's "tremendous strides in modernizing economies, while maintaining steady growth and overcoming inflation" and then going on to accept that "in an open international system, the struggle for macroeconomic stability and increased productivity was necessary." It is only within this context that he calls for a greater recognition of the fact that "the provision of decent work and social protection" can be described as "the greatest guarantors of social progress and the best means of consolidating the gains of the past decade." The trouble is that those gains accrued very disproportionately to the continent's upper income groups and to international capital. And the lack of social and human progress that Mr. Somalia is deploring would appear to be an endemic feature of the current neoliberal incarnation of an "open international system." Moreover, he might have noted that the "struggle for macroeconomic stability and increased productivity" is apparently not being won, despite the high costs being imposed on so many societies.

In the Latin American context, as in Africa, the evidence has made it increasingly difficult to avoid the conclusion that the policies themselves need to be reassessed. But, as before, the "official" response is to reject this apparently obvious conclusion in favor of yet another injunction asking (other) people to "stay the course"—however long and difficult the transition may turn out to be. Thus, at an Ibero-American summit in Venezuela in 1997, there was widespread agreement as to "the facts." The World Bank's representative declared that: "We are very concerned about the increase in income inequality and the lack of progress in income distribution in this region over the last decade" (Koch-Weser 1997: 7).[15]

And these conclusions echoed those reached by UNCTAD, which reported in 1997 that "while there was a pronounced tendency for inequality to increase in Latin America during the debt crisis of the 1980s, the subsequent recovery has not been sufficient to reverse this tendency" (UNCTAD 1997: 109). However, most of those at this summit were anxious to insist that these observations should, on no account, lead to a loss of confidence in the orthodox policy regime. As Colitt (1997: 7) states: "despite the rise in income inequality, multilateral lending institutions warn of back-tracking. After reshaping the state and empowering local government through decentralization in the past decade . . . the region must now implement 'a much more difficult, second generation of reforms.'" But the problem with such a total ideological commitment to a particular policy regime, regardless of the evidence, is that it may ultimately be overwhelmed by the "real world."

It is, of course, unknown how long the fuse on this time-bomb may be. But we can be certain that even when it explodes, the true ideologues will learn nothing because their beliefs are immune to the evidence. Hence they would simply blame the failure of their policies on the social unrest, or on some aspect of the process of social disintegration, like corruption, government failure to enforce contracts or public sector inefficiency. What they do not appear to understand is that wise policies must take such issues into account. These are not exogenous factors, to be blamed when things go wrong. They are an essential part of the policy process and any policy regime that does not deal with them is ultimately indefensible.

The most sobering thought is that these extremely disappointing outcomes have emerged in an extended period of apparent prosperity; a period when foreign capital was flooding into the continent on a very large scale. And one has to wonder what to expect when the next major financial crisis erupts, which is undoubtedly only a matter of time. The results will undoubtedly be grim, since that next crisis will impinge on societies that are often already stretched to breaking point after so many years of unsuccessful adjustment. Their governments will be less able to respond constructively to such developments because 15 years of neoliberal restructuring have left them with less moral authority, fewer resources, weaker administrative capabilities (largely due to downsizing, persistent budget cuts, and rock bottom civil service morale), and fewer sovereign powers. And many potentially useful policy instruments have now been proscribed by new international treaties and institutions which threaten anyone who would try to use them with massive economic retaliation.

The implosion of the Communist bloc

In the former Soviet Union the situation is, if anything, even more dramatic. Here the scale of the economic collapse has been almost unimaginable and hardly needs elaboration since it has been so widely documented.

> Economic surveys read like disaster reports. Gross national product, which fell by about half between 1990 and 1995, dropped by 6 percent last year. Industrial production, which had slid by even more during the 1990–5 period, fell by another 9 percent. The collapse of investment and light industry is even more dramatic. True, these figures must be taken with a grain of salt, since a parallel economy is gaining ground . . . Fiscal fraud has reached epidemic proportions. Companies don't pay taxes, either because they cannot afford to or because they speculate, "lending" money to the

state by buying bonds. With its coffers empty, the state is slashing social services and delays payments. The elderly and disabled have to wait for pensions, public servants for their salaries. Industrial workers whether in the private or public sector, fare no better.

(Singer 1997: 20)

The impact on the social and political fabric of the nation is maybe even more ominous. A recent report speaks of "a deepening and corrosive threat to Russia's young democracy and free-market economy: the breakdown of law enforcement and the proliferation of private armies and protection rackets prone to ruthless gangland tactics" (Hoffman 1997: AO1). But, as elsewhere, the true ideologues are not swayed by the evidence. Even in the face of these extreme outcomes, they merely demanded even more radical reforms, or more time, or they blame "unfavorable circumstances" for having undermined their "rational policies," for turning even more power over to the market, even though that market is often not competitive and even though the "social capital" (Stiglitz 1998a, 1998b) that is needed if markets are to function effectively, or in the public interest, either does not exist, or is actively being destroyed.

Asia: the erstwhile exception that proves the rule

Asia has, of course, been the great exception to this relentless litany of woe, and it is a significant exception since it is home to more than one half of the world's population and many of its people have made dramatic gains over the past quarter century. But, even so, it is not immune to global pressures, and financial speculation has also become a major problem in that region in recent years. Moreover, Asia's positive experience up to this point does not invalidate the view that the neoliberal policy regime represents a systematic threat to people and their societies if it is allowed to run its course unchallenged. Indeed, properly understood, the Asian experience actually supports the thesis that a politically managed "social market" represents the only potentially sustainable, defensible and desirable form of capitalism; and that the deregulated neoliberal market is a predatory, unstable, and destructive force that is ultimately socially and polit-ically damaging—and economically inefficient. Indeed, as Asia is forced, or per-suaded, to further liberalize its financial markets, it may also have occasion to learn this bitter lesson at first hand one day in the not too distant future.

The causes of the crisis

In the decades following World War II Asia financed the transformation of technologically and economically underdeveloped low-income economies into intensely competitive industrial economies with significant national technological capabilities. These allowed it to generate and to appropriate technology rents and to remain competitive even while real wages and per capita incomes rose in a sustained and dramatic way. Moreover, this growth was primarily financed from domestic resources that were mobilized by financial systems which acted as very effective financial intermediaries: they sustained high levels of national savings on the basis of low interest rates, while channeling those resources into the real economy in a very effective and strategic manner, working closely with their respective developmental states.

To understand what caused the crisis and the responses to it we need also to consider the changes that were occurring in the international system. Thus we need to understand that once the WTO had successfully concluded the Global Telecommunications Agreement it immediately set its sights on negotiating a Global Financial Services Agreement. The deadline was set for December 1997, but by April 1997 the London *Financial Times* reported that the talks had stalled largely because of a distinct lack of enthusiasm in Asia. This was described as a matter of grave concern to the WTO officials and to the financial services industry, which was actively and publicly promoting these negotiations. In response, this industry established a small but influential group of senior executives who were sent out to lobby Asia's leaders and to gain their support.

In July 1997, the Thai baht came under attack—and the rest is history. Mahathir's charge (at the December Fund meetings in Hong Kong) that the attack on the Asian currencies was politically motivated was ridiculed by George Soros and others. But there can be no doubt that politics played an important role in these events. The financial markets clearly wanted more unrestricted access to Asian markets, which were growing rapidly while economic conditions in much of the rest of the world were increasingly precarious. The industry was working with the WTO to this end, while the United States had made no secret of its desire to see these markets liberalized. It is not a "conspiracy theory" to suggest that these political circumstances were relevant to the emergence of the crisis—and to its eventual outcome. Indeed, those political factors must be integrated into any fair or independent assessment of these events.

Given the turmoil that followed the Asian crisis, and the sudden need for urgent "rescue packages," the Asian government opposition to a Financial Services Agreement eroded rapidly and an Agreement was duly signed just a few minutes after the original midnight deadline. The real meaning of these events was clarified a few months later when Larry Summers, the US government's Deputy Secretary of the Treasury, announced that in just a few months, the Asian crisis had achieved more policy change in Korea than two decades of tough bilateral bargaining between the United States and Korea.

Of course no one strand of this argument can stand on its own. While the international financial services industry, and the US government, had a clear and declared interest in bringing about certain changes in Asia's financial markets, that alone does not explain the crisis. For that we need to understand the process through which the opportunity to exploit a crisis to this end, presented itself. And that opportunity ultimately presented itself because of the severe imbalances that emerged in their domestic economies as these countries opened their previously stable and highly successful financial sectors to the outside world. In this sense, domestic imbalances and contradictions rightly assume great significance as the immediate triggers of the crisis. But it is important to remember that those "domestic" problems reflected both external and internal developments.

The truth is that speculative bubbles had been growing in a number of Asian economies since the early 1990s. In fact, when Japan's bubble economy had collapsed in the early 1990s, the *Far Eastern Economic Review* (*FEER*) reported a large exodus of "financial gunslingers" who were quoted as saying that the Japanese market would be dead for some time to come; because of the mountains of bad debt that the bubble had left in its wake, they were off to other Asian centers.

By 1997 it was obvious that many Asian markets were ripe for a major "adjustment." Indeed, for two years before the 1997 crisis, I used to say at every opportunity that it was foolish to extrapolate the Asian miracle into the future without recognizing that "water runs downhill in Asia, just like anywhere else in the world" and that "speculative bubbles must collapse in Asia, just as anywhere else in the world."

> Watching the wild developments on the world's bond and stock markets in 1997 one would have to agree with the cynics. Stock market valuations are simply outlandish and historically without precedent by now; bond markets have lost touch with reality, as large issues from bankrupt countries are regularly heavily over-subscribed; and property markets in many parts of the world, but especially in Asia, have reached dizzying heights from which they have a long way to fall. In May of 1997, the conservative *Asia Times* suggested that a "global financial meltdown" now had to be considered a real possibility, and anyone without a vested interest in the process would have to agree.
>
> (Bienefeld 1997: 27)

The important point to understand is that this was a global problem, manifesting itself in many different parts of the global economy. At its heart lay a rising tide of global liquidity which has become the dominant feature of the world economy and which was created when national authorities effectively lost control over the issuance of money in the 1970s. The problem could now manifest itself so virulently in Asia because many of the Asian economies had been persuaded, cajoled or pressured into opening their financial sectors to the outside world. This had not been so before, and that was a major reason why most of Asia, apart from the Philippines, had found itself in a relatively favorable position in the early 1980s when the debt crisis had engulfed Latin America and Africa, ushering in their "lost development decades."

Moreover, Asia did not stagnate or decline as a result. It did not even suffer from a lack of access to capital. In fact, Asia was the engine of the world economy, attracting foreign capital to complement its high domestic savings, and using those resources to build relatively stable, dynamic, strategically directed economies in which the benefits of growth were widely shared and in which rapidly growing domestic markets could sustain favorable investment climates.

By 1997 these models had been compromised by financial liberalization. The resulting large imbalances in their financial sectors began to have an increasing impact on their real economies—first through the balance of payments, then through the price distortions caused by property speculation and finally through the impact of escalating debt burdens on institutions and firms, which became explosive once exchange rates began to fall.

In short, any discussion of the causes of the Asian crisis should place heavy emphasis on "domestic factors," especially if it is looking to identify the immediate triggers of the crisis. But the domestic factors that emerge from such an analysis are neither inherently Asian nor purely domestic. They are reflections of the incompatibility between the open, volatile international capital markets and "the Asian models." And the fact that it is those models that are now being deconstructed is nothing short of a tragedy.

It is a tragedy because those "Asian models," despite their various shortcomings, were the only models that have actually allowed a few societies to achieve "genuine development" over the past 50 years. And the fact that they are now being aggressively dismantled augurs ill for the future of the developing world, including that of Asia. That is the most serious consequence of the Asian crisis; and that is what one has to bear in mind in thinking about appropriate responses to that crisis.

The future of the crisis and concluding remarks

If the current dismantling of the Asian model is carried to completion, Asia will be Latin Americanized. In essence, the Asian countries will lose the great advantage that some of them had under the previous model, namely their ability to make coherent, strategically informed decisions; to mobilize savings effectively; and to engage their populations in national development processes that were both dynamic and fair enough to sustain people's support and to harness their energies. Some people erroneously ascribed these outcomes to "Confucian culture" but I believe that, if current trends continue, Asia will soon discover that these advantages will soon disappear as their societies polarize and become increasingly unstable and unpredictable.

There is, of course, another alternative—one in which some of the key Asian countries follow China in recognizing the importance of reversing those current trends and rebuilding a more vibrant Asian model, anchored in a regional structure that provides liquidity on the basis of a different set of conditions. Such conditions require recipient countries to rebuild the ideological, institutional and infrastructural foundations that supported the earlier successful Asian models.

At the very center of such a project lies the task of rebuilding monetary stability and reconstructing the links between national financial systems and national real economies. And that requires a degree of disengagement from an international financial system that is now awash in liquidity, is endemically unstable, and in which the power to create credit has become effectively unlimited and uncontrolled. Until that problem is addressed and solved, the world will be condemned to suffer repeated and escalating bouts of instability that will continue to impose huge welfare losses on the weakest, stifle investment and growth and fuel inequality and conflict.

At some point Polanyi's double movement will see societies react by reasserting control over their circumstances. We can only hope that this day will come sooner rather than later. And we must recognize that Asia may well take the lead in that process.

Of course we must also hope that those who are profiting so handsomely from the current anarchy will not be prepared to deploy their smart bombs and their star wars technologies to defend their current poisonous privileges. But that has to be regarded as a very real possibility.

Nor can this process be excused on the grounds that it is necessary for ensuring high levels of future investment and growth. In fact, this argument was always controversial and has recently been further weakened by an accumulation of empirical research suggesting that income inequality is frequently detrimental to growth and prosperity. A study in 1994 of 56 countries found "a strong negative relationship between income inequality and growth in GDP per head" (Persson and Tabellini 1994: 21), and this merely echoed the conclusions reached by several other authoritative studies. As a result:

> Many economists are now revising their views, having begun to see greater income equality as compatible with faster growth—and perhaps even contributing to it . . . "It's a major shift in economists' perspectives" Joseph Stiglitz, a member of the President's Council of Economic Advisers, said. "There are lessons here for the United States . . . Not only did trickle-down economics not solve the problems of the poor or the middle class, but it was bad growth policy." Some researchers . . . argued that in Asian countries, there was a direct cause-and-effect link between faster growth and policies that reduce inequality. "One of the strongest lessons from Asia is that equality is not only a corollary, but may actually stimulate economic growth" said Professor Sabot of Williams College, the co-author of a study with Ms. Birdsall, "Inequality and Growth Reconsidered."
>
> (Nasar 1994: 17)

Elsewhere, doubts about the desirability and the sustainability of the neoliberal revolution have arisen even among some prominent former advocates, in the face of the accumulating evidence. Thus, John Gray, a former advisor to Mrs. Thatcher, now regards these policies as misguided and unsustainable because they tend to destroy the social values, networks, and institutions on which the efficient operation of markets ultimately depends. Moreover, like Keynes, he sees the free flow of international capital as the main mechanism that is undermining the government's ability to protect these networks.

> History exemplifies an equally important fact: Free-market economies lack built-in stabilizers. Without effective management by government, they are

liable to recurrent booms and busts—with all their costs in social cohesion and political stability . . . The current era of free capital flows cannot survive much longer. Internationally coordinated movement toward a new regime of regulation is the only alternative to the disastrous prospect of tit-for-tat protectionism.[16]

(Gray 1998a: 17–18)

A similar conclusion was reached by Paul Krugman in a recent article ("The Return of Depression Economics") in which he warns against the comfortable assumption that we need no longer fear a serious, cumulative deflationary spiral, like the one that led to the Depression of the 1930s. While reflationary policies will normally avert such a possibility, the complexity and the scale of international finance entanglements have once again reached the point where totally unpredictable and incomprehensible disturbances have become a real and dangerous fact of life. As a result:

> it is hard to avoid concluding that sooner or later we will have to turn the clock at least part of the way back: to limit capital flows for countries that are unsuitable for either currency unions or free floating; to reregulate financial markets to some extent; and to seek low but not too low inflation rather than price stability. We must heed the lessons of Depression economics, lest we be forced to relearn them the hard way.

(Krugman 1999: 74)

However, despite such straws in the wind, the neoliberal advance continues as new international treaties and institutions try to lock governments ever more firmly into that policy regime. The Asian crisis has actually been used as a lever to open up the financial systems of these economies and within the main international financial institutions the demand for the further liberalization of markets remains in the ascendant. Meanwhile, welfare reform in the United States is continuing to remove the vestigial safety net that had been protecting labor from becoming a "pure commodity," and similar reforms are reducing worker protection in much of the world.

Bibliography

Agarwala, R. and Schwartz, P. N. (1994) "Sub-Saharan Africa: A Long-term Perspective Study," paper written for the Learning Process on Participatory Development, World Bank: Washington DC, May, mimeo.

Anonymous (1997) "Why the Recovery is not a Recovery," *NACLA: Report on the Americas* 30: 4, Jan/Feb.

Azpiazu, D., Basualdo, E. M., and Nochteff, H. J. (1998) "Menem's Great Swindle: Convertibility, Inequality and the Neoliberal Schock," *NACLA Report on the Americas* 31: 6, May/June.

Bienefeld, M. A. (1983) "Efficiency, Expertise, the NICs and the Accelerated Development Report," *IDS Bulletin* 14 (1), Institute of Development Studies: Sussex, UK.

—— (1986) "In Defence of 'Nationalism' as a Trade Union Perspective," in R. Southall (ed.) *Trade Unions and the New Industrialization of the Third World*, London: Zed Press.

—— (1997) "The State and Civil Society: The Political Economy of the 'New Social Policy,'" working paper no. 60, Development Research Series, Research Center on Development and International Relations, Aalborg University, Denmark.

Cieza, D. (1998) "Argentine Labor: A Movement in Crisis," *NACLA Report on the Americas* 31 (6), May/June.

Colitt, R. (1997) "Latin American Reforms 'Fail to Cut Income Disparities'," *The [London] Financial Times* November 13.

Gray, J. (1998a) "Not for the First Time, World Sours on Free Markets," *The Nation* October 19.

—— (1998b) *False Dawn: The Delusions of Global Capitalism*, London: Granta Books.

Hoffman, D. (1997) "Banditry Threatens the New Russia: Law Enforcement Collapse Erodes Democracy, Free Market Economy," *Washington Post* May 12.

ILO (1999) "Despite Decade Long Reforms, Social Progress is Stalling in Latin America, Caribbean," August 23 and 26.

James, H. (1996) *International Monetary Cooperation since Bretton Woods*, Washington DC: IMF and Oxford University Press.

Keynes, J. M. (1933) "National Self-Sufficiency," *New Statesman* July 8 and 15.

Koch-Weser, C. (1997) quoted in R. Colitt, "Latin American Reforms 'Fail to Cut Income Disparities,'" *Financial Times* November 13.

Krugman, P. (1999) "The Return of Depression Economics," *Foreign Affairs* (January/ February).

Kuhn, T. ([1962] 1970) *The Structure of Scientific Revolutions*, 2nd edn, Chicago IL: University of Chicago Press.

Lal, D. (1983) "The Poverty of 'Development Economics'," *Hobart Paperbacks* 16, London: Institute of Economic Affairs.

Legrand, C. (1997) "Poor Demand Share of Argentina's Wealth," *Manchester Guardian Weekly* July 27.

Lord Lever, B. (1989) Commonwealth Secretariat.

Mandel, M. J. (1996) "The High-Risk Society," *Business Week* October 28.

Nasar, S. (1994) "Economics of Equality: A New View," *The New York Times* January 8.

O'Brien, P. (1988) cited in *The Toronto Globe and Mail* June 22.

Persson, T. and Tabellini, O. (1994) "Is Inequality Harmful for Growth?" *American Economic Review* 84 (3) June.

Singer, D. (1997) "Yeltsin's Summit, Russia's Vale," *The Nation* March 31.

Southall, R. (ed.) (1988) *Trade Unions and the New Industrialisation of the Third World*, London: Zed Books.

Stiglitz, J. (1998a) "Knowledge for Development: Economic Science, Economic Policy and Economic Advice," Address to the World Bank's 10th Annual Bank Conference on Development Economics, Washington, DC, April 20.

—— (1998b) "More Instruments and Broader Goals: Moving Towards a Post-Washington Consensus," *1998 WIDER Annual Lecture*, Helsinki, Finland, January.

—— (1999) "Whither Reform: Ten Years of the Transition," keynote address to the World Bank Annual Conference on Development Economics.

The Toronto Globe and Mail (1995) January 16.

UNCTAD (United Nations Conference on Trade and Development) (1997), *Trade and Development Report*, UNCTAD: Geneva.

Wade, R. (1994) "The World Bank and the Art of Paradigm Maintenance," *New Left Review*.

World Bank (1988) *Adjustment Lending: An Evaluation of Ten Years of Experience*, Washington DC: World Bank.

—— (1989a) *World Development Report 1989*, Washington DC: World Bank.

—— (1989b) *Sub-Saharan Africa: From Crisis to Sustainable Development*, Washington DC: World Bank.

Part II

Critical perspectives on the role of politics

4 The space for politics

Globalization, hegemony, and passive revolution

Anne Showstack Sassoon

[The question] is one . . . of seeing whether "what ought to be" is arbitrary or necessary; whether it is concrete on the one hand or idle fancy, yearning, daydream on the other. The active politician is a creator, an initiator; but he neither creates from nothing nor does he move in the turbid void of his own desires and dreams. He bases himself on effective reality, but what is this effective reality? Is it something static and immobile, or is it not rather a relation of forces in continuous motion and shift of equilibrium?

(Gramsci 1971: 172)

A common error in historico-political analysis consists in an inability to find the correct relation between what is organic and what is conjunctural . . . [I]f [such] error is serious in historiography, it becomes still more serious in the art of politics, when it is not the reconstruction of past history but the construction of present and future history which is at stake. One's own baser and more immediate desires and passions are the cause of error, in that they take the place of an objective and impartial analysis—and this happens not as a conscious "means" to stimulate to action, but as self-deception.

(Gramsci 1971: 178–9)

Putting politics back in

At the heart of contemporary debates on globalization is the question of the role of politics and the possibility of shaping our present and future, no more so than on the political left where the question of the possibility of a "third way" is on the political agenda (Massey 1997; Weiss 1997). It is striking how exchanges, for example in *Monthly Review* in the United States (Du Boff and Herman 1997; Tabb 1997a, 1997b; Wood 1997; Piven and Cloward 1998), or in major books and articles in Britain (e.g. Archibugi and Held 1995; Held 1995; Hirst and Thompson 1996; Goldblatt 1997; Goldblatt, Held, McGrew, and Perraton 1997; Gray 1998) grapple with questions similar in many respects to those posed by Gramsci in the 1930s in a very different context. The important task of considering the category of globalization historically—in connection with changes in the state and in the international order, and hence of developing a critique of concepts as they develop over time—and concretely as part of rethinking social and political theory more generally is parallel to Gramsci's own work in rethinking politics, even when it is not particularly influenced by his ideas (David Harvey, ch. 1, this volume; Peterson 1996, 1997; Kilminster 1997). Globalization may be formulated in terms of economic tendencies, financial deregulation, or technological and cultural change, as a description of a process or as a project (Massey 1997; Scott 1997b). However it is defined, the analysis of differentiated impacts on national realities and the possibility, or lack of possibility, for specific types of political intervention are, on the one hand, deeply rooted historical trends and, on the other hand, a function of more immediate political developments. As such, this has important points in common with the themes that Gramsci was considering in the 1920s and 1930s when he was confronted by a version of "there is no alternative."

What follows is a brief intervention in a debate in which I am an interested outsider—one who can offer a few observations related to some insights from Gramsci's work. But first a couple of disclaimers are in order. There is a growing body of work in international relations which is inspired by Gramsci and uses his concepts. Much of this literature goes back to Robert W. Cox's seminal essay written in 1983, although other influences have also been important (Murphy 1998), and has continued to be developed by Stephen Gill and others (e.g. Augelli and Murphy 1993, 1997; Cox 1993, 1997; Gill 1993a, 1993b, 1993c, 1997a, 1997b; Gill and Law 1993; Sakamoto 1997). In Italy recent writing is also putting Gramsci onto a global plane as questions are asked about the possible transcendence of the role of the nation-state (Montanari 1997a, 1997b; Telò 1997). Of course there is the risk that the historical roots of Gramsci's ideas are obscured and that they are transferred onto inappropriate objects (Germaine and Kenny 1998). When, however, it is acknowledged that his ideas are indeed rooted in his historical context (Cox 1997), and that Gramsci's concept of hegemony, going beyond its traditional use in international relations, is understood as depending on active consent (e.g. Augelli and Murphy 1993; Cox 1993; Gill 1997a), this interchange between Gramsci's work and international relations has been fruitful (Rupert 1998). Indeed, a major contribution which much of this literature makes is to remind us that Gramsci was a political thinker concerned with the nature of political power and political strategy, an approach which is congenial to my own (Sassoon 1987, 2000b). My intention here, however, is not to engage with this writing as such, or to endorse or to criticize the way his ideas have been translated and applied beyond his immediate objectives, regardless of how important such a critique may be (Germaine and Kenny 1998; Rupert 1998).

Secondly, going beyond this literature, a full discussion of Gramsci's possible contribution to contemporary debates on globalization would entail examining his ideas on political analysis and political intervention, and his attempt to discern long-term organic tendencies and to differentiate those which were more immediate, contingent, and short term, and therefore more closely determined by political forces. A central aspect of this could be formulated as the attempt to analyze the "new" to understand what indeed is historically original and novel in social reality and what is the reproduction of the "old" even if in different forms, to understand the intersections of elements of continuity and change. Of great relevance to today's debates on globalization is his concern to provide the tools necessary to delineate the lines of political freedom and constraint so that analysis of "effective reality" avoids the false dichotomy between pessimistic resignation and optimistic voluntarism. These are themes which are both examined in depth and run through the *Prison Notebooks* (e.g. Gramsci 1971: 136–40, 169–73, 175–85; Sassoon 2000d).

The aim here is to connect some general comments on the debate on globalization to a brief discussion of Gramsci's concepts of hegemony and of passive revolution with regard to what I will argue is an essential but sometimes overlooked aspect of what are undoubtedly also harsh international realities: globalization as the mark of an historical transition in which acquiescence to features of this transition can derive not only from the domination of powerful economic and political forces but relate to what are perceived as real improvements in people's lives. At the same time, the danger exists, however, that, because of the relation of forces, such a transition takes the form of what Gramsci called a passive revolution, in which the potentially progressive aspects of such profound historical change are undermined by strategies governed by a logic which contributes to the reconstitution of relations of domination and subordination which subvert the possibilities of progressive outcomes (Sassoon 1987: 204–17). These are long and complex arguments which can only be sketched in a preliminary form here.

A "symptomatic" reading of the debate

These dimensions can easily be lost in general theoretical overviews that miss the political significance of phenomena which can only be seen by a shift in focus. A few observations on the debate on globalization lead to some points which run the risk of being obvious to those "inside" these discussions, but the intention is to make them explicit and to raise some questions from the "outside" which, it is hoped, will contribute to a richer debate in the future.

Important aspects of this debate could be framed in the following way. The central concern in discussions about globalization with regard to the role of politics relates to the possibility of political intervention by national governments and international organizations. The answers given derive from analyses of national and international trends and tendencies which allow for, are affected by, or inhibit such intervention, itself conceived of in terms of determined ends or goals. Thus the analyses themselves do not stand outside of the desire to intervene although they cannot be reduced to the effects of such an aim. One factor which affects such analysis, and indeed, the very definition of the "occupation" of academics and other specialist thinkers, is the "belonging" of those who undertake it, be it subject specialisms, the influence of national discourses and perspectives, the taken for granted assumptions which only appear or can be seen clearly if we step outside our usual "habitats" to notice the specificities of our approaches. The effects of how, in this sense, the analysis is "situated" extend across many, different contemporary debates, for example the one on civil society (Sassoon 2000a).

In the literature in English, at least, those who "do" the theory are more likely than not to come from the Anglo-American world—a manifestation of the dominance of Anglo-American social science, and a reflection of the international power and influence in particular of academic production from the United States. Those, on the other hand, who offer concrete analyses of different national realities tend to speak to their own experience from smaller countries or "peripheral" parts of the world (Sassoon 2000a). Yet far from being "peripheral" in terms of theoretical implications, it is often those supposed applications of grand theory which demonstrate the greater theoretical sophistication. Sensitive examinations of different national realities can reveal the complexities and limits of the effects of international pressures without underestimating the constraints that are faced (e.g. Hellman 1994; Bagchi 1997; Gurnah 1997; Harding and Le Galès 1997; Jalan 1997; Kassim 1997; Roseneil 1997; Stewart and Garrahan 1997; Street 1997; Tao and Ho 1997; Kwang-Yeong Shin, ch. 8, this volume). Studies such as these do not replace a focus on international trends and tendencies but paint a finer and more subtle picture than that which might otherwise be produced (Poppi 1997; Scott 1997b). Once the picture "on the ground" is brought into focus, this work can counter-balance any tendency to underestimate the complexity of the effects of globalization and hence to formulate better questions about the possible extent and limits imposed by general international tendencies on political intervention. Such intervention, to refer back to Gramsci's concept of hegemony, must take account of the need for national governments to maintain popular support, and also the possibility that the stability of different regimes will depend on the success or not of managing change and preserving power through a strategy of passive revolution.

It is understandable, particularly in a period of major transitions, in which what is being lost is often felt much more strongly than the new which is still emerging in all its contradictions, that the negative features of contemporary developments take prominence and that the only alternatives presented are a return to the past or insurrectionary opposition. We who do the analysis no less than the rest of society can easily feel overwhelmed by the forces in the field, and by the sense of loss as the old goal posts disappear. What can be detected at times, however, is a nostalgia for an earlier period when "the state was really a state," that is, a desire for the power of the state to make public policy as a relatively autonomous instrument in the social democratic or Keynesian mode. It is possible that if it is no longer an instrument in some traditional sense, our very self-definition as intellectuals and specialists offering "advice" is undermined along with traditional concepts of politics. It has also been pointed out that such nostalgia can signify the failure to mourn adequately what has been lost and hence the inability to move on (Wheeler 1994).

In discussing globalization the attempt to find a "subject" of a process which appears, to borrow a Kleinian term, barely containable, can leave open the question of who are the actors: global élites, bureaucrats, state managers, financial classes or other societal forces? The subject, the "it" of globalization as a political project can be associated with various actors at the same time as it appears either out of control, or so powerful that only insurrectionary movements seem to offer a measure of opposition however unlikely it is that these movements could somehow reverse what are presented as all powerful tendencies. Certainly as economies on the Pacific Rim totter, there is a growing conviction—ranging from financiers like George Soros to the business pages of serious newspapers to center-left politicians—that new international regulatory arrangements are necessary.

At the same time, an issue is raised that concerns which groups within national terrains make use of external pressures, real or presumed, to push forward their own agendas. This is posed not only in less developed countries but also in Europe, for example in debates about European integration or the transformations taking place in Central and Eastern Europe, and indeed in North America with regard to NAFTA. How are these pressures described, mediated, and countered? These were precisely the kinds of questions which Gramsci was asking in the 1930s. We can only make sense of all of this if we, like Gramsci, try to disentangle the processes and look for differential rhythms, impacts, and logics and are open to messages which contradict the desire for generalization. That is, a richer and fuller comprehension can only be arrived at if complexity and contradiction form an integral part of our methodology. Following Gramsci, it can be argued that such complex analysis requires that *no* development be reduced to its "bad" or, indeed, to its "good" effects. For example, it is not at all obvious that we face some inevitable "race to the bottom," however powerful the pressures may appear (Hirst and Thompson 1996). There are always tendencies and countertendencies, as Gramsci argued when considering the impact on Italy and other European countries in the 1930s of trends toward what he called Americanism and Fordism (Gramsci 1971: 280–6). Parallel arguments can be found in the extensive contemporary literature about the embeddedness of economic and other institutions, about the significance of human capital for investment decisions, about social justice and greater equality and security as preconditions for effective economies and risk taking by individuals (e.g. Glyn and Miliband 1994).

Much of this can be seen better if the focus shifts to another level of analysis. To take an example with regard to gender, if we are not going to patronize all those poor women or, indeed, all those poor men and women, particularly in the lesser developed countries, who are affected by trends toward globalization, we need to analyze the effects of global processes in all their complexity. Most particularly, we need to avoid either implicitly romanticizing some "before" or failing to recognize that sentient human beings are making choices in conditions of severe constraint but which also contain the possibility of new freedoms.

Surely the conditions in rural society with oppressive traditional social relations, not to speak of poverty, severely limit the realm of freedom of women and especially younger people more generally, whose wider horizons than previously mean that they are open to new experiences, however difficult the outcomes. These could be among the factors which help to explain migration in search of better lives. That those lives are not all better and in some ways worse should not cancel out either the improvements or the new contradictions which arise.

As Marx and Engels amongst others stress, historical and social change implies loss, gain and new possibilities. Gramsci's own approach to trying to comprehend popular phenomena, while avoiding any populism or reducing people to victims, was to imagine himself in the shoes of the person "in the street" and to ask what that person, or group of people, might get out of a particular situation. Indeed, one model for Gramsci, which might appear surprising, was the fictional character Father Brown, who put himself into the mind of the perpetrator of a crime and looked for the evidence which did not fit immediate preconceptions or abstract schema. As an aside, the scattering of references to G. K. Chesterton in the *Prison Notebooks* (especially in the fuller Italian edition) demonstrates a significant aspect of Gramsci's thought: even those whose politics are quite alien could provide important keys to a better understanding (Gramsci 1971: 362; Gramsci 1975: 19, 406, 698, 888, 1822, 2127, 2130, 2200, 2372, 2377, 2455, 2705, 2998, 3008). The contradictory effects of major periods of transition on the daily lives and on the perceptions of those who are potentially the protagonists to whom governments have to respond are important aspects of understanding the different strategies of various political actors (Hellman 1994). The cost of not undertaking such a complex, sensitive analysis in which new freedoms as well as new constraints are investigated is to feed "there is no alternative." This can result in de facto collusion in the success of a strategy of passive revolution which responds to pressures from below by incorporating popular demands. Such a strategy can succeed in improving the lives of enough of the population to be able to make hegemonic claims as long as economic conditions permit. The outcome of what Gramsci also refers to as revolution-restoration can therefore be the maintenance of power through the reconstitution of relations of domination and subordination in new forms.

Hegemony as an exchange, passive revolution as a danger

This brings us back to Gramsci's concept of hegemony. As I have argued above, Gramsci in fact transforms the traditional meaning of hegemony into something very different from the usual connotation in international relations (Sassoon 2000c, 2000e). His concept implies that in the twentieth century, however restricted the political space (and he had no illusions about this: given that he was writing in a fascist prison!), any long-term mode of governing requires consent if it is to be durable. A hegemonic power is different from one which is merely dominant (Teló 1997). His reformulation is derived from an analysis of what he considers fundamental transformations in national and international political realities which produce new questions and leads to new understandings about the nature of political power from the end of the last century (Sassoon 1987).

Above all, following in the footsteps of other complex thinkers such as Marx and Engels, I would add that Gramsci never reduces individuals or social groups or, indeed, states to victims. They may be subordinated, they may be oppressed, but he always stresses that the basis of hegemony, which is the acceptance of a relationship, is rooted in concrete reforms (Augelli and Murphy 1993). He is convinced, for example, and has the courage to argue from a fascist prison, that if sections of the Italian population support fascism, it is not just because of coercion or because those "in the know" (implying the left) often assume that they are mistaken, but because fascism addresses some of their needs, precisely in the manner of a passive revolution. The implication is that no analysis of political power is complete unless the bargains which are struck by even the most authoritarian regimes with major sectors of their populations are acknowledged. And no strategy of opposition will succeed if it does not take account of the real improvements in people's lives, even in conditions of oppression and even if in some respects their situations worsen.

The intersection of the national and the international

There is another analytical dimension of Gramsci's work which is still relevant. As a communist in the 1930s, Gramsci could not help but also be concerned with the relationship between the national and the international terrains. To focus on just one important note, in a very different context from today's debates on globalization, Gramsci wrote the following:

> In reality, the internal relations of any nation are the result of a combination which is "original" and (in a certain sense) unique: these relations must be understood and conceived in their originality and uniqueness if one wishes to dominate them and direct them. To be sure, the line of development is towards internationalism, but the point of departure is the "national"—and it is from this point of departure that one must begin. Yet the perspective is international and cannot be otherwise.
>
> (Gramsci 1971: 240)

Gramsci was in fact referring in this note to the debate between Trotsky and Stalin. Gramsci frequently used quotation marks to denaturalize concepts (Sassoon 2000d), and those around "national" are significant. The national terrain, as it was being redefined, was still the starting point for political intervention because the basis of the hegemony of a state was founded on the historic bloc of forces, which it succeeded in weaving together around a national, collective project. The maintenance of consent, whether through elections or by other means, was rooted in the national terrain, and was also the point of departure for international politics which fed back into the ability of the state to survive. At the same time, major historical transitions or watersheds, such as that marked by the Russian Revolution, or what Gramsci described as Americanism and Fordism (Gramsci 1971: 279–318), two of the parameters of a new international order in the period in which he was writing, implied an international perspective and, tendentially at least, the undermining of the nation-state.

Beyond the question of "socialism in one country," the tensions in the communist movement of translating international directives into national politics are well documented. It is also well known that these tensions affected Gramsci's relations with other communist prisoners and resulted in his being isolated. But the complex relationship between the national and the international could not help but engage Gramsci for other reasons: the problematic inheritance of the emergence of Italy as a nation-state from the time of Machiavelli to the Risorgimento when Cavour's intelligence in taking advantage of the changing international situation was a key factor in the dominance of the historic "right" of the outcomes of national unification, and the changing relationship between the Catholic Church, an international organization par excellence, and the Italian state was so important politically. The significance of both processes was certainly grasped by Mussolini, and by Gramsci.

Furthermore, no one writing about politics in the 1920s and 1930s could avoid thinking about World War I. During the war, and never completely reversed afterward, there had been an enormous expansion in the role of the state in the very moment when the slaughter of millions undermined its legitimacy and, not accidentally, produced demands for further democratization (for example, the expansion of male and female suffrage) and institutional reforms of various kinds, as well as critiques of "parliamentarism" by left and right which led in quite different directions. And there was also, of course, the emergence of the United States as an international power with the potential of becoming hegemonic, that is, becoming a model—not just through the weight of coercion but through the influence of both "Americanism," with, from a European perspective, its liberal connotations (Montanari 1997a, 1997b), and the dynamic of new production and managerial techniques, or "Fordism," which also had significant implications for politics and culture. Indeed, the debates in the 1920s and 1930s about Americanism and the consequences of Fordism parallel in many ways today's debates on globalization.

One of the most fundamental political questions of the period which preoccupied Gramsci concerned the range of potential political responses to these international trends. Gramsci was convinced that simple opposition or attempts to cling to the "old" were self-defeating, as the inadequacy of the strategy of the American trade unions demonstrated. There should be no mistake. Gramsci was quite clear about the brutality implied in de-skilling and other aspects of Fordism, yet he also argued that there were potentially progressive elements which, however, could only be harnessed by a very different approach (Sassoon 2000c, 2000e). He was trying to escape the dichotomy "accept or be defeated," no doubt also worried by the fascination in the communist movement and in the Soviet Union for "rational" or "scientific" production techniques.

Americanism and Fordism were examples of passive revolution. Gramsci examines the differential impact of these international trends on different European countries and on the social forces within them as a precondition for arriving at a strategy which is capable of harnessing what was progressive within them and which would therefore counteract the possibility of a passive revolution. Gramsci is quite explicit in writing that while the analytical concept of passive revolution may usefully be employed to understand strategies to reconstitute dominance, it must not be adopted as a political program by the left. Paraphrasing a passage from Marx's Preface to *A Contribution to a Critique of Political Economy*, Gramsci discusses passive revolution in terms of the relationship between what he calls the marginal possibilities for further development which any social formation "always" enjoys, and the possibilities of creating something qualitatively new (Gramsci 1971: 106–7, 114, 222). That is, the survival and transformation of capitalism despite such severe social and economic crises produce both new forms of oppression and exploitation and new spaces for progressive politics. If understood properly as possibility and potential, these new spaces could, but not necessarily would, provide the opportunity to develop a progressive politics to neutralize the strategy of managing change through promoting a passive revolution. Suffice it to say here that discussions of globalization could do worse than take a page from Gramsci's book and begin to ask not only what dangers must be confronted but what spaces open up or not for politics in the contemporary messy, contradictory, and highly differentiated world. Above all, to conceptualize an alternative, the advantages as well as the disadvantages which large sectors of the population experience in different national contexts must be appreciated and taken as a starting point for alternative strategies.

Gramsci at our disposal

No one thinker and certainly not one whose works were rooted in historical realities that to a great extent have now been superseded, can be sufficient for today's needs. Nonetheless, Gramsci's writings are a precious resource in thinking about the novel features of our situation as well as the reproduction of old relations of domination and subordination in new forms, that is, in the assessment of the multifaceted features of the conjuncture, not least in reflecting on the relationship between "scientific" analysis and political intervention. He was trying to understand the impact of major historical changes: World War I, the Russian Revolution, the rise of fascism, the relative stability of capitalism despite major political and economic crises, what he calls Americanism and Fordism. All of them challenged old modes of analysis and old ways of "doing" politics no less than features of the contemporary world. He, too, was concerned to avoid being swept aside and rendered irrelevant by what appeared overwhelming and irreversible change. His courage in facing the future and trying to understand the defeats of the past serves as a useful example. He helps us to pose questions about which concepts and methods can help us to understand the present historical moment. In particular, he helps us to explore what is new in all its contradictions, difficulties, and possibilities without confusing the relatively super-ficial, contingent, and short term for the profound, the fundamental, so that we can recognize the watersheds which mean that there is no turning back while understanding that there are nonetheless different paths forward.

One thing is essential methodologically and even more important politically: not to take anything for granted. Much of the literature on globalization aims precisely at avoiding this danger. The alternative is a self-fulfilling prophecy in which any space for progressive politics is foreclosed. That is the message of a number of recent works, whose analyses, of course, can be contested (Hirst and Thompson 1996; Weiss 1997). Whatever the diagnosis or the prognosis of our condition, we must examine the contradictory effects of globalization as process or project, intertwined as these dimensions are. Expressed in a different way, Gramsci, building on Machiavelli, explored what he calls the art of politics, which makes use of the results of political science, but also understands that effective reality is never a given but depends on what has been built. Gramsci writes, for example, that concrete analysis is not an end in itself but depends on how it can lead to "practical activity." Another formulation is found in the tension, and tension there is, between "pessimism of the intellect" and "optimism of the will." That is, what is possible is also related to what is desired (Sassoon 2000c).

Bibliography

Archibugi, D. and Held, D. (eds) (1995) *Cosmopolitan Democracy. An Agenda for a New World Order*, Cambridge: Polity Press.

Augelli, E. and Murphy, C. N. (1993) "Gramsci and International Relations: A General Perspective with Recent Examples of US Policy Toward the Third World," in S. Gill (ed.) *Gramsci, Historical Materialism and International Relations*, Cambridge: Cambridge University Press.

—— (1997) "Consciousness, Myth and Collective Action: Gramsci, Sorel, and the Ethical State," in S. Gill and J. H. Mittelman (eds) *Innovation and Transformation in International Studies*, Cambridge: Cambridge University Press.

Bagchi, A. (1997) "Globalization, Regionalization and Social Change in Labour Markets in the Asian Context," paper presented to the international workshop: "Globalization and Social Change," Research Center on Development and International Relations, Aalborg University, May 15–16.

Cox, R. W. (1993) "Gramsci, Hegemony and International Relations," in S. Gill (ed.) *Gramsci, Historical Materialism and International Relations*, Cambridge: Cambridge University Press.

—— (1997) "Gramsci's Thought and the Question of Civil Society in the Later Twentieth Century," paper prepared for the conference: "Gramsci e il novecento," Cagliari, April 15–18, 1997.

Du Boff, R. and Herman, E. S. (1997) "A Critique of Tabb on Globalization," *Monthly Review* 49 (6), November.

Germaine, R. D. and Kenny, M. (1998) "Engaging Gramsci: International Relations Theory and the New Gramscians," *Review of International Studies* 24.

Gill, S. (1993a) "Epistemology, Ontology, and the 'Italian School,'" in S. Gill (ed.) *Gramsci, Historical Materialism and International Relations*, Cambridge: Cambridge University Press.

—— (1993b) "Gramsci and Global Politics: Towards a Post-Hegemonic Research Agenda," in S. Gill (ed.) *Gramsci, Historical Materialism and International Relations*, Cambridge: Cambridge University Press.

—— (ed.) (1993c) *Gramsci, Historical Materialism and International Relations*, Cambridge: Cambridge University Press.

—— (1997a) "Gramsci, Modernity and Globalisation," paper prepared for the conference, Gramsci e il novecento, Cagliari, April 15–18.

—— (1997b) "Transformation and Innovation in the Study of World Order," in S. Gill and J. H. Mittelman (eds) *Innovation and Transformation in International Studies*, Cambridge: Cambridge University Press.

Gill, S. and Law, D. (1993) "Global Hegemony and the Structural Power of Capital," in Gill S. (ed.) *Gramsci, Historical Materialism and International Relations*, Cambridge: Cambridge University Press.

Gill, S. and Mittelman, J. H. (eds) (1997) *Innovation and Transformation in International Studies*, Cambridge: Cambridge University Press.

Glyn, A. and Miliband, D. (eds) (1994) *Paying for Inequality. The Economic Cost of Social Inequality*, London: IPPR/Rivers Oram Press.

Goldblatt, D. (1997) "At the Limits of Political Possibility: The Cosmopolitan Democratic Project," *New Left Review* (September/October).

Goldblatt, D., Held, D., McGrew, A., and Perraton, J. (1997) "Economic Globalisation and the Nation State: The Transformation of Political Power?" *Soundings* 7 (Autumn).

Gramsci, A. (1971) *Selections from the Prison Notebooks*, London: Lawrence and Wishart.

—— (1975) *Quaderni del carcere*, Turin: Einaudi.

Gray, J. (1998) *False Dawn. Delusions of Global Capitalism*, London: Granta Books.

Gurnah, A. (1997) "Elvis in Zanzibar," in A. Scott (ed.) *The Limits of Globalization. Cases and Arguments*, London: Routledge.

Harding, A. and Le Galès, P. (1997) "Globalization, Urban Change and Urban Policies in Britain and France," in A. Scott (ed.) *The Limits of Globalization. Cases and Arguments*, London: Routledge.

Harvey, D. (1997) "Globalization in Question," Department of Development and Planning, Aalborg University, Aalborg: Development Research Series, 56.

Held, D. (1995) *Democracy and the Global Order*, Cambridge: Polity Press.

Hellman, J. A. (1994) *Mexican Lives*, New York: The New Press.

Hirst, P. and Thompson, G. (1996) *Globalisation in Question*, Cambridge: Polity Press.

Jalan, R. (1997) "An Asian Orientalism? Libas and the Textures of Postcolonialism," in A. Scott (ed.) *The Limits of Globalization. Cases and Arguments*, London: Routledge.

Kassim, H. (1997) "Air Transport and Globalization: A Sceptical View," in A. Scott (ed.) *The Limits of Globalization. Cases and Arguments*, London: Routledge.

Kilminster, R. (1997) "Globalization as an Emergent Concept," in A. Scott (ed.) *The Limits of Globalization. Cases and Arguments*, London: Routledge.

Massey, D. (1997) "Problems with Globalisation," *Soundings* 7 (Autumn).

Montanari, M. (1997a) "Crisi dello stato e crisi della modernitá," paper prepared for the conference "Gramsci e il novecento," Cagliari, April 15–18.

—— (1997b) "Introduzione," in A. Gramsci (ed.) *Pensare la democrazia. Antologia dai "Quaderni del carcere,"* Turin: Einaudi.

Murphy, C. (1998) "Understanding IR: Understanding Gramsci," *Review of International Studies* 24 (3).

Peterson, V. S. (1995) "Reframing the Politics of Identity: Democracy, Globalisation and Gender," *Political Expressions* 1 (1).

—— (1996) "The Politics of Identification in the Context of Globalization," *Women's Studies International Forum* 19 (1–2), January–April.

—— (1997) "Whose Crisis? Early and Post-Modern Masculinism," in S. Gill and J. H. Mittelman (eds) *Innovation and Transformation in International Studies*, Cambridge: Cambridge University Press.

Piven, F. F. and Cloward, R. A. (1998) "Eras of Power," *Monthly Review* 49 (8).

Poppi, C. (1997) "Wider Horizons with Larger Details: Subjectivity, Ethnicity and Globalization," in A. Scott (ed.) *The Limits of Globalization. Cases and Arguments*, London: Routledge.

Roseneil, S. (1997) "The Global Common: The Global, Local, and Personal; Dynamics of the Women's Peace Movement in the 1980s," in A. Scott (ed.) *The Limits of Globalization. Cases and Arguments*, London: Routledge.

Rupert, M. (1993) "Alienation, Capitalism and the Inter-state System: Toward a Marxian–Gramscian Critique," in S. Gill (ed.) *Gramsci, Historical Materialism and International Relations*, Cambridge: Cambridge University Press.

—— (1998) "(Re-)Engaging Gramsci: A Response to Germaine and Kenny," *Review of International Studies* 24 (3).

Sakamoto, Y. (1997) "Civil Society and Democratic World Order," in S. Gill and J. H. Mittelman (eds) *Innovation and Transformation in International Studies*, Cambridge: Cambridge University Press.

Sassoon, A. S. (1987) *Gramsci's Politics*, 2nd edn, London: Unwin Hyman, and Minneapolis: University of Minnesota Press.

—— (2000a) "Back to the Future: Gramsci and the Debate in English on Civil Society," in A. S. Sassoon, *Gramsci and Contemporary Politics. Beyond Pessimism of the Intellect*, London: Routledge.

—— (2000b) *Gramsci and Contemporary Politics. Beyond Pessimism of the Intellect*, London: Routledge.

—— (2000c) "The Challenge to Traditional Intellectuals: Specialisation, Organisation, Leadership," in A. S. Sassoon, *Gramsci and Contemporary Politics. Beyond Pessimism of the Intellect*, London: Routledge.

—— (2000d) "Gramsci's Subversion of the Language of Politics," in A. S. Sassoon, *Gramsci and Contemporary Politics. Beyond Pessimism of the Intellect*, London: Routledge.

—— (2000e) "The Politics of the Organic Intellectuals," in A. S. Sassoon, *Gramsci and Contemporary Politics. Beyond Pessimism of the Intellect*, London: Routledge.

—— (2000f) "The People, Intellectuals and Specialised Knowledge," in A. S. Sassoon, *Gramsci and Contemporary Politics. Beyond Pessimism of the Intellect*, London: Routledge.

Scott, A. (ed.) (1997a) *The Limits of Globalization. Cases and Arguments*, London: Routledge.

—— (1997b) "Introduction. Globalization: Social Process or Political Rhetoric?" in A. Scott (ed.) *The Limits of Globalization. Cases and Arguments*, London: Routledge.

Shin, K-Y. (1997) "Globalization and Class Politics in South Korea," paper presented to the international workshop "Globalization and Social Change," Aalborg University.

Stewart, P. and Garrahan, P. (1997) "Globalization, the Company and the Workplace: Some Interim Evidence from the Auto Industry in Britain," in A. Scott (ed.) *The Limits of Globalization. Cases and Arguments*, London: Routledge.

Street, J. (1997) "'Across the Universe': The Limits of Global Popular Culture," in A. Scott (ed.) *The Limits of Globalization. Cases and Arguments*, London: Routledge.

Tabb, W. K. (1997a) "Globalization is an Issue. The Power of Capital is the Issue," *Monthly Review* 48 (4), June.

—— (1997b) "Contextualizing Globalization: Comments on Du Boff and Herman," *Monthly Review* 49 (6), November.

Tao, J. and Ho, W. (1997) "Chinese Entrepreneurship: Culture and Economic Actors," in A. Scott (ed.) *The Limits of Globalization. Cases and Arguments*, London: Routledge.

Telò, M. (1997) "Gramsci e il futuro dell'occidente," paper prepared for the conference "Gramsci e il novecento," Cagliari, April 15–18.

Weiss, L. (1997) "Globalization and the Myth of the Powerless State," *New Left Review* (September/October).

Wheeler, W. (1994) "Nostalgia isn't Nasty—The Postmodernising of Parliamentary Democracy," in M. Perryman (ed.) *Altered States. Postmodernism. Politics. Culture*, London: Lawrence and Wishart.

Wood, E. M. (1997) "A Note on Du Boff and Herman," *Monthly Review* 49 (6), November.

5 Globalization and the revival of traditional knowledge

Andrew Jamison

Introduction

During the nineteenth and twentieth centuries, modern science was spread around the world, first as part of Europe's imperialist expansion and, later, in the post-war era, as part of the "globalization" strategies of transnational corporations. Science is central to globalization, providing both a knowledge base for new products, as well as a cornerstone for the ideologies of positivism, scientism, and modernism which have helped to legitimize the destruction of other forms of knowledge. It has been in the name of science that a myth of progress has been constructed and upheld, according to which the diverse array of "non-scientific" human knowledges have come to be labeled "traditional" with all the negative and derogatory connotations that the term has come to imply.

Until recently, these traditional forms of knowledge have tended to be viewed as leftover legacies of the past that impede the advancement of science, and as dangerous transgressions from the modern methods of truth-seeking. The so-called project of modernity and its corresponding forms of rationality have often been portrayed as a battle against the past, a future-oriented struggle to free society from the constraints of cultural traditions. For the social theorist Anthony Giddens, traditional knowledge is characterized by what he terms a "formulaic notion of truth." Traditional knowledge is not derived from experience or experimental observation, but from magic and religious ritual. In traditional societies, Giddens contends, authority rests with the guardians of these mysterious truths, "be they elders, healers, magicians or religious functionaries" (Giddens 1994: 65). One of the achievements of modernity has been to replace this traditional knowledge with the objective methods of science: "science was invested with the authority of a final court of appeal" (Giddens 1994: 87). What Giddens and, for that matter, so many other "modernists," find so disturbing in the contemporary world is that the authority of science has been undermined, without any viable replacement coming to the fore, thus leaving room for the resurgence of traditionalism.

Through the paradigmatic lens of modernist ideology, traditional knowledge and modern science are seen as polar opposites. The revival of interest in traditional knowledge in recent decades is reduced to anti-modern traditionalism, and seen as a direct enemy of the universal values and progressive achievements of modern science. The problem with such a view is that it is unable to recognize the cultural specificity of modern science itself, and thus unwittingly feeds into the technological arrogance of the globalizing transnational corporations. Even more serious, perhaps, is that the modernist is incapable, and unusually uninterested in distinguishing among the different varieties of traditional knowledge that are currently being reinvented or rediscovered. As I see it, it is increasingly important for the contemporary global citizen (as well as for contemporary social theorists, not to mention scientists and engineers) to take traditional knowledge seriously, and it is thus necessary to question the modernist bias of much of the contemporary globalization "discourse" (cf. Eyerman and Jamison 1998).

To begin with, we need to understand that it was a particular kind of scientific "tradition," born and bred in Western Europe, which, over the past 200 years, has become the globally hegemonic form of knowledge production. Philosophically, modern science has its own characteristic procedures of experimentation and "falsification," its own specific theories of justification and verification, that are by no means the only way to achieve an understanding of reality (Popper 1963; Hacking 1983). Sociologically, modern science is grounded in culturally specific norms of objectivity and "organized scepticism," and is structured in particular disciplines, institutions, and discourses that are also intimately connected to the cultural and political traditions of Western Europe (Merton 1957; Traweek 1988). Economically, modern science has for a hundred years or more been transformed into a "productive force;" what distinguishes modern science from traditional knowledge in the material domain is its essential technological, or instrumental, orientation, and this also is by no means the only way that systematic inquiry into natural processes can be combined with material production (Böhme et al. 1978; Scheler 1980).

Modern science is a composite form of knowledge production, which links curiosity to production, or the most basic scientific research to commercial technological applications. In regard to globalization, it is especially the scientistic belief in the intrinsic superiority of scientific-technological rationality over all other forms of thought, as well as the centrality of "instrumental rationality" in the global political economy—the crucial role of research and development as a driving force of economic growth and expansion—that is most significant. Traditional knowledge is programmatically rejected by both the theorists and practitioners of globalization, even though, in many areas of production and everyday life, the modern science of transnational firms and globally oriented academic institutions is increasingly being challenged by other modes of inquiry and practice.

It is well to remember that modern science was not diffused all at once; it was rather a gradual and long-term process, by which a "mode" of knowledge production that developed in Europe, with its particular theories and methods, as well as its particular relations to the rest of society, systematically took on a globally hegemonic status (cf. Mendelssohn 1976). In the process, other modes of inquiry were explicitly banished in many places, but more commonly they continued to exist at the margins of society, even though they received little if any support from the state or the imperial authorities. Even today, schools for training or initiation in various traditional medical and crafts techniques operate in many parts of the world, much as they have done for hundreds, even thousands, of years. It is somewhat beyond the scope of this chapter to attempt to present these activities in any detail. Rather, forms of traditional knowledge production will be discussed as they have been rediscovered or reinterpreted in a more or less conscious search for alternatives to global modern science.

It is as part of the efforts to counteract broader processes of globalization that traditional knowledge will be considered. Here it is possible to delineate two main approaches: a *traditionalist approach*, which has sought to revive the pre-colonial past in a more or less unadulterated form, and an *integrative approach*, which has sought to combine elements of indigenous knowledge traditions in one or another developmental framework. There has been a tension between the two approaches, and in most developing countries there continue to be conflicts over the most appropriate way to develop "non-Western" ways of doing science.

The communist model of development, first put into practice in the Soviet Union and then in China, Vietnam, Cuba and, to varying degrees, in several African countries, tended to promulgate a weak integrative approach: traditional techniques in medicine, agriculture, and industry have been tolerated only when they could contribute to a new "socialist" or "people's" science of some kind. Although patterns of development have varied from country to country, the standard procedure was to build up formal systems of modern science and technology, while allowing some informal systems of training, diffusion and service in traditional approaches, what was once called "walking on two legs" (cf. Science for the People 1974). The dichotomy has roughly corresponded to the division between the urban and rural economies. The general ideology of socialist development has been modernist, depicting science and technology as intrinsically progressive, and relegating traditional belief systems as belonging to a premodern past (cf. Blomström and Hettne 1984).

In many of the non-communist developing countries, the scientistic value system associated with modern science has more explicitly been distinguished from its practice; certain elements of Western philosophy, religion and belief have been characterized as belonging to a "colonial mentality" and attempts have been made to encourage indigenous religions and belief systems. At the same time, the natural and engineering sciences have been developed almost exclusively along Western lines, since most of the leading scientists in developing countries were, at least until independence, educated in Western countries. Usually, traditional philosophy and art has been encouraged alongside the modern sciences, not to mention religions and rituals, which has meant that even though the formal systems are based on the Western policy and organizational models, the research and education "culture" is influenced in many ways by traditional beliefs and ways of life (cf. Mendelsohn and Elkana 1980; Salomon et al. 1994).

Post-colonialism

The questioning of modern science and the revival of traditional knowledge can be seen, somewhat schematically, to have gone through three different phases since the end of World War II. In a first phase that lasted in most countries at least until the second half of the 1960s, there was little concern with developing alternatives to modern science at either an institutional or material level; it was only the Western philosophy that was challenged and countered by reinterpretations of traditional belief systems. In Africa, Nkrumah's and Senghor's attempts to formulate an indigenous African philosophy involved both the reinvention of African tradition as well as the conscious application of selected elements of that tradition to contemporary political and social projects: "Africanization" (Mazrui 1978).

For my purposes, the attempts to develop African philosophy and revive traditional forms of religion are interesting in seeking to provide a different cultural framework for the development of science, not a different science. It is also important to note that they are the result, for the most part, of interaction with critical European traditions; the Western-trained leaders and cultural spokesmen of the newly independent countries of the Third World have applied or at least made use of certain tools of Western cultural criticism in seeking to foster the traditions of their own peoples. In Africa, the rediscovery of the past was inspired by Western anthropology (Mudimbe 1988). Those who came to formulate African philosophy were influenced especially by the works of the anthropologist Levy-Bruhl, and they were affected more generally by the cultural relativism that was a rather common feature of European philosophy and sociology between the two World Wars (Tambiah 1990).

While some leaders of newly emerging countries thus sought to develop alternatives to the philosophical dimensions of modern science, the articulators of socialist development strategies sought to impose a different agenda for putting science to use. The writings of Franz Fanon, which had a major influence in Third World intellectual circles during the first period of independence, can be taken as representative of this socialist position. For Fanon in Algeria, much like Mao in China, Nehru in India, and Castro in Cuba, traditional approaches to knowledge were part of the undeveloped and backward society; the starting point was the observation that traditional society had been "thrown into confusion" by the experience of colonization. In the colonial period, Fanon wrote,

the dominant group arrives with its values and imposes them with such violence that the very life of the colonized can manifest itself only defensively, in a more or less clandestine way. Under these conditions, colonial domination distorts the very relations that the colonized maintains with his own culture.

(Fanon 1970: 111)

For Fanon, the liberation struggle in Algeria had helped solve the problem by taking the side of modern medicine.

> Witchcraft, *maraboutism* (already considerably discredited as a result of the propaganda carried on by the intellectuals), belief in the *djinn*, all things that seemed to be part of the very being of the Algerian, were swept away by the action and practice initiated by the Revolution . . . The notions about "native psychology" or of the "basic personality" are shown to be vain. The people who take their destiny into their own hands assimilate the most modern forms of technology at an extraordinary rate.
>
> (Fanon 1970: 124, 126)

What liberation and independence provided was thus not a return to tradition but a different approach to modernity, a different way to *use* modern science. It is certainly no accident that it was Western-trained medical doctors, lawyers, engineers and scientists who were among the leaders in most of the Third World struggles for independence. They were modernists, who had imbibed the teachings of Marxism and positivism, and who saw their revolutions, among other things, as crucial steps toward assimilating modern science and technology into their "underdeveloped" societies. Most of them saw traditional knowledge as a kind of unfortunate heritage that was to be transcended and supplanted; bred of ignorance and superstition, it was to be replaced by systematic scientific inquiry and modern technology. Marx, in the nineteenth century, had of course been a critic of capitalism, but his criticism had not been directed toward science and technology; indeed, central to his critique was the belief that capitalism could not make satisfactory use of the new productive forces that it had unleashed on the world. It was rather the task of the working class to put the revolutionary discoveries of modern science to more effective and widespread use (Jamison 1982: 36–48).

In the twentieth century, first in Russia and then in the colonies, Marxism was disseminated to other groups of oppressed peoples, but its attitude to science and technology was not particularly affected in the process. It was only as a "critical theory" among European socialists (such as Max Horkheimer, Theodor Adorno, and Herbert Marcuse, and their disciples) that Marxism became involved in questioning modern science and technology. But this was a very different Marxism than that developed in the revolutionary movements of national liberation (see Gouldner 1980). The revolutionary movements that came to power after World War II, many of which explicitly identified themselves as Marxist, were propagators, even propagandists, for modern science and technology and, for the most part, rejected and opposed traditional forms of knowledge production.

Anti-imperialism and appropriate technology

A second wave of opposition to modern science began to take shape as a part of the anti-imperialist movements of the 1960s. Already in the early 1960s, the

Cuban revolution was greeted as a "revolution in the revolution" by the French student, Regis Debray, and, as the 1960s progressed, new kinds of social movements took form throughout the world—in both the north and the south—that were critical of "neoimperialist" development strategies. What was at issue was not primarily the science and technology that were central to development, but the orientation to the imperialist center, the dominance that the imperialist countries continued to exercise over the newly independent countries of the Third World. In order to continue the struggle beyond independence to a true national liberation it was necessary, among other things, to take the pre-colonial past much more seriously, and to question some of the modernist assumptions that had hitherto guided the development of science and technology.

It was the Vietnam War that brought these issues to a head. The United States, now seen as the dominant imperialist power, mobilized a massive destructive force that was highly dependent on the most advanced science and technology. In response, the Vietnamese mobilized their indigenous skills and traditional knowledge and in the process came to stand for a new kind of popular approach to military resistance, the "people's war." Mao in China had also come to launch his Great Proletarian Cultural Revolution, closing the universities and sending students to the countryside to learn from the people rather than from the "bourgeois" professors who were still supposedly in power in the cities. Where the Vietnamese were forced to defend themselves by rediscovering traditional methods of guerrilla warfare, the Chinese people were forced to take part in a massive and largely disastrous social experiment. For both countries, the experiments produced a great deal of suffering, wasted effort, and human and natural destruction; to speak in Karl Popper's terms, they were massive social experiments, which failed to falsify Western science. Indeed, in both countries, the enthusiasm for modern science and technology has, if anything, been greater after the revolutionary experiments than before (cf. Jamison and Baark 1995). In their time, however, both efforts provided models for other countries to emulate, and contributed to a more general search for alternative or appropriate approaches to science and technology (Dickson 1974; Sigurdson 1980).

In the 1970s, appropriate technology, by which was usually meant the creative combination in particular contexts of traditional and modern techniques to meet the problems at hand, developed into a multifaceted social movement— and not only in developing countries (Pursell 1993). For some, it came to mean labor-intensive technology, and thus often a more participatory approach to knowledge and skill generation. Here, traditional knowledge represented the tacit or practical competence of the artisan, and was opposed to the scientific-technical expertise of the transnational corporations. For others, appropriate technology came to mean a more environmentally-conscious technology, and thus a rediscovery of traditional agricultural and even manufacturing techniques. This type of traditional knowledge is still influential within the global environmental movement; the often idealized view of the past that informs this quest for ecological technology is of a human–nature interaction that is seen as having been more harmonious than the exploitative and anthropocentric relations necessitated by a globalized mode of capitalist production (cf. Norberg-Hodge 1991). For still others, appropriate technology came to mean a small-scale technology, and a more localized form of material production and social organization, thus challenging the large dams and other mammoth development projects that had proved so damaging and destructive to the cultures of the newly independent countries (Schumacher 1973). Appropriate technology came to be supported by the specialized agencies of the United Nations as well as by a number of non-governmental action groups and organizations; and for a time, the search for alternatives to Western-style development was a major concern throughout the developing world (cf. Jequier 1976).

The proponents of appropriate technology sought to break the link that had been formed already in the early modern period in the seventeenth and eighteenth centuries between the development of science and the development of practical techniques. Appropriate technologists argued—and, for the most part, continue to argue today—for a return to a more locally-based kind of knowledge, and to a conception of technology that focuses on the collective craftworker rather than the scientist or engineer as the main source of innovation. Appropriate technology has tended to be seen as a process of development from below, a non-scientific, or, at least, non-expert, participatory form of technical activity that makes better use of the available human and natural resources than a technology development from above, directed by scientific experts with little awareness of local conditions and capabilities (cf. MacRobie 1981). As a social movement, appropriate technology had difficulty in meeting the challenges of the new advanced technologies of microelectronics and biotechnology that began to appear in the international marketplace in the late 1970s. These technologies were based on the latest scientific understanding and thus seemed to imply a re-Westernization or a reaffirmation of the globally hegemonic modern science. The ideas of appropriate technology, in the course of the 1980s, tended to be marginalized, and now serve not so much as a real global alternative to modern science and technology but as a kind of collective memory. Part of the problem is that the alternatives quickly grew too specific. Rather than develop a comprehensive set of appropriate technologies and encourage each country to ransack its own traditions and find those ideas and approaches that seemed most fruitful to develop further, all too many appropriate technology enthusiasts sought to develop immediate solutions, "technical fixes" to contemporary problems. The units that still survive are primarily those that have sought to stimulate appropriate processes for technological development and training rather than appropriate products. But what was also stimulated was a much more thorough historical reconnaissance than had ever been encouraged before, and that search for a usable past continues to this day (cf. Alvares 1979; Goonatilake 1984; Pacey 1990).

Particularly important were the efforts made to reinterpret the precolonial scientific traditions. In Latin America, as part of the effort to save the tropical rain forests from extinction, the ethnobotanies of the Amerindians were rediscovered, and research institutes have been established to carry out agricultural programs based on the revitalized traditional knowledges (cf. Posey 1989). In China, acupuncture and herbal medicine have not only become fully legitimate parts of medical science and treatment, but they have been transferred to the rest of the world as a visibly non-Western way to treat—and understand—the human animal. In Africa and Central America, the pre-colonial astronomical and cosmological theories have been rediscovered, and some of the mysteries of modern astrophysics are beginning to receive different kinds of explanations when filtered through other cosmological frameworks. Of course, much of this new fascination with traditional knowledge, like a good deal of the broader "new age" movement with which its spokespersons are often associated, exaggerates the "scientificity" of pre-modern knowledge systems (cf. Capra 1982). But there is no doubt that there is a growing acceptance of the value of pre-modern techniques, and an increasing interest in understanding or decoding their hidden, and long-lost "rationalities."

Fundamentalism and the return to tradition

With the Iranian revolution in 1979, the search for alternatives to Western science can be said to have moved into a third and still unfolding phase. More polarized and explicitly conflictual, the new more "fundamentalist" tendencies and movements seek to revive or reconstitute an alternative, traditional form of knowledge production that opposes both the philosophical, technological and sociological dimensions of modern science. What is taking place can be seen as the emergence of comprehensive alternatives to modern science, or what Leif Stenberg has recently termed, in relation to perhaps the most visible such alternative, the articulation of an "Islamic modernity" (Stenberg 1996).

Ziauddin Sardar, one of the most vocal spokesmen for Islamic science, has identified four streams of thought among those who would develop an alternative to modern science in the Middle East (Sardar 1989), and these have recently been further delineated in a doctoral dissertation by Leif Stenberg. One—"the quest for a sacred science"—is identified with the Persian scholar S. H. Nasr, who has focused attention on the philosophical or spiritual dimensions of Islamic science; Nasr has long questioned the exploitative attitude to nature that characterizes modern science (Nasr 1968), and for Sardar and other younger critics there is a tendency in Nasr's writings to reduce science to cosmology, and equate the alternative Islamic science with a general, occultist interest in "gnosis." All too many spokesmen for Islamic science, according to Sardar, weaken their criticism by not satisfactorily specifying the alternative. Their position becomes merely another restatement of the old debate between religious experience and scientific knowledge, which merely seeks to replace one belief system with another (Nasr 1976).

A second group, composed primarily of people who are both Muslims and scientists, and often leaders within their own countries' scientific establishments, are those who continue to pursue business as usual. The critiques of Western science that have been promulgated over the past two or three decades are simply brushed aside, according to Sardar, and the scientists in Islamic countries continue to live schizophrenic lives, Western scientists by day, practicing Muslims by night.

Abdus Salam, one of the leading physicists of the Arab world, can be taken as a representative of this position (Salam 1989). For scientists like Salam, science is seen as global and universal; but, all too often, Muslims and people in developing countries are excluded from contributing to and participating in its development:

> . . . there truly is no disconsonance between Islam and modern science . . . What gives one hope is that there *are* Muslim scientists working principally (though not exclusively) in developed countries who have registered the highest attainments in sciences. This implies that it is basically environmental factors in our societies which need to be corrected.
>
> (Salam 1989: 323, 348)

The position of the French physician Maurice Bucaille is similar to Salam's, but attempts to link Islamic religious faith more directly to modern science. In a series of influential books, Bucaille has sought to show how Islam and science are interconnected, and how the Koran prefigures many modern scientific theories and discoveries (Stenberg 1996: 221ff.).

The other positions identified by Sardar and Stenberg are, in many respects, more interesting for the purposes of this chapter. They involve those who would establish a new metaphysical starting point for scientific inquiry which would have far-reaching consequences for the actual pursuit of scientific research. If I follow their arguments, the difference is one of degree; one group, associated with the attempts to institutionalize Islamic science in the International Institute of Islamic Thought, would alter the relations between scientific fields, the selection of problems, and the depth of moral and religious reflection attached to scientific research, and would conduct a fully-fledged series of alternative research programs; while the other group, to which Sardar himself belongs and which he calls the Ijmali position, would seek to create an entire new science, by which the very "facts" of nature would be different. Ijmalis, according to Sardar, "have a unique position of our own which is derived solely from the ethical, value and conceptual parameters of Islam. The essence of Ijmali thought is reconstruction, complexity (sic) and interconnection, or what Riaz Kirmani has called complementarity" (Sardar 1989: 155).

Islamic science, as perhaps the most ambitious alternative, or the ethnoscience tradition currently being reinvented, has thus already spawned internal dissension and, judging from Sardar's treatment of his adversaries, there is a rather large amount of aggression in an enterprise that claims to be based entirely on a love of God, or Allah, the "one and only God." Indeed, in comparison with his first book, *Science, Technology and Development in the Muslim World* (Sardar 1977), the program of Islamic science that he outlines in more recent works appears to have increased in rhetoric but lost something in practical achievement and focus.

In this respect the attempt to develop an Islamic science seems to be repeating much of the same process that the attempt to develop an appropriate technology or "science for the people" went through in the 1970s. In both cases, a critical identification of problems has apparently led to an overly ambitious formulation of an alternative which has proved impossible to realize in practice. While the alternative becomes ever more extreme and absolute in terms of rhetoric, it thus fails to solve the particular problems that were initially attributed to modern science and in need of amelioration (Stenberg 1996).

The four schools of thought can be taken as representative of the different alternative approaches to modern science that have developed, albeit in very different ways in different countries, as new religious movements have exercised a growing political and, not least, cultural influence. On the one hand, there is what might be called a spiritualist position: the particular traditional teachings are not as important as the general ambition to counter materialism and "materialist" science with a revival of spirit, occultism, and religious faith. On the other hand, there are the realists, who continue to practice modern science while professing a set of moral values, as it were, on the side. Science and values continue to be separate spheres of existence for this second group, which still seems to include many of those who actually work as scientists and engineers in most developing countries. It is among students that one might expect the strongest resonance for the other two, somewhat newer schools of thought; and, as such, there seems to be a significant generational dimension to the revival of ethnosciences, or traditional knowledge. The one, the critical or integrative school, sees the development of alternatives by taking the Western tradition seriously, pointing to its weaknesses, both methodologically and practically, and seeing a new ethnoscience as an explicit combination of modern and traditional approaches. The other, with its more dogmatic or traditionalist orientation, sees the alternative, Islamic science as a self-enclosed activity that in some way can separate its own ethnoscience from others.

India as an example

In order to bring some of the general discussion a bit closer to reality, it might be useful to focus on the experiences of one particular developing country. India has been chosen not merely for the size and diversity of its population and the richness of its culture, but also because almost all of the themes that have been taken up in the general debates about modern science can be found there. Indeed, it could be argued that India's struggle for independence was, to a greater extent than elsewhere, also a struggle for the resurrection of Indian civilization. At the very least, it can be said that traditional techniques, beliefs and customs were mobilized in the political struggle more explicitly there than elsewhere. Under the inspiration of Mohandas (later Mahatma) Gandhi the peoples of the Indian subcontinent were encouraged to revive traditional technical practices and even managed to put aside, for a time, some of their religious antagonisms in order to achieve national independence. Gandhi was Western-trained and learned about Western philosophy and modern science while studying law in Britain. Gandhi also became acquainted with Western traditions of cultural criticism, associated with such names as Ruskin, Tolstoy and Thoreau. The "experiments with truth" that made up Gandhi's life were, in large measure, a conscious effort to combine these critical Western ideas with a very personal interpretation of Hindu belief. Gandhi embodied an alternative science and technology in his own person, but he was not particularly successful in writing about it or in institutionalizing it. He has served in post-independence India as both a legend and personal model, but his legacy remains controversial.

Gandhi was not alone in his attempts to develop alternative approaches to science and technology in colonial India, although it was his vision that has perhaps been most influential. Ashis Nandy has contrasted Gandhi's "critical traditionalism" to the more absolute glorification of tradition represented by the art historian and Buddhist scholar Ananda Coomaraswamy (Nandy 1987). Where Gandhi made use of Indian traditions in an open-ended, reflective way, Coomaraswamy's tradition, according to Nandy, "remains homogeneous and undifferentiated from the point of view of man-made suffering." "Today, with the renewed interest in cultural visions, one has to be aware that commitment to traditions, too, can objectify by drawing a line between a culture and those who live by that culture, by setting up some as the true interpreters of a culture and the others as falsifiers, and by trying to defend the core of a culture from its periphery" (Nandy 1987: 121–2).

Gandhi's critique of modern science was fundamental and comprehensive. He rejected science both in theory and practice, recombining the romantic or poetic critique of secularization with critiques of the institutionalized elitism and the "technicist" orientation of Western science. It was the lack of morality, the lack of idealism of Western civilization that Gandhi objected to; and Western science was, for him, a central part of that immoral value system. As Nandy puts it:

> As a general rule, Gandhi was against technologies which replaced the uniquely human aspects of man. Not only because such replacement turned a person into a mechanical part of the production machine, but also because it turned him into a mechanical, "dead" consumer of utilities. For Gandhi, technology had to be judged both on the grounds of what it did and what it symbolized.
>
> (Nandy 1987: 138)

The double nature of Gandhi's critique is important in understanding the subsequent Indian discourse(s) on modern science and traditional knowledge. Unlike the Marxist or positivist leaders of most other independence movements, Gandhi sought to develop an alternative way of life in which traditional techniques and beliefs had a central place. His critique of Western civilization was thus not merely a critique of its immorality but also of its epistemology. "Traditional technology, too, was for him an ethically and cognitively better system of applied knowledge than modern technology. He rejected machine civilization, not because he was a saint making occasional forays into the secular world, but because he was a political activist and thinker with strong moral concerns" (Nandy 1987: 160).

India, of course, did not follow Gandhi's lead in the first two decades of independence. Instead, under the leadership of Jawaharlal Nehru, ambitious efforts were made to implant what Nehru called a scientific temper in Indian society. Nehru's scientism, and that of his leading scientific and political advisers, was deep and unambiguous. "It is science alone that can solve the problems of hunger and poverty, of insanitation and illiteracy, of superstition and deadening custom and tradition, of vast resources running to waste, of a rich country inhabited by starving people. I do not see any way out of our vicious circle of poverty except by utilizing the new sources of power which science has placed at our disposal" (Nehru, quoted in Krishna and Jain 1990: 7–8).

For Nehru, Indian civilization, with its superstitions and religious strife, was in need of radical change; a "scientific temper" needed to be imposed on the Indian society, and his governments did their utmost to develop both scientific institutions as well as a popular understanding and appreciation for science. From the late 1940s, scientific and technological research were organized roughly along the lines of the Soviet model, with central planning and strong state control over priorities and orientation.

> The Indian experience of science policy up to the late 1960s, which was based on the close alliance between elite scientists and the political leadership, had the major objective to expand the infrastructural base for science, technology and education. The leadership of Nehru provided the necessary political will and economic assistance to ensure continuous expansion of scientific organisations and funding of science and technology.
>
> (Krishna and Jain 1990: 15)

It would be an oversimplification to say that Nehru's death in 1964 led to a revival of Gandhian thought. But as the 1960s progressed, a number of challenges emerged to the developmental strategies and emphases that had guided India since independence. The wars with China and Pakistan fostered nationalistic tendencies, and a variety of popular peasant movements began to wage struggles against the central and regional authorities. The international wave of student and anti-imperialist protest also played its part, so that by the early 1970s, India was a society torn by inner conflict. Most significant from our perspective was the revitalization of the Gandhian undercurrent, spearheaded by Jaraprakash Narayan, or JP as he came to be called, with his "total revolution" which aimed to revive village economic life and grass-roots initiatives. The revival of Gandhism was an important factor in the protests against the large dams and government-sponsored social forestry programs as well as the emergence of environmental movements, especially the famous Chipko "tree-huggers" in northern India. In 1978, Prime Minister Indira Gandhi, after having ruled the country through an unpopular state of emergency, was defeated by the oppositional

Janata party, which in many ways tried to apply Gandhian ideas during its few short years in power, before being torn apart by internal dissension.

It was in this general spirit of criticism and change that the political scientist, Rajni Kothari, gathered together a number of Western-trained humanists and social scientists at the Center for the Study of Developing Societies (CSDS) in Delhi. Kothari had been the chairman of the social science research council and had been a key actor in the infrastructure-building of the Nehru era. In the 1970s, however, Kothari and his colleagues at CSDS grew increasingly disillusioned with the path that Indian development had taken, and began to reconsider the Gandhian intellectual legacy. Indeed, throughout the country, perhaps particularly among science and engineering students who were finding their knowledge increasingly irrelevant to the needs of their country, the received position about the crucial role of modern science in Indian development began to be questioned. It was particularly among engineering students that the appeal of appropriate technology seems to have been felt most strongly, and in the 1970s a number of different units were established (cf. MacRobie 1981).

At the end of the 1970s, three books appeared that served to articulate a new kind of intellectual critique of Western science in India. In 1978, J. P. S. Uberoi, professor of sociology at Delhi University, published *Science and Culture*, in which he developed an all-encompassing critique of modern science, or, more specifically, of the positivist tradition, which he traced back to the Reformation and the separation of subject and object. According to Uberoi:

> I am persuaded that so long as the problem of the alternative is seen in India or elsewhere in purely practical extrinsic terms, whether political, social or economic, modern Western science itself will remain a stranger and liable to exploit us for its own ends. Its so-called diffusion, implantation or assimilation in the non-Western world will very properly remain a failure or turn into something worse. On the other hand, if the intrinsic intellectual problem of the positivist theory and praxis of science and its claims come to be appreciated by us, leading to a dialogue with native theory and praxis, whether classical or vernacular, then modern Western science will find itself reconstituted into something new in the process.
>
> (Uberoi 1978: 86)

The following year, 1979, the Bombay-based journalist and political activist Claude Alvares, who had gone off to Holland to study philosophy, provided what would become a catalyst for much of the new critical thinking in his doctoral dissertation, *Homo Faber: Technology and Culture in India, China and the West 1500–1972*. Alvares's book opened up an arena for critical reappreciation, among intellectuals, of the non-Western scientific traditions in India. It presented what Alvares called a new anthropological model of technological development, and explicitly called for the integration of ethnosciences, or indigenous knowledge traditions, in the development of appropriate technologies and developmental strategies. For Alvares (1979: 45), "the model of social and technological development idealized out of the industrial revolution in England, the United States and certain parts of Western Europe is no longer the sole means by which the Southern countries and nations of Asia, Africa and Latin America can hope to survive." Alvares traced the historical development of technology in India, China and England, and sought to show how cultural traditions and, in particular, the experiences of imperialism and colonialism had affected all three countries in fundamental ways. Such historical relativization was necessary, according to Alvares, if the non-Western countries were to escape their historical dependency on the West.

> The displacement of the West in its monopoly over the productive process will be accompanied by the displacement of its monopoly position as the arbiter of what is proper for the Southern nations in the realm of culture, ideas and ideals. The wider dispersal of the ability to produce goods will be accompanied by the wider dispersal of the ability to produce ideas.
>
> (Alvares 1979: 221)

A third book of the Janata period, Ashis Nandy's *Alternative Sciences*, brought the critique of modern science down to a micro or individual level. Nandy analyzed the different ways in which Jagadis Chandra Bose, the plant physiologist, and Srinivasa Ramanujan, the mathematician, had become "alien insiders" in the world of Western science. His was not a straightforward critique, but rather a more subtle psychological analysis which carried a number of different messages. On the one hand, Nandy showed how two Indian scientists had been constrained in their work by their Indianness, but on the other, he also indicated how Indian tradition had provided opportunities for creative "dissent" from Western science (Nandy 1980). It is the theme of creative dissent that has continued to concern Nandy in his later writings. In the meantime, however, India has returned to the modernist ambitions of the Nehru period; and, as a result, the academic critiques of Nandy and Uberoi have had little substantive impact on Indian science and technology policy.

More significant in recent years has been the emergence of a critique of modern science in the various social movements. The movements of religious fundamentalism have garnered the most attention, but, at least in India, their interest in science and knowledge has apparently not been particularly strong. They seem to have primarily adopted a spiritualist, or traditionalist, position, opposing, sometimes quite violently and aggressively, various symptoms and attributes of modern science and technology, and offering religious beliefs and rituals as alternatives. Integrative approaches have developed within other kinds of movements. On the one hand, there are the so-called people's science movements which have been particularly active in southern India, beginning with the founding of the Kerala Sastra Sahitya Parishad (KSSP) in 1962. Here the emphasis has been on critical popularization, linking modern science in selective ways to popular myths and traditions and bringing scientific expertise to bear on protests against government-sponsored irrigation and forestry projects. The people's science movements are not critical of science; they are rather critical of the ways in which Western science has been misused in Indian society. Much like the Red Guard during the cultural revolution in China, but with less rhetoric and often, it seems, more popular support, the people's science movements are seeking to develop a socialist science, a "science for social revolution," according to the KSSP's main slogan (Jaffry et al. 1983).

What has emerged in other parts of India, as an outgrowth of the environmental movements in the forests and on tribal lands, has been a very different kind of alternative. Here the various critiques of Western science that have been developed in the West have been integrated into the "cognitive praxis" of environmental activism (cf. Eyerman and Jamison 1991). As articulated by the physicist turned green activist, Vandana Shiva, "maldevelopment is intellectually based on, and justified through, reductionist categories of scientific thought and action. Politically and economically, each project which has fragmented nature and displaced women from productive work has been legitimized as scientific by operationalizing reductionist concepts to realize uniformity, centralization and control" (Shiva 1988: 14). In her book, *Staying Alive*, Shiva combines an ecological and feminist critique of Western science and discovers an alternative feminine attitude to nature in traditional Indian thought. "Contemporary Western views of nature are fraught with the dichotomy or duality between man and woman, and person and nature ... In Indian cosmology, by contrast, person and nature (Purusha-Pakriti) are a duality in unity" (Shiva 1988: 40).

Shiva's argument is that social forestry and the green revolution in agriculture have been masculine, reductionist projects that have separated women (and men) from their natural roots as well as destroying valuable natural resources. In the protests of rural women, especially the Chipko movement in northern India, Shiva sees the "countervailing power" of women's knowledge and politics:

> Women producing survival are showing us that nature is the very basis and matrix of economic life ... They are challenging concepts of waste, rubbish and dispensability as the modern west has defined them ... They have the knowledge and experience to extricate us from the ecological cul-de-sac that the western masculine mind has manoeuvred us into.
>
> (Shiva 1988: 224)

Shiva and other scientists who have joined forces with the environmental movements in India have developed a range of research institutions and alternative organizations for the dissemination of their ecological alternative. Particularly significant has been the Delhi-based Center for Science and Environment (CSE), which has produced the widely-read reports on *The State of India's Environment* and the journal, *Down to Earth*, as well as a large number of magazine and newspaper articles through its press service. The Center is now increasingly involved in propagation programs for a creative mobilization of traditional techniques in food production, forestry, and, most recently, water management (Agarwal and Nurain 1997).

Together with the appropriate technology groups that are still dotted around the Indian countryside, the environmental movements represent a practical critique of Western science in India. Here, as elsewhere, the critique is Western-inspired and many of the critics Western-trained; but at least to my way of thinking, it has produced an ongoing dialogue with Indian traditions that is likely to grow in importance in the years ahead, and not just in India. Both Vandana Shiva and the CSE are actively involved in international non-governmental activities, and take part in the networks of "radical ecologists" that have challenged the programs, among others, of the World Bank and the International Monetary Fund (cf. Jamison 1996). What Shiva and the CSE and others are attempting to infuse into the contemporary discussion of globalization is a critique of the "localism" of the west. The radical ecologists see much of the new interest in sustainable development as a new form of colonialism or "green imperialism" at the same time as they urge a selective use of traditional knowledge in both the industrial and the developing countries.

Conclusion

Up till now, the revival of traditional knowledge has tended to be partial and, as in the case of appropriate technology, often overly specific. There has also often been a gap between the rhetoric of the critics and the viability of their alternative practices. There are also increasingly major tensions between traditionalists and integrationists, between those who would reject all modern science as "Western imperialism" and those who would seek to creatively combine modern science and traditional knowledge. And there is, to be sure, a good deal of anti-science, not to say irrationalism, to be found among those who would revive traditional knowledge. For most of the revivalists considered in this chapter, however, rationality itself is not the issue as much as the uses to which rationality is put and the institutional contexts in which it is organized, and not least the relations between scientific-technological rationality and the main agents of globalization: the transnational corporations. It is within strategies of empowerment and a more local "development from below" that the selective revival of traditional knowledge is seen as an important ingredient. Modern science, in becoming intertwined with the agents of globalization, has too often come to play a destructive role in too many contexts.

In an article published in 1979, the German philosopher Gernot Böhme contrasted alternative approaches to science with alternative traditions in science (Böhme 1979). For Böhme, the alternative to science is obscurantism; there had been, throughout modern history, sufficient alternative traditions within science to sustain visions of the good society. The difficulty was in realizing the good science while avoiding the "bad" applications and priorities. In the years since, there has been a much greater movement to address environmental issues in developing countries, and the rediscovery of traditional knowledge has, if anything, grown more intense. While the level of rhetoric has been raised, however, the practical achievements have been few and the impact of the "revival" on globalization and on the theory and practice of modern science has been relatively insignificant. There is now a noticeable "pro-science" backlash, a visible mobilization against those who challenge the global hegemony of modern science, which is likely to weaken even more the role that traditional knowledge can play in pursuit of one or another form of sustainable development. And that would be unfortunate, for there is certainly need for a more modest, even more humane science; it is often the arrogance and intolerance of planners and experts that is in need of correction, not always their substantive knowledge. There is need for a more open dialogue with other forms of knowledge production, a dialogue that becomes ever more urgent, but also increasingly difficult to achieve.

Bibliography

Agarwal, A. and Nurain, S. (eds) (1997) *Dying Wisdom: Rise, Fall and Potential of India's Traditional Water Harvesting Systems*, Delhi: Centre for Science and Environment.

Alvares, C. (1979) *Homo Faber. Technology and Culture in India, China and the West 1500–1972*, Bombay: Allied Publishers.

Beck, U., Gidden, A., and Lash, S. (1994) *Reflexive Modernization: Politics, Tradition and Aesthetics in the Modern Social Order*, Cambridge: Polity Press.

Blomström, M. and Hettne, B. (1984) *Development Theory in Transition*, London: Zed Books.

Böhme, G. (1979) "Alternatives in Science, Alternatives to Science," in H. Nowotny and H. Rose (eds) *Counter-movements in the Sciences*, Dordrecht: Reidel.

Böhme, G., van den Daele, W., and Krohn, W. (1978) "The 'Scientification' of Technology," in W. Krohn et al. (eds) *The Dynamics of Science and Technology*, Dordrecht: Reidel.

Capra, F. (1982) *The Turning Point. Science, Society and the Rising Culture*, London: Wildwood House.

Dickson, D. (1974) *Alternative Technology and the Politics of Technical Change*, Glasgow: Fontana.

Elzinga, A. and Jamison, A. (1986) "The Other Side of the Coin: The Cultural Critique of Technology in India and Japan," in E. Baark and A. Jamison (eds) *Technological Development in China, India and Japan*, London: Macmillan.

Eyerman, R. and Jamison, A. (1991) *Social Movements: A Cognitive Approach*, Cambridge: Polity Press.

—— (1998) *Music and Social Movements: Mobilizing Traditions in the Twentieth Century*, Cambridge: Cambridge University Press.

Fanon, F. ([1959] 1970) *A Dying Colonialism*, Harmondsworth: Penguin.

Giddens, A. (1994) "Living in a Post-traditional Society," in U. Beck et al. (eds) *Reflexive Modernization: Politics, Tradition and Aesthetics in the Modern Social Order*, Cambridge: Polity Press.

Goonatilake, S. (1984) *Aborted Discovery*, London: Zed Books.

Gouldner, A. (1980) *The Two Marxisms*, New York: Oxford University Press.

Hacking, I. (1983) *Representing and Interpreting*, Cambridge: Cambridge University Press.

Jaffry, A., Rangarajan, M., Ekbal, B., and Kannan, K. P. (1983) "Towards a People's Science Movement," *Economic and Political Weekly* 18 (11).

Jamison, A. (1982) *National Components of Scientific Knowledge: A Contribution to the Social Theory of Science*, Lund: Research Policy Institute.

—— (1996) "The Shaping of the Global Environmental Agenda: The Role of Non-governmental Organizations," in S. Lash et al. (eds) *Risk Environment Modernity: Toward a New Ecology*, London: Sage.

Jamison, A. and Baark, E. (1995) "From Market Reforms to Sustainable Development. The Cultural Dimension of Science and Technology Policy in China and Vietnam," in I. Nørlund et al. (eds) *Vietnam in a Changing World*, London: Curzon Press.

Jequier, N. (1976) *Appropriate Technology: Problems and Promises*, Paris: OECD.

Kragh, H. (1980) *On Science and Underdevelopment*, Roskilde: RUC Forlag.

Krishna, V. and Jain, A. (1990) "Country Report: Scientific Research, Science Policy and Social Studies of Science and Technology in India," paper prepared for the first meeting of the Comparative Research program on Scientific Community, Paris, April.

MacRobie, G. (1981) *Small is Possible*, New York: Harper and Row.

Mazrui, A. (1978) *Political Values and the Educated Class in Africa*, London: Heinemann.

Mendelsohn, E. and Elkana, Y. (eds) (1980) *Sciences and Cultures*, Dordrecht: Reidel.

Mendelssohn, K. (1976) *Science and Western Domination*, London: Thames and Hudson.

Merton, R. (1957) *Social Theory and Social Structure*, New York: The Free Press.

Mudimbe, V. (1988) *The Invention of Africa. Gnosis, Philosophy and the Order of Knowledge*, Bloomington: Indiana University Press.

Nandy, A. (1980) *Alternative Sciences*, New Delhi: Allied Publishers.

—— (1987) *Traditions, Tyranny and Utopias*, Delhi: Oxford University Press.

Nasr, S. (1968) *Man and Nature. The Spiritual Crisis of Modern Man*, London: George Allen and Unwin.

—— (1976) *Islamic Science: An Illustrated Study*, London: World of Islam Festival.

Norberg-Hodge, H. (1991) *Ancient Futures: Learning from Ladakh*, San Francisco: Sierra Club Books.

Pacey, A. (1983) *The Culture of Technology*, Oxford: Basil Blackwell.

—— (1990) *Technology in World Civilization*, Oxford: Basil Blackwell.

Popper, K. (1963) *Conjectures and Refutations: The Growth of Scientific Knowledge*, London: Routledge and Kegan Paul.

Posey, D. (1989) "Alternatives to Forest Destruction: Lessons from the Mebengokre Indians," *The Ecologist* 19 (6).

Pursell, C. (1993) "The Rise and Fall of the Appropriate Technology Movement in the United States, 1965–1985," *Technology and Culture* 34.

Salam, A. (1989) *Ideals and Realities. Selected Essays*, Singapore: World Scientific.

Salomon, J., Sagasti, F., and Sachs-Jeantet, C. (eds) (1994) *The Uncertain Quest: Science, Technology and Development*, Tokyo: United Nations University Press.

Sardar, Z. (1977) *Science, Technology and Development in the Muslim World*, London: Croom Helm.

—— (1989) *Explorations in Islamic Science*, London: Mansell.

Scheler, M. (1980 [1923]) *Problems of a Sociology of Knowledge*, London: Routledge and Kegan Paul.

Schumacher, E. (1973) *Small is Beautiful. Economics as if People Mattered*, New York: Harper and Row.

Science for the People (1974) *China: Science Walks on Two Legs*, New York: Avon Books.

Shiva, V. (1988) *Staying Alive. Women, Ecology and Development*, London: Zed Books.

Sigurdson, J. (1980) *Technology and Science in the People's Republic of China*, London: Pergamon.

Stenberg, L. (1996) *The Islamization of Science: Four Muslim Positions Developing an Islamic Modernity*, Lund: Lund Studies in History of Religions.

Tambiah, S. (1990) *Magic, Science, Religion, and the Scope of Rationality*, Cambridge: Cambridge University Press.

Traweek, S. (1988) *Beamtimes and Lifetimes. The Worlds of High Energy Physics*, Cambridge MA: Harvard University Press.

Uberoi, J. (1978) *Science and Culture*, Delhi: Oxford University Press.

—— (1984) *The Other Mind of Europe: Goethe as a Scientist*, Delhi: Oxford University Press.

6 The concept of materialist state theory and regulation theory

Joachim Hirsch

The world is changing rapidly. During the 1970s, world capitalism went into a cyclical crisis, which is still unsolved. As a part of this crisis, the Soviet system broke down and the hegemonic position of the United States was seriously questioned by new competitors such as Japan or Western Europe. Some of the so-called newly industrializing countries seemed to be closing in on the First World countries, while others, like the Latin American ones, were severely hit by the debt crisis of the 1980s and its results. Parts of the former capitalist periphery now find themselves uncoupled from any industrial development. Important regions of the world-system are threatened by marginalization and misery. National states are splitting off and breaking down, resulting in a growing number of wars and civil wars. Whole nations and regions are fighting against peripheralization and trying to fit themselves into new dependency relations to the capitalist core regions. This is a main reason for the recent outburst of nationalism, racism, and fundamentalism. Military conflicts, such as in the Balkans and in Eastern Europe, can only be understood within this context.

The "new world order," which former US President Bush announced at the beginning of the second Gulf War, in fact looks much more like a growing global disorder. As a result existing theories of the world-system seem to be considerably disoriented.

One result of the ongoing crisis and the processes of restructuring is the fact that it becomes more difficult than ever to speak of a "First" or a "Third World" as separate parts of the global system. That does not mean at all that "Third World-like" conditions of production and living are disappearing, as some authors like to argue. But the relation between capitalist core and periphery becomes more complex and fluctuating. Inside the core there are developing "Third World" areas, like in New York, Los Angeles, or London, and at the same time some parts of the former capitalist periphery seem to become, at least, capitalist sub-regions.

The crisis of the old world order also provoked a disorder within the traditional frameworks of economic, social, and political theory. The theory of international relations has, for example, some problems in dealing with the new situation "after hegemony" which followed the economic decline, particularly the breakdown of the former superpowers. Keynesianism lost its dominant position in the field of economic theory and was replaced by neoclassical and monetarist theories. These have, in turn, remarkable problems in trying to explain what is going on. It is obvious at least that the market does not solve all problems of society. Classical theories of imperialism, development, or underdevelopment no longer seem to be valid and are in many aspects empirically refuted. That holds for both of the dominating concepts in this area, which can be generalized as the "modernization" and "dependency" approaches. Therefore we have to ask whether there are any new theoretical frameworks which are able to meet the shortcomings of all these traditional approaches.

The question here is whether regulation theory can contribute to a solution. This theory was developed as a reaction to the world economic crisis of the 1970s and was intended to meet the shortcomings of existing economic theories. And, interestingly enough, regulation theory can be understood as an attempt to renew the Marxist tradition's theory of capitalism. Whether these ambitions really meet expectations needs to be discussed.

In this chapter I will not refer systematically to the reasons, dynamics, and outcomes of the actual globalization process. It should, however, be underlined that globalization as deregulation of international money and capital flows can be interpreted as a means fundamentally to reorganize world capitalism after the crisis of the 1970s. Thus it implies a wide-ranging restructuring of both social relations and political systems. From this perspective it has to be explained as a strategy of class struggle. Its central aim is to break up the political structures and class relations characteristic of "Fordist" post-war capitalism.

It should be kept in mind, therefore, that this process is not the result of any economic logic or historical trajectory. It is a decisive political strategy, put through by the internationalized sectors of capital, cooperating with neoliberal governments. Its aim is a worldwide and systemic rationalization process based on internationalization, deregulation, and flexibilization, which is expected to reestablish the profitability of capital. This obviously has important effects for all national societies, states, as well as the world-system (for more details see Hirsch 1995a).

The theoretical framework of regulation theory

Understanding the conceptualization of regulation theory is a rather complex matter. In fact it is not a comprehensive and completed construct, but rather a many-sided and in some respects even loose frame. In itself, it incorporates very different theoretical approaches, for example the so-called "value theoretic" and the "price-theoretic," the more economic and the policy- and state-theory-oriented ones, and so on (cf. Jessop 1990, 1997). It is, of course, beyond the scope of this chapter to map out these differences, and it is likewise impossible to have a critical discussion of the theoretical problematics of the whole concept (see Esser et al. 1994). What can be done here is to sketch out some of its basic features.

It is important to realize that regulation theory, which was mainly launched by a group of French researchers during the 1970s and 1980s, is itself a reflection both of the crisis of world capitalism which developed in these years and the connected reorganization of international structures of dominance and dependency. The pioneering book on US capitalism by Michel Aglietta (Aglietta 1976) aimed to explain the hegemonic power of the United States in the post-war era. His thesis was that this dominant position was mainly due to the development of a superior mode of political, social, and economic regulation within the US, i.e. the so-called "Fordist" approach. Because in the first half of this century the US was able to develop a very special and new type of capitalist society there was a long-lasting growth period and a decisive superiority in work productivity and technological dominance. It was, therefore, the organization of the whole society in economic, social, and political terms which made the US overwhelmingly competitive. Other nations were forced to adapt to these structures. This resulted in the establishment of what is called the "American century" or "global Fordism." International economic and political dominance was seen not so much as a result of the pure size of the economy, the availability of masses of capital, of educated manpower, of natural resources, or pure military power but as mainly determined by internal socio-economic structures and processes. Regulation theory shifted the focus from international relations between states and economies, taken as given entities and closed units, to the level of internal societal, economic, and political structures.

Regulation theory points out that capitalism is not a homogeneous and stable structure, and that its historical development is neither determined by objective laws nor by the unfolding of a simple "core structure." In historical and spatial relations, capitalism indeed shows very different and various social prototypes. If, however, capitalism is spatially and historically different, if its specific national formations are both diverse and changing, what are the theoretical tools enabling us to understand it? The fundamental object of regulation theory was to develop a framework for the analysis of specific historical formations of capitalism, their development, their crises, and transformations.

Seen against this background, the most fundamental question raised by regulation theory was: how can capitalism, as a highly fragmented society characterized by competing and struggling individuals, enterprises, and opposite classes, be stable at all and how does it reproduce itself? That was the question posed by classical political economy and by Marx. The basic thesis is that this cannot be explained by pure economic mechanisms, as Marx as well as liberal economic theory seem to have done. What needs to be explained above all is why and how individuals, or economic actors, adjust to contradictory, repressive and exploitative social relations, and why they behave in a manner that makes the accumulation of capital possible. In addition, it has to be made clear why class conflict under capitalism does not destroy the whole system at any moment. This is what makes it necessary to analyze norms of social behavior, social institutions, and social value setting.

Regulation theory underscores the discontinuities in the history of capitalism which make it necessary to investigate, both temporally and spatially, historical capitalist formations, their interrelations, and their processes of crisis and development. It proceeds from the assumption that each of these formations is characterized by a complex interrelationship between a "regime of accumulation" on the one hand and a "mode of regulation" on the other—each containing their historically diverse forms of capital-valorization, class relations, political-social processes, and crises.

Lipietz defines an "accumulation regime" as a "mode of systematic distribution and reallocation of the social product, which over longer periods of time generates determinated relations of correspondence between changes in the conditions of production (the volume of deployed capital, distribution between branches and levels of production) on the one hand, and changes in the conditions of final consumption (consumption norms of wage dependants and other classes, collective social expenditures, etc.) on the other hand." By "mode of regulation" he means "the entirety of institutional forms, networks, and explicit or implicit norms which secure the compatibility of modes of behavior within the framework of an accumulation regime, one corresponding to the state of social relations as well as to their properties of struggle and conflict" (Lipietz 1985: 120ff.). The state is the center of regulation insofar as one finds in its institutional setting the concentration of social relations of power and class in which social compromises are codified and forcefully stabilized. It is, therefore, not an autonomous actor but a field in which class relations materialize institutionally (Poulantzas 1978). The state's concrete structure and manner of functioning is a constituent of the historically corresponding mode of accumulation and regulation, and it changes with these.

Every capitalist society requires an institutional-normative social network, one capable of coordinating the conditions of capital accumulation with the diverging strategies and actions of individuals, groups, and classes in competition and struggle with one another. The development of an institutional mode of regulation cannot, however, be functionally "derived" from the economic conditions of the process of capital valorization. Rather, it results from social movements, struggles, conflicts, and the consequently emerging social forms, structures of compromise, institutions, and normative attitudes. The stability of a historic formation of capitalism presupposes the generation of a corresponding and reciprocally stabilizing mode of accumulation and regulation. These modes, however, do not exist in functional correspondence to one another. Rather, they constitute a relationship of articulation—their emergence follows its own conditions and regularities. Thus, the generation of a relatively stable capitalist formation has the character of an "object found" (*objet trouvé*, as Lipietz says). In correspondence with power relations and class compromises, capitalist societies manifest markedly different temporal-spatial differences in their modes of accumulation and regulation.

Regulation theory investigates the conditions of relative stability found in a given context of societalization, one structurally characterized by crisis and uncertainty. Accumulation regimes and modes of regulation contain specific dynamics of their own which are not reducible to functional relations. This means that capitalist societies are stable only conditionally and within a limited period. "Cyclical" crises of capitalist formations are to be conceived as the disarticulation of modes of accumulation and regulation, and it is mainly this process which sets limits to the valorization of capital within the economic, technical, and political-social conditions given under that formation. The solution to such major crisis lies in the thoroughgoing reorganization—driven by political and social struggles—of the mode of accumulation and regulation. This means that neither the continued stability nor the final collapse of capitalism is structurally predetermined. Given the differing conditions of accumulation and regulation, each historical formation has its own particular form of crisis.

National and international regulation

Despite the fact that the focus of regulation theory originally was directed at the analysis of international dependency relations (cf. Aglietta 1976; Lipietz 1987), a thorough and developed approach to the analysis of the international system has not yet been written. But it seems to be possible to sketch out such a concept using elements developed in the context of analyzing both special national forms and the global crisis of Fordism (Robles 1994). From the perspective of regulation theory, the global capitalist system is conceived as a complex compound of national relations of reproduction with their own modes of accumulation and regulation. Such national formations constitute an essential starting point for the analysis of the world-system; this, however, does not mean that global capitalism is simply the sum of national formations. The emphasis lies on national formations because of the fact that only on that level the social relations between individuals and classes in their institutional textures combine with one another in such a manner that a balance of social compromise and structures of political decision-making become possible, without which a continuing reproduction of capital and class relations cannot be guaranteed. In this sense, regulation theory can be markedly contrasted, for example, to world-system theory (Wallerstein 1979).

A decisive dynamic of international relations and their transformation proceeds from the processes of development and crises found in national formations (Mistral 1986: 170ff.). At the same time, however, the stability of national formations depends upon the degree of success with which particular modes of accumulation and regulation become tied to the structure of the world market and the international division of labor so that capital accumulation and economic growth become possible. At the international level, a doubled set of connections arises: a national "growth model" presupposes its integration in an international division of labor, while at the same time the latter is determined by the development of national relations of reproduction. The character and manner of this integration—that is, the connection of "national" with "international" accumulation and regulation—depends upon social processes and conflicts unfolding at the national level, ones which are certainly not independent of international political and economic constellations. Global capitalism is thus to be grasped as a compound of processes at diverse levels and with diverse actors—nation-states, firms, national and international organizations and institutions (Lipietz 1987: 25). The capitalist world-system is a complex knot of national modes of accumulation and regulation, one containing a distinctive space for national developments (Mistral 1986: 172ff.): "A field of possible positions, in other words a range of mutually compatible national regimes, does exist, but positions within it are not allocated in advance. The ruling classes of various countries can refer to a number of 'models'." Likewise, "social alliances within the dominated countries develop strategies which may, depending on the state of the international class struggle, lead either to dependency or autonomy" (Lipietz 1987: 24). In contrast to classical theories of imperialism, world-system or dependency, regulation theory approaches the global capitalist system not as a spatially and temporary homogeneous hierarchical model or a simple core–periphery relation, but rather as a variable network. International movements of capital are constantly modified via national formations, i.e. through their specific accumulation regimes and modes of regulation, as well as the balance of social forces and politics expressed by them. This makes possible not only the decline of dominant regions, but also the "catching-up" development of peripheral areas, as for example in the "newly industrializing countries."

At the same time, the differences between national capitalist formations are a fundamental prerequisite of global accumulation and are permanently reproduced within this process. The development of global capitalism must therefore be highly uneven, and the international capitalist system necessarily manifests strong relations of inequality, dominance, and dependency. In historical development, some countries became dominant insofar as they succeeded at developing a coherent mode of accumulation and regulation, and geared it to the international system, securing a strong and steady economic growth. This placed them in a situation where they were able to establish norms of production, technology, division of labor, and consumption in a trans-regional form, allowing them to make the economic potential of other countries become the condition of their own expansion (see Aglietta 1976). Hence, not merely military strength, size, or wealth in resources is crucial for international dominance. It is, however, mainly the internal social and political relations and the constellation of class forces which are decisive. From this perspective, the political system and the organization of the state, the manner in which class relations become institutionalized, and the forms of social relations and compromise formation are meaningful. The international dominance of one national "model of growth" produces not only economic, but also political and cultural dependencies, and this puts a substantive pressure of competition and conformity on other countries. Thus economic dependency can be described as a structural incoherence both between the internal mode of accumulation and regulation as well as in dependent countries' connection with the conditions of the world market and the patterns of capital reproduction and division of labor. The forms which such dependencies and relations of competition assume are dependent upon the globally dominant mode of accumulation and regulation, and they become transformed along with it—as, for example, in the transition from classical colonialism to "neo-colonialism" as part of the establishment of US-dominated Fordism following World War II.

Nation state, state system, and international regulation

As divergent socio-economic areas and the existence of competing nation-states mark the capitalist world-system, it lacks the relative coherence which usually characterizes national reproduction structures. Lipietz has pointed out that the structure of the world market "is simply the effect of the interactions between several relatively autonomous processes, of the provisional stabilized complementarity and antagonism that exists between various national regimes of accumulation" (Lipietz 1987: 25). This remark, however, has to be made more specific: it is not so much the national form of accumulation and regulation which constitutes that antagonism. Rather, from the outset, this antagonism is based on the global process of accumulation and class struggle which is expressed by national formations in a contradictory and conflicting manner. This is why the global accumulation process requires its own interstate and supra-state institutions and mechanisms as a prerequisite for relatively stable commodity, money, and capital transactions (Mistral 1986: 181ff.). On a global level, the accumulation of capital must also be politically regulated to a certain degree. In practice, this occurs through interaction between national governments and central banks, international institutions, national and multinational corporations, unions, and other groupings. But as the regulation of class relations remains bound to the nation-state and the contradictions of accumulation processes continuously lead to inter-state conflicts, these international regulatory systems can develop only limited coherence and density. They are much more fragmented and incomplete in comparison to those existing on the nation-state level (Robles 1994). The durability of national accumulation and regulation structures is thus linked to the existence of an international regulatory system, which, at the same time, is undermined by those national structures.

In the past the contradictory relationship between national and international regulation had the effect that a long-term stabilization of international regulative "regimes" was only possible if these were guaranteed by a hegemonic power. This was the case for the UK up to the turn of the twentieth century or for the US during the Fordist era. Hegemony is rooted in the enforcement of a determinate socio-economic structural and growth model by the economically and politically dominating states. They not only shape the international regulatory structures but they also support these with their own resources. This implies a readiness—if necessary—to forgo short-term advantages in favor of the long-term stability of the international system. However, the deployment of simple economic and military power is an insufficient guarantor for the durability of international accumulation and regulation modes. These remain fundamentally interlinked with an institutionalized structure of compromise that also concedes opportunities for growth and development to dependent and underdeveloped countries (Mistral 1986: 180; see also Cox 1987; Gill 1993).

The decline of US hegemony since the 1970s is a result of the structural dynamics of the Fordist system of international regulation supported and controlled by the US. Under the conditions of a liberalized world market guaranteed by the US, this decline was, not least, a consequence of western Europe's and Japan's swift advance by way of their very specific own Fordist models of regulation and growth, which called US dominance into question. That the end of US hegemony coincides with the dissolution of the Soviet Union is only seemingly a paradox. The Soviet Union proved incapable of keeping pace in the helter-skelter technological race by which the capitalist centers reacted to the crisis during the 1970s. The Soviet Union's disappearance further intensifies the competition between the now dominating poles of the capitalist "triad" (Ohmae 1985). The crisis of the Fordist–Keynesian model of regulation both in the capitalist economies and on the international level has led to a situation in which national competitive strategies have asserted themselves in the world market with increasing disregard for its stability. This has pushed large segments of the capitalist periphery toward economic and social catastrophe.

The prospects for the reestablishment of a stable international regulatory system on the basis of the presently developing "triad" are very uncertain. The regulation of international monetary transactions is especially problematic, as both a "world state" and a globally ruling guarantor power are lacking. A precondition for the establishment of such a system would be the successful reorganization of the system of international regulatory agencies. However, this would entail a long-term willingness on the part of the dominant economies to work together in a kind of "cooperative hegemony." Yet, in practice, this path stands in stark contrast to the trend toward the regional disintegration of global capitalism (cf. Altvater 1991; Amin 1992; Garten 1993). Not least, the precarious stability of the present international system stems from the imbalance between the absolute military predominance of the US and its relatively reduced economic position. With regard to the capitalist economies, this implies a certain reciprocal pressure to cooperate, to prevent the outbreak of open military conflicts, to force adherence to minimal forms of international regulation, and, especially, to make possible ad hoc action aimed at securing common interests with regard, for example, to the accessibility of natural resources or the pacification of threatening conflicts in the periphery. The second Gulf War characterizes this new international structure in the same way as did the "peace-making" military interventions under the formal umbrella of the UN that followed it.

Because of the fact that the nation-state form politically mediates the global accumulation process, "international regulation" is structurally fragmented and weak, and this is one main reason for recurrent global crises. The question is whether the ongoing process of globalization will change this structure. In discussion of the so-called "hollowing out" of the nation-state it is argued that globalization will weaken the nation-state system to the extent that this political level becomes more and more meaningless, thereby making space for a more integrated and homogeneous international regulation system which is able to manage global capitalism, or even contribute to the emergence of a "world state." Against this viewpoint it should be kept in mind that the political form of the nation-state and the existence of a plurality of states is a structural component of capitalist society which cannot be abolished without overcoming capitalist class relations. The contradiction between global accumulation and national political forms is, therefore, fundamental and will remain so as long as capitalism exists.

Even if the relationship between the establishment of the centralized and bureaucratized nation-state and the development of global capitalism is not simply causal, these two phenomena are closely interrelated. The creation of centrally controlled and delineated state territories provided some of the most basic conditions for the establishment of distinct and strong capitalist economies. Of course, from the outset, these "national" economies could develop only in the context of the emerging world market. External trade and early colonialism formed an important basis for capital accumulation and industrialization (Gerstenberger 1973; Braunmühl 1978; Wallerstein 1984). Finally, a highly complex relationship between the development of the capitalist nation-state and "bourgeois" (i.e. parliamentary-pluralist) political democracy also exists; this relationship derives from the fact that democratic and social class struggles can develop successfully only within this relatively distinct economic and institutional terrain (see especially Held 1991; Rueschemeyer et al. 1992). To be sure, this relationship has been characterized by numerous contradictions, as evidenced by the always critical relationship between democratic principles and capitalist relations of production. Nevertheless, fundamental normative orientations—equality, social relations governed by the rule of law, general freedoms, and respect for universal human rights—even if they are often not put into practice, remain bound to the nation-state. Ironically, the nation-state at the same time functions as a substantial protective barrier, as these orientations largely do not exist outside of nation-state borders. General human rights can survive only if codified as civil rights within a nation-state. In the Third World the relationship between nation-states has remained one of (colonial) dependency, violence, and war. Oppression and the rule of the strongest have been only marginally counterbalanced by institutional and legal systems. The relative importance of values based on democracy and civil society have remained confined to a small number of economically and politically powerful states.

A discussion of these complex relationships between nation-state, capitalism, and democracy requires several fundamental state-theoretical explanations. My thesis is that the pluralist system of nation-states, characterized by the principle of territoriality and relatively delimited external borders, as well as the specific "relative autonomy" of a centralized power-apparatus vis-à-vis all societal groups and classes—in sum, a structural divide between "politics" and "economics"—is the specific form of the political realm under capitalist relations of production. Lacking space for more detailed explanations, I will merely point out the main features of the argument, namely, that we can distinguish between a historical-genetic and a structural aspect of this highly contradictory relationship (for a detailed discussion see Hirsch 1974; Poulantzas 1978; Holloway/Picciotto 1978; Jessop 1982; Hirsch 1995a, 1995b).

First, I will argue that the emergence of a state apparatus formally separated from all social classes—including the capitalist class—and the resulting institutionalized division between "politics" and "economics" is a structural requirement for the stable reproduction of capitalist societies. The decisive reason for this division derives from the prerequisite of an economic reproduction based on private labor, exchange, and the law of value, which requires an institutionalization of physical coercive power that is separated from the immediate agents of production—capitalists and wage laborers (Hirsch 1995a, 1995b). At the same time, this "relative autonomy" of the state and the establishment of its "monopoly on legitimate physical force" (Max Weber) is a decisive precondition for the "regulatability" of class relationships, i.e. the legitimization of power and the enforceability of social compromises. However, these structural conditions of stability and reproduction of capitalist societies are not at all functionally guaranteed. They only emerge—if at all—within and through complex social struggles which are determined by the strategies of conflicting actors. Thus the development of each capitalist society and its characteristic social forms is tied to specific historical conditions, class struggles, political forces, and international relations.

Significant for our question is that the political and ideological regulation of capitalist relations of production only becomes possible through an outward delimitation and concurrent establishment of class overarching "national" interests. The fragmentation of "world society" into nation-states allows and substantiates coalitions that cross class lines, whereby these coalitions become the basis of every stable socio-political "balance of compromise" under capitalist conditions. Nation-states are not merely "instruments" for securing competitive advantages by sections of the global bourgeoisie (Wallerstein 1984: 17), but are also expressions of competition-related and class-overarching social compromises. In sum, we can say that the political organization of the nation-state is both based on and strengthens global capitalist class linkages and divides.

Thus, externally, the plurality of economically competitive nation-states explains both the partial solidarity within a bourgeoisie in its struggle against other "national" bourgeoisies and a generalized interest in prosperity and growth which can become the basis for class-overarching social compromises. Internally, the institutional apparatus of bourgeois democracy—with its regulated modes pertaining to decision-making, transition of power, and compromise-procedures—acts as an important element by which the autonomy of the state apparatus and, concurrently, a relatively flexible stabilization of economic and social reproduction are secured. At the same time, relatively continuous capitalist growth acts as an important material precondition for the stabilization of democratic conditions and the necessary social compromises these conditions require. Global capitalism's political division into a plurality of nation-states thus appears as an important prerequisite for the stabilization of its specific political form—a form characterized by the separation of politics and economics as well as the particularization of the state—and also provides the historical basis for the emergence of bourgeois-democratic structures.

The development of a plurality of individual states is therefore an expression of competition and class conflict and thus a basic structural feature of capitalism (Dabat 1991: 12). It allows the establishment of sub-markets to which labor and capital have different degrees of access, and provides an unlimitedly mobile capital basis for operating within the socio-political regulatory modes of nation-states while playing off one state—seen as class fractions—against the other. In other words, global capital benefits structurally from the "competition of national locations." On the other hand, this competition serves to underpin the social structures of coalition and compromise characterizing national regulation modes. All in all, there is sufficient evidence to advance the assumption that the global process of accumulation is dependent upon the parallel existence of divergent "national" modes of accumulation and regulation. Measured on a world-wide basis, the accumulation process is neither subordinate nor superordinate to the nation-state. Rather, "global" and "national" accumulations together form a complex and contradictory unity.

Despite certain similarities on the surface, this state-theoretical conceptualization stands in contrast to the neo-institutional state theory and the "theory of international regimes" (see, for example, Keohane 1982; Krasner 1982; Rittberger 1993). On the basis of their relatively simple action-theoretical assumptions, these theories can neither explain the constitutionalizing conditions for institutionalization processes in society nor their structural antagonisms and dynamics. The nation-state is simply defined as "given," its character as a specific historical form of power and rule is nebulous, and the complex relationship between global and inner-state political-economic processes remains underexposed. This neglects the fact that political processes of institutionalization in capitalism are the form in which social antagonisms become "regulatable" but not permanently solvable, which explains the fundamental inclination of institutional systems on the national and international level to fall into crisis (Hirsch 1993, 1995a). The international regime theory is more far-reaching in that it stresses the need for relatively autonomous regulatory mechanisms beyond national power politics; but it hardly goes further than descriptive case studies. Its theoretical deficits with regard to both economics and the state are obvious (for a critique of regime theory see Strange 1982; Wend and Duvall 1989; Robles 1994).

Why national states?

The question remains, why does this political form of competitive power apparatus characterized by specific internal structural features take on a "nation"-state gestalt? This cannot be fully explained with reference to the peculiarities of the economic reproduction process alone. Rather, the answer is closely connected to the question of how the formation of "society" is at all possible given the social structure of capitalism. Capitalist relations of production do not only produce the space and time matrix specific to bourgeois society (Poulantzas 1978: 85ff.);

they also lead to a thorough and historically new individualization of social subjects as competitive market participants. The power of the market enforces a basically unlimited mobility and exchangeability of societal producers and tends to dissolve existing social relationships, ties, and milieus. As commodity owners, bourgeois individuals are at the same time isolated atoms and "world citizens." The capitalist economy permanently undermines the social relationships, cultural institutions, and common cultural heritage that make possible the specific formation and conscious self-reflection of society. This is why the modern nation and nation-state is the terrain upon which social relations under capitalist market conditions must be reproduced anew through the development of overarching cultural commonalties and traditions, as well as in contra-distinction to the "foreign." "Nationality" becomes the ideological expression for the way in which capitalist society constitutionalizes and views itself as society, and in which it gains contours and borders in the eyes of its members. Respect for societal rules and institutions is based less and less on particular traditions of local commonality and on a matrix of personal relationships, but—following the logic embedded in the capitalist matrix of space and time—adheres to the principle of a homogeneous-linear national tradition and a tightly delimited territorial affiliation. As this develops in delimitation of the foreign—inside and outside of state borders—and as it is based upon a coercive socio-cultural homogenization, there is a close relationship between the modern nation-state and totalitarianism as well as racism (Poulantzas 1978: 85ff.; Balibar 1993).

It would be wrong and empirically easily refutable to consider the nation-state as a product and an expression of a preconceived nationhood. If "nations" struggle for their own state, this historically always occurs in the context of a developed system of capitalist states that is determined by coercively formed homogenization, suppression, and competition. Modern nations are substantially the product of centralized state apparatuses and their strategies of homogenization and marginalization. These "invent" and construct unitary national cultures by marginalizing, eliminating, and suppressing deviance. The modern state becomes a nation by a process in which existing socio-cultural spaces and historical traditions are selectively and differentially put together to form a new construct, a process that takes place, for example, with respect to the development of a common national language. The contradictory nature of this process lies in the fact that the state—as a bureaucratic coercive apparatus—cannot install new socio-cultural relationships but can only utilize, reconstruct, and rearrange them; this leaves the state fundamentally bound to the obduracy of these relationships. Completely homogenized nation-states have thus never existed.

In light of the ongoing globalization offensive, the nation-state is by no means disappearing. It is, however, undergoing considerable changes with regard to its traditional roles, meaning, and significance. The structural transformations of global capitalism have drastically reduced the margins for economic and social state intervention, which is true even in the context of large and powerful nation-states. The liberalization of money, capital, commodity, and service-sector transactions subjects national policies with an ever-increasing rapidness to the dynamic of the world market and international corporate strategies. Intensified international competition and the growing flexibility of global capital has raised "locational politics" or "national forms of competitive advantage" (i.e. the provision of optimal conditions for the valorization of capital within a nation-state framework) to a central political priority for all national states (Porter 1990; Reich 1991). This shift in political priorities may be seen as a decisive cause for the failure of regulatory models primarily based on the Keynesian welfare state, which developed in the capitalist centers during the Fordist era after World War II. In effect, the Fordist "security-state" (Hirsch 1986), which was oriented toward a coherent economic and social development within national boundaries, seems to be superseded by a substantially new type of capitalist state, the "national competitive state" (Hirsch 1995a). This type of state concentrates on the mobilization of all productive forces for the purposes of international competition, which sets aside the former politics of materially based social and political integration. The triumph of neoliberal doctrines has provided the ideological basis for this transformation of capitalism.

Crises of international regulation

Ultimately, a regulation and state theory conception of the capitalist world-system has decisive consequences in terms of crisis theory. "Cyclical" crises of capitalism are characterized by reciprocally conditioned and reinforcing disturbances of national and international relations of accumulation and regulation to which the established and specifically formed socio-economic processes are indebted. The crisis of a national formation can be understood as the dynamic of valorization-driven processes of accumulation within the framework of an accumulation regime colliding with the conditions of the system of regulation, collisions which finally impede the possibilities of capital valorization. The more a historical mode of accumulation and regulation becomes universalized and the hegemony of a dominant country, the more encroaching and enveloping become its specific crisis tendencies. At the same time, the international regulation system manifests its own moments of instability: the position of the hegemonic power can be increasingly subverted by stronger competitors. These are usually unsuccessful not only because they simply copy the dominant model, but also because their internal political-social structures do not allow them to develop effective alternatives. The erosion of hegemonic positions is nevertheless caused by internal as well as external factors. The resulting destabilization of international regulation in turn affects the national economies. The crisis of a global historic formation of capital—such as that of Fordism during the 1970s and 1980s—can be interpreted as a reciprocally conditioned and reinforcing interplay of internal and external disturbances of the mode of accumulation and regulation. The consequences are not only a global impediment of capital accumulation, along with reinforcing international economic disparities and conflicts, but also a crisis of institutions at a national as well as international level. A "solution" to cyclical crises presupposes in this regard not only a reorganization of national modes of accumulation and regulation, but also how these themselves remain tied to the reconstruction of a functioning system of international regulation.

Conclusion

Finally, let me sum up some of the main explanations that regulation theory and materialist state theory can offer regarding the capitalist world-system and its dynamics:

1   It can show that structure and development of the capitalist world-system are determined by the contradiction between the global accumulation process and the nation-state political form which is fundamental for its regulation. The system of international regulation is therefore fragmented and weak. This contradiction becomes more pronounced as the processes of globalization and internationalization becomes more and more intensified. The more the regulation of the global accumulation process becomes problematic and international migration flows and ecological catastrophes are threatening, the less the nation-state form is able to deal with this evolution. At the same time, this political form is embedded within the capitalist mode of production and capitalist class relations and, therefore, cannot be overcome as long as they exist.

2   It can explain the development of international hegemony structures, as it did by analyzing the base of US hegemony and the causes of its decline. This can be seen in the fact that Japan and some European countries were able not only to copy the US model but also to develop their own types of Fordism—in both cases patterns of a highly state-regulated economy very different from each other. This development was able to function within the structure of global Fordism guaranteed by the US. This meant that the reconstruction of the world market based on the Bretton Woods system and the rapid internationalization of capital became possible within the framework of this regime. The regulationist theory of hegemony takes into consideration the emergence of the so-called capitalist "triad" and how it functions, namely as a competitive relationship not so much between equal capitalist economies, but between very different social formations trying to develop their own modes of post-Fordism.

3   It can explain why international hegemonic structures and dependency relations cannot be stable over time, since they are founded in specific accumulation regimes and regulation modes which must change in a crisis-ridden way. Accumulation regimes have their own logic of development and it is very unlikely that their relation to existing modes of regulation can be stable over time. Hegemony can work when one nation is able to develop a superior social model, to make it internationally dominant, and to give dependent nations a chance to develop within this framework. "Hegemony" is therefore much more than economic, political, or military dominance. It must be

understood in a strictly Gramscian sense. Really established hegemony is a relation which provides, to some extent, mutual benefits if the hegemonic nation is prepared to make some material sacrifices as was done by the US in the post-war period. The present situation, on the other hand, is characterized by the fact that the US is no longer able or willing to fulfil this task. This concept of hegemony could, therefore, provide an interesting approach in order to update or supersede traditional theories of imperialism.

4   It can show that the crisis of Fordism was to a decisive extent a crisis of international regulation, and that its breakdown—mainly marked by the end of the Bretton Woods system—intensified processes of crisis at national levels. The breakdown of Fordist international regulation was mainly due to the fact that US hegemony was weakened and that at the same time the internationalization of capital was growing under the auspices of global Fordism. In turn, that means that a solution to the present crisis is only possible if a relatively stable system of international regulation can be reestablished. And that renews the problem of hegemony, which has become more difficult in the present "triadic" structure of world capitalism.

5   It can explain that the end of Fordist hegemony, the pluralization of capitalism, and the breakdown of international regulation lie behind the growing international inequalities and the obvious failure of traditional concepts of development. The reason is that with international competition growing fast, nation-states are severely weakened in terms of independent domestic economic and social policies while no power is able to guarantee a stable international economic order.

6   It can, equally, explain the reasons for the few Third World success stories found mainly in some East Asian countries; this refers to the exceptions to the traditional theories of the world-system. The reason for the success of the so-called East Asian "tigers" is not to be found, as neoliberal doctrines proclaim, in the effectiveness of pure market forces, but much more in specific cultural traditions and social structures—like, for example, a strong state which is equipped with a remarkable grade of relative autonomy against all social classes and which is able effectively to organize the whole of society (such as the enforcement of land reforms with its decisive consequences for class structures, etc.). On the other hand, the failure of import substitution strategies of development, which was characteristic of most Latin American countries, can neither be simply explained by the negative effects of state interventionism and protectionism nor by economic dependency on the outside. Again, more important are internal social structures and power relations, such as the predominance of an agrarian oligarchy, a weak, privatized and corrupt state administration, a highly segmented post-colonial social structure, religious traditions, etc.

To summarize: regulation theory understands the international system not as a stable hierarchy but as a complex and changing network of social formations which are characterized by special modes of accumulation and regulation. Internal social structures and power relations are fundamentally important for each country's position within the world-system and, in turn, strongly influences the development of its own mode of accumulation and regulation. Because of the fact that accumulation/regulation complexity, on both national and international levels, is structurally crisis-ridden, the structure of the capitalist world-system cannot be stable over time. Cyclical crises of capitalism are necessarily crises of hegemony which shift the whole dependency structure.

Bibliography

Aglietta, M. (1976) *Regulation et crises du capitalisme: L'Experience des États-Unis*, Paris: Insee.

Altvater, E. (1991) *Die Zukunft des Marktes*, Münster: Verlag Westfilisches Damphboot.

Amin, S. (1992) *Das Reich des Chaos. Der neue Vormarsch der ersten Welt*, Hamburg: VSA.

Balibar, E. (1993) *Die Grenzen der Demokratie*, Hamburg: Argument Verlag.

Beaud, M. (1987) *Le système national/mondial hierarchisé*, une nouvelle lecture du capitalisme mondial, Paris: La Découverte.

Braunmühl, C. V. (1978) "On the Analysis of the Bourgeois Nation State within the World Market Context," in J. Holloway and S. Picciotto (eds) *State and Capital. A Marxist Debate*, London: Edward Arnold.

Cox, R. W. (1987) *Production, Power, and World Order. Social Forces in History*, New York: Columbia University Press.

Dabat, A. (1991) *Capitalismo mundial y capitalismos nacionales*, Mexico D.F.: CRIM.

Esser, J., Görg, C., and Hirsch, J. (eds) (1994) *Politik, Institutionen und Staat. Zur Kritik der Regulationstheorie*, Hamburg: VSA Verlag.

Garten, J. E. (1992) *Cold Peace. America, Japan, Germany and the Struggle for Supremacy*, New York: Times Books.

Gerstenberger, H. (1973) "Zur Theorie der Historischen Konstitution des Bürgerlichen Staates," *PROKLA* 8/9.

Gill, S. (ed.) (1993) *Gramsci, Historical Materialism and International Relations*, Cambridge: Cambridge University Press.

Held, D. (1991) "Democracy, the Nation State and the Global System," in D. Held (ed.) *Political Theory Today*, Cambridge: Polity Press.

Hirsch, J. (1974) *Staatsapparat und Reproduktion des Kapitals*, Frankfurt/M.: Suhrkamp.

—— (1986) *Der Sicherheitsstaat*, 2nd edition, Frankfurt/M.: Athenaeum, Taschenbücher Syndicat EVA.

—— (1990) *Kapitalismus ohne Alternative?* Hamburg: VSA Verlag.

—— (1993) "Internationale Regulation. Bedingungen von Dominanz, Abhängigkeit und Entwicklung im globalen Kapitalismus," *Das Argument* 198.

—— (1995a) *Der nationale Wettbewerbsstaat-Staat, Demokratie und Politik im globalen Kapitalismus*, Amsterdam and Berlin: Edition ID-Archiv.

—— (1995b) "Nation State, International Regulation and the Question of Democracy," *Review of International Political Economy* 2 (2).

Holloway, J. and Picciotto, S. (eds) (1978) *State and Capital. A Marxist Debate*, London: Edward Arnold.

Jessop, B. (1982) *Regulation Theories in Retrospect and Prospect. The Capitalist State: Marxist Theories and Methods*, Oxford: Robertson.

—— (1990) "Regulation Theories in Retrospect and Prospect," *Economy and Society* 19 (2).

—— (1997) Survey Article: "The Regulation Approach," *Journal of Political Philosophy* 5 (3).

Keohane, R. O. (1982) "The Demand for International Regimes," *International Organization* 36 (2).

Krasner, S. D. (1982) "Regimes and the Limits of Realism: Regimes as Autonomous Variables," *International Organization* 36 (2).

Lipietz, A. (1985) "Akkumulation, Krisen und Auswege aus der Krise. Einige methodologische Anmerkungen zum Begriff der "Regulation'," *PROKLA*, no. 58.

—— (1987) *Mirages and Miracles. The Crises of Global Fordism*, London.

Mistral, J. (1986) "Régime international et trajectoires nationales," in R. Boyer (ed.) *Capitalismes fin de siècle*, Paris: Presses Universitaires de France.

Ohmae, K. (1985) *Die Macht der Triade. Die neue Form des Wettbewerbs*, Wiesbaden: Gabler.

Porter, M. E. (1990) *The Competitive Advantage of Nations*, London and Basingstoke: Macmillan.

Poulantzas, N. (1978) *Staatstheorie. Politischer überbau, Ideologie, sozialistische Demokratie*, Hamburg: VSA Rittberger.

Reich, R. (1991) *The Work of Nations*, New York: A. A. Knopf; Oxford: Clarendon Press.

Rittberger, V. (1993) *Regime Theory and International Relations*, Oxford: Clarendon Press.

Robles, A. C. (1994) *French Theories of Regulation and Conceptions of the International Division of Labour*, Basingstoke: Macmillan.

Rueschemeyer, D., Stephens, E. H., and Stephens, J. D. (1992) *Capitalist Development and Democracy*, Cambridge: Polity Press.

Strange, S. (1982) "Cave! Hic Dragones: A Critique of Regime Analysis," *International Organization* 36 (2).

Wallerstein, I. (1979) *The Capitalist World-Economy*, Cambridge: Cambridge University Press.

—— (1984) *The Politics of World Economy*, Cambridge: Cambridge University Press.

Wend, A. and Duvall, R. (1989) "Institutions and International Order," in E. O. Czempiel and J. N. Rosenau (eds) *Global Changes and Theoretical Challenges*, Lexington MA: Lexington Books.

Part III

East Asia: the last bastion of dirigisme

7 Globalizing India

A critique of an agenda for financiers and speculators

Amiya Kumar Bagchi

Globalization as process and as policy

The term "globalization" has been tortured and made to assume many different meanings since it was first coined. At the risk of adding to this fragmentation, we can distinguish two different generic classes of meanings attributed to it. One is the spread of human civilization, artefacts, institutions, patterns of living, information, and knowledge across the planet (and the stratosphere surrounding it). The other is a policy deliberately aimed at spreading certain institutions, certain modes of doing business, producing and trading commodities, services and information across all the states of the world. An analyst can trace the process of globalization in the various senses of the first generic class without accepting the agenda implicit in the second.

Following the usage of other analysts, we can distinguish the following features within "globalization" in its analytical sense:

1   There is a spread of international trade in goods and "commodities" in the Marxian sense (the latter are distinguished by the fact that they are produced with the help of inputs traded in the market and are destined primarily for sale).
2   People migrate from one country or region to another, temporarily or permanently.
3   Money or means of payment are exchanged on an increasing scale between different countries or regions (when different regions within the same country have different media of exchange, as happened in India under British rule until the eve of World War I).
4   Capital flows from one country to another to help produce goods and services.
5   Finance—not necessarily linked to the production of goods and services— flows between different countries.
6   Transnational companies arise which increasingly engage in the activities listed so far.
7   Technology is traded as commodities between different countries. Increasingly, with the spread of the patent regimes governed by the Paris Con-

vention as modified by the provisions of the World Trade Organization, frontier technologies take an increasingly proprietary form.

8   The spread of print and electronic media.

9   The growth in international trade and production of services of all kinds—shipping, insurance, banking, healthcare and, of course, finance.

As is clear from this list, the categories sometimes overlap, but if we do not list them separately we are likely to miss out on the multifaceted nature of globalization as a process.

As with other aspects of capitalist development, globalization displays many features of combined and unequal development. The growth of international trade may be said to be the earliest feature of the process of commercial internalization. It has, however, often been associated with an exchange of money at a fast pace, and also with migration of people. For example, in the three centuries after the discovery by Europeans of navigable routes from Europe to the western hemisphere and around Africa to Asia, commodities traveled mainly from Asia to Europe, silver from the Americas to Europe and thence to Asia, and enslaved Africans were subjected to forced migration from Africa to the Americas. Within Europe itself, the Netherlands became the financier of European wars and of the economic progress of competing nations, especially of England (before the Netherlands became industrialized enough to attain the status of a leading commodity-producing nation), and thereby helped hasten its own economic and political decline.

We can produce a chronology of the stages of globalization, from increasing commercialization of a basically self-sufficient economy through its increasing involvement in international trade flows and attendant specialization in particular branches of production, to its involvement in flows of portfolio and direct investment, its integration in international production structures through an increasing tempo of exchange of inputs as between firms (often affiliates of the same firms), the increasing domination of its production, exchange and banking structure by transnational non-financial corporations and transnational banks, and finally to its entanglement in seemingly uncontrollable flows of finance across its borders (Bagchi 1994). But this evolutionary sequence is not linear, and neither is it inevitable nor irreversible. In the case of India and the international economy as a whole the flow of international trade accelerated from the 1870s to 1913 and had decelerated from the middle of the 1920s (Bagchi 1993). In India's case, however, the ratio of foreign trade to national income tended to decline over the period from the 1950s to the early 1970s, but it increased slowly again from the late 1970s.

The ebbs and flows in the components of a national economy's involvement in international trade, production and finance are influenced strongly by broad developments in the world economy as well as by domestic policies. For example, from the beginning of British rule, foreign trade was used as the chief conveyor belt for the remittance of the tribute extracted from the Indian empire to Britain. But its importance as the transmission mechanism for this extraction grew during the spread of the gold standard to the major industrializing economies of the North Atlantic and the acceleration in the rates of growth of their national income and resulting demand for industrial inputs and primary commodities. By contrast, the worldwide depression in trade in agricultural products, which set in from 1926 (i.e. some years before the Great Depression starting in 1929), badly affected Indian exports. Again, the rise in the ratio of Indian foreign trade to national income in the late 1970s was much less induced by policy than by developments in the world economy and especially by the growth in demand for Indian exports in West Asia and some other oil-exporting regions. However, global recession in the early 1980s brought down demand. In 1985–6, India's exports made up 4.7 percent of the country's GDP. The corresponding figure rose to 6.8 percent on the eve of the spate of liberalization measures adopted in June–July 1991. Exports as a share of GDP rose to 10.3 percent in 1996–7, but have stagnated at around that level in the last two years, with a slowdown in the growth of both exports and national income.

What then are the policies which have promoted the globalization of the Indian economy in its various aspects in recent years? Virtually all the elements of the policy of economic liberalization, which started in an attenuated form in 1985 and were adopted as an official policy stance from 1991, have promoted globalization of Indian capitalism in all its aspects. We devote the next section to a rapid sketch of these policy measures.

The so-called economic reforms in India since the 1980s and some of their results

In India, partly as a legacy from the days of World War II and partly as the outcome of moves to ration scarce resources and direct them to planned uses and to curb the power and the socially damaging behavior of foreign capital and monopoly houses, a number of regulations sought to delimit the fields of operation of the private and the public sectors, allocate investment and finance, and control the inflow and outflow of foreign funds.

From the late 1970s, however, some of these regulations were relaxed and the foreign exchange value of the rupee was allowed to drift downward on a crawling-peg basis. In 1981 India obtained an Extended Funding Facility credit of Special Drawing Rights (SDR) 5 billion from the IMF, but did not draw the last installment of the loan and no major changes took place in the array of policies pursued by the government. However, in 1985 a series of moves began which essentially amounted to an expansive, debt-dependent fiscal policy directed at stimulating the growth of the economy (for a description of the policy changes, see Datta 1992; Bagchi 1995: section 5; and Nayyar 1996: chs 2 and 3).

The changes effected in 1985 covered all the major fields of regulation except the capital market. The rigor of the Monopolies and Restrictive Trade Practices Act (1969) was considerably reduced, making it virtually irrelevant as far as the expansion of monopoly houses was concerned. The government encouraged foreign investment into many areas from which such investment had earlier been barred. It considerably liberalized the imports of capital goods and materials, especially of those needed for large projects in electricity generation, and in industries utilizing natural gas and oil. Along with these moves, the burden of taxation on high-income and propertied groups was considerably lessened. The government resorted to higher and higher doses of deficit financing to defray its expenditures and this led to a rapid accumulation of internal, and even more ominously, external, debt.

By the beginning of 1991, India was faced with the prospect of defaulting on its debt obligations and, as a consequence, was unable to secure even short-term loans except on very onerous terms. In June–July 1991, in order to restore confidence among India's debtors and in the rupee, the government entered into an agreement with the IMF for a standby first-tranche credit of SDR 551.93 million (about US\$ 754 million) and drawings under the compensatory and contingency financing facility totaling the equivalent of SDR 1,352 million (about US\$ 1,847 million). Later in the year, the IMF granted another standby credit authorizing drawings up to the equivalent of SDR 1,656 million (about US\$ 2,262 million) (International Monetary Fund, Press Release No. 91/64, October 31, 1991). In accordance with the memorandum of understanding reached with the IMF, the government of India carried out a series of policy reforms. The rupee was devalued by about 24 percent. Initially, a dual exchange rate was introduced, with a lower rate being available to exporters. By the beginning of 1993, the currency was made convertible for current account transactions and the two rates were unified. Quantitative restrictions on imports were moderated or removed altogether, and import tariffs were brought down across the board. Earlier restrictions on foreign investment were done away with and a Foreign Investment Promotion Board was set up in order to attract foreign capital.

Internal deregulation accompanied these changes in the foreign trade and payments regime. Many of the industrial sectors which had earlier been reserved for public enterprises were now thrown open to the private sector as well. The government sold off large proportions of shares in public enterprises to private purchasers, including mutual funds and foreign financial institutions. The system under which firms had to seek permission of the government for establishing new enterprises beyond a certain size, or investment above a certain limit, was abolished, except for a specified group of industries. The provision under the Monopolies and Restrictive Practices Act imposing restrictions on investment and production on firms of groups with assets above Rs. 1 billion was abolished.

A degree of financial liberalization seeking to unify capital and money markets was also effected. Control over new capital issues was abolished; banks were allowed to deal in shares by setting up mutual funds; foreign financial institutions were allowed to enter the stock market and buy up shares of Indian companies, subject to some mild restrictions; banks were permitted to set their own rates for accepting deposits and lending money, but the central bank, of course, still has control over minimum cash reserves or rediscounting facilities and thus can influence the supply of base money and terms of lending; and lending to "priority sectors" at preferential rates has been continued but de-emphasized in actual transactions by banks. The government has also tried, though not very success-fully so far, to bring down subsidies to agriculture, by raising water rates for public irrigation facilities, electricity tariffs, and fertilizer prices. Subsidization of phosphatic fertilizers has been discontinued with a strongly negative effect on their use.

The Indian experience compared with that of other countries of South Asia

We have so far discussed the Indian situation in isolation from the other coun-tries of South Asia. However, because of a long historical legacy, and continual interchange among the peoples of these countries, they share many characteris-tics, including policy-induced but fragmented globalization. Among the South Asian countries the first serious policy package aimed at globalization was intro-duced in 1977 in Sri Lanka under the presidency of Junius Jayawardena. But several halting attempts at liberalization of the trade and investment regime were also made in Pakistan, attempts that were often stymied by unsustainable macroeconomic imbalances. In Bangladesh a more thoroughgoing liberalization program was introduced in the 1980s under the military regime and continued by the democratic regimes that succeeded it.

Given the background, it is useful to examine some country-specific indices of aspects of globalization mentioned earlier. The first set of such indices relates to the shares of exports and imports to GDP (Table 7.1). In many of the countries of South Asia these ratios were increasing before the onset of the formal policy of globalization as Tables 7.1 and 7.2 reveal. Historically, Sri Lanka had a high

Table 7.1 Bangladesh, India, Pakistan, and Sri Lanka: annual average exports and im-ports, 1970–1994 (% of GDP)

Country	Exports					Imports				
	1971–80	*1980–5*	*1985–90*	*1990–4*	*1994*	*1971–80*	*1980–5*	*1985–90*	*1990–4*	*1994*
Bangladesh	5.4	6.8	7.6	8.8	10.3	13.4	18.9	17.4	17.3	18.2
India	5.8	6.3	6.8	8.7	8.6	6.7	9.2	9.5	10.3	9.2
Pakistan	10.6	11.9	13.8	16.3	18.0	19.1	22.9	22.2	23.3	22.0
Sri Lanka	28.4	28.3	25.9	28.9	28.0	34.7	43.2	36.2	37.8	41.7

Sources: Muqtada and Basu (1994: table 3.2); World Bank (1996)

Table 7.2 Nepal: annual average exports and imports, 1977–1995 (% of GDP)

	1979/80–1983/4	*1984/5–1988/9*	*1990/1–1994/5*
Exports	4.7	5.2	9.0
Imports	16.4	18.1	24.8

Source: Guru-Gharana and Shrestha (1996: table 4.1)

Table 7.3 Foreign direct investment (FDI) inflows into South Asia, 1983–1994

	Average annual inflow (US$ million)						
	1983–8	*1989*	*1990*	*1991*	*1992*	*1993*	*1994*
Bangladesh	1	—	3	1	4	14	6
India	92	252	236	155	261	586	947
Nepal	1	—	6	2	—	—	1
Pakistan	106	210	244	257	335	346	313
Sri Lanka	39	20	43	48	123	195	122

Source: UNCTAD (1995: 394–5)

ratio of foreign trade to GDP because of the importance of plantation crops such as tea, coffee, and rubber. The ratio of exports and imports to GDP in South Asian economies remains much lower than in typical East and Southeast Asian economies. Moreover, except for the case of exports from Bangladesh, Pakistan, and Nepal, there is no strong time trend in foreign trade flows in these economies. In most cases, imports of merchandise were higher than exports to start with, and the absolute increases in imports have generally been higher than those in exports so that balance of payments deficits have continued to trouble them, even after the process of liberalization had been underway for some time. The gap between exports and imports has generally been bridged by remittances from migrant workers, and by foreign aid including foreign loans, supplemented in the case of Sri Lanka and India by some inflows of foreign portfolio and direct investment.

Not only is the overall share of trade in GDP lower and increasing more slowly than in the fast-growing economies of East and Southeast Asia but the share of developing Asia (countries east of Iran) as a whole in Asian trade is also generally lower than the share of East and Southeast Asia in that trade. In 1994, whereas the share of total exports of East and Southeast Asia, barring Japan, going to Japan and developing Asia (as defined above) was 54.6 percent, that of total exports of South Asia going to the same group of countries was only 27.7 percent. Correspondingly, while the share of developing Asian countries and Japan in the imports of East and Southeast Asia was 58.4 percent, the share of imports of South Asia coming from the same region was 33.4 percent (ADB 1996: 186–7). Moreover, intra-South Asian trade was also rather meagre in value: the share of exports of countries of South Asia going to one another was only 4.2 percent in 1994. Thus South Asia did not gain much either from the dynamism of East and Southeast Asian economies or from a thriving intra-regional trade.

With regard to another index of the active globalization process—inflows and outflows of FDI—we note that these were also rather feeble in the South Asian region. Table 7.3 reproduces the figures of FDI inflows as indicated in UNCTAD (1995).

Table 7.4 Workers' remittances (WR), South Asia and the Philippines, 1980–1993 (% of GDP and exports)

Country	Year	WR as % of GDP	WR as % of merchandise exports
Philippines	1980	1.9	10.6
	1985	2.6	17.4
	1990	3.3	17.8
	1993	4.7	22.3
Bangladesh	1980	2.2	36.1
	1985	4.0	50.2
	1990	3.7	46.6
	1993	4.2	44.1
India	1980	1.6	32.7
	1985	1.1	25.6
	1990	0.7	12.4
	1993	1.2	13.4
Pakistan	1980	8.9	82.1
	1985	8.7	97.2
	1990	5.5	40.4
	1993	3.3	23.7
Sri Lanka	1980	3.5	13.1
	1985	3.9	17.7
	1990	4.6	19.9
	1993	5.4	19.3

Source: ADB (1996: 207); World Bank (1995) *World Tables 1995* (for estimates of figures for India in 1993)

We have not reproduced the figures of FDI outflows because they are quite insignificant. It is difficult to discern any real time trend of FDI inflows into any economy except perhaps for India and Sri Lanka. But also in their case, they pale into insignificance compared with the inflows into say, Indonesia, Malaysia, Singapore or Thailand.

We now come to another aspect of globalization that we examined earlier, i.e. labor migration out of and into the South Asian countries. Internationally comparable and reliable figures of movements of labor within the subcontinent (for example, from Nepal and Bangladesh into India, or any reverse movement) are not available; nor are the figures of total migration outside the subcontinent for recent years (the latest internationally comparable figures available up to 1985 or 1986, are given in the studies assembled in Amjad, 1989). However, a substitute is available in the form of figures of workers' remittances for Bangladesh, India, Pakistan, and Sri Lanka (World Bank 1995 gives the figure for workers' remittances for Nepal as zero, which cannot be the case; rather it means that these figures are not officially collected). Table 7.4 presents the ratios of workers' remittances to the GDPs and exports of the South Asian countries. The Philippines, the country with perhaps the largest share of migrants in the labor force is

Table 7.5 Unemployment in Pakistan, the Philippines, and Sri Lanka by gender, 1990–1994 (as % of total labor force)

	1990			1991			1992		
	Total	*Men*	*Women*	*Total*	*Men*	*Women*	*Total*	*Men*	*Women*
Pakistan	3.1	3.4	8.9	6.3	4.5	16.8	5.9	4.3	14.7
Philippines	8.1	7.1	9.8	9.0	8.1	10.5	8.6	7.9	9.8
Sri Lanka	14.4	9.1	23.5	14.1	10.0	21.2	14.1	10.6	21.0

	1993			1994		
	Total	*Men*	*Women*	*Total*	*Men*	*Women*
Pakistan	4.7	3.8	10.3	4.7	3.8	10.3
Philippines	8.9	8.2	10.0	8.4	7.9	9.4
Sri Lanka	14.7	9.1	25.2	13.6	9.9	20.8

Source: ILO (1995)

Note: the 1990 figures for Pakistan are not comparable with the figures for other years because of a difference in the method of computation

also included. The figures indicate that, in Bangladesh and Pakistan, workers' remittances play an even bigger role in generating income and acting as supplements to export earnings than in the case of the major labor-exporting Philippines. The gender character of migration from all the countries varies. Among the migrants from Sri Lanka, women make up a considerably larger percentage than is the case for other South Asian countries. There is also a large out-migration of women from the Philippines. In both cases this is partly a reflection of the higher level of education of women than in most of the other labor-exporting lands but partly also the result of high levels of unemployment of women in both countries (see Table 7.5). Pakistan also has a high level of unemployment of women, but there the percentage of women in paid employment is rather low compared with the two other countries.

These figures of high unemployment among women, co-existing with the reported feminization of labor, especially in labor-intensive export-oriented industries such as garments in Fiji, Bangladesh, Sri Lanka, and Nepal, reveal the contradictory impact of globalization on gender equity at low levels of economic development. On the one hand, the rapid penetration of market forces into rural areas and small towns often leads to the displacement of women engaged in subsistence activities in agriculture and in artisanal work such as handloom-weaving or other craftwork. On the other hand, if globalization is spearheaded by the growth of labor-intensive manufactures, then entrepreneurs bent on maximizing profits engage low-skilled, low-wage female labor. This leads not only to the feminization of labor but also, in the presence of grinding poverty, the juvenization of labor. In this situation, where education and cultural practices allow them to join the stream of migrants, migration overseas can provide a means of escape and a path to higher incomes for women.

Toward financial liberalization in India: the illusion of security through securitization

In India, up to 1991, the banking system was closely regulated by the Reserve Bank of India (the central bank) and the Ministry of Finance, and the money and capital markets were segregated. Banks were not allowed to hold shares in private firms as part of their statutory holding of liquid assets against their liabilities. The Reserve Bank of India laid down two aggregate constraints on the operations of commercial banks. The first was the minimum cash reserve ratio to liabilities (CRR), and the second was a legally stipulated minimum ratio of the value of approved securities to the total liabilities of banks—the second liquidity ratio (SLR). There was also a distinction between the so-called term-lending institutions (such as the Industrial Finance Corporation of India (IFCI), the Industrial Development Bank of India (IDBI), and the Industrial Credit and Investment Corporation of India (ICICI)) and the commercial banks, who were supposed to extend mainly short-term credit. The rates of interest paid by banks on various classes of deposit and the rates of interest charged by them on different categories of loans were also specified. There was also a regulation that at least 40 percent of the credit extended by the commercial banks would be given to the so-called priority sectors such as agriculture, small-scale industry, transport operators and so on, at rates of interest which were lower than those charged to other borrowers.

Issues of new capital through the stock market were also regulated by an official Controller of Capital Issues. Banks could act as underwriters of capital issues but could not hold equities as major assets, which would tend to infringe the requirement of keeping a minimum SLR as officially stipulated. Foreign investors were not usually allowed to hold more than a small percentage of equity in an Indian company.

In moves to deregulate the Indian economy, most of the regulations, controls, and devices of segregation between the money and capital markets, and between domestic and foreign investors, were eased if not removed altogether. Banks were allowed to set their deposit rates and their lending rates within certain limits, the requirement of setting aside 40 percent of the credit for priority sectors was eased, and because of the perception that reducing the fiscal deficit of the government would lead to lower borrowing requirements of the public sector, by 1997 the SLR was brought down from 38 to 25 percent (Reserve Bank of India 1997b). The CRR was also brought down to 10 percent in a move to increase the liquidity of the banks in a regime of generally high interest rates. From May 1992, foreign institutional investors were allowed to participate directly in the Indian stock market. Already in 1987, public sector banks (which made up the major part of the banking sector since all major banks had been nationalized) had been allowed to set up mutual funds for subscribing to bonds and equities. Non-banking companies were allowed to mobilize funds through deposits and other schemes, and other non-banking financial companies (NBFCs) were permitted to operate in the capital and money markets. Banks and NBFCs were allowed to raise money through certificates of deposit in India and abroad (by means of the so-called global deposit receipts or GDRs). Under the neoliberal regime, money market mutual funds (not necessarily linked to banks) were allowed to be set up in the private sector as well. In order to allow companies to tap new sources of funds and give potential investors everywhere access to profit-making opportunities, many new stock exchanges were set up, covering all major cities and regions.

The logic of financial liberalization

The rationale behind all these moves was partly oriented towards allocation and partly oriented toward promotion of entrepreneurship and thrift. It was assumed that higher rates of interest on deposits with banks and other financial interme-diaries would encourage people to save more. At the same time freedom to set rates of interest on the parts of banks and NBFCs were meant to encourage competition and better allocation of the savings mobilized as between the capital and money market agents. The unification of capital and money markets also aimed at better allocation of resources and faster growth. Finally, the govern-ment of India had already been offering attractive rates of interest to foreign and non-resident Indian depositors of foreign currency deposits. Their privileges were further strengthened, and in a bid to attract both foreign direct and portfolio investment, they were now allowed to enter many sectors of the economy previ-ously closed to them, and likewise they were allowed to hold progressively larger shares of equity in such firms. The current BJP-led central government has allowed foreigners to hold 100 percent equity stakes in most sectors of industry and services, including infrastructural facilities. A program of progressive priva-tization of major public sector corporations, such as the State Bank of India, Indian Oil Corporation, Oil and Natural Gas Corporation, and Bharat Heavy Electricals, was set in train. From 1992 foreign institutional investors were allowed to buy and sell shares in the market, and their permitted stakes have been hiked progressively over the years. In the United States and Britain, the unification of the money and capital markets had already occurred in the 1980s. Consequently, large transnational clearing banks, merchant banks, and mutual funds had got used to operating in both money and capital markets on their own behalf and that of their clients. It was supposed by policy-makers that these banks and fund managers would find investing in the Indian money and stock markets attractive if they were allowed to have the same freedom of operation in India as they enjoyed abroad. (In fact, the origins of the so-called "bank scam" of 1991–2 can be traced back to 1987 when some of the transnational banks abused the new facility extended to them of the right to manage portfolios of stocks and bonds for their assets, and the Reserve Bank of India authorities turned a blind eye to these abuses in order not to offend the potential foreign investors.)

Reaping the harvest of badly regulated financial liberation in India

When the government of India adopted the step of abolishing official regulation of capital issues by companies, and indicated that further measures liberalizing industrial and financial regulation were in the offing, it started a boom in the stock market, and the share prices of many companies doubled and trebled within a few months. This share market boom collapsed around May 1992. It was revealed soon after that the boom had been fueled by a small group of bull operators who had been financed mainly by a few foreign banks such as the Citibank, ANZ Grindlays Bank, Bank of America and major public sector banks such as the National Housing Bank and the Bank of Baroda, often in violation of the central bank regulations and prudential norms. A sum of at least Rs. 5000 crores (Rs. 50 billion) lent by the banks to brokers in the stock market remains to this day still unaccounted for. It is symptomatic that M. J. Pherwani, the then chairman of the National Housing Bank, who had been a key player in the extension of the jurisdiction of the stock market (having recently chaired two high-powered committees, appointed by the Reserve Bank of India in relation to this affair (Misra 1997: 353)), died under suspicious circumstances as soon as the so-called "bank scam" came into public view. The lesson of this bit of history is that if government regulation breeds corruption, so does the operation of private interests. Only an official watchdog with sufficiently strong panel powers can check the worst abuses committed by unscrupulous dealers and bankers.

After the revelation of the "bank scam," the Government of India decided to endow the Securities and Exchange Board of India, which had been established in 1988, with some real powers of monitoring and regulation of stock markets. The history of the operation of the Indian stock market has nevertheless been dotted with brokers often unable to meet their commitments, allegations and proved instances of insider trading, and deliberate manipulation of stock prices by bears and bulls. Stock prices have gone through several incidents of booms and troughs, the biggest boom occurring between 1993–4 and 1994–5 (Table 7.6). But since then, with some fluctuations from time to time, the share prices have been in a downward movement, and 1998 witnessed new troughs reached by the share market.

The value of primary capital issues in the stock market has also followed a zigzag course, as revealed by Table 7.7. From 1991 to the middle of 1993, India passed through an industrial recession, and then industrial growth picked up from 1993 to 1996, but from 1996 industrial growth rates declined again. Some of the acceleration of industrial growth from 1993 was a reaction to recession and inventory depletion in the earlier two years, but some was caused by the continued tariff protection afforded to major consumer durables and transport industries, such as cars and motor-cycles, trucks, and so on; some growth was

Table 7.6 Index numbers of prices of industrial securities, India, 1990/1–1996/7 (averages of weeks ended Saturday, Bombay Stock Exchange; Bose: 1981/2 = 100)

	Index numbers	Sensitive index (Sensex) of ordinary share prices
1990/1	500.30	
1991/2	776.20	
1992/3	1,142.30	
1993/4	1,051.30	
1994/5	1,537.30	
1995/6	1,189.60	
1996/7	1,146.80	3,469.00
1997/8	1,061.00	3,813.00
June 1997	1,069.10	4,001.00
March 1998	n.a.	3,817.00
13 October 1998	n.a.	2,832.03

Sources: Reserve Bank of India, 1991/2–1996/7, *Reports on Currency and Finance*, Mumbai; Reserve Bank of India, 1998, *Annual Report 1997–8*, Mumbai; *Business Standard*, 14 October 1998, Calcutta

Table 7.7 New capital issues by non-government public limited companies, India, 1991–1998

	No. of issues	Amount (Rs. billion)
1991/2	514	61.93
1992/3	1,040	198.03
1993/4	1,133	193.30
1994/5	1,676	264.17
1995/6	1,677	161.72
1996/7	851	104.57
1997/8	102	31.38

Sources: Reserve Bank of India, 1997, *Reports on Currency and Finance, 1996–7*, vol. II, Statement 127, Mumbai; Reserve Bank of India, 1998, *Annual Report 1997–8*, Appendix Table V.8

also caused by the rapid diffusion of information technology users among the affluent sections of the middle class. A larger inflow of foreign funds and good monsoons sustaining agricultural production both boosted growth during those three years and helped moderate inflation. There was also a higher rate of growth of exports, helped by the devaluation of the Indian rupee and a strong growth in world trade. However, once these factors were exhausted, growth faltered, and from 1997 India entered into a renewed phase of slowdown in industrial growth, which turned into a recession in 1998. These developments have been exacerbated by the Asian economic crisis starting in Thailand in July–August 1997, and spreading to South Korea, Indonesia, and Malaysia. The latest major victim of the global slump and turmoil in foreign exchange markets has been Russia which in effect suspended the servicing of its foreign debt in September 1998.

The international turmoil in stock markets and the irony of external debt burdens

All these developments have had their impact on stock markets across the world and in India. The market for primary security floatation has virtually collapsed in India as Table 7.7 clearly indicates. The prices of stocks all across the world were hammered. According to *The Economist* (September 5, 1998), almost US$ 4 trillion had been wiped off the total value of share prices across the world in the preceding two months—a sum equivalent to the GDP of Japan, the second largest economy of the world. According to estimates published in the *Human Development Report 1998* (UN 1998: table 20), the total value of the external debt of the developing countries in 1995 was US$ 1,583 billion. In the same Report (Table 37), the total external debt of Eastern Europe and the CIS was US$ 263.861 billion in 1995, with the debt of the Russian Federation estimated at US$ 120.461 billion. According to press reports, the latter figure had risen to $150 billion on the eve of the suspension of the debt servicing by Russia in 1998. Assuming a similar rate of growth of foreign debt for other Eastern European countries, the total external debt of all those countries in 1998 would come to about US$ 330 billion; a similar assumption would bring up the debt of the developing countries to US$ 1,980 billion; while the total external debt of all the developing countries and Eastern Europe (including Russia) would be US$ 2,310 billion. Thus the loss in global share value alone would have more than compensated for the total value of the external debt of all the major indebted countries. The outstanding external debt of the Latin American countries and of the Asian economies in trouble from 1997 had been one of the chief contributory factors to the Mexican crisis of 1995 and the crisis of the East and Southeast Asian economies (Bagchi 1998). Yet the watchdogs of the financial world, such as the IMF, the World Bank, and the leaders of the G7 countries did not dare to write off any significant part of the debt of the heavily indebted countries, for in their view this would have undermined the very integrity of private ownership and hence of the global capitalist order.

Managing volatile markets in India

What happened in other major stock markets in the world had its parallel and its impact on the Indian stock market as well. As mentioned earlier, the industrial slowdown started in 1996–7 when the official index of industrial production grew only by 6.4 percent in that year compared with a growth of 12.5 percent in 1995–6; in 1997–8, the index grew only by 5.7 percent (Government of India 1998: table 1.2). This slowdown squeezed the profitability of many industrial companies whose shares were traded on the stock market, and increased the volume of non-performing assets of banks. Moreover, because of the current-account convertibility of the rupee and the increasing penetration of Indian stock markets by foreign financial institutions (FFIs) looking for higher profits, the foreign exchange market, the share market, and the market for government securities became much more closely interlinked than ever before.

In response to external shocks arising from the South-East Asian crisis and in recognition of the interlinkages, a series of monetary policy measures were undertaken impinging on liquidity, foreign exchange and money market rates . . . During the first quarter (April–June 1997), excess supply conditions existed in the forex market, and inter-bank call money rates were low. Liquidity was abundant and the Reserve Bank sold government securities to absorb liquidity through open market operations. Outstanding amounts of repos [i.e. government securities deposited with the Reserve Bank by banks and other approved organizations for short periods on condition that they would buy them back] were also high. The first two months of the second quarter of the year reflected more or less the same trends. However, there was noticeable depreciation of the rupee in September 1997 . . . and also, some sales of foreign currencies by the Reserve Bank. Reflecting the resulting liquidity drain, the average outstanding repos stood low and the reverse repos outstanding increased sharply, the turnover in the call money market too showed a decline. In the third quarter, the months of November and December again witnessed pressures developing in the exchange markets with the FEDAI [Foreign Exchange Dealers' Association of India] indicative rates depreciating sharply against the US dollar. Foreign currency sales were marked in these months, the liquidity effects of which were partially offset by reverse repo operations. The turnover in the call money market during these two months was also lower than that in the month of October 1997. In January 1998 the foreign exchange market again came under severe pressure, necessitating the Reserve Bank to undertake strong monetary policy measures leading to a sharp withdrawal of liquidity and increase in interest rates. As a consequence, call rates increased sharply, and in line with the development, the turnover in the money market recorded a further decline. As offsetting measures, foreign currency purchases were undertaken together with reverse repo operations. The impact of monetary management was such that in February orderly conditions were restored in the foreign market and liquidity showed an improvement . . .

(Reserve Bank of India 1998: 76–7)

I have deliberately included this long quotation from the *Annual Report* (1998) of the Reserve Bank of India, in order to show the yo-yo movements and the necessity for constant intervention in the foreign exchange and money markets, caused by the linking of the domestic money and capital markets with foreign exchange markets and the instability in the currency markets in recent times. The Indian monetary authorities have so far managed to prevent a sudden devaluation of the rupee and extreme turmoil in the value of the rupee in the foreign currency markets. But they have done so by resorting to a rather high-interest regime, and preventing transfers of capital abroad except through certain permitted channels. But the relative stability in the external value of the rupee against the background of the Asian currency crisis has been associated with a huge depreciation in the Indian stock prices and has required deliberate action to prevent the collapse of India's oldest and largest government-controlled mutual fund, the Unit Trust of India.

Is there a distinction between fully integrated money and stock markets and a casino?

Fervent believers in the unification of the capital and money markets and de-regulation of all prices and quantities in the financial markets have been victims of fallacious reasoning with grave implications for the financial stability of the whole world, including, of course, India. The reasoning contains a number of fallacies which, together, would explain all the troubles the world economy has undergone under the unregulated capitalist dispensation since 1973, and espe-cially since the onset of financial liberalization in the era of Reagan and Thatcher, and their mimetic successors. The first and fundamental fallacy is a confusion between equality of prices of goods and services, and of rates of all assets as a consistency relation in a state of equilibrium as defined by neoclassical econo-mists, and the possibility of achievement of that equality through a regime of unbridled competition. The fallacy is best seen in the operation of markets for liquid assets and was brought out clearly by John Maynard Keynes in his classic work on the theory of involuntary unemployment in a capitalist economy (Keynes 1936: ch. 12). In a market for liquid assets, if every person correctly expects the rate of return to be higher than that of some other asset, then nobody will hold the second asset, and prices of assets will fluctuate violently. If, on the other hand, the relative prices of different assets happen to be such that everybody is indifferent as to the holding of any two assets, then the allocation becomes absolutely fixed or indeterminate, and the competitive mechanism ceases to operate as a signaling mechanism for changing the portfolio mix.

Thus, determinate allocation of assets requires that different persons should hold different beliefs about the way the rates of return on different assets will change. This is the mechanism by which, for example, at any moment the margins between bonds and equities, or expected rates of return of those two classes of assets, or between equities of different companies are determined. This difference in expectation of different investors, and their hopes of making a profit out of utilizing their knowledge of what they believe to be the correct state of nature is what drives the speculative motive, as Richard Kahn brought out in a classic article (Kahn [1954] 1972).

However, states of nature in asset markets are not simply the world of objects, physical assets and their true productive powers. The theorists who want to reduce all uncertainty to an actuarial expectation commit two related fallacies even in conceptualizing how such "objective facts" are translated into expected values. First, they assume that individuals make correct calculations of the actu-arial values, given the probability distribution of the relevant states of nature. But people in fact make systematic mistakes in this regard (Tversky and Kahneman 1974). Secondly, the neoclassical finance theorists assume that if people know something to be against their self-interest, they will avoid it. However, faced with known risks, for example, of accident in their place of work such as the threat of nuclear radiation, many workers have been found to display what has been called "cognition dissonance" and fail to take well-tried precautions (Akerlof and Dickens 1982). Many investors behave very similarly when faced with the prospect of loss in the securities market.

Apart from these faulty judgements about the state of nature, the market for securities has the peculiar characteristic that people's beliefs and judgements enter vitally into the determination of returns. An investor may believe correctly, let us say, that a company set up to exploit the Himalayan snow for irrigating the desert in the northwest of the Indian subcontinent will be very profitable after the next two years. But if all the other investors and the bankers of the company hold opposite beliefs, then the lone investor with confidence in its future will come a cropper if he does not sell out his shares while the going is good, because the company will go bust owing to the lack of confidence of other investors. The lone investor will not be able to use his correct belief for the benefit of himself or the community unless he happens to be in the multi-billionaire class, or he can get other backers who share his own beliefs. (Of course, if he is a multi-billionaire he may persuade other people to his point of view even if he happens to be wrong!)

Another fallacy propagated by adherents of the neoclassical theory of the firm and the valuation and control of the firm through the agency of the stock market is that the latter throws up the "true value" of the firm through competition between investors. If the managers of the firm use the assets of the firm inefficiently and do not reward the equity-holders in accordance with the true returns obtainable from those assets, then the firm would be taken over by competitive bidders. By operating in this way the stock market will also bring about the optimal behavior of the agents (namely, the managers) and minimize their tendency to neglect the interests of the principals, that is, the owners or shareholders of the firm (Manne 1965; Jensen and Meckling 1976). However, this theory falls foul of the fact that, as pointed out long ago by Keynes, if there are some investors who hope to gain simply by bidding for and holding the shares of the taken-over firm for a short time, and then selling them, the market will not reveal the "true value" of the firm. All that will happen when a market for corporate control develops is that the managers will be more interested in defending themselves, or benefiting from, the activities of raiders than in looking after the long-term growth of the productivity of the firm. Moreover, it has been clear, after the conceptualization of the idea that relations between sellers and buyers, lenders and borrowers, or principals and agents are necessarily fraught with the asymmetric distribution of information between the players on the two sides of the bargain that security markets suffer as much from such problems of asymmetric and incomplete information as the market for credit (Gertler 1988).

Once these basic peculiarities of the market for securities are grasped, it becomes easy to understand why financial markets should be subject to herd behavior of investors, speculative attacks by bulls and bears, contagion effects of rumors, and sudden panics caused, let us say, by investigations into the sexual behavior of an American president. Thus security markets can be expected to be volatile and the more the behavior of firms is constrained by the way speculators and raiders, or even ordinary investors behaving like a herd, operate, the more the behavior of real investment simulates the operation of a casino, as Keynes pointed out more than six decades back. To call a financially liberalized world "casino capitalism" (Strange 1989) sounds then tautologous for capitalism itself becomes a giant casino.

Given the above proclivities of securitized markets, the "spreading of risks" and their minimization, viewed from the perspective of an individual profit-seeker, become transformed into the spreading of risks and uncertainty throughout the system: the invisible hand bringing about order changes into a hand wreaking mayhem and disorder.

The disorderliness of the stock market does not, of course, remain confined to itself but has its impact on the real economy, especially if the securitized firms are major foci of investment. Falls in asset values of firms through a contraction in sales make them less attractive as loci of investment, and the credit channels of firms become constricted. The contraction in real investment leads to a fall in income and a rise in unemployment; the fall in the prices of assets and debts leads to a contraction in the borrowing capacity of bankers and lending capacity of financial institutions (Fisher 1933; Bernanke 1983; Bagchi 1996) and acts as a depressor of the system and adversely affects expectations of an upturn in business confidence.

Advocates of financial liberalization tend to believe that linking local asset markets with foreign stock markets, by opening up local capital and money markets to foreign operators and the reciprocal permission granted to domestic investors to operate in foreign financial markets (including currency markets), allows the further spreading of risks and accrual of gains to everybody through competition and arbitrage leading to equalization of rates of return, adjusted for the risk of changes in exchange rates. New opportunities of arbitrage attracted many European and American pension funds and other financial institutions to Asian stock and currency markets, and to the Indian stock markets as well. Exploitation of these opportunities by foreign investors has failed to bridge the enormous differences in interest rates or real rates of return as between, say, London, New York, Tokyo, and Frankfurt, on the one hand, and Jakarta, Karachi, Mumbai, and Lagos on the other. If interest rates corrected for exchange risk fail to be equalized internationally, there is even less evidence of any tendency toward convergence of per capita incomes as between developed and less developed countries (UNCTAD 1997). Putting everything into the casino of an internationally unified stock market can only create instability without bringing about equality of asset returns, let alone per capita incomes. Even in periods of relative financial stability, the process of convergence of rates of return or incomes per capita among the regions of the most financially and economically developed countries has been found to be much stronger than internationally. One reason for this is that within a single country, say, the United States or Canada, the state can, through fiscal redistribution, try to equalize infrastructural facilities and income support measures between different regions (Atkeson and Bayoumi 1993; Bayoumi and Masson 1994; Bayoumi and Klein 1995; Obstfeld and Rogoff 1996: box 5.2). But such redistributive measures are conspicuous by their absence in the international arena.

The availability of fiscal measures by governments nationally but lack of such mechanisms internationally stands as a strong reason against the full integration of national and international financial markets. Furthermore, a national government can try to redistribute debts and credits (in a bid, for example, to restore the financial health of banks with large proportions of non-performing assets) by discriminating between different categories of domestic borrowers and creditors. However, under current international law, and given the increasingly forceful use of the provisions of the World Trade Organization, it cannot discriminate between domestic and foreign operators in the economy. Moreover, under the convention of clubbing, virtually all debts owed to foreigners as the sovereign debt owed by the government of the country, external debt has a higher priority for settlement than domestic debt. Even if this convention had not acquired the status of a legal norm, governments which have permitted the accumulation of external debt through the operation of a liberalized financial market have felt compelled to honor even those debts which did not carry a public guarantee. The cases of Chile and the Philippines in the 1980s are two outstanding examples of inclusion of all external debts under the umbrella of the sovereign debt.

The recent Indian experience with equity markets and the desperate attempt of the liberalizers to introduce capital account convertibility

After six years of experience with the liberalized regime, the Reserve Bank of India, on February 28, 1997, appointed a committee "with a view to examining the various issues relating to capital account convertibility" (CAC 1997: annexure I). The committee consisted of three bankers, and two economists, who were both known supporters of the policy of liberalization; thus there was very little scope for the committee to seriously examine the arguments for keeping controls on capital account convertibility (CAC). The report of the committee was submitted within a remarkably short period, on May 30, 1997 (that is, within a period of three months). The committee's examination of the experience of developing countries with capital account convertibility was remarkably superficial. It was confined to the period of the 1990s and skated over many episodes in Latin America and elsewhere in which such countries as Argentina, Brazil, and Chile had already introduced CAC in the 1970s and had then had to suspend it because of unsustainable balance of payments deficits, capital flight and so on. It even failed to draw the right lessons from the mediocre growth record of such countries as the Philippines and Mexico which had introduced CAC. The committee laid down certain preconditions for the introduction of CAC in India, but failed to prioritize them properly. It concluded for example, that "strengthening of the financial system" and not "a strong balance of payments position" is the most important precondition for CAC (CAC 1997: 130). An examination of the East and Southeast Asian countries revealed, however, that only regions or countries such as Taiwan, Hong Kong and the People's Republic of China which have been able to maintain a strong balance of payments position have so far escaped the need to appeal to the IMF to ease them out of their difficulties. Moreover, Taiwan, China and indirectly Hong Kong also have maintained various controls over inflows and outflows of capital from their respective territories (Bagchi 1998).

Despite some recognition on the part of the Committee that the preconditions for attainment of CAC had not been fulfilled in India, it recommended that "its implementation be spread over "a three-year period 1997–98, 1998–99 and 1999–2000" (CAC 1997: 131), while these preconditions are attained. This reasoning is fallacious on several counts of which only two will be mentioned here. First, India's record in bringing down the balance of payments and fiscal deficits during the liberalization period has been extremely mixed so far. The policy stance of the government is to minimize the taxes on the rich while enriching them further, and hence there is little prospect of achieving a fiscal or macroeconomic balance through its policies. Given the state of the world economy since 1997 there is also little prospect of a turnaround in the export performance and hence of attaining a balance of payments surplus for India. Secondly, even supposing India manages to attain better indices of performance in its balance of payments, in its budgetary balances, its rate of inflation (which has gone up again) and in its growth rate, all the indices can tumble down if or when an international financial panic occurs, or when, for some reason, the international financial community regards India's prospects with a jaundiced eye.

Earlier we noted the gymnastics that the Reserve Bank of India has had to perform in a bid to keep order in the markets for foreign exchange, government securities, and credit, in the wake of the Asian currency crisis. Many of the same neoliberals who had been baying for CAC are now patting themselves on the back for keeping control on capital movements and hence avoiding the kind of predicament that Thailand, Indonesia or South Korea got into. However, some of them have not given up. The chairman of the committee on CAC, for example, recently chided policy analysts for giving up the idea of making the Indian rupee convertible in the near future (Tarapore 1998).

We will end this section by examining the idea, in the Indian context, that securitization and unification of financial markets can deliver greater security for investors. The largest and oldest Indian mutual fund is the Unit Trust of India (UTI) whose total investments grew from Rs. 213.75 billion on June 30, 1992 (that is, one year after the onset of economic reforms) to Rs. 487.24 billion on June 30, 1997 (Reserve Bank of India 1993a: 318; 1997: 131). With the lifting of ceilings on new capital issues by firms and on interest rates paid to depositors or charged to creditors, the UTI invested increasingly in equities rather than fixed-interest debentures. The share of equities in its total investment rose from 27.8 percent on June 30, 1992 to 48.9 percent on June 30, 1997. As we have seen, however, share values went on a downward slide again from 1997, and this made it increasingly difficult to keep up the redemption value of its leading scheme for small investors (e.g. US-64) and fears were expressed about the ability of UTI to continue redeeming them except at much-depreciated prices. In the US-64 scheme itself the share of equities had increased from 65.7 percent on June 30, 1998 to 68 percent on June 30, 1998 (*Business Standard* 1998). Between June and September 1998, the values of the shares of India's leading companies such as Reliance, Telco, ITC, LandT, and so on declined by very large percentages—in some cases by over 60 percent. When the news of UTI's portfolio was publicized in the papers, share prices went into a tailspin, partly because of general panic, and partly because a foreign institutional investor offloaded shares on a large scale (*Business Standard* 1998). In fact, it is suspected that bear runs on the Indian stock market have been increasingly led by foreign institutional investors.

Ultimately, the rush for redemption of US-64 paper and the general slide in stock prices had to be contained by pledging the support of the government and the public sector banks (which dominate the money market) behind the UTI (*Telegraph* 1998). Thus ironically enough, the damage caused by thoughtless securitization and linking up with foreign financial agencies could be contained only through state action, and not through the wizardry of alchemists of finance. How long and to what extent an enfeebled state in a liberalized regime can continue to act as a fire-fighter remains a moot question in India as elsewhere.

Acknowledgement

Non-incriminating thanks are due to Professor Nirmala Banerjee for her helpful comments.

Bibliography

ADB (1996) *Asian Development Outlook 1996 and 1997*, New York: Oxford University Press for the Asian Development Bank.

Akerlof, G. A. and Dickens, W. T. (1982) "The Economic Consequences of Cognitive Dissonance," *American Economic Review* 72 (3), June.

Amjad, R. (ed.) (1989) *To the Gulf and Back: Studies on the Economic Impact of Asian Labour Migration*, New Delhi: ILO/ARTEP and UNDP.

Atkeson, A. and Bayoumi, T. (1993) "Do Private Capital Markets Insure Regional Risk Evidence from Europe and the United States?" *Open Economies Review* 4 (3).

Bagchi, A. K. (1992) "Transnational Banks, US Power Game and Global Impoverishment," *Economic and Political Weekly* 27 (22), May 30.

—— (1993) "Transnationalisation en Asie du Sud," in S. Amin and P. Gonzalez Casanova (eds) *Mondialisation et accumulation*, Paris: L'Harmattan.

—— (1994) "Globalising India: The Fantasy and the Reality," *Social Scientist* [Delhi], 22.

—— (1995) "Employment and Economic Reforms in India," background paper for *World Employment Report 1996*, Geneva, International Labour Office.

—— (1996) "Fluctuations in Global Economy: Income, Debt and Terms of Trade Processes," in S. Sen (ed.) *Financial Facility, Debt and Economic Reforms*, London: Macmillan.

—— (1998) "Growth Miracle and its Unravelling in East and South-east Asia: Unregulated Competitiveness and Denouncement of Manipulation by International Financial Community," *Economic and Political Weekly* 33 (18), May 2.

Bayoumi, T. and Klein, M. W. (1995) *A Provincial View of Capital Mobility*, Working Paper no. 5115, National Bureau of Economic Research.

Bayoumi, T. and Masson, P. R. (1994) *Fiscal Flows in the United States and Canada: Lessons for Monetary Union in Europe*, Discussion Paper No. 1057, Centre for Economic Policy Research.

Bernanke, B. S. (1983) Non-monetary Effects of the Financial Crisis in the Propagation of the Great Depression, *American Economic Review* 73.

Business Standard (1998) "US-64 Equity Exposure 68%," *Business Standard*, Calcutta, October 8.

CAC (1997) *Report of the Committee on Capital Account Convertibility*, Mumbai: Reserve Bank of India.

Datta, B. (1992) *Indian Planning at the Crossroads*, Delhi: Oxford University Press.

Fisher, I. (1933) "The Debt-deflation Theory of Great Depressions," *Econometrica* 1 (4).

Freixas, X. and Rochet, J. C. (1997) *Microeconomics of Banking*, Cambridge MA: MIT Press.

Gertler, M. (1988) "Financial Structure and Aggregate Economic Activity: An Overview," *Journal of Money, Credit and Banking* 20 (3).

Government of India (1998) *Economic Survey 1997–98*, New Delhi, Government of India, Ministry of Finance.

Guru-Gharana, K. K. and Shrestha, A. P. (1996) "Globalisation with Equity: Policies for Growth in Nepal," (mimeo.), Kathmandu: Nepal Foundation for Advanced Studies.

ILO (1995) *Yearbook of Labour Statistics 1995*, Geneva: International Labour Office.

Jensen, M. C. and Meckling, W. H. (1976) "Theory of the Firm: Managerial Behaviour, Agency Costs and Ownership Structure," *Journal of Financial Economics* 3.

Kahn, R. F. ([1954] 1972) "Some Notes on Liquidity Preference," reprinted in Kahn *Selected Essays on Employment and Growth*, Cambridge: Cambridge University Press.

Keynes, J. M. (1936) *The General Theory of Employment, Interest and Money*, London: Macmillan.

Manne, H. G. (1965) "Mergers and the Market for Corporate Control," *Journal of Political Economy*, 73.

Misra, B. M. (1997) "Fifty Years of the Indian Capital Market," *Reserve Bank of India Occasional Papers* 18 (2 and 3), June and September.

Muqtada, M. and Basu, P. (1994) *Macroeconomic Policies, Growth and Employment Expansion: The Experience of South Asia*, Geneva: International Labour Office.

Nayyar, D. (1996) *Economic Liberalization in India: Analytics, Experience and Lessons*, Calcutta: Orient Longman.

Obstfeld, M. and Rogoff, K. (1996) *Foundations of International Macroeconomics*, Cambridge MA: MIT Press.

Reserve Bank of India (1993) *Report on Currency and Finance, 1992–93*, vol. I, Bombay: Reserve Bank of India.

—— (1997a) *Report on Trend and Progress of Banking in India 1995–96 (July–June)*, Mumbai: Reserve Bank of India.

—— (1997b) *Report on Currency and Finance, 1997–98*, vol. II, Mumbai: Reserve Bank of India.

Strange, S. (1989) *Casino Capitalism*, Oxford: Blackwell.

Tarapore, S. S. (1998) "Hosannas for Capital Control," *Business Standard*, Calcutta, October 9.

Telegraph (1998) "Govt., Public Sector Banks Pledge Support to UTI," *Telegraph*, Calcutta, October 14.

Tversky, A. and Kahneman, D. (1974) "Judgment under Uncertainty: Heuristics and Biases," *Science* 185.

UN (1998) *Human Development Report 1998*, New York: Oxford University Press for the United Nations Development Office.

UNCTAD (1995) *World Investment Report 1995*, New York: United Nations.

—— (1997) *Trade and Development Report 1997*, Geneva and New York: United Nations Conference on Trade and Development.

World Bank (1995) *World Tables 1995*, Washington, DC: World Bank.

—— (1996) *World Development Report 1996*, New York: Oxford University Press for the World Bank.

8 Globalization and class politics in South Korea

Kwang-Yeong Shin

The later part of the twentieth century saw the advanced capitalist societies undergoing a fundamental transformation due to globalization, with far-reaching effects on domestic politics as well as international relations. Globalization is an economic process, which extends economic networks across the whole world and integrates them into a synchronized economic system, destroying indigenous economies, shaking up domestic political orders, and creating regional economic blocks at the same time.[1] Globalization was initiated by multinational corporations in the core countries in the 1980s and 1990s. The increasing interconnectedness of the international economy has been accelerated by the development of the technology of micro-electronics, the communication industry, and the increase in trade among nations.

However, the local response to the global changes differs from country to country according to the position within the world-system and local political dynamics. While the welfare state system in Western Europe suffers from the tumbling national economy due to globalization (Cox 1987; Esping-Anderson 1992; The Group of Lisbon 1995), the newly democratized countries (NDCs) experience serious threats to their democratization due to the increasing market competition and instability of the national economy (Petras, 1997). In general, it seems to be clear that globalization in the 1980s and 1990s hampered the newly emerging democracies by undermining the strength of the labor unions and democratic social forces. It might be argued that under the increasing tendency of globalization in East Asia, authoritarian capital begins to replace the role of the authoritarian state in mobilizing public opinion and exercising political power over the people. The capital logic of competition and accumulation achieves a hegemonic position in society with the help of the developmental state even after the democratic transition.

This notwithstanding, resistance against globalization has been prevailing in many countries. It also differs from country to country according to the domestic strength of the labor movement and the national political conjuncture. Opposition takes a variety of forms and follows different paths; for example, it can take the form of a peasant revolt like the Zapatistas in Chiapas, Mexico, or a workers' strike like the general strike in January 1997 in South Korea, or it may express itself through political ascendance of leftist parties as in recent elections in Europe.

Thus, globalization has become a politically contested concept rather than a concept to capture the formation of the global economy. It also has not been free from political ideology because social classes and social groups advocate particular features of globalization for their own interests.

In this chapter we will analyze globalization and resistance to it in South Korea, revealing the cross-cutting effects of globalization on domestic politics and the union movement. The consequences of globalization are not linear and one-sided but opposing and conflicting. It is contradictory in the sense that the effect of globalization is not always in favor of capital. It is also conflict-embedded in the sense that state and capital do not monopolize the meanings of globalization and that resistance by labor unions and social movements shape the popular discourse on globalization. The trade unions do have power to fabricate the understanding of globalization with the help of democratic forces. In Korea, globalization has not only been an economic process but also a political process in which social actors mobilize symbolic resources as well as organizational capacity to impose their interpretation and interests on state policy. The authoritarian developmental state in the 6th Republic tried to avoid democratic consolidation of political and economic institutions and rules, advocating the necessity for restriction of popular demands under "the crisis of the national economy" as defined by the state managers and business. The state and the Chaebols, the Korean conglomerates, have been disseminating for years the perception of the coming crisis of the Korean economy as being due to globalization which was interpreted as unlimited competition.

Democratization and globalization in South Korea

In the late 1980s, South Korea encountered two different transformative social dynamics: democratization and globalization. The society underwent the political transition from authoritarianism to democracy as a consequence of the democratic struggle of more than three decades. A democratic coalition succeeded in removing the military regime in 1987. People's power was strong enough to override the oppressive regime of Chun Doo Hwan. Since the inauguration of Roh Tae Woo's government, the democratic coalition began to recognize the fact that democratization requires continuous popular mobilization to prevent a "reverse course" of democratization. The ongoing democratic transition has been a turbulent process in which the ruling bloc tried to maintain its power while democratic forces challenged it.

The Korean path of democratization reveals a prototype of limited democratization due to its failure to overthrow the old regime. The former ruling bloc regained power through a political transfusion in 1990. President Roh, who won the 1987 election, suffered from a low level of support after he won the election with the support of only one-third of the voters. Owing to the split between the two opposition leaders, Kim Dae Joong and Kim Young Sam, Roh Tae Woo needed the support of only 32 percent of the total votes to win the election. But the ruling party failed to get a majority in the parliamentary election of April

1988, and the opposition parties formed an ad hoc coalition against the ruling party in the new parliament. In order to overcome its political weakness, Roh and two minor party leaders made a political deal to form a new majority party. As a result of this reshuffling of the political parties, the authoritarian ruling party was able to maintain its political hegemony during the subsequent processes of democratization, controlling both the timing and the contents of democratization.

Although there were continuous struggles for democratization, Roh's government mobilized counter-attacks against those struggles, controlling the political discourses of democracy and exacerbating the perception of economic crisis. It introduced the concept of globalization into the political agenda in order to evoke feelings of crisis among the people. Under Roh's regime, globalization (defined as unlimited competition) became an instrument for attacking radical labor movements for undermining the economic growth achieved by the previous regimes. It also blamed their radical political demands for undermining the "business climate" of South Korea.

However, the democratic forces, which included the labor unions and student organizations, accepted the global trend of economic interconnectedness. But this acceptance was based on a redefinition of globalization as a political reform to demilitarize the regime and guarantee civil rights in accordance with the international discourse. Their first and most urgent demand was the abolition of the authoritarian legacy. Discursive warfare as well as street skirmishes have since prevailed in Korea as a result of the activities of the democratization movements. Because the content of democracy is not pre-ordained by some law or by politicians, the day-to-day struggles for democracy include critiques of the logic both of capital as well as of the authoritarian state.

While Korean society was experiencing globalization, another global process of increasing economic interaction among nations emerged. It was not until the Uruguay Round that the Korean government acknowledged the necessity of deregulating its economy and abolishing import barriers. The notion of globalization had been alien to Korean governments and politicians in the past, because the military regime tightly controlled the flow of information and travel during the Yushin system.[2] Soon after the Seoul Olympic Games, the Korean government established economic relations with socialist countries including those of Eastern Europe and China. On the one hand, the South Korean government initiated the establishment of diplomatic relationships with the socialist bloc to contain North Korea. The "Northern Policy," imitating the Eastern Policy of Willy Brandt in West Germany, was launched by Roh Tae Woo. In the 1990s, regional economic integration such as the EC and NAFTA drastically transformed the market environment of the Korean manufacturers who were highly dependent upon foreign trade. On the other hand, the relationship between the United States and South Korea began to change, as the Cold War rapidly lost its significance as the organizing principle of international order. In 1989, the US government overhauled the preferential tariff treatment given to South Korea under the General System of Preferences (GSP). Furthermore, as the United

Table 8.1 Trade between Korea and the United States

	Trade with America (US$ million)			Proportion of the US market (%)			
	Export	Import	Balance	Korea	Japan	China	Taiwan
1987	183.1	87.6	95.5	4.4	20.8	1.6	6.0
1989	206.4	159.1	47.3	4.2	19.8	2.5	5.1
1991	195.6	188.9	−3.4	3.5	18.8	3.9	4.7
1992	180.9	182.9	−2.0	4.1	18.3	4.5	4.6

Source: Korean Development Institute (KDI) (1994) *Economic Policy in the Period of Opening*, Seoul, p. 223

States' trade deficit against South Korea became larger and larger, Washington strongly demanded that the Korean government take measures to change state regulation of trade and reduce the trade surplus against America.[3] In 1992, there were 70 US import regulations on Korean products, including anti-dumping claims and quote restrictions, whereas there had been only three during the 1980s. The US government applied the "Super 301 code" to threaten the Korean government in order to impose its demands. The tension between the United States and Korea heralded the post-Cold War era in which economic competition came to outweigh military alliance.

The way in which the historical conjuncture derived from US pressure and the end of the Cold War can be used depends upon the strategic capacity of social actors as well as the ideological matrix of a society. Because globalization as a new terminology is fluid as well as alien to all social and political actors, a dominant understanding of globalization has not yet formed. As the pressure from the United States became more visible than ever and the numbers of international agreements on trade increased, the Korean ruling bloc began to launch "the movement for globalization." Using recent episodes as evidence of international intervention in the national sovereignty and economy, the mass media used the metaphor of presenting this as the second period of external pressure similar to the enforced opening of the Lee Dynasty by imperial Japan in 1878.[4] The argument was that the difference between the two openings related to the context. It was implied that modern Korea would now utilize this opportunity for development, since the state and society were ready to respond to the new challenge.

Nevertheless, the question of which sector and to what extent the Korean economy could be opened was a political issue, because according to the state decision some social groups would benefit, while others would lose. The most pressing problem was the peasant question. The opening up of the agricultural market would be damaging to a Korean peasantry which was already rapidly declining in numbers. On the other hand, the opening up of the manufactured goods market would significantly damage the interests of Korean capitalists in the domestic economy. The Korean state chose the capitalist sector as the national interest at the expense of the peasantry in order to secure the competitive position of Korean-made manufactured goods in the international market. Joining the World Trade Organization (WTO), the state gave up its protection of the Korean peasantry whose numbers were falling drastically and whose political influence was consequently weak. The state also accentuated the necessity of wage constraints to improve the competitiveness of Korean products in both European and American markets. Labor conflicts and strikes were criticized as a major cause of the slowdown of the economy.

Globalization and the politics of labor law reforms

Democratization implies a dual transformation in South Korea: in the realm of politics the transition from authoritarianism to a competitive electoral system and in the industrial sector the transition from authoritarian to democratic industrial relations.

The authoritarian developmental regime (hereafter ADV) pursued economic growth by mobilizing human as well as economic resources. In order to achieve a favorable business climate, the ADV oppressed workers' collective actions by excluding the working class from the political sphere. Labor unions have been tightly controlled by state organizations such as the police. Independent unions were not legally permitted and their leaders have been prosecuted under the national security law.

After 1987, Roh's government did not restrict the deployment of the riot police to resolve industrial disputes as it had previously done. Roh's government was besieged by the pressures of democratization. President Roh could not but prosecute the former president Chun Doo Hwan who commanded the Kwangju massacre in May 1980. He tried to distance himself from Chun Doo Hwan. Because the parliament was controlled by the opposition parties, Roh took a defensive position with a minimalist movement toward democratization. To use Gramsci's term, the core of the minimalist action was a "war of position," in other words a strategy of attrition.

In 1988, progressive social forces became active for reforming the Draconian labor law of the repressive military regime. The opposition parties also accepted the need for a reform of labor regulation. But the content of the revised labor law did not include the radical demands of the labor unions since the conservative opposition party did not agree with the other opposition party with respect to issues such as the political participation of labor unions and enterprise unions.[5] However, President Roh exercised his power of veto to reject the revised Labor Relations Bill and only signed the revised Labor Standard Law in 1989. He chose to improve individual labor rights, denying improvement of collective rights such as the freedom of union organization and collective actions. The big capitalist groups strongly urged Roh not to sign the revised bill, arguing that the revision of labor legislation would lead to the collapse of the national economy. Independent labor unions did not show strong enthusiasm for law reform because they faced difficulties in defending their new organizations at the enterprise level. They suffered from too many changes in the union leadership and from attacks from industrialists. Management organized the "company rescue team," comprised of white-collar workers and company security personnel, to attack striking workers. The state used riot police to quell strikes at the major sites including the Hyundai Motor Company and the Korean Broadcasting System. Following the illegal visit of preacher Moon, a leading figure of the opposition movement, to North Korea in March 1989, Roh's regime mobilized the strong anti-communist sentiments among the people. Accusing strikers of being controlled by North Korea, it also sent the riot police to crack down on the strikers in many regions.

In 1990, the Ministry of Commerce and Ministry of Labor tried to revise the collective labor laws as well as the labor standard law according to the demands from the Chaebols who wanted measures to improve the flexibility of human resource management and a reduction in labor costs. Announcing that working conditions in Korea were much better than in many of its competitors, the two ministries tried to extend working hours by reducing national holidays and paid vacation.[6] These proposals failed due to the resistance from the people. Instead the ministries wanted to introduce flexible working time in order to reduce labor costs during the period of economic recession. But the Ministry of Commerce retreated as workers' resistance escalated.

In 1993, the new president, Kim Young Sam, who had spent more than 20 years in the struggle for democracy, introduced political slogans such as "New Korea," "New Economy," and "New Labor Policy" in his inauguration speech in February 1993. He launched an ambitious reform plan to rationalize bureaucracy and economic regulations. He introduced the real name bank account system and the real name land system in the first half of that year. The newly appointed minister of labor, who had been a former human rights lawyer, announced a non-interventionist policy in disputes between managers and workers. This represented a drastic change in the state's labor policy—from one of "oppression and exclusion" to one of "autonomy and participation." As the state withdrew from involvement in industrial relations, the capitalist class had to find a way to exercise its power toward the seemingly neutral state and the militant workers. For the first time, the Korean capitalists encountered an hostile political and social environment.

The response of capital came in the form of sabotage against state policy by the drastic reduction of investment in production. In the fourth quarter of 1992, machine facility investment dropped by 10.2 percent to its lowest level for 30 years. In the first quarter of 1993, it dropped further by 12.4 percent. Even in the second quarter, it could not regain the level of the previous year with a rise of only 1.2 percent.[7] The investment strike, in turn, began to affect macroeconomic indicators, displaying a slowdown of economic growth and the expected increase of unemployment. The rate of economic growth in 1993 was 3.4 percent, which was the lowest since 1980. Increasing capital mobility into the Southeast Asian nations further aggravated the problems of a national economy that was already suffering from the recession. Kim Young Sam, who had been oriented toward economic growth, was shocked by the decrease of investment and the expected economic recession. Restricting the reform drive, he began to solicit capital investment in the manufacturing sector, inviting the Chaebols to the Blue House. They strongly warned the government not to discourage the capitalist investment and to improve the business climate immediately.

This collective action successfully prevented the state from carrying out continuous reforms. The capitalists further demanded the replacement of the minister of labor with a conservative one. The strike at the Hyundai Motor Company in May 1992 was the test case of the new labor policy. Management of the company did not make any concession to workers' demands and invoked state intervention for two months. The state eventually used compulsory arbitration procedure and sent the riot police to crush the strike. The strike lasted for two months and ended with the massive arrests of workers. This event displayed the total failure of the new labor policy. Since Kim's government pursued economic growth as a state goal as the previous regimes had done, it could not but surrender to the capitalist interests. The first reform effort was thus interrupted by the capitalist concerted collective obstruction and resistance. Eventually the minister of labor was replaced by one of the old guard who had served under the 5th and 6th Republics. The revision of the labor law was postponed until 1994 (*Donga Daily News* 1996: 150).[8]

As Korea joined the Uruguay Round in 1993 and the WTO in 1994, the state utilized "internationalization" (*Kukjehwa*) as a political propaganda tool to quash labor strikes by arguing that the Korean economy was in crisis due to the low "state of competitiveness." After the aborted first reform, Kim Young Sam announced upon his return from a summit meeting of the Asia Pacific Economic Cooperation (APEC) the "second reform" to upgrade Korean society to the level of the advanced countries. However, the major concern of the second reform was to enhance the competitiveness of Korean goods in the international market. The state policy for internationalization contained deregulation of government intervention in the economy and privatization of state corporations. TV commercials and newspaper advertisements were used to publicize the urgency for improvement in the competitiveness of Korean products in the international market. Workers were also asked to share the burden of international competition. In reality, this simply meant a restriction on wage increases and labor strikes.

Replacing the term internationalization, Kim Young Sam introduced the key word of "globalization" (*Segeihwa*) in 1995, demanding further improvement in national competitiveness.[9] In order to formulate policies for globalization, he established the "globalization committee" as a presidential advisory committee. In the same year the state organized a movement for an extra half-hour's working time and, in 1996, organized the movement for a 10 percent increase of competitiveness. In fact, this political rhetoric held little of substance. Nevertheless, they became key words in the mass media which were predominantly conservative and anti-labor in their political stance. As globalization became a prevailing discourse, unions and workers were worrying about the negative public perception of their collective actions. Strikes were portrayed as group egoism detrimental to adjustment to globalization.

The Chaebols also launched a massive "discursive warfare" against the unions, propagating the necessity of wage constraints and flexible automation. The National Confederation of Employers (NCE) organized seminars on competitiveness and flexibility with major national newspapers reporting the contents of the papers presented in those discussions. The NCE chose academics with a pro-capitalist perspective and utilized the mass media to advertise their opinions. Public seminars or conferences were traditional methods for mobilizing public opinion before contacting law makers and government bureaucrats to deal with the major issues. Concerted efforts by the capitalists were aimed at influencing the perception of the people who were suspicious of the Chaebols' behavior. The "British disease" was frequently mentioned in order to tame the militant labor movement.

As oppression of labor unions continued, workers responded by organizing the new confederation of independent trade unions. In November 1995, the Korean Confederation of Trade Unions (KCTU), technically illegal, was established independently of the existing state-controlled and state-sponsored Korean Federation of Trade Unions (KFTU). The formation of the KCTU heralded a new era for the labor movement in South Korea since the new union announced social reform as a goal of its organization. In addition to wages and working conditions, it dealt with major social and economic issues such as social security, economic concentration by the Chaebols, consumer prices, housing problems, educational reforms, and democratization of the mass media, etc. Criticizing the state and the capitalist class, the KCTU insisted that major social problems can only be solved through the initiative of the working class.

When South Korea joined the OECD in 1996, a precondition for membership was that the Korean government must change its authoritarian labor law.[10] Kim Young Sam organized a Presidential Commission on Industrial Relations Reform (PCIR) on May 9, 1996, to change the old labor law.[11] The committee included representatives from the government, academic institutions, employer organizations, unions, and public interest groups, as well as representatives from the newly established confederation of the independent unions. The two confederations of trade unions, the KFTU and KCTU submitted proposals for revision of the labor law, which did not reveal differences between the positions of the two confederations of trade unions. However, the Korean Confederation of Employers (KCE) submitted its own proposal maintaining the major codes of the authoritarian labor law and adding measures to maximize flexibility of manpower management.[12]

As the PCIR meetings continued, the conflicting interests between labor and management loomed larger with respect to key issues and did not converge at all before the scheduled date. The major demand of the capitalist class were maintenance of the old labor union law and change of the labor standard law to allow individual firms to utilize manpower flexibly. The capitalist organizations insisted that the major rationale for the reform of industrial relations should be improvement of international competitiveness in the period of globalization. Without improving competitiveness, they argue, the Korean economy will collapse sooner or later because of the high wages and low efficiency. Thus, the Chaebols demanded the restriction of union activity and legalization of flexible manpower management, which included loosening the regulations concerning standard working hours[13] and dismissal without severance payment.[14] Furthermore, the Federation of Korean Industries, the Chaebols' umbrella organization, demanded a five-year wage freeze as one way of overcoming the economic crisis.

In contrast the unions called for the abolition of the old labor oppressive codes established during the military dictatorship and the establishment of democratic industrial relations. They strongly demanded abolition of the codes concerning the prohibition of plural unionism, unions' political activity, and a third party's involvement in union affairs. They also insisted on the legalization of the teachers' union and public sector unions.

However, the final concession regarding major codes could not be reached. As the committee was dominated by capitalist forces, the representatives of the KCTU exited from the committee. Denouncing the capitalist stance of the committee, they mobilized massive rallies to protest the detainment of the authoritarian labor codes which in the past were applied to suppress labor movements. The PCIR sent the draft version of the labor law reform to the government on November 12, 1996 without having resolved the major disagreements between labor and capital.

Kim Young Sam urged the cabinet to revise the labor law as soon as possible. He wanted to put an end to the debate on the labor law reform in 1996 before the presidential election in 1997. In order to prevent this question from becoming an explosive issue in transforming the electoral game, he tried to change the labor law before this election. The government committee, with the prime minister as chairman, was established in order to finalize the official version of the revised labor bill on November 11, 1996. Nonetheless, the committee could not finalize the government document because of disagreement from the outset among committee members on several codes.[15] The government drafted the labor bill on December 3, 1996, compromising the conflicting interests of the ministries. The distinctive feature of the labor bill drafted by the government was to codify employers' interests, legalizing the free layoff of workers due to managerial difficulty, the introduction of new technology, and downsizing. It also allowed employers to introduce a system of flexible working hours to reduce labor costs[16] and to replace striking workers. Nonetheless, labor demands were partially included in the government's draft in order to attenuate the possible workers' protests. For example, multiple unionism was legalized at the industrial level in 1997 and will be at the enterprise level in 2002. Third party intervention is allowed but confined to those organizations registered with the Ministry of Labor. Teachers have been able to organize unions from 1999 but are not allowed to strike.

The government committee presented its version of the labor bill to parliament, postponing revision of the contested codes. The ruling party passed the bill through parliament at dawn on December 26, 1996. The ruling party members sneaked into parliament at 6 o'clock in the morning in order to avoid possible resistance from opposition parties and in just seven minutes voted on this bill and 11 others, including the revised national security bill.[17] In fact, this version of the bill by the ruling party was more pro-capital than that of the government. It extended the period prohibiting a union's political activity from three years to five years. It also retained the oppressive codes banning plural unionism until 2000, prohibition of political activity by the labor unions, and prohibition of the teachers' union. It only codified the relaxation of the labor standard by permitting employers a flexible employment practice and the sacking of workers without redundancy payment, which was conventionally given. The new labor law mainly responded to the demands of the capitalist class and rejected the demands of the unions.

The passage of the labor law reform bill and the national security bill impacted on the population in two senses. First, the Korean people were shocked by the way in which the ruling party had railroaded the bills through parliament. This was a totally illegal and undemocratic method frequently used by the previous authoritarian regimes in which the ruling party alone passed many bills without due process. Even though there were protests from opposition parties and social groups, the authoritarian governments ignored them by raising new issues. Secondly, Koreans were angry about the content of the labor bill and the national security bill which revived the possibility of despotic control of the labor movement and political opposition. Instead of reforming the authoritarian legacies in the realm of law, the ruling party attempted to restore them completely and fully implement the Chaebols' interests.

Workers' resistance and global solidarity

Directly after the passage of the labor bill, the KCTU announced a general strike. Organized by the KCTU in December 1996 and January 1997, this was the first successful nationwide general strike. The KCTU succeeded in receiving massive popular support because the industrial action represented the prevailing anti-authoritarian sentiment of the people as well as workers' discontent. The ruling party chose the date for the passage of the bills through parliament in order to minimize the impact of the "railroading" on national politics and the next presidential election. The date of December 26, 1996, being just after Christmas, was probably chosen on the basis that the people's discontent would have waned during the year-end holidays. Contrary to these expectations, the KCTU reinforced the protest movements by orchestrating nationwide strikes in major industries. Because Korean unions are organized on an individual enterprise-based system, it was a mammoth task to implement nationwide strikes. Thus the KCTU adopted more flexible tactics than ever before in order to maintain people's support.[18] It postponed the attempted strike of the Seoul Subway Union and the National Bank Unions in order not to damage the people's daily lives, while it ordered the Korean Broadcasting Unions to strike in order to demonstrate the strength of the protest against authoritarian labor law. Contrary to government expectations, the state-sponsored KFTU joined the general strike in mid-January when it realized that the people's anger was not abating. The KFTU announced a 48-hour strike on January 14. Thus, for the first time in Korean labor history, the KFTU and the KCTU formed an ad hoc united front against the state—and the general strike in January 1997 thus represented a confrontation between the state and united unions. The subsequent call for nationwide strikes by the KCTU leaders was answered by workers' active participation for two months.

The most distinctive characteristics of the general strike were the concerted efforts of blue-collar workers, white-collar workers unions, and social movement organizations. Major broadcasting unions and newspaper unions started sympathy strikes from January 1. As the early retirement system, called honorary retirement, had been introduced even in the Chaebols' enterprises since 1995, white-collar workers were no longer safe from lay-off and lifetime employment could no longer be guaranteed. Thus, unions such as the Commerce of Business, the Association of the Insurance Company Unions, the Union of Professions, and eight state-owned corporation unions joined the general strike.

Social movement organizations, environmental organizations, cultural associations, university faculty associations, religious leaders, etc., all expressed solidarity with the strikers. One-third of all Catholic priests, who were the leading religious group during the struggle against the military dictatorship, signed the appeal for the revision of the revised labor law and joined the campaign. The Roman Catholic cardinal of Korea urged the government to resolve the situation peacefully when he met with Kim Young Sam. Despite the state's attempt to minimize the influence of the union leaders on public opinion, the general strike was fully supported by the people.[19] As such the general strike can be considered as representing the people's resistance to the authoritarian state and to the Korean capitalist class. Contrary to the expectation of the government and ruling party, the popularity of the general strike did not wane during the whole period of the conflict. Kim's regime encountered its most serious resistance and its lowest popularity rating since its inauguration in 1993.

Interestingly, international organizations played an important role in restricting the choice of policies for the Korean state. The committee member of the OECD labor consultants (TUAC) supported the KCTU's general strike, denouncing the undemocratic passage of the authoritarian labor bill by the ruling party. The secretary of the committee demanded revision of the labor law according to the ILO conventions of December 27, 1996; he visited the Myoung-Dong cathedral on January 11, 1997, where the leaders of the KCTU had established their headquarters from where they organized the general strike, in order to display support for the strikers. The International Confederation of Free Trade Unions (ICFTU) filed a complaint to the ILO which accused the Korean government of violating conventions 87 and 89 on December 28. The chairman of the American Federation of Labor-Congress of Industrial Organizations

(AFL-CIO), John Sweeny, demanded that Kim should veto the bill, criticizing the undemocratic method and content of its passage which hindered democratization and undermined worker's rights. The World Federation of Trade Unions (WFTU) declared "solidarity" with the Korean workers on strike. Massive demonstrations in front of South Korean embassies were organized by unions in 13 countries including France, New Zealand, Hong Kong, and the Philippines.[20]

The OECD decided that the revised labor law in Korea did not fully meet international standards. Although it is not compulsory for members to accept recommendations by the OECD, it nevertheless undermined the legitimacy of the revised labor law and the government's accountability. Also, the international media began to report the details of the confrontation between the state and workers in Korea. As state action became the focus of worldwide media attention, the government could not use riot police to arrest the leaders of the KCTU. And as more international organizations became involved, the general strike in Korea came to be interpreted as part of the worldwide struggle between the labor movement and neoliberalism as well as a conflict between the authoritarian state and the labor unions in South Korea.[21]

Unable to use the warrants issued for the arrest of the main union leaders, and having besieged the Myoung-Dong cathedral for more than two months, Kim Young Sam sought to compromise by promising a revision of the labor law in parliament. Since the ruling party was controlled by President Kim, his decision to revise the labor law was implemented in parliament. As the issue was again transferred to the legislature, the unions could be marginalized. The labor law therefore became an object of political negotiations between the ruling party and the opposition parties. Because labor did not have any political channel to the existing political parties, the unions were no longer major actors during the process of parliamentary bargaining. The opposition parties had not presented any alternatives before the passage of the former bill, and they were not active in reforming the authoritarian labor law (although they had rejected the proposal of the ruling party). On the one hand, they did not want to reveal conflict and disunity among themselves, because their power came from their combined opposition to the ruling party. On the other hand, the opposition parties are conservative, and each has a different political genesis as far as political background and ideology are concerned.[22] However, the ongoing general strike supported by the masses put pressure on the opposition parties and the ruling party. In the end, the political parties succeeded in producing a compromised revision of the labor law. Although it took into account the demands of labor, it was still not satisfactory in the eyes of the unions. The labor unions did not accept some of the new codes such as the prohibition against forming a teachers' union and the permission given to employers to discharge employees without paying severance payment. Notwithstanding this dissatisfaction, the unions could not but accept the law as a reality because its implementation had followed procedural rules and both the opposition parties and the ruling party had participated in the revision of the labor law.

The general strike and after

As a proclaimed social reformist trade union, the KCTU took the national economy into account in its conduct of the strike in order to maintain the support of the people. The maximalist strategy—to continue the general strike until all the demands had been met—might have isolated the KCTU from other social groups and weakened its precarious partnership with the other union, the KFTU. When parliament declared its intention to discuss the revision of the revised labor law, the KCTU decided to suspend its scheduled strike on January 28 and call for a nationwide strike on February 18, in case this revision proved to be unacceptable. The union controlled the number and scale of weekly and monthly strikes, thereby minimizing the impact on the national economy but maximizing the impact on the political sphere.

The ruling party and the opposition parties did not finalize the revision of the labor law until March 8, much later than the due date. Although the new labor law was passed through with concessions, demands by labor unions were not fully met. Because of institutional constraints within unions, labor leaders embarked on a more active strategy to form a working-class party. Without a political organization, the unions would never be able to maximize the gains of the successful general strike, and so, together with other social organizations, the unions sought to participate in national politics under their own political wing. The KCTU, which took a hegemonic position in the labor movements, initiated a political strategy independent of the existing opposition parties.

The process of the revision of the authoritarian labor law in Korea reveals the complex dynamics of interactions between the unions, the capitalist class, the state, political parties, and international organizations. Even though the state and the capitalists utilized globalization as an opportunity to mobilize around neoliberalism, the unions and the international organizations also used the age of globalization as a chance to counteract authoritarianism by demanding the revision of the labor laws in accordance with the international standard. The ILO strongly urged the Korean government to change its undemocratic labor law and ratify the ILO codes associated with basic workers' rights.[23]

Conclusion

Although the Korean economy was already internationalized before democratization, this occurred mainly in conjunction with the Cold War system controlled by the United States. The collapse of the socialist bloc drastically changed the capitalist world system. Globalization as a "new hot war" proceeds at an unprecedented pace and scale, destroying traditional national boundaries and expanding the economic networks into the whole world.

Globalization endangers newly democratizing societies, invoking the dominance of neoliberalism which allows the unlimited exploitation of workers by capital at the international level as well as at the national level. South Korea, experiencing democratization as well as globalization at the same time, reveals the most contested case of the cross-current effects of globalization on domestic class politics. As the authoritarian developmental state loses its administrative capability to intervene in the market, so private capital moves in to replace the role of the state in exercising ruthless power over the workers through the state apparatus. The state lost major leverage during the democratization, whereas capital gains power under the umbrella of globalization.

However, the process in South Korea has not turned out to be linear and one-sided because of the challenge from the labor unions. There have been continuous, discursive struggles and class conflicts. These are bound to be renewed as a result of the financial crisis of 1997 which continues to place additional pressure on industrial and social relations. While the capitalist class defines globalization as unlimited or limitless competition in the world market and as the justification for wage restriction and worker conformity, labor unions define it as the improvement of labor rights to the level of international standards. The Kim government adopted the capitalist view of globalization and propagated it in order to change the state apparatus. As the state uses globalization as political legitimization and allows capital to take an hegemonic position, labor unions could challenge the neoliberalist state by mobilizing the latent discontent of the people as well as of workers.[24]

The South Korean case reveals that globalization in the newly democratizing countries significantly limits the development of democracy. Thus the neoliberal version of globalization in South Korea is no longer neoliberal but anti-liberal in its political ideology. If we extrapolate the South Korean experience of globalization, we can conclude that globalization without any restriction is apt to endanger democracy in general, generating imbalances in power between the capitalist class and the working class. However, ruthless globalization carried out by the state and capital can generate massive workers' resistance. With the help of popular support, the struggle against globalization in South Korea succeeded in revoking ascendance of neoliberalism which leads to social polarization, worsening wealth distribution and generating larger residual groups which cannot survive without state welfare, and last but not least intensifying class conflicts. The general strike in Korea teaches us that the offensive position of unions with the support of the people is the best defense against authoritarian politics and neoliberal economics.

Bibliography

Axford, B. (1995) *The Global System: Economics, Politics and Culture*, New York: St. Martin Press.

Burton Jr, D. F. (1994) "Competitiveness: Here to Stay," in B. Roberts (ed.) *New Forces in the World Economy*, Cambridge MA: The MIT Press.

Cotton, J. (1992) "Understanding the State in South Korea," *Comparative Political Studies* 24 (1).

Cox, R. (1987) *Production, Power, and World-Order: Social Forces in the Making of History*, New York: Columbia University Press.

Donga Daily News (1996) *Donga Annual Report.*

Esping-Anderson, G. (1992) "The Emerging Realignment Between Labour Movements and Welfare States," in M. Ragine (ed.) *The Future of Labour Movements,* London: Sage.

The Group of Lisbon (1995) *Limits to Competition,* Cambridge MA: MIT Press.

Hangyerae Daily News (1997) *Hangyerae 21,* various issues.

Hirst, P. and Thompson, G. (1996) *Globalization in Question,* London: Polity Press.

KDI (1995) *Major Indicator in Economic Trends,* May.

Kofman, E. and Youngs, G. (1996) *Globalization: Theory and Practice,* London: Pinter.

Korea Labour Institute (1997) *The Profile of Korean Human Assets: Labour Statistics.*

—— (1997) *KLI Labour Statistics.*

Korean Development Institute (KDI) (1994) *Economic Policy in the Period of Opening,* Seoul: Mirae (in Korean).

—— (1995) *Major Indicators in Economic Trends,* May.

Korean Labour and Society Institute (1997) *Progress of Korean Labour Movement,* Special Issue for Labour and Society Studies, January.

Krugman, P. (1994) "Competitiveness: A Dangerous Obsession," *Foreign Affairs* 73.

Mittelman, J. H. (ed.) (1997) *Globalization: Critical Reflections,* Boulder CO: Lynne Rienner.

Ohmae, K. (1990) *The Borderless World,* London: Collins.

—— (1993) "The Rise of the Region State," *Foreign Affairs,* Spring.

Petras, J. (1997) "Alternative to Neoliberalism in Latin America," *Latin American Perspectives* 24 (1).

Shin, K. Y. (1997) "Industrial Relations and Political Transition," in *Korea Sasang,* Summer (in Korean).

—— (forthcoming) "Industrialization and Economic Development in the East Asian Nations: The Case of Korea and Taiwan," in Eun Mee Kim (ed.) *Four Tigers,* New York: Academic Press.

World Bank (1995) *World Development Report: Workers in an Integrating World,* Oxford: Oxford University Press.

9 Globalization, democratization, and labor social welfare in Thailand[1]

Johannes Dragsbaek Schmidt

In the period preceding the crisis in July 1997, Thailand had enjoyed two decades of strong economic growth though marked by growing disparities in wealth and power. In this context one important characteristic of Thai politics has been the confrontation between increasing demands for public social welfare and democratization and the hegemonic anti-entitlement ideology of the political elite which is operating in an international environment of competitive austerity.

This chapter examines the twin aspects of social welfare and democracy, and the location of the "Thai-style" developmental state in the framework of globalization. First, it situates this particular type of state in relation to export-orientation and social welfare; this is followed by a brief critique of the evolution of the concept of democracy and proposes a definition of (Western-style) democracy first and foremost as an ideology or discourse. "Democratization" it is suggested needs to be applied as an actor's concept and as a social and political process. Finally, an attempt is made to assess the recent role of labor in making social and political demands on governing elites and the reverse role of these elites' efforts to secure popular compliance. However, at the same time elites are under a constant double-pressure either to comply or act against external demands regarding *universal* standards of democracy and social welfare, and the hegemony of neoliberal globalization which limits some policy options and threatens others.

Globalization and the Southeast Asian growth model

We seemingly live in a world where *globalization* is presented by the dominant neoliberal discourse like the bullet train from Osaka to Tokyo. "If you miss it, it's gone and there is no way to catch up." According to this view, the world belongs to those who are willing to give up their loyalties to community and nation—people and places—who seek identities in the global marketplace.

It is within the framework of a changing global environment—politically, economically, as well as industrially—that *social change* occurs. The manner and processes through which social change is brought about are also highly important, as are the ramifications of social change on social classes and on other emerging social and economic groups. Globalization results in increasing social disparities causing severe economic dislocation and social instability, and equally serious ecological imbalances. It is in this context that the relationship between globalization and social welfare becomes important, both in order to understand responses at the nation-state level and also because it creates more resistance from social groups and classes against globalization. While much has been written on globalization and on the crisis of the welfare state, the relationship between these two contemporary phenomena has not been well articulated, especially not in Southeast Asia.

The major argument in this chapter is that Southeast Asian leaders have deliberately pursued economic growth by emphasizing international competition through a calculated export-led strategy and avoided what is termed generous social welfare programs. This essentially anti-entitlement attitude has laid the groundwork for a stable social order based on the family and a specific set of shared social values. Policy-making in this regard has promoted a political culture which claims that social policy reduces productivity.

Before the crisis, the Washington Consensus hailed East Asia as a success based on the limited role of the state, low public expenditures, lax regulation, and low taxation. The market-allocated wealth automatically and efficiently *trickled-down* and thereby minimized social inequalities. Implicitly the objective of this neoliberal position has served to rationalize the competition between the different national socio-economic units in the world economy thereby offering transnational capital the best conditions possible. Since investment in manufactured production and services increasingly favors countries with low wages, and with minimal social security, health, safety, and environmental costs, competition becomes a zero-sum social game (Schmidt 2000).

Trade competition likewise creates immense pressures on states and firms to restructure in the West. East Asia's relative success in terms of high economic growth can be viewed as a challenge to the "advanced" countries, a challenge that is perhaps stronger and more antagonistic than was the case with *real-existing socialism* in the former Soviet-type economies. The reason is that it involves, among other things, traditional trade and commercial rivalry as well as clashes for global market shares and market penetration, and it raises the question of which model of capitalism has been the most efficient and replicable for other catching-up economies (Schmidt forthcoming).

This is probably why, beginning in the mid-1980s, global neoliberal discipline was induced in bureaucracies and institutions in East Asia. Globalization was also a factor in limiting social policy options by disseminating expectations and behaviors. This discourse emanating from the Washington Consensus described above plays a considerable role in the current restructuring of the East and Southeast Asian state.

Although the international ideological environment is primarily in favor of neoliberal globalization there are also pressures from the West on public authorities in the East to increase labor and other social rights. Public social welfare expenditures have seemingly become an important element in global economic competition and in hegemonizing the ideological sphere which defines the norms and values in relation to the international political economy. This is also one explanation why anti-welfare ideology has become the main motivation behind the debate about Asian *values*. When Mahathir and Lee Kuan Yew speak of the discipline and self-control that distinguish East Asia from what is considered Western social decay and breakdown they actually speak to a regional and domestic audience in order to justify authoritarianism and repression of political and social rights.

Thailand's dilemma of having to face the external and neighboring pressures of economic competition at the same time as demands for welfare are growing, is related to its type of economy. Various statistical studies show that much of Thailand's growth has been driven by a massive increase in domestic labor force participation as well as capital, critical parts of which have come from abroad. But these inputs have been difficult to sustain (Asher 1997: 9). This not only implies a leveling off of high rates of growth, but also makes a transition to a higher level of social security more difficult, as such a transition could acutely impinge on the international competitiveness of the economy (Asher 1995: 16). This situation has become even more complicated since the financial-cum-social crisis of July 1997, on which I will comment only briefly in the final part of this chapter.

Export-orientation and social welfare in Thailand

Thai governments and policy-makers have historically been able to interpret the past in order to justify their lack of enthusiasm for Western-type welfare states. In 1983 the prime minister expressed Thai elite thinking regarding stigmatism by noting that "culturally the Thai behavior and way of life are inactive . . . Lack of ambition is the big enemy of the Thai way of life . . . The democratic government must take some action by the establishment of the Department of Public Welfare as the tool for action" (Wongchai 1985: 357 and 363). The implication of this paternalistic political culture of the elite has been a policy more inclined to individual charity and comparatively very low social expenditures.

At the beginning of the 1980s, the Thai Department of Welfare spent less than 0.5 percent of the total government budget on social benefits (Wongchai 1985: 363). In the 1990s, official social security schemes (covered by the Social Security Act) became available only to formal sector workers in the civil service and those working in enterprises employing ten or more workers. Those working in the informal sector did not receive protection under the labor law, nor were they covered by social security provisions. The consequences have been extreme problems of social exclusion due to uneven development and unfair institutional arrangements, such as inadequate provision of basic social goods (Pongpaichit et al. 1995: 151 and 159). Such comparatively very low expenditure on social welfare is not a coincidence but is closely related to the predominant but extremely fragile development model which is based on export and high-speed growth.

The implementation of the export-oriented industrialization (EOI) strategy in Thailand has differed in a number of ways from the experience of Korea and Taiwan as newly industrialized countries (Bernard and Ravenhill 1995; Schmidt 1997). In the Thai case, according to Piriyarangsan and Poonpanich (1994: 249– 50), "the external factors for policy reform were the inflow of international capital and the relocation of light industries into the country. The internal factors were pressure from the local business sector, liberal technocrats and foreign advisors advocating a more liberal development strategy." High domestic savings and investment were not significant factors.

Labor discipline and peaceful industrial labor is always a prerequisite for EOI development based on cheap labor. The disciplined labor pool in Thailand since the mid-1970s was the result of the political exclusion of labor through the indirect intervention of the state. First, the state created a legal framework for industrial relations which encouraged weak and fragmented unionism. Another form of indirect control of labor was the establishment of institutional conditions for wage negotiation in the labor market. Only in a few instances was wage bargaining in accordance with the minimum wage policy implemented under the supervision of the tripartite National Wage Committee. This also explains why, historically, labor union activity in Thailand has been weak and why organized labor has only recently been able to influence the public agenda of social welfare significantly. This situation also had serious implications for labor's bargaining leverage and the resulting wage levels.

Minimum wages represent a relatively small proportion of average wages, and have shown no upward trend in real terms, and have lacked serious implementation (Khan 1995: 88). The stress on EOI led to a policy of wage restraint (in contrast to South Korea, where wages have risen as a result of labor shortages, but where the process of industrialization is much more advanced) and unsuccessful attempts to promote institutional frameworks which could limit conflicts in industrial relations (Deyo 1989). In short, the policy has been marked by restraint and a laissez-faire environment with below minimum wages, child labor and an authoritarian work environment.

Although there have been periods of repression and periods of free organization of labor in Thailand, the development strategy of the political elite and business has always marginalized labor. The same type of labor market regulation (usually tight and repressive with brief periods of looser policies) has severely weakened trade unionism and made it susceptible to cooption by the state. The key problem, no matter how one defines democracy, has been political representation. Labor and other marginalized groups (farmers) have never had an institutionalized voice in the political arena, except for a brief period between 1973 and 1976. Historical evidence shows that this is not a matter of "new politics" but is related to repression and the outlawing of alternatives to the dominant discourse of non-distributive growth, exports and elite paternalism.

The relative liberty enjoyed by Thai trade unions in the period 1973–6 was undermined by the pro-military government that followed at the end of 1976. In 1991, the National Peace-Keeping Council (NPKC) banned industrial action by

prohibiting strikes and disuniting the relatively stronger public trade union movement and its much weaker counterpart in the private sector.

After the downfall of the NPKC in 1992 and the reinstallation of a civilian
regime, labor cutbacks in the textile industries, associated with the development
of new managerial styles, resulted in strikes and protests by workers. According
to former director-general of the Labor Department Nikom Chandravithun
(quoted in Bierling 1995: 104), "there is now an awakening among low level
workers about their rights and privileges under the law . . . There is a rise in
expectations . . . only an estimated 30 percent of companies paid the minimum
wage of Baht 125 a day . . . In the textile industry, workers on average were paid
only Baht 4,000 a month for a 60-hour week, often in poor working conditions."
But as Piriyarangsan and Poonpanich (1994: 223) point out, the main problem is
that, "although the number of wage earners increased, proletarian concentration
in the Marxist sense rarely occurred in Thailand."

Labor market regulation has focused on oppression of trade union organization or alternatively coopting labor under state guidance. The fight for labor
welfare, i.e. improvement in pay and working conditions, has been a dangerous
and sometimes deadly affair.

By comparison, one of the contributing determinants behind the low levels
of inequality in Japan and the NICs (Taiwan and South Korea) was the
insignificance of foreign private capital. This deviation from the NICs and Japan
on the distributional factor raises the question of whether foreign investment
improves general welfare (and in particular the welfare of workers) or whether it
contributes to further uneven development. How do these problems relate to
Thailand? This question is closely linked to the conditions of work and labor
organization.

Labor regulation and EOI: a regional perspective

In Southeast Asia working conditions are, in general, unregulated; working hours
of up to 60–65 hours per week are not unusual, productivity demands are
intense, and welfare conditions are dehumanizing (as seen in the widespread
abuse of child labor). In Thailand it has been estimated that more than 1 million
children between the ages of seven and eleven years—approximately 20 percent
of the non-agricultural workforce—were employed in the urban sector (Turton
1984: 35). This background partly explains the "re-emergence" in the mid-1990s
of militant unionism (Hewison 1989) which in the longer term may challenge
neoliberalism and globalization as embodied in the TNC policies toward labor
and social welfare.

An example of TNC misconduct was a fire at a Thailand toy factory which
killed 188 workers; management had locked them inside the plant and had not
maintained the sprinkler system. Such bad working conditions can also be interpreted as a result of the extremely low level of unionization in Thailand and "the
race to the bottom"—for instance, in 1990, there were over 700 (enterprise-
based) unions with a total membership of 300,000. However after the abolition

of the state enterprise unions in 1991 only 645 unions remained with a total membership of 160,000. The enterprise union approach was adopted in the private sector by Japanese TNCs toward workers and unions in the overseas subsidiaries of these companies. But one study reveals that employment arrangements, working conditions and industrial relations practices in three Thai subsidiaries did not equate with those existing in the parent company in Japan (Williamson 1991: 17–25).

In contrast to Japan, Korea, and Taiwan, all countries in ASEAN are characterized by high income inequalities. Thailand's significant economic growth has concentrated nearly 60 percent of its wealth in the hands of 20 percent of the people. Data on Singapore, Malaysia, and Thailand show that over one-third of household incomes accrue to the richest 10 percent of the population. Such skewed income distribution reflects sharp internal social and economic divisions along ethnic, regional, and class lines which several decades of rapid growth have apparently done little to remove and indeed have aggravated (Booth 1995: 43). These emerging inequalities are reflected in calls for change not only from labor, but also from other societal forces.

There are several factors—the media and the NGOs, for instance—which play an important role in the construction of the hybrid welfare state in Thailand. Pressures for social reform come from a variety of other domestic forces. Women's emancipation and, in particular, the rising expectations of burgeoning labor organizations, and to some degree peasants' collective protests, all have considerable importance; but these forces have been severely restrained under so-called "exclusionary democracy" (Deyo 1995: 141). Even in high profile, authoritarian Singapore, women's groups have put pressure on the government to extend social security to single mothers, but without success. The People's Action Party (PAP) government stresses that it is not labor which is the problem. Trade unions are essentially controlled by the state and have no real bargaining powers. The government's biggest worry, however, is popular culture—television, rock music, the buy-now-pay-later advertisements, conspicuous consumption, the desire for more material goods. The government sees this as eroding the traditional virtues of hard work, thrift, personal responsibility, and family ties. Together with pressures from the West on Singapore to set up a welfare state, these are the challenges which the discourse on Asian values tries to confront (Tong 1994: 420 and 422). However, in other parts of East and Southeast Asia the major pressures for social welfare and democratization come from labor.

The growing importance of organized labor in South Korea and Taiwan put pressure on the governments to increase welfare standards (Kim 1995: 133–61; Frenkel 1995: 178–9). This was also evident in the overthrow of the Marcos regime in the Philippines through the People's Revolution leading to growing popular expectations of a more just and less unequal social system. The conjunction of this pressure with the financial crisis in 1997 created a very explosive situation.

Thailand likewise experienced several confrontations around the end of the 1980s and in the 1990s between the state, capital, and labor:

[While] unions have been able to preserve previously won gains and security through resistance to privatization, outsourcing and flexibilization, they evoke continued coercive state controls. Thus, for example, Thai labor repression has been sustained in the state enterprises sector, where unions effectively blocked privatization efforts and provided national leadership in labor's successful struggle to force the passage of expanded social security legislation in 1990.

(Deyo 1995: 141)

This background suggests another explanation for the military coup d'état which occurred soon after.

The impact of neoliberal globalization in Thailand has led to increasing demands for privatization of the energy sector, but unions are fiercely trying to halt privatization. Thamyudh Suthivicha, president of the State Enterprises Employees Association, delivered an ultimatum to the government: "Drop EGAT's privatization before 18 April or the union will more than double the number of protesters on Bangkok's streets from the present 20,000—mostly members of the Assembly of the Poor" (Pothong 1997). The result of privatization would be the laying-off of workers in other sectors as well.

Labor welfare and the role of TNCs

As noted above, until 1997 labor regulation in Southeast Asia had emerged in different forms. In Indonesia, it was direct military intervention; in Thailand, less than 5 percent of industrial workers were in unions; in Malaysia, labor market relations were mediated through bureaucratic unionism similar to Japanese-style enterprise unionism, combined with harsh internal security laws that have been used to incarcerate labor activists; in the Philippines, weak enterprise unionism was combined with state-sponsored violence in the form of vigilante action against alternative radical labor organizations. Despite the differing forms, they all reveal a high degree of coercive state intervention against the interests of labor (Lambert 1993: 34, fn. 9), and as mentioned, this strategy is closely related to the interests of foreign capital.

Hence, the aim of labor legislation in the region has essentially been to attract foreign capital and to develop the EOI sectors. In the case of TNC operations several studies found that, since 1985, a significant number of Japanese firms have sought to undermine union organization with a range of tactics. These include sacking union leaders, forming pro-company second unions, employing temporary workers to break strikes, and matching union wage demands with their own counter-demands which would result in worse conditions. While Japanese TNCs may preach cooperative industrial relations, Williamson (1991) and Kosaisuk (1990) found that it is evident that they actually do the opposite of what is regarded as normal labor-management relations back home in Japan.

Foreign direct investment by transnational corporations tends to be less sensitive to social concerns and to political pressures of national and regional authorities.[2] Thus, TNC workers in Southeast Asian "would-be-NICs" are more exploited and inhibited from participating in labor union activities than their few colleagues in the Northeast Asian NICs; they are effectively prevented from having autonomous workers' organizations to defend their standards of living through collective action. TNC workers are almost wholly dependent upon the goodwill of management. Data show that all the states in the region intervened directly in slightly over one-half (51.9 percent) of labor actions between 1968 and 1983. Workers were fired in 49.0 percent of the events; detained in 12.2 percent; injured in 8.2 percent; and forced out of work in 32.7 percent. At least one form of repression occurred in two-thirds (67.3 percent) of the cases.[3] Most of these labor actions took place in foreign-owned factories, but despite this TNC workers still seem to be better off than workers in the domestic business sector.

Charles Gray, executive director of the AFL-CIO's Asian-American Free Labor Institute (noted for its pro-business stance), noted in 1990[4] that TNCs "generally insist the host government suppress the right of workers to organize and join unions, even when that right is guaranteed in the country's own constitution and laws." The organization that coordinates trade in GATT (WTO) does not have a single rule that "covers the subsidies that transnational corporations get through pressures on Third World governments to permit 19th century-type exploitation of labor." In China's Guangdong province, hailed as one of the miracles of capitalist success, when the government found that "the factory of a leading toy manufacturer was engaged in labor law violations—such as 14-hour workdays and seven-day workweeks—it approached the managers to ask them to respect the law. The managers refused, and said that if they were unable to operate the way they wanted they would close their Chinese factories and move to Thailand"—a country where there are no such unreasonable demands.

Labor and social welfare in Thailand

The suppression of trade unions in Thailand for the purpose of EOI policies has caused the erosion of real wages. The industrial working-class is small, with a restrained political potential and mobilization. It has been easy for the state and policy elites to establish domination over the labor movements. Unions in Thailand have also traditionally been small and fragmented, and occasionally have come under the influence of factions in the military and the government (Crouch and Morley 1993: 285).

Thus the lack of bargaining power of the working class is also accentuated by both unemployment and widespread underemployment. Considering the sectoral distribution of production structures and the labor force it is significant that Thai society has not experienced a substantial shift to agro-industrialism. The proportion of the workforce in manufacturing and construction is below 15 percent. More than half of the total working population is in agriculture (and some claim the figure is as high as 80 percent), thus showing a much lower level of employment transition and mobility. Importantly, it shows that productivity is very low in the rural areas, a problem associated with the fact that Thai farmers are still waiting for the implementation of land reforms.

The tactics used by the Thai government and employers remain current in other Southeast Asian countries, but the new response by labor against cooption and repression is also duplicated throughout the region.

However, due to international pressure and the present period of democratic development, there are signs that the legitimacy of state-sponsored and employer-dominated labor unions is being eroded and that independent, representative organizations are emerging within an atmosphere of growing militancy.[5] Several international organizations such as the AAFLI, ICFTU, and ILO have been lobbying Western governments to impose trade sanctions as a protest against the widespread disbanding of unions, the ban on strikes, and other government-induced industrial government action. There is no doubt that labor welfare campaigns and common strategies aimed at the establishment of social security systems and other solidarity measures have been increasing, not only in Thailand, but all over the Southeast Asian region (Brown and Frenkel 1995: 82–106).

In Thailand, evidence shows that because the state policies have proved inadequate for improving the income and welfare of employees to catch up with inflation, workers' demands initially concentrated on wage increases. But this pattern has been changing. This is clear from the fact that "major issues of labor disputes from 1987 to 1989 concerned welfare (33 percent), wages (20 percent), conditions of employment (18 percent), and other issues (29 percent)" (Piriyarangsan and Poonpanich 1994: 241). The struggle to obtain social security protection in Thailand dates back to the 1950s, but in the late 1980s renewed pressure through public demonstrations and campaigns from the Labor Congress and Trades Union Congress resulted in the promulgation of the Social Security Act of 1990 (Brown and Frenkel 1995: 104). The first phase was implemented in 1992 and covers health insurance, maternity benefit, disability benefit, and death benefit. The scheme is financed by employers, employees, and the government, with each paying 1.5 percent of wages as contributions, but there is serious debate about the second phase (Asher 1995: 16).

Globally, "flexibility" has become the buzzword for dismantling the welfare state, including the sort of hybrid welfare state that exists in Thailand. However, this is now being contested from below by demands for democratization and social reform. The problematic about social welfare in Thailand has closely followed the neoliberal ideology of globalization, which is essentially a matter of identifying needs, solving problems, and creating opportunities at the individual level. The causes behind the needs for support are believed to rest overwhelmingly on individuals and subcultural defects and dispositions. Responsibility is deflected from states and national economic, administrative, and legal organizations to individuals and groups. Little or no attention is paid to the interacting consequences of economic and social change for families, employment, taxation, housing, social security and public services. Laissez-faire individualism and the legitimization of discrimination are in fact the intellectual sources of this tradition. This is why the macroeconomic dogma, characterized by neoclassical and neo-institutionalist explanations, claims that high economic growth leads to significant general improvements in the living conditions and incomes of the poor. However, the Thai experience contests the validity of this assertion. Thus, despite high growth rates the reduction in poverty, though significant, has been comparatively modest. The rate of decline has not been enough to bring about any significant fall in the absolute number of the poor.

This particular Thai version of social welfare is in practice closely based on welfare theories about social philanthropy which, implicitly and sometimes explicitly, contradicts democratization and politicization from below. It is difficult to discern anything specifically Asian in this, except for the fact that this version rests on a particular ideology—authoritarian paternalism—which is used as a repressive tool to discipline labor's demands for social security and, more generally, demands which could humanize and socialize work and living conditions and economic relations.

The twin quests for democracy and social welfare: the switching pattern

The explanation as to why democracy and democratization in certain periods develop and in other periods are destroyed, demands a more open-ended debate and framework. European history has shown that democracy as well as fascism, colonialism, and imperialism have been political components of the various modernization processes. Seen in this light democracy is a rather recent phenomenon. As Carole Pateman (1996: 8) has argued, "political scientists frequently present citizenship in the West as a slow, gradual incorporation of various sections of the population; on the contrary, it was as much a matter of exclusion as inclusion." In the last century or so, Japan has experienced constant economic growth, but Japanese-style capitalism does not produce or even seem to need political democracy in order to function. In other words, the periods of greatest economic growth in Japan have coincided with periods of authoritarianism, not with periods of democracy, as Western theory suggests. Is the same causality at work in Thailand? If this (Western) tautology is wrong how then is it possible to understand the Thai process of democratization?

In the general discussion of the evolution of societies in the global system, this question historically speaking was rather recently raised. Can the widespread democratization process yield similar end-products in different parts of the world which are endowed with vastly different heritages and history, or will we see the emergence of variant democratic models? Further, will democratization lead to increased social welfare?

Most conventional definitions of democracy project an ideal-type model for emulating by all states and nations, while radical theory sees democratization as a never-ending process emanating from below—that is, defined as a concept involving power relations and constellations within society. Democratization means social, political and human rights, the right to free speech, organizational freedom (i.e. labor rights), and other popular demands directed to the state. In general, democratization—the devolution of state power from military dictators and one-party bureaucracies to civilian democrats—can be seen as a political response to a generic economic crisis, while democracy as a regime-form can be seen as part and parcel of the hegemony of neoliberalism (i.e. by the concerted effort of state bureaucrats to demilitarize, privatize, and demercantilize the state and the economy in an effort to respond to globalization and resolve outstanding economic problems and to lay the basis for economic growth) (Scaeffer 1993: 170).

Instead of presenting democracy as an ideal political system that humans only imperfectly realize, the aim here is to conceptualize democracy and democratization as being repeatedly reinvented. Instead of treating the political institutions and practices as largely a product of separate national histories and cultures, this chapter has focused on how economic changes flow across national frontiers and the ways in which those in power, in different countries, influence one another. Instead of reducing democracy to well-defined routine practices and institutions such as elections and parliaments, it is actually social movements which repeatedly challenge and transform existing institutions.

Democracy carries within it not only the conflicts of the present moment but also the legacy of past waves of democratization, which have shaped what is meant by democracy. It is mirrored in any comparison of regime-forms and levels of (semi/soft/hard etc.) authoritarianism, transitions, creations of temporary political pacts, democracy, etc. Thailand, for example, exhibits quite different patterns of *democracy* in its mainstream definition.

Thailand has been a case of a political regime in transition. Until the mid-1970s, the regime comprised a narrow elite drawn from the army officer corps in alliance with senior bureaucrats. Virtually all other sectors were excluded from policy-making, and the regime was based on paternalism and authoritarianism. Thailand went through three major political events—in 1973, 1976, and 1992—and each was treated differently by the state. Although these are examined in detail elsewhere,[6] the reason why Thailand and other Southeast Asian societies have switched between democracy and authoritarian regimes is essentially a social problem.

No country in Southeast Asia (except perhaps Malaysia, Singapore, and Vietnam) has a binding and well-functioning social contract as Rousseau defined it. The legitimacy of the governments and state bureaucracies in Thailand and Indonesia, and to a certain extent also in the Philippines is based on economic growth and an attempt to promote social order (Schmidt 1998: 54).

Some scholars suggest that the traditions of royalty in Thailand and the Pancasila ideology in Indonesia perform a similar function. But these models are extremely fragile, because they are personalized and thereby point to a permanent state of uncertainty, which is furthermore exaggerated by heavy interference from the United States and the Washington Consensus. The United States is both a role model in a love and hate relationship, and a very important actor in internal Thai politics.

As a matter of fact, what is often forgotten in international debates about democracy is that one of the biggest obstacles to democracy in the Third World since World War II has been and still is the United States. The list of incidents where US intervention in the name of the Cold War has followed the outcome of general elections is long indeed—Guatemala, Iran/Persia, Grenada, and Chile, just to mention a few. Even so, the American democratic model and experience had little impact in Asia, apart from the Philippines. According to Samuel Huntington, American democracy has been shaped by an English heritage, empty spaces, and free land, the absence of an aristocracy, massive immigration, vertical and horizontal social mobility, minimum government, and a pervasive middle-class liberal ethos. No similar combination of factors exists anywhere in Asia (Huntington 1994: 37–8). In fact, permanent democracy is rare, and instead a series of "switches in and out of democracy" has been the pattern (Johnston 1993: 161). This helps to explain the historical and contemporary dilemma of Thai democracy, based on the interaction of socio-economic and political influences.

As pointed out by Johnston and as indicated in Figure 9.1 the reason for this switching pattern is related to the fact that the state has to balance its roles for *promotion of accumulation* and *legitimization of capitalism*. At point 1 in the diagram, the country concerned is a democracy. The government has to react to the expectations of the electorate which put it there and will determine its future; it does this by creating welfare and corporate state structures. These actions may stimulate inflation if expectations are met in part by the government creating money to stimulate demand in the economy; and this generates further wage demands to sustain current expectations, let alone rising ones. The government must increase its taxation levels and borrowing requirements to meet some of these demands, thereby making the country less attractive to investors, both external and local. The consequence is capital flight and a rationality crisis: there are fewer jobs to create the wealth from which to meet the rising expectations. The government cannot be too harsh in its treatment of the population because of its fears of electoral consequences. Political and civil disorder is likely, however, until eventually democracy is replaced—almost invariably by the military, probably covertly linked to one or more of the capitalist core states—in order to bring order and stability (Johnston 1993: 162).

Furthermore, Johnston notes that the new government is able to encourage investment by imposing repressive policies on the local population and thus providing the stability needed to attract capital. Jobs are created and prosperity slowly grows, especially for the middle classes and to a lesser extent for those who obtain work. The welfare and corporate structures are weak, however, and the expectations of many may not be met. The government may promise a *return to democracy* once prosperity is restored and stability is ensured, but the growing resentment against the repressive policies may reflect an impatience with the pace of delivery, especially if the economic benefits of those policies accrue to a small number only. The government may well then face civil disorder, which is increasingly costly to police: eventually it may be forced to yield, so resulting in

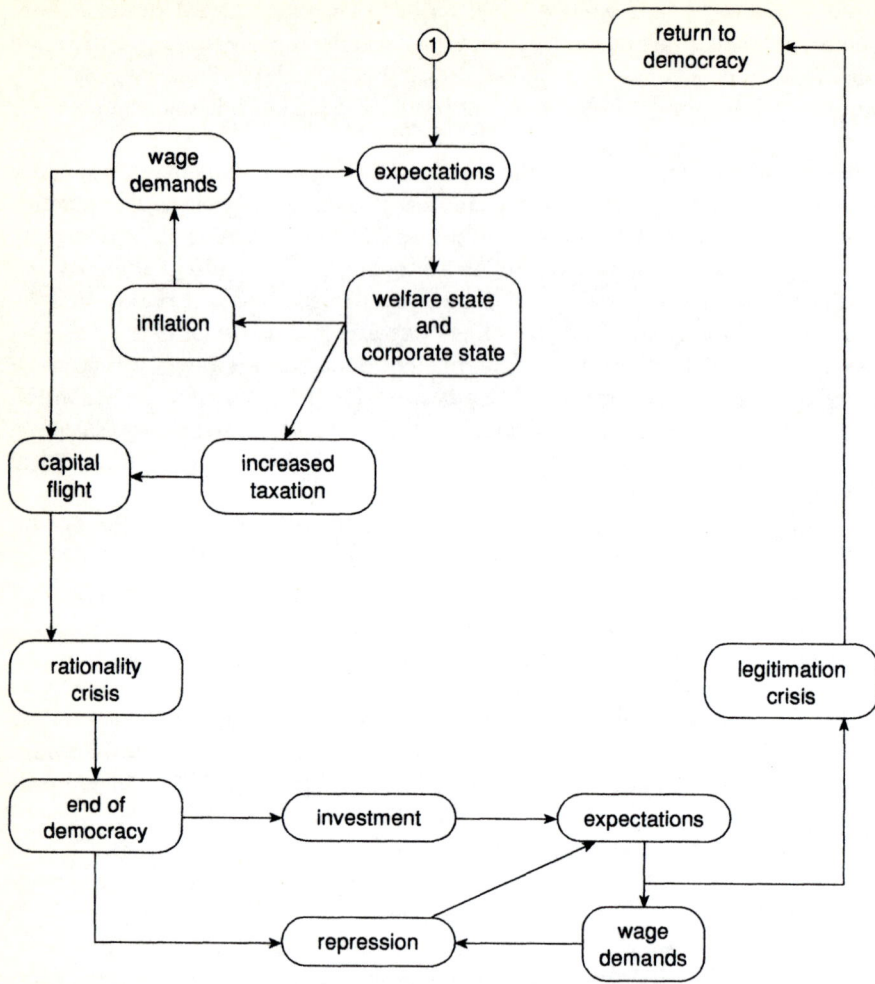

Figure 9.1 The democracy–dictatorship sequence in Third World states
Source: adapted from Johnston (1993)

a reintroduction of democracy, returning the country to the starting point of the cycle (Johnston 1993: 162–3). This model seems to provide a very good explanation of the directions taken in Thailand's history since the social democratic revolution in 1932.

Labor and social welfare under pressure

Apart from the Philippines, the other countries in the region have not yet had to face the problem of powerful domestic vested economic interests other than the politico-bureaucratic one, but capitalist growth is creating them.[7] Interestingly these emerging classes have given birth to a new literature about the role of the middle class and the nouveaux riches. The international media and mainstream American political science in particular appear to uphold these emerging actors as the real champions of democracy, equality and freedom.

These claims are increasingly being disputed by other observers who term the so-called transitionary societies of Southeast Asia, as the dictatorships of middle-class democracy.[8]

It is not the intention here to downplay the role of these much celebrated middle classes and nouveaux riches, but as Robison and Goodman (1996: ch. 1) have concluded, the emerging middle classes are most likely to tolerate author-itarian rule and xenophobic nationalism. Traditionally, experience from Europe and elsewhere tells us that it is not necessarily the wish of the middle classes and the petty bourgeoisie to share their social status or push for social reforms. On the contrary, democratization, social welfare, and pressures for a more egalitar-ian growth model, are usually the spoils of hard-fought battles from below—i.e. labor and the peasantry. This is the historical evidence from Scandinavia and, partly, Latin America; although other instances show that authoritarian regimes in collaboration with external forces in Northeast Asia created egalitarianism but without participatory politics and public welfare.

In parallel, the uprising against the Suchinda regime in 1992 was not, as is often claimed by the international media, initiated by the middle class. Rather, it was organized mostly by workers and students.[9] In fact the role of workers has been deliberately downplayed by the public media, as can be seen by the treat-ment of the number of casualties in Thailand: "Those injured came from all levels within society, and can be sub-classified as laborers (42%), unknown (16%), businesspersons (14%), students (12%), lawyers (8%), government officials (4%), taxi drivers (3%), the police and the military (1%)."[10]

Whether or not political and social change is initiated within the middle class or organized from below, Thailand's reliance on EOI strategies has important implications for the rest of the world economy. The non-welfare approach not only of Thailand but also of East Asia as a whole, and the low tax levels have resulted in a number of European, North American and Japanese low-skilled jobs being exported to East Asian sites. As this chapter suggests, coercive incen-tives to work and save, and less welfare-state-inspired interventionism are all strategies of economic competition. Hence, the worry about losing jobs to South-east Asia is real, but at the same time Southeast Asians worry about losing jobs to still younger rising economies where wages are even lower. Some 800,000 people are employed in Thailand's textile and clothing industries, yet in 1993 more than 1,500 workers were laid off. According to various estimates before the financial crisis, employers talked of up to 30,000 more job losses over the next couple of years, and at the beginning of 1998 various sources estimated that over 2 million workers would be laid off, largely because of heavy private sector borrowings and lax state regulation.

It must be noted, however, that wages and productivity gains, not to mention patenting licenses and development of new technology in Thailand are by no means comparable to the gains of the NICs. Furthermore, as stressed in the

Bangkok Post (May 26, 1992) in the aftermath of the Black May incident when the Thai military carried out a bloody crackdown on demonstrators: "no matter which way one looks at it, Southeast Asia has entered a period of increased social and political instability." Business does not like instability.

The real threat to social welfare systems is the capacity of TNCs to plan on a global rather than a national scale, together with the hollow doctrine of free trade abroad and protectionism at home. Southeast Asia remains a challenge to the West, but one that is manageable and very easy to regulate if too much is at stake. The major menace is not to the external international environment but to Southeast Asian societies themselves. For it is from labor that the pressures come for a fairer distribution of the high economic growth experienced over the past decades, pressures that can challenge the established socio-political structures. I will end this chapter by presenting an example from Thailand, where the confrontation between organized labor and anti-democratic forces has been most significant.

Before the Chatichai regime was ousted in 1991 by the military, the prime minister and his advisors tried to include labor organizations in their policy dialogue. But this increased role was rejected by a number of employer groups and, significantly, the leading army generals from NKPC. General Suchinda led a spirited rejection of the Social Security Bill in the Senate, after it had been passed by the lower house, claiming it was a mere vote-winning strategy. In fact the role of the Thai military in this regard has historically been one of excluding labor and removing their right to strike. The reliance on a "hard" developmental state in political and cultural terms, combined with the exclusion of the majority of the population from the polity, and the open-door character of the neoliberal discourse, has had grave consequences for the so-called "Thai model."

In spring 1997, Thailand's economy came under severe attack from international currency speculators and its economy has slowed sharply. According to the *International Herald Tribune*, large-scale job losses, rising unemployment, labor protests, and social unrest could spread to other parts of Southeast Asia in a chain reaction. The workers at a September rally in Bangkok, mostly from factories and state enterprises threatened to bring "hundreds of thousands of laborers onto the streets" if the government did not bend to their demands.[11]

Such protests and rallies by workers and farmers demanding government help in the face of economic hardship are an indication of economic dislocation, not only in Thailand but all over Southeast Asia.

Rapid growth in the region has both created and masked social tensions. "Despite enormous achievements in alleviating poverty, Southeast Asia is widely considered by its residents to be a deeply unequal place . . . There is widespread resentment of a perceived 'wealth gap' between the plutocratic few who have made fortunes and the disadvantaged many who have not. To some extent, the fact that everybody was getting richer eased the tensions." "The problem is that reductions in living standards of between 10 percent and 25 percent are not something that politicians can easily sell to their relatively poor populations."[12]

According to the *Asia Times* misplaced labor policies of successive Thai governments, combined with a poor performing economy, are guilty in a number of incidents. In December 1996, for instance, a mob of 2,000 workers set fire to the Sanyo Electric Company headquarters in Bangkok over disputed bonus payments. Three months prior to this incident, employees at the Japanese-owned Thai Suzuki Motors Company's motorcycle factory outside Bangkok had resorted to similar strong-arm tactics by keeping management officials locked inside the factory premises for several days. In recent years there has been an increase in these kinds of incidents, as well as in the number of strikes and labor agitations.[13]

Since the 1970s, a tripartite body consisting of government, employer, and labor representatives has been active in settling disputes through dialogue, but many workers view this as inadequate. Workers have a deep distrust of government representatives, who are seen as being too biased in favor of management. About 20,000 cases reach the labor courts every year but judicial institutions, apart from being slow in settling pending cases, are also being criticized for the decisions they hand down.

The major problem is that to prevent politicization of workers, special laws have been (and continue to be) invoked in order to ban the association of unions with political parties. But as mentioned before, it is only recently, and occasionally, that the Thai political elite has allowed workers to organize, and only when there is political stability and economic growth.

What is important here is the fact that according to the *Asia Times* the problems are very well illustrated in the Chatichai government's enactment of the Social Security Bill which, as noted above, should look after basic wage, safety, insurance and employment rights of workers. Initially it was considered a significant victory for the country's labor movement, but in practice the law refers only to large industrial enterprises. In the small-scale and informal sectors no labor laws are adhered to and thousands of workers in major export industries such as garments, fisheries, toys, gems, and jewelry are working in contravention of the minimum wage and of health and safety conditions. A 1997 survey of Thai industry found that fewer than 43 percent of the Thai workforce was actually being paid the stipulated minimum wage. The obvious result is that "in the coming days, as more and more Thai companies cut costs and lay off workers to survive the economic downturn, such disputes are likely to increase. In the absence of credible intervention by state agencies, it is only the presence of organized unions capable of protecting workers' interests that will prevent the smoldering grievances of workers from igniting into actual fire."[14]

Demands for democracy and social welfare go hand in hand. During the current financial-cum-social structural crisis, which is in fact a crisis of global capitalism, labor is organizing and challenging the past 25 years of the Southeast Asian model of accumulation.

Concluding remarks

Southeast Asia's nascent labor movements, although weak at the moment, are a source of real concern for governments. South Korea, for example, experienced over 7,000 strikes between the summer of 1987 and late 1989 (almost ten per day). This has cast dark shadows over the dream of the "Pacific Century." In Southeast Asia governments are confronted by a whole new set of pressures— from increasing strikes, and labor and farmers' protests, to the new linkages between trade, loans, aid, foreign policy, and to other demands from abroad to enforce labor laws, improve working conditions, social welfare in general, and democratization from below.

The major issue has long been political stability, which has been top priority for policy-makers. In a political system consisting of an elite mostly recruited from the civil and military bureaucracy, the problem is political representation of the marginalized majority of the population. Their rights have effectively been sacrificed on the altar of economic growth and stability, which was deemed a necessary prerequisite for development.

Today Thailand stands in a vacuum. For a period of 25 years the country relied on a low-wage, labor-intensive EOI growth strategy which meant that the majority of the population was either repressed or denied political organization and representation. Students, labor, and farmers tried three times to set up preliminary social movements and political forms of institutions, but without success. The result has been what might be termed a contradiction between "urban semi-democracy" and "rural political decay."

The problem is whether the new (16th) constitutional reform will provide the necessary change which is needed to prepare Thailand's move to a more diversified and advanced economic and industrial system. Opposing this reform process are the entrenched interests—"the dark forces" located in the Ministry of Interior which control the provincial and rural areas, big business and the military. In favor is a more diversified group of intellectuals, students, parts of the middle class, various farmers' organizations, and not least organized labor. This is essentially "civil society." No one pretends that solving the contradictions between these two opposing camps is going to be easy; there is no simple recipe. Free media, NGOs, "the voice of the man in the street," "the general public," and "an open society" are all said to be the actors pushing for democracy. But even if one accepted these highly ideological (Western/American) concepts, in the case of Thailand, they don't hold much meaning. Political representation is the problem. According to trade union leaders and leaders of people's organizations it could solve the problem of interest-based politics which involves a real change of the old "bureaucratic policy."

The unresolved issues in the current type of development model in Thailand are linked to the contradictions between the rural and the urban (Bangkok) contexts: comprehensive land reform; a qualitative change away from the reliance on low-wage labor; the unresolved issues of social welfare. And not least, the big question of the situation: Who is going to pay the bill for the current economic crisis?

Confirmation of the vulnerability of the Southeast and Northeast Asian societies became obvious in the summer of 1997 with the financial and social crisis which impacted on the entire region. And it is more than likely that the aid package from the International Monetary Fund, accompanied by stringent conditions, accentuated the potential conflictual tendencies in these societies. This affects the balance of power between different social actors. Not least, the Thai elite will be surprised in the coming months and years to learn that the crisis originated in the programs imposed by the IMF and World Bank, which liberalized the capital account as fully as possible in order to achieve full integration in global financial markets. Furthermore, the reason why Thailand and the rest of East and Southeast Asia have virtually no unemployment insurance, social safety nets, and very little provision for old-age pension insurance should be found in the Washington-based multilateral institutions and not in the domestic context. Over the past 10 to 15 years, the IMF and the World Bank have constantly cast doubt on the benefits of social welfare programs and emphasized their negative budgetary consequence.

History has a habit of overturning the most confident predictions and the only safe prognostication is that we will always continue to be surprised at least by some future developments in the international system of capitalism. An economic system which requires social polarization is possible *only* in societies with high levels of marginalization. The consequences do not make for harmony. As a report from a meeting of major US businessmen in 1983 disclosed, corporate leaders have begun to fear that capitalism and democracy may be incompatible in the long run. That belief has not been discussed in public by businessmen then or since. Competitive austerity has its natural limits on a global scale even in the era of neoliberalism.

Bibliography

Asher, M. G. (1995) "Social Security Systems: A Regional Challenge," *Bangkok Post* May 18.
—— (1997) "ASEAN Countries must Adjust to a Globalized Economy," *Asia Times* January 8.
Bernard, M. and Ravenhill, J. (1995) "Beyond Product Cycles and Flying Geese. Regionalization, Hierarchy, and the Industrialization of East Asia," *World Politics* 47, January.
Bierling, J. (1995) "The 'Developing Powers': Thailand, Malaysia, the Philippines and Indonesia," *Current Sociology* 43 (1).
Booth, A. (1995) "Southeast Asian Economic Growth: Can the Momentum be Maintained?" *Southeast Asian Affairs*, Singapore: ISEAS.
Brown, A. and Frenkel, S. (1995) "Union Unevenness and Insecurity in Thailand," in S. Frenkel, *Organized Labor in the Asia-Pacific Region*, New York: ILR Press.
Callahan, W. A. (1994) "Imagining the *Demos* at the Demos: Mob Discourse in Thai Politics," *Alternatives* 19 (3).
Chomsky, N. (1991) *Deterring Democracy*, London and New York: Verso.
Cotton, J. (1991) "The Limits to Liberalization in Industrializing Asia: Three Views of the State," *Pacific Affairs* 64 (3).
Crouch, H. and Morley, J. W. (1993) "The Dynamics of Political Change," in J. W. Morley (ed.) *Driven by Growth, Political Change in the Asia-Pacific Region*, New York: M. E. Sharpe.

Deyo, F. C. (1989) *Beneath the Miracle, Labor Subordination in the New Asian Industrialism,* Berkeley: University of California Press.
—— (1995) "Capital, Labor, and State in Thai Industrial Restructuring: The Impact of Global Economic Transformations," in D. A. Smith and J. Borocz (eds) *A New World Order? Global Transformations in the Late Twentieth Century,* Westport CT: Greenwood Press.
Dhiravegin, L. (1992) *Demi Democracy,* Times Academic Press, Singapore.
Doner, R. F. (1991) "Approaches to the Politics of Economic Growth in Southeast Asia," *The Journal of Asian Studies* 50 (4).
Frenkel, S. (1995) "Exclusion in Thailand," in G. Rodgers, C. Gore, and J. B. Figueiredo, *Social Exclusion: Rhetoric, Reality, Responses,* Geneva: ILO.
Gray, C. (1990a) *Far Eastern Economic Review,* September 13.
—— (1990b) "The Guangdong Dynamo," *South,* November.
Hewison, K. (1989) *Bankers and Bureaucrats. Capital and the Role of the State in Thailand, Monograph Series 34,* Yale University Southeast Asian Studies, New Haven CT: Yale Center for International and Area Studies.
Huntington, S. P. (1994) "American Democracy in Relation to Asia," in R. Bartley, Chan Heng Chee, S. P. Huntington and Shijuro Ogata, *Democracy and Capitalism, Asian and American Perspectives,* Singapore: ISEAS.
Johnston, J. (1993) "The Rise and Decline of the Corporate-Welfare State: A Comparative Analysis in Global Context," in P. J. Taylor (ed.) *Political Geography of the Twentieth Century, A Global Analysis,* London: Belhaven Press.
Khan, A. R. (1995) "Structural Adjustment, Labor Market, and Employment," *Asian Development Review* 13 (2).
Kim, H.-J. (1995) "The Korean Union Movement in Transition," in S. Frenkel (ed.) *Organized Labor in the Asia-Pacific Region.* New York: ILR Press.
Kosaisuk, S. (1990) *Labour Against Dictatorship,* Friedrich Ebert Stiftung, Labour Museum Project, Bangkok: Arom Pongsangan Foundation.
Kowalewski, D. (1989) "Asian State Repression and Strikes Against Transnationals," in G. A. Lopez and M. Stohl (eds) *Dependence, Development and State Repression: Contributions in Political Science,* no. 209, New York: Greenwood Press.
Lambert, R. (1993) *Authoritarian State Unionism in New Order Indonesia,* Working Paper no. 25 (October), Asia Research Centre, Murdoch University, Perth, Australia.
Lambert, R. and Caspersz, D. (1995) "International Labour Standards: Challenging Globalization Ideology?" *The Pacific Review* 8 (4).
Laothamas, A. (1992a) *Business Associations and the New Political Economy of Thailand,* Boulder CO: Westview Press.
—— (1992b) "The Success of Structural Adjustment in Thailand: A Political Explanation of Economic Sucess," in A. J. MacIntyre and K. Jayasuryia (eds) *The Dynamics of Economic Policy Reform in South-East Asia and the South-West Pacific,* Singapore: Oxford University Press.
MacIntyre, A. J. and Jayasuryia, K. (eds) (1992) *The Dynamics of Economic Policy Reform in South-East Asia and the South-West Pacific,* Singapore: Oxford University Press.
Nun, J. (1968) "Latin American Phenomenon: The Middle Class Military Coup," in J. Petras and M. Zeitlin (eds) *Latin America. Reform of Revolution?* New York: Fawcett.
Pateman, C. (1996) "Democracy and Democratization," *International Political Science Review* 17 (1).
Piriyarangsan, S. and Poonpanich, K. (1994) "Labour Institutions in an Export-oriented Country: A Case Study of Thailand," in G. Rodgers (ed.) *Workers, Institutions and Economic Growth in Asia,* Geneva: ILO.

Pongpaichit, P., Piriyarangsan, S., and Treevat, N. (1995) "Patterns and Processes of Social Exclusion in Thailand," in G. Rodgers, C. Gore, and J. B. Figueiredo, *Social Exclusion: Rhetoric, Reality, Responses*, Geneva: ILO.

Pothong, V. (1997) "Union Uses Shock Tactics to Halt Thai Power Selloff," *Asia Times* March 18, 1997.

Richardson, M. (1997) "Southeast Asia: Domino Effect?" *International Herald Tribune* September 16, 1997.

Robison, R. and Goodman, D. S. G. (1996) *The New Rich in Asia: Mobile Phones, McDonalds and Middle-class Revolution*, London: Routledge.

Scaeffer, R. (1993) "Democratic Devolutions: East Asian Democratization in Comparative Perspective," in R. A. Palat (ed.) *Pacific-Asia and the Future of the World-System*, Westport CT: Greenwood Press.

Schmidt, J. D. (1993a) "Theory and Reality of Democracy and Thai Democratization," *Kasarinlan: A Philippine Quarterly of Third World Studies* 8 (3), Manila, Philippines.

—— (1993b) "State and Democracy in Thailand," *Copenhagen Papers in East and Southeast Asian Studies* 8, East Asian Institute, Copenhagen University, Tusculanum Press, Spring.

—— (1996) "Paternalism and Planning in Thailand: Facilitating Growth Without Social Benefits," in M. Parnwell (ed.) *Uneven Development in Thailand*, Aldershot: Avebury.

—— (1997) "The Challenge From Southeast Asia: Between Equity and Growth," in C. Dixon and D. Drakakis (eds) *Uneven Development in Southeast Asia*, London: Gower Avebury Press.

—— (1998) "The Custodian State and Social Change—Creating Growth Without Welfare," in J. D. Schmidt, J. Hersh, and N. Ford (eds) *Social Change in Southeast Asia*, Harlow Essex and New York: Longman.

—— (2000) "Neoliberal Globalization, Social Welfare and Trade Unionism in Southeast Asia," in B. Gills (ed.) *Globalization and the Politics of Resistance*, London: Macmillan; New York: St. Martin's Press.

—— (forthcoming) "Global Neoliberalism and Social Welfare," in J. D. Schmidt and J. Hersh (eds) *Globalization and Social Welfare in East and Southeast Asia*, London: Routledge.

Seaman, W. (1996) "The Current Crisis in Indonesia," interview with Benedict Anderson, *Zmagazine*, December 1996.

Sivaraman, S. (1997) "Lack of Thai Unions Lets Labor Problems Get Out of Hand," *Asia Times* May 1.

Tong, G. C. (1994) "Moral Values: The Foundation of a Vibrant State," address delivered at a National Day rally, August 21, 1994, quoted in "Social Values, Singapore Style," *Current History* 93 (587).

Turton, A. (1984) "Limits of Ideological Domination and the Formation of Social Consciousness," in A. Turton and S. Tanabe (eds) *History and Peasant Consciousness in South-East Asia*, Osaka: National Museum of Ethnology.

Wade, R. (1990) "Governing the Market," *Economic Theory and the Role of Government in East Asian Industrialization*, New Jersey: Princeton University Press.

—— (1996) "The Role of the State in East Asian Capitalism: Lessons for Eastern Europe," in J. Hersh and J. D. Schmidt (eds) *The Aftermath of "Real-Existing Socialism" in Eastern Europe: Between Western Europe and East Asia*, London: Macmillan; New York: St. Martin's Press.

Williamson, H. (1991) "Japanese Enterprise Unions in Transnational Companies: Prospects for International Co-operation," *Capital and Class* 45, Autumn.

Wongchai, Y. (1985) "Thailand," in J. Dixon and Hyung Shik Kim (eds) *Social Welfare in Asia*, London: Croom Helm.

Part IV

Geopolitics and intersocietal conflicts

10 States and governance in the era of "globalization"

Philip McMichael

Introduction

Much of the recent process of global restructuring has involved the transformation of states and their patterns of governance. Arguably, this is because current global economic integration is a political project in which states author changes in regulatory institutions appropriate to global market participation. Historically, states have always mediated social and political relations with local and global dimensions. The relative balance of these dimensions has varied across space (the state system) and time. The colonial system, for example, combined European mercantilism with colonial export economies. Decolonization involved a movement to reverse the colonial condition and emulate European national protectionism. Today, we find that movement in decline as states adopt policies that weaken national protections and strengthen global market relations. This chapter will examine this movement as a contradiction between the governance of markets (the "global state") and the governance of space (the *nation*-state).

Over the past two centuries, the dominant form of the state has been the nation-state, pioneered in Western Europe and its settler states (Tilly 1975; Giddens 1987; Friedmann and McMichael 1989). Much of our state theory has derived from this historical fact, including the conventions of the national unit of analysis of social structure and process. Further, much of our normative understanding of state-building has derived from this historical experience (Moore 1967; Rueschemeyer et al. 1992), and continues to frame how we think about ideal democratic forms of association and governance. Indeed, the mid-twentieth century process of decolonization, which involved the attempt to universalize the nation-state, drew its normative or ideological power from the apparent success of the European model of national development (e.g. Escobar 1995). Arguably, this attempt has been universal in form, but not in substance—given the incomplete forms of civil society, the fragility of democratic rule, and the shallow roots of formal economic arrangements in the post-colonial states, not to mention the global power structure within which this attempt occurred (Migdal 1988; Davidson 1992).

National developmentalism, as a strategy, is currently in decline. This has as much to do with its relatively weak roots within the post-colonial world as it has to do with its role as an organizing myth (McMichael 1996). Instituting a universal nation-state system was certainly an effective way of organizing the post-World War II world on behalf of the First World development establishment. However, from hindsight we can see that this "development project" has been quite limited in its impact, concentrating on core regions of the global economy, identified by Ohmae as a band of middle-class consumers in the Triad zone of the European Union, North America and the Asia-Pacific region (1995: xvi–xvii).

The incompleteness of national developmentalism is of great significance today in underlining the limits of current attempts to reinvigorate public institutional capacity in the wake of the 1980s debt crisis. As the principal development agency, the World Bank is now a convert to institution-building in the South as a stabilizing mechanism for the globalization project at large. The problem is that globalization itself is premised on public reforms that tend to deplete national resources through the erosion of the tax base and the privileging of productive activities geared to (global) market, rather than social, priorities. In my view, the Bank's new interest in "state effectiveness" is part of a broad strategy of stabilizing unstable social conditions in order to sustain the new organizing myth of "globalization" as the path to economic well-being. This strategy is implicit in the following passage from the *World Development Report 1997*:

> The cost of not opening up will be a widening gap in living standards between those countries that have integrated and those that remain outside. For lagging countries the route to higher incomes will lie in pursuing sound domestic policies and building the capability of the state. Integration gives powerful support to such policies—and increases the benefits from them— but it cannot substitute for them. *In that sense, globalization begins at home. But multilateral institutions such as the World Trade Organization have an important role to play in providing countries with the incentive to make the leap.*
>
> (World Bank 1997: 12, italics added)

My premise is that globalization is not a thing in itself, rather it is first and foremost a political project pursued by a global elite. The target is the nation-state and its policies of social regulation, which fetter profitability under current economic conditions. The two principal constraints on profitability have been the institution of wage labor and the system of capital controls associated with the Bretton Woods regime. The wage labor institution is a historical complex including nationally protected industries, minimum wage laws, public benefits and subsidies (the social wage), and the like. Capital control is a related construct whereby states, via their access to the capital market and legal restrictions on capital flight, put limits on the disposition of capital investments. With the rise of global productive capacity, and a global money market, these constraints have come under serious attack.

This line of argument has two dimensions. First, the global restructuring of capital circuits involves a simultaneous restructuring of labor and its conditions for existence: in a word, re-regulation. As Hoogvelt (1997: 148) argues, the fact of new global circuits "removes the need for capital to worry about the repro-duction of labor power or domestic markets." Second, globalization is an institutional phenomenon, and, through the re-regulation associated with global economic integration, it is transforming the conditions of governance. In short, to the extent that labor rights are diminished by the globalization project, there is a growing differentiation between the governance of the market and the governance of populations. It is important to caution the reader that I refer to a contested tendency, not an inevitable result.

Regulation and governance

Arguably, the relation between regulation and governance has undergone an inversion in the so-called era of "globalization." Post-World War II capitalist regulation proceeded from, or expressed, constitutional government, anchored in substantive principles of citizenship. But governance is conditioned now by global regulatory mechanisms, as institutions of national regulation have progressively weakened. Global regulation, based in subordinating national policies to the maintenance of global circuits of capital (e.g. "sound finance"), is transforming the conditions of governance.

Michel Aglietta's notion of "social regulation" conceptualized regulation in terms of the politics of the wage relation, including monetary relations. Through monetary regulation "the state forms part of the very existence of the wage relation," which, on a global scale, was "accompanied by the consolidation of a system of states" (Aglietta 1979: 32). In other words, regulation takes particular political forms, depending on the organization of the wage relation, which in turn depends on the organization of the state system.

It is widely acknowledged that the contemporary capitalist order has departed from the national form of social regulation associated with the Bretton Woods regime, governed by national priorities of economic management. These, in turn, were anchored in the substantive principles of citizenship associated with the era of liberalism (Rueschemeyer et al. 1992; Wallerstein 1995). Since the breakdown of the Bretton Woods regime, monetary relations within and among states have been relatively unregulated, and the stability of the global financial system depends on a series of *ad hoc* interventions by multilateral institutions and the G7 powers, sometimes via financial condominium. My argument is that these interventions enlist states in the elaboration of a global, rather than a national, wage relation (where the organization and remuneration of labor is increasingly governed by global capital movements). And, to the extent that this global wage relation depends on the removal of labor protections there is a growing crisis of governance in its traditional constitutional form.

Emergent forms of governance involve the rules of "market rationality" that abstract from the populations to which they are applied. These rules seek to remove uncertainties in circuits of capital, rather than express democratic input. That is, where constitutionalism was the governance of space (national territory), market rule is the governance of flows. We currently experience the contradictions arising from both forms of governance operating at once. The logic of market rule is the minimalization of traditional constitutional rule, and its replacement by alternative institutional forms. These are outlined below.

The demise of developmentalism and national regulation

Developmentalism was institutionalized in the development project in the post-World War II world economy. The development project was a construct through which the world capitalist economy was stabilized at that time. Like any social construct the institutions of market economy are historically specific. Just as early capitalism emerged within distinct political frameworks—pre-nineteenth-century mercantilism (trade organized to enlarge national wealth), nineteenth-century liberalism (free-trade imperialism to enlarge capitalist markets)—so mid-twentieth-century capitalism was organized within the framework of the (now universal) nation-state system.

In the post-war years, the stabilization of world capitalism occurred on global and national levels, via an internationally negotiated regime of "embedded liberalism" (Ruggie 1982). This regime combined the principles of mercantilist and liberal organization, subordinating international trade to systems of national economic management, anchored in strategic economic sectors like steel and farming. Its centerpiece was the management of national economic growth. Together, international and national institutions regulated monetary and wage relations to stabilize "national capitalisms" within this liberal trade regime. As former colonies achieved independence, they adopted, or were forced to adopt, the nation-state as the universal form of political organization. While this provided continuity to the political organization of the world's subject populations, it was by no means an equal, or uniform, state system.

The monetary regime, instituted through the Bretton Woods agreements in 1944, established the principle of fixed exchange rates and mechanisms whereby the IMF could maintain stable currency exchange by extending short-term loans to those states with payments imbalances (Block 1977). National economies, geared to stabilizing the wage relation through rising investment (in mass production) and state subsidies (to promote full-employment and rising consumption), were supported by a stable trade environment. This formula, despite its uneven implementation, is often characterized as a mix of Keynesian/Fordist political economy (Harvey 1989).

Alongside this multilateral arrangement were the geopolitical realities of the Cold War. The United States, in particular, deployed Marshall aid to redistribute dollars to capital-poor regions of the world (from Europe, through East Asia to Africa). This established the dollar as the international reserve currency and promoted freedom of enterprise, which became the litmus test of the so-called free world (Arrighi 1982). Export credits, extended to Marshall Plan recipients, facilitated the transfer of American technology. In turn, the World Bank (along with other such multilateral financial assistance institutions) disbursed long-term loan funds to encourage the habit of developmentalism (Rich 1994).

Thus, in the mid-twentieth century the foundations of capitalism were reformulated through a wholesale institutional reconstruction of the world order. Forms of international regulation (especially of monetary relations) were combined with national (wage relation) regulation. Developmentalism emerged within this institutional framework. "First World" (and Cold War) planners perceived their goal as raising and protecting living standards, and to this end pursued massive (military and economic) assistance programs. Developmentalism thus instrumentalized the nation-state as its agent through a set of complementary relations with bilateral and multilateral institutions.

Developmentalism unraveled via its own internal contradictions. As freedom of enterprise and transnational corporate integration grew, the proliferation of offshore money markets undermined the integrity of the Bretton Woods monetary regime. The growth of an unregulated global money market also encouraged a process of financialization: a contagious preference for liquid rather than fixed capital on the part of private and institutional investors. Giovanni Arrighi (1994) has identified financialization with the decline of a hegemonic state, as the resulting geo-political uncertainty discourages fixed investment. In the 1970s, private loans to industrializing states expressed this decoupling of money capital from productive capital, as global financiers banked on the NIC phenomenon and the expectation that governments would not default on loans. The stage was set for the debt crisis.

The debt crisis reversed the development project (cf. Arrighi 1990). Debt management served to reconstruct global, and hence national, monetary relations. The IMF assumed a *de facto* role of banker to the world, determining, with the World Bank, conditions by which states could renegotiate their outstanding loans, and/or service their debt. These conditions were universally imposed and adopted, as states privatized public assets, slashed social budgets, cut wages, devalued national currencies, and promoted exports. In these ways, the mechanisms of the debt regime institutionalized the power and authority of global management within states' very organizations and procedures, weakening commitments to national welfare. In other words, governance of global circuits began to override national governance concerns.

Global regulation and governance

The 1980s management of debt under the terms of monetarist ideology and policy was a dress rehearsal for a full-blown globalization project in the post-Cold War era. Since the 1990s, with the elaboration of free trade agreements (FTAs) and the creation of the World Trade Organization (WTO), the winds of global competition have intensified. The ideological goal of world scale liberalization is backed up by the institutionalization of market rules. This involves an explicit reorganization of states in order to facilitate the freedom of circuits of money capital and commodity capital.

Globalization is not specific to our era. But globalization as a view of ordering the world is. It is a historical project, just as the development project was. The development project was a view of ordering the world, but it was understood, institutionalized, and embraced as a process to be replicated in nation-states. The developmentalist elites were essentially state managers who shared an interest in stabilizing the world capitalist order, one in which First World working classes and colonial and post-colonial populist movements were demanding inclusion. These elites gathered at the United Nations and the Bretton Woods conferences in 1944, with the stated goal of raising living standards one society at a time, heading off labor and anti-colonial struggles, and establishing a realm of free enterprise to assure the flow of strategic resources to the military-industrial centers of the Free World.

The elites associated with the globalization project are of a different order. In addition to state managers (those embracing liberalization), there are the new financial and transnational corporate elites as well as the managers of newly empowered multilateral institutions like the IMF, the World Bank, and the WTO. The Bank's 1992 *World Development Report* stated: "this relationship (between corporations, the Bank and the Fund) is being strengthened to achieve greater cohesiveness in global economic policy-making." As proponents of globalization —formed in the conjuncture framed by the Trilateral Commission, debt crisis management, and the Uruguay Round of negotiations regarding global trade and investment regulation—these elites constitute what is arguably an incipient global ruling class (a segment of the transnational capitalist class described by Sklair 1997). They are concerned with the viability of the global financial system.

Global regulation, then, involves reproducing capitalism on a global scale. Since monetary relations remain relatively unregulated, and governed by the hyper-mobility of finance capital, global regulation means avoiding financial collapse. In turn this means underwriting and rescheduling debt, and facilitating global capital flows. In other words, the social content of global regulation is the subversion of national protections and public welfare. Subversion of national regulation (developmentalism) emerged as a corporate project in the 1970s, blossomed in the 1980s under the debt regime (targeting the Third and Second Worlds, but with recursive effects on the First World), and became a full-blown project on a global scale in the 1990s. It takes several forms, all of which contribute to a growing crisis of governance.

US President Reagan's monetarist counter-revolution symbolized the challenge to the substantive aspects of national regulation. A centerpiece of this was the Reagan administration's deployment of the Uruguay Round to rewrite domestic policy (Paarlberg 1992; Ritchie 1993: 7), using the rhetoric of loyalty to GATT liberalization measures to dismantle social policies and governmental regulations that "distorted" US trade relations. Unable to dislodge a powerful national farm lobby, Reagan directed the attack from the outside, via supranational institutional pressure. Not only did the Reagan administration see the Uruguay Round as a vehicle for rewriting US farm and food policy, but also it "planned to trade away a number of important domestic industries, including textiles, auto, steel, and forestry in exchange for improved market access for US-based finance and service sector transnational corporations" (Ritchie 1993: 7).

The GATT Uruguay Round complemented the debt regime, preparing the ground for the elaboration of market rule. While the multilateral financial institutions rehearsed the conditions for global regulation by imposing a standard of adjustment conditions on one state after another, the GATT negotiators devised a set of rules designed to liberalize the entire system of states. Free trade was the slogan, but freedom of investment and the protection of intellectual property rights were as significant in laying the foundations of a global market regime.

The new rules that would facilitate and guarantee global circuits of capital are bureaucratic in form. They privilege economic value over social value, reducing nations and their intercourse to an abstract market rationality. Their elaboration, and their interpretation, are profoundly unrepresentative. Bureaucrats in global agencies exert a growing influence as makers or custodians of the new market rules—this was clear from the imposition of liberalization measures on indebted states with little or no scrutiny by the citizens of those states. And this practice became extended in the WTO, which has independent jurisdiction and oversees trade in manufactures, agriculture, services, investment, and intellectual property protection. The WTO has global governing power insofar as its rules are binding on all members, and it has the potential to overrule state and local powers regulating environment, product and food safety. Its staff is made up of unelected bureaucrats, who have no constituency to answer to other than an abstract set of free trade rules and their proponents. Its proceedings deny citizen participation.

Through the WTO, global managers assume extraordinary powers to manage the web of global economic relations across the countries, at the expense of those state organizations, including their democratic achievements. They also wield a certain structural power in acting as the vehicle of global development. On April 24, 1996, the WTO director-general, Mr. Renato Ruggiero, stressed that regional initiatives by states should aim for a borderless world, "to lessen the constraints of space and time on their traders and to widen the access of their citizens to the most important raw material of the 21st century—information." This goal is premised on the privatization of development assistance. He remarked, "In a world where budgetary constraints increasingly limit traditional development aid financing, foreign direct investment is more than ever the key to development" (WTO Web Page Press Release, April 24, 1996).

Global visions notwithstanding, the world's population is not joining the global economy *en masse*. Nevertheless, many of those outside of the global economy are adversely affected, or actively marginalized, by the reduction in public capacity associated with this transformation in governance patterns. About 80 percent of the more than five billion people in the world live outside global consumer networks (Barnet and Cavanagh 1994: 383). Or, as James Speth from UNDP has remarked: "We still have more than half the people on the planet with incomes of less than $2 a day—more than 3 billion people." The *1996 Human Development Report* documents an enlarged gap between the world's (and the United States's) rich and poor, with 89 countries being worse off than they were a decade or more ago, but with 358 billionaires worldwide controlling assets greater that the combined annual incomes of countries containing 45 percent of the world's population. As Speth claims: "An emerging global elite, *mostly urban-based and interconnected in a variety of ways*, is amassing great wealth and power, while more than half of humanity is left out" (Crossette 1996: 3; italics added).

Mexico, the showcase of liberalization, FTA-style, has experienced an intensification of inequality since it joined NAFTA, with the government admitting that the numbers of Mexicans living in extreme poverty had grown by 5 million over the following 15 months. NAFTA has contributed to social (and geographical) polarization: symbolized by the collapse of the Mexican market for relatively cheap Volkswagen Beetles, and the expected 50 percent growth in sales of Mercedes-Benz. Liberalization not only has real class effects, but also divides populations, as one journalist puts it, "between those whose lives are increasingly tied to the United States economy and those who are entirely dependent on the fortunes of Mexico" (DePalma 1996).

As states embrace the globalization project, the governance of populations is increasingly subordinated to the governance of capital circuits. Liberalization shrinks public resources and capacities, removing protections and subsidies, and elites pirate the privatized resources. As markets integrate, and controls diminish, entrepreneurs prosper in the new spaces of accumulation. There are several forms expressing this change in the content of governance. For the most part states author, or assist, these alternative forms. I identify four parallel and/or nested forms here.

EPZs and disguised informalization

Export processing zones (EPZs) have been in place for almost 40 years. As specialized industrial estates they typically have minimal customs controls and are exempt from labor regulations and domestic taxes. As social and economic enclaves within their own countries, their low-paid, highly exploited and predominantly female workers constituted the new global labor force. While this world factory strategy on the part of host governments contributed to the new international division of labor, we now see a generalization of EPZ conditions in the wake of the debt crisis, referred to as "maquiladorization." We also see that the EPZ incubated a process of "disguised informalization" whereby the absence of civil rights for labor in the EPZs has been a model for the more general casualization of labor that is a significant trend across the world, and particularly in the South (Srinivasan 1996). There are some signs, however, of effective resistance to this disorganization of labor. As a consequence of the bad press that certain lines of apparel have had recently, a US presidential task force, including human rights groups, labor unions and corporate representatives, has undertaken to try to establish minimum (voluntary) standards, including the right to unionize and engage in collective bargaining (Greenhouse 1997: 1, 7). In August

1997, workers for the US-based Phillips Van Heusen Corporation succeeded in ratifying the first collective bargaining agreement in Guatemala's *maquiladora* sector, concerning organizing rights, job security, grievance procedures, wage levels, and so forth (US/Guatemala Labor Education Project 1997).

In addition to the process of maquiladorization that undercuts and/or pre-empts labor rights and therefore constitutional governance, the EPZ was the thin edge of the state-shrinking wedge, insofar as it involved tax concessions. In the 1970s for example, the Mexican government's most favorable concession for *maquila* investment was in Sonora, where TNCs were offered 100 percent tax exemption for the first ten years, and 50 percent for the next ten (Baird and McCaughan 1979: 135). Again, the EPZ represented a model of the ideal of liberalization, with erosion of the tax base as one of its legacies. The existence of such concessions reproduces the "race to the bottom" logic in tax concessions. This results in serious erosion of the basis for governance in the relationship between taxes, citizenship, and the nation-state.

Region-states

In many respects the EPZ was an incipient "region-state," which Ohmae (1995: 80) argues is the natural economic zone in a borderless world. The San Diego/ Tijuana zone grew out of the *maquiladora system*, and China's southern Special Economic Zones have in fact become the building blocks of the south China regional economy centered on Hong Kong (Pepper 1988). Ohmae claims that

> Because of the pressures operating on them, the predictable focus of nation-states is on mechanisms for propping up troubled industries . . . [whereas] Region states . . . are economic not political units, and they are anything but local in focus. They may lie within the borders of an established nation-state, but they are such powerful engines of development because their primary orientation is toward—and their primary linkage is with—the global economy. They are, in fact, its most reliable ports of entry . . . For global managers, the bright, attractive—and manageable—spots on today's development maps are not countries but bounded regions like Shanghai/Pudong, which are appealing in themselves as a market, as a base from which to provide manufactured goods and services, and as a functioning link to the borderless economy.
>
> (Ohmae 1995: 99, 89, 105)

These regional zones are "manageable" precisely because they embody many of the concessions associated with the EPZ, which are generalized now as agreements between national governments—yet another component of the governance of flows. Beijing, for example, allows China's official regions—each an "island of opportunity" in its own right—the right of independent negotiation with foreign providers of capital and infrastructure expertise (Ohmae 1995: 104).

Yet regional economic zones, like the Growth Triangle of Singapore, Johore (southern Malaysia) and the nearby Riau islands of Indonesia, go beyond the more abstract globalism of the EPZ concept to capture regional advantages. Ohmae argues: "In the past, you might have been attracted to these locations by their low rates of taxation or by their proximity to raw materials or cheap labor. Today, the attraction is increasingly the intimacy of their knowledge- and culture-rooted connection with several of the most appealing regions of growth in the world" (1995: 109). Ohmae's use of the term "region-state" is telling insofar as he is describing perhaps the purest form of flow governance, devoid of the legitimation pressures associated with macro-regional free trade agreements that must pass legislative scrutiny.

Free trade agreements (FTAs)

FTAs represent an intermediate form of state-authored globalization—applying the logic of liberalization on a macro-regional basis. Arguably the FTA phenomenon has three stimuli. First, it may reflect a defensive strategy by firms and states who distrust the intentions of other firm/state regional clusters and who move to secure their own contiguous free trade area. Second, it may reflect new strategies of regional investment as TNCs employ flexible and decentralized investment and production strategies to optimize access to the fastest growing markets. The recent importance of Mexico and China as investment locations attests to the significance of the new regional complexes of the North American Free Trade Agreement (NAFTA) and the Asia-Pacific Economic Conference (APEC), respectively. Third, and most important for my argument, FTAs institutionalize the rules governing global circuits of capital.

NAFTA exemplifies the trend conceptualized by Gill (1992) as the "new constitutionalism," by which economic rules are institutionalized in bureaucratic regimes beyond accountability to citizens of member states. But these rules are not simply imposed from above, so to speak. Agreement involves national political debate, but one very much framed by the discourse of competitiveness in the global economy, and sometimes built around symbolic concessions to global regimes. During the debates preceding the signing of NAFTA, the opposition candidate, Cuauhtémoc Cárdenas, argued that "exploitation of cheap labor energy, raw materials, technological dependency, and lax environmental protection should not be the premises upon which Mexico establishes links with the United States, Canada, and the world economy" (quoted in Resource Center 1993: 2). Nevertheless, in Mexico, the reform of Article 27 of the Constitution, privileging private investment in land over the traditional rights of *campesinos* to petition for land redistribution within the *ejido* framework, signaled that Mexico was prepared to submit to a global property regime. And, since the passage of NAFTA, the Mexican federal environmental law of 1988, supposedly guaranteeing that free trade would not harm the Mexican or the border environment, has been subject to continuing attempts to dismantle it—including a congressional modification, issued in January 1996, eliminating environmental impact assessment requirements, and decentralizing (and therefore disempowering) enforcement to state and local governments under the oxymoronic concept of "auto-regulation," and further restricting citizen scrutiny (Kelly 1996).

A potential global property regime is anticipated in the FTA process. Chapter 11 of NAFTA requires that foreign investment be accorded "national treatment"—that is, that it has the same legal standing and treatment as that given domestic investors. Article 1106 prohibits establishing performance criteria for foreign investment—such as export ratios, or links to local suppliers, or utilization of technology appropriate to the host country's resource base. In an assessment of Chile's formal negotiations to join NAFTA, which began in June 1995, Hansen-Kuhn and Leiva note:

> While accession to NAFTA would pose limited immediate problems in this regard as the principle of national treatment is generally consistent with current Chilean investment law, it would serve to tighten and lock this policy in place and block future governments from adopting alternative economic strategies that include, for example, plans for targeted industrial development. If Chile accedes to NAFTA, it will be prohibited from maintaining its current controls on flows of speculative foreign capital. One of the few remaining restrictions on foreign investment in Chile requires that foreigners maintain their investments in the country for at least one year, although profits can be repatriated at any time. Article 1109 of NAFTA prohibits this kind of limitation on the sale of investments. In fact the Clinton government has been pressuring the Chilean government to eliminate this restriction as a precursor to its accession to NAFTA despite the fact that this provision in Chilean law has discouraged the kind of volatile investment that so exacerbated the Mexican peso crisis.
>
> (Hansen-Kuhn and Leiva 1995)

Thus, the FTA not only institutionalizes a global property regime, but it also subordinates national governance to the governance of flows, namely the capital market.

Mexico is, of course, the paradigm case. NAFTA did not decree absolute opening of the Mexican economy. For example, Mexico agreed to gradually allow foreign bank entry up to a 15 percent share by 1999, and it also reserved exemptions for several state enterprises, including railroads and their satellite operations—even though NAFTA decrees that state enterprises operate "solely in accordance with commercial considerations" and refrain from using "anticompetitive practices" (quotes from Panitch 1996: 97). However, the 1994 peso crisis, stemming from the NAFTA dress rehearsal and stimulated by the Chiapas rebellion, compelled the Mexican government in 1995 to try to raise funds by allowing 100 percent ownership of Mexican financial institutions and selling off its railroads and its satellite operations. The weakening of the nation-state[1] is thus both a legal and a logical outcome of the FTA phenomenon, and anticipates a multilateral-based property regime.

Multilateral institutions

A multilateral-based global property regime involves some centralization of state power in global institutions, strengthening their ability to shape state administrative priorities. This tendency is exemplified by the World Bank's new lending criteria, whereby the Bank has shifted away from project loans to policy loans. Further, the Bank's *1992 World Development Report* stated that: "Good governance, for the World Bank, is synonymous with sound development management" (George and Sabelli 1994: 150). The Bank, as the most influential development agency in the world, insists on shaping governments rather than simply economic trajectories—a practice it refined during the 1980s by way of its Structural Adjustment Loans (see, for example, Cahn 1993).

The formal power of the multilateral institutions structures policy discourses across the debtor states. A more far-reaching, substantive, power is presaged in the negotiation over the terms of the WTO. In particular, the dispute over the reach of the WTO regarding investment is central to the institutionalization of a global property regime. While the WTO is as yet only empowered to rule on "trade-related investments" (TRIPS), the European Commission (backed by the United States and Japan) proposed a Multilateral Agreement on Investments (MAI) that would relax all restrictions on foreign investment in any member state, and grant the legal right for foreigners to invest and operate competitively in all sectors of the economy. The proposal came in the form of a paper entitled "A Level Playing Field for Direct Investment Worldwide," arguing that foreign investment is essential to today's corporate strategies, with global communications creating a near global marketplace. Multilateral rules should go beyond right of entry provisions to allow "accompanying measures" such as freedom to make financial transfers, rendering transparent domestic regulations, and so forth (Khor 1995b).

A response by 30 NGOs made three key points: first, that such a proposal would threaten national sovereignty in the determination of economic and social policies; second, the WTO is an inappropriate institution for overseeing such an agreement since it has the power of trade sanctions to discipline states in relation to these proposals, and that this is a misuse of an organization designed to establish trade, not investment, rules; and third, the proposal illustrates the unaccountability of the WTO, where select interests such as trade officials of a few major countries, and powerful financial lobbies can promote their interests through WTO rules (Khor 1995a). As a consequence of this pressure, US officials pushed for the MAI to be negotiated through the OECD, in order "to obtain a high-standard multilateral investment agreement that will protect US investors abroad" (quoted in Clarke 1997). Initially, this investment code will service the wealthy Triadic states, and will therefore avoid collective southern pressures to dilute it by allowing entry to other states on a case-by-case basis, provided the standards are upheld.

As Clarke (1997) points out in an evaluation of the revised MAI proposal, under these new global investment rules (which take their cue from NAFTA), the

"ability of governments, for example, to use investment policy as a tool to promote social, economic and environmental objectives will be forbidden under the
MAI," and further, that MAI "amounts to a declaration of global corporate
rule ... designed to enhance the political rights, the political power, and the
political security of the TNCs on a worldwide scale." The code includes proposals to institutionalize rights of corporations (and financiers) as investors, with a
legal status equivalent to that of nation-states, except that governments are not
granted rights to sue such investors for damages on behalf of their citizens—in
Clarke's words, "the draft MAI points to a massive transfer of 'rights' from
citizens to investors in the new global economy." Further, as the draft Agreement states, "Any new liberalization measures would be 'locked in' so they could
not be rescinded or nullified over time" at the point of changes in government by
participating states, which will not be able to withdraw for five years from the
MAI, while the rules for existing investments must stand for an additional 15
years.

Governance in the global economy

We have seen that there is a clear tension between the governance of space and
the governance of flows. The tension centers on questions of sovereignty and
power. But this is not a synchronic issue—it must be understood in historical
terms. Institutionalization of the governance of capital circuits threatens to erode
social gains from historical struggles that constitute popular, sovereign government, or its potential. While much of this dynamic pivots on the dismantling of
the developmentalist, or welfare, state, as a condition of enhancing money and
commodity circuits, this is not simply a zero-sum relation. It also involves a
rather more subtle transformation of the content of citizenship.

It is axiomatic that modern citizenship rests on a historical pedestal of social
mobilization by political parties, labor movements, trade unions, and women's
and civil rights and other social movements. The decline of organized labor,
under the combined onslaught of the micro-electronics revolution and policies of
liberalization, and the restructuring of the political discourse, has weakened the
capacity of this social base to counterpose protection as a principle of social
organization to efficiency. In this context, the construction of the global consumer contaminates the content of citizenship. An elision is occurring, from
embedding citizenship in the notion of a social contract to disembedding citizenship in the abstractions of market rule, emptying its meaning of its historical and
institutional substance. This is clearly evident in the attempts to socially engineer
Eastern European transition, and to substitute—overnight—market rule for central planning. Thus the World Bank characterized Romania's 1993 privatization
plan as a model for the creation of responsible "nations of shareholders" *qua* new
world order citizens (Drainville 1994: 63).

The reconstruction of citizenship (via waves of "democratization") occurs still
at the national level in a context in which populations are prohibited from
circulating at will.[2] In my view, this process is not so much to revitalize popular

governance, as to stabilize the global project. This can be illustrated from the UN Social Summit.

In March 1995, the United Nations held a World Summit for Social Development in Denmark. The agenda was summed up in the call by then UN Secretary General Boutros Boutros-Ghali for "a new social contract," recognizing that global poverty has worldwide consequences. Although no funds were forthcoming, the argument was that agencies like the UN have a responsibility to address global conditions of poverty and fight discrimination. Programmatically, the "Social Summit" attempted to redefine aid, rejecting the term "foreign aid" and promoting the idea of reallocating money and other resources globally. Social conditions within former Third World countries will enter into decisions about international financial assistance, including the ability of wealthy elites to help.

In an idea resembling the 1980s debt-for-nature swap, the suggestion was that every dollar of cancelled debt should be spent on social services, and forgiven debt should be matched by reductions in arms expenditure. Sub-Saharan Africa was named as the major development challenge (Crossette 1995a). In an era when "foreign aid" faces growing skepticism, the prime minister of Denmark, Poul Nyrup Rasmussen, explained the rationale for continuing aid:

> We have a good argument now, a very concrete one, for ordinary people, which is, if you don't help the Third World, if you don't help northern Africa, if you don't help eastern and central Europe with a little part of your welfare, then you will have these poor people in our society.
>
> (Crossette 1995b)

If the globalization project has any appeal to people in the north beyond the idea of efficiency—which may not remain credible over time—it lies in the appeal to northern security concerns. This involves the belief that southern needs must be taken into account if only to stem the tide of migration. Since northern economic conditions are hardly robust (except in the United States which models the casual labor market), freedom of labor movement is an unlikely political platform—even though under the terms of the globalization project freedom is extended to money, capital, and goods. The security question, then, compels the global managers to focus on a new form of loan conditionality: assistance where governments attend to stabilizing their populations. This has been included in the World Bank's new lending criteria; for example, Lewis Preston, the Bank president in the early 1990s, declared "sustainable poverty reduction is the benchmark by which our performance as a development institution will be measured" (quoted in George and Sabelli 1994: 150). In other words, globalization begins at home.

For the immediate future, it appears then that global management will focus on stabilizing the system of states across the world. This involves two levels of action. First is the elaboration of the vision of a global community. For example, in 1995 the Commission on Global Governance, which included leaders from North and South, published its report *Our Global Neighbourhood*, in which it called for the development of a "global civic ethic." The Commission argued that this is a necessary social cement involving non-governmental political association at a time when "groups of many kinds are reaching out and establishing links with counterparts in other parts of the world" (Commission on Global Governance 1995: 55). How effective this will be without a framework for institutionalizing representation is another (but urgent) matter. It is noteworthy that there is a parallel restructuring of the United Nations system under consideration. With the South's recent demand for an Economic Security Council grounded, global managerialist thinking has argued that the UN should confine itself to social and politico-military matters, leaving economic and technological governance to the WTO, the World Bank and the IMF, TNC representatives, and a Council representing this nexus—which is in clear violation of the Covenant on Economic, Social and Cultural Rights (Kothari 1995: 9).

Second, under conditions in which it is not only the north/south gap that commands attention but also the widening gap within countries, states are the ultimate gatekeepers for destabilized populations. Short of military intervention, attaching governance conditions to financial assistance is a new chapter in the continuing story of management of the global order. For example, on July 15, 1997, the Argentinean government agreed to a deal with the IMF whereby the latter would provide a line of credit that depended on evidence of "good governance." This included shifting public spending priorities toward improving the health and education of the workforce, "overhauling the tax system, improving court practices, strengthening private property rights and opening Government ledgers" (Lewis 1997: D1). Because this arrangement improves Argentina's ability to attract lower loan rates in private credit markets, it is being touted as a "model for developing countries in Latin America and possibly other areas, giving private business and investment a bigger share of the role that the monetary fund has played" (Lewis 1997: D1).

Conclusion

The overwhelming paradox is that states are not well-suited to governing flows, and yet flows are becoming a dominant reality of the new world order. Arrighi (1994) suggests this may be a cyclical phenomenon, where the "capitalist" principle (financial liquidity) overrides the "territorial" principle in an unstable post-hegemonic world order, where the center of accumulation (the US home market) erodes, and speculation on an unknown financial future heightens. Nevertheless, the governance of flows threatens to unravel the social foundation of territorialism.

Democratic politics has hitherto been based in social relations grounded in the governance of territories. Guéhenno has argued that the "territorial foundation of political modernity . . . is under attack from new forms of economic modernity"—namely, networks of information, or flows. The territorial basis of taxation, which is the substance of the national state's governing capacity, is "called into question today on three counts": the mobility of [certain] people, capital, and the attribution of added value in the internal transfer accounting operations of TNCs (Guéhenno 1995: 10). In this context of capital flows jeopardizing the tax base of the state, Guéhenno claims: "in the age of networks, the relationship of the citizens to the body politic is in competition with the infinity of connections they establish outside it . . . the political space is immediately threatened with extinction, for there is no market that can establish the 'value' of the national interest and circumscribe the scope of solidarity" (1995: 19, 23).

Under these circumstances, social solidarities become defined in rather more exclusivist terms. Identity politics, crystallized by the official and unofficial migration of labor workers under conditions of global economic uncertainty and rising unemployment, contaminates the universalism of citizenship as a historic social relation. Nation-states function more as population containment zones than as potentially inclusive communities of national citizens. Governance of populations deteriorates into the regulation of differential citizenship status, defined along culturist lines of ethnic or racial distinction.

The governance of flows thus dilutes the governance of space. Under these conditions there is considerable uncertainty as to how this contradiction will be resolved. This is why multilateral agencies like the World Bank are focusing on the question of governance, supporting a subtle transformation from national governance to market governance. The state is not disappearing; rather, these forces would turn the nation-state into a global state, where state administrations author market governance alongside the global managers.

However, new political relations crystallize in this encounter between the governance of flows and that of space. Flows operate above and below states, paralleling processes of decentralization of authority on the one hand, and global coordination on the other. Precisely because of the ubiquity (and especially the velocity) of flows, they generate instabilities. Market integration is often accompanied by social protest or disintegration, the consequences of which are more easily transmitted through the greater exposure of integrated financial circuits. For example, the 1994 Zapatista uprising contributed to the destabilization of the Mexican money market as investors withdrew their short-term dollars (with the aid of the Bank of Mexico), precipitating the peso crisis and its *tequila* effect throughout South American financial markets. Thus, it is likely that as the governance of flows intensifies, so will counter-movements to reassert popular governance, creating serious uncertainties for capital circuits. This contradictory state of affairs remains the surest way to demystify globalization as a one-dimensional organizing myth, with a dangerously abstracted model of governance.

Bibliography

Aglietta, M. (1979) *A Theory of Capitalist Regulation*, London: New Left Books.
Arrighi, G. (1982) "A Crisis of Hegemony," in S. Amin, G. Arrighi, A. G. Frank, and I. Wallerstein (eds) *Dynamics of Global Crisis*, New York: Monthly Review Press.
—— (1990) "The Developmentalist Illusion: A Reconceptualization of the Semiperiphery," in W. G. Martin (ed.) *Semiperipheral States in the World Economy*, Westport CT: Greenwood.
—— (1994) *The Long Twentieth Century. Money, Power, and the Origins of Our Times*, London: Verso.

Baird, P. and McCaughan, E. (1979) *Beyond the Border*, New York: NACLA.

Barnet, R. J. and Cavanagh, J. (1994) *Global Dreams. Imperial Corporations and the New World Order*, New York: Simon and Schuster.

Block, F. L. (1977) *The Origins of International Economic Disorder. A Study of United States' International Monetary Policy from World War II to the Present*, Berkeley and Los Angeles: University of California Press.

Brecher, J. and Costello, T. (1994) *Global Village or Global Pillage. Economic Reconstruction From the Bottom Up*, Boston: South End Press.

Cahn, J. (1993) "Challenging the New Imperial Authority: The World Bank and the Democratization of Development," *Harvard Human Rights Journal* 6.

Clarke, T. (1997) "The Corporate Rule Treaty. The Multilateral Agreement on Investments (MAI) Seeks to Consolidate Global Corporate Rule," *Trade-Strategy* [www.igc.apc.org].

Commission on Global Governance (1995) *Our Global Neighbourhood*, Oxford: Oxford University Press.

Crook, C. (1993) "New Ways to Grow. A Survey of World Finance," *The Economist*, Special Supplement, September 25.

Crossette, B. (1995a) "UN Parley Puts Focus on Africa," *The New York Times*, March 9.

—— (1995b) "Talks in Denmark Redefine 'Foreign Aid' in Post-Cold War Era," *The New York Times*, March 10.

—— (1996) "UN Survey Finds World Rich–Poor Gap Widening," *The New York Times*, July 15.

Davidson, B. (1992) *The Black Man's Burden. Africa and the Curse of the Nation-State*, New York: Times Books.

DePalma, A. (1996) "Income GAP in Mexico Grows, and so do Protests," *New York Times*, July 20.

Drainville, A. C. (1994) "International Political Economy in the Age of Open Marxism," *Review of International Political Economy* 1 (1).

Escobar, A. (1995) *Encountering Development: The Making and Unmaking of the Third World*, Princeton: Princeton University Press.

Friedmann, H. and McMichael, P. (1989) "Agriculture and the State System. The Rise and Decline of National Agricultures, 1870 to the Present," *Sociologia Ruralis*, 29 (2).

George, S. and F. Sabelli (1994) *Faith and Credit. The World Bank's Secular Empire*, Boulder CO: Westview Press.

Giddens, A. (1987) *The Nation-State and Violence*, Berkeley: University of California Press.

Gill, S. (1992) "Economic Globalization and the Internationalization of Authority: Limits and Contradictions," *Geoforum* 23 (3).

Greenhouse, S. (1997) "Voluntary Rules on Apparel Labor Proving Elusive," *New York Times* February 1.

Guéhenno, J. M. (1995) *The End of the Nation-State*, Minneapolis: University of Minnesota Press.

Hansen-Kuhn, K. and Leiva, F. (1995) "NAFTA and the Chilean Economy," *Development GAP Factsheet* [www.igc.apc.org].

Harvey, D. (1989) *The Condition of Postmodernity*, Oxford: Basil Blackwell.

Hoogvelt, A. (1997) *Globalisation and the Postcolonial World*. Basingstoke and London: Macmillan.

Kelly, M. E (1996) "Another NAFTA Mask Removed" [www.igc.apc.org].

Khor, M. (1995a) "Countering the North's New Trade Agenda," *Third World Network*, November 9.

—— (1995b) "India, Malaysia, Brazil Diplomats Against New Issues in WTO," *Third World Network*, November 9.

Kothari, S. (1995) "Where are the People? The United Nations, Global Economic Institutions and Governance," paper presented to conference "The UN: Between Sovereignty and Governance," La Trobe University, July 2–6.

Lewis, P. (1997) "IMF Seeks Argentine Deal Linking Credit to Governing," *New York Times*, July 15.

McMichael, P. (1996) *Development and Social Change. A Global Perspective*, Thousand Oaks CA: Pine Forge Press.

Migdal, J. S. (1988) *Strong Societies and Weak States. State–Society Relations and State Capabilities in the Third World*, Princeton: Princeton University Press.

Moore, B. Jr. (1967) *Social Origins of Dictatorship and Democracy. Lord and Peasant in the Making of the Modern World*, Boston: Beacon.

Ohmae, K. (1995) *The End of the Nation-State. The Rise of Regional Economies*, New York: The Free Press.

Paarlberg, R. (1992) "How Agriculture Blocked the Uruguay Round," *SAIS Review* 12.

Panitch, L. (1996) "Rethinking the Role of the State," in J. H. Mittelman (ed.) *Globalization: Critical Reflections*, Boulder CO: Lynne Reinner.

Pepper, S. (1988) "China's Special Economic Zones," *Bulletin of Concerned Asian Scholars* 20 (3).

Raghavan, C. (1996) "Forward to the 19th Century?" *Third World Network*, November 9.

Resource Center (1993) "Free Trade: The 'ifs', 'ands', and 'buts'," *Resource Center Bulletin* nos. 31–32.

Rich, B. (1994) *Mortgaging the Earth. The World Bank, Environmental Impoverishment and the Crisis of Development*, Boston: Beacon.

Ritchie, M. (1993) *Breaking the Deadlock. The United States and Agricultural Policy in the Uruguay Round*, Minneapolis: Institute for Agriculture and Trade Policy.

Ruggie, J. G. (1982) "International Regimes, Transactions and Change: Embedded Liberalism in the Post-war Economic Order," *International Organization* 36.

Rueschemeyer, D., Stephens, J. D., and Stephens, E. H. (1992) *Capitalist Development and Democracy*, Chicago: University of Chicago Press.

Sinclair, T. J. (1994) "Passing Judgement: Credit Rating Processes as Regulatory Mechanisms of Governance in the Emerging World Order," *Review of International Political Economy* 1 (1).

Sklair, L. (1997) "Social Movements for Global Capitalism: The Transnational Capitalist Class in Action," *Review of International Political Economy* 4 (3).

Srinivasan, R. (1996) "Export Processing Zones in the Context of Foreign Trade Liberalization in India: Role of a Casualized Labor Force," unpublished Ph.D. thesis, Cornell University.

Tilly, C. (ed.) (1975) *The Formation of the Nation-State in Western Europe*, Princeton: Princeton University Press.

US/Guatemala Labor Education Project (1997) "Break-Through in Guatemala!" *Labor Alerts* [www.igc.apc.org].

Wallerstein, I. (1995) *After Liberalism*, New York: Vintage.

World Bank (1997) *World Development Report. The State in a Changing World*, New York: Oxford University Press.

11 Civilizational conflicts and globalization: a critique

Jacques Hersh

[T]o the natives, however, of both the East and the West Indies, all the commercial benefit, which can have resulted from those events [their discovery by Europe] have been sunk and lost in the dreadful misfortunes which they have occasioned . . .

(Adam Smith [1776] 1937: 189)

The aim of this chapter is to discuss the apparent paradox between capitalist globalization which can be seen everywhere, and the eruption of conflicts and contradictions at all levels. How is this phenomenon to be understood? The attempt will be made to assess the answers given by mainstream American political scientists to this question. There are two approaches which confront each other on interpreting the international situation. In this context, the term mainstream is applied to the main body of scholars and publicists whose work is based on a problem-solving endeavor in contrast to critical theory which considers the structures causing the problem and point to the necessity of overhauling them. As a proponent of the latter approach puts it:

> Critical theory steps outside the confines of the existing set of relationships to identify the origins and development potential of these phenomena. While problem-solving theory assumes the functional coherence of existing phenomena, critical theory seeks out the sources of contradiction and conflict in those entities and evaluates their potential to change into different patterns.
>
> (Sinclair 1996: 5–6)

Although the two theoretical frameworks need not be mutually exclusive in all cases, it should nevertheless be remembered that theory in social sciences is not neutral. As Robert Cox (1995b: 31) points out: "Theory is always *for* someone and *for* some purpose."

The reason for taking seriously the conventional discourses found in the production of ideas and concepts developed within the academic community of the hegemonic power of the world system is that they have a tendency to trickle down and form part and parcel of the ideological and political way of thinking in the subordinate units. This is especially the case when a new situation arises demanding clarification and conceptualization. In the Foucault understanding, discourse is a group of statements providing a language of meaning for talking about/or representing a specific kind of knowledge about a topic or subject (see Hall 1992: 291–5). This was of significance in the vacuum which arose as a result of the transformation which took place as the world entered the last decade of the twentieth century.

The certitudes deriving from the East–West bipolar world had to be revised after the fall of the Berlin Wall and the meltdown of "real existing socialism." The explanations offered by political scientists of international relations, which had almost exclusively focused on the contradictions affecting this relationship, had predicted neither these events nor the new situation which came to the fore. The fate of the communist regimes in Eastern Europe and Russia led to the need for a new conceptualization of the capitalist world system. An attempt in this direction was made soon after the demise of the socialist regimes. The idea that, with the disappearance of any alternative to capitalism, the history of mankind had reached the pinnacle of its apogee found some proponents. This was how Francis Fukuyama interpreted the new situation in his original essay "The End of History" (1989). According to this perception, Western-type liberal democracy is seen as endowed with a kind of universality which the rest of the world was bound to follow.

The thesis was not so readily accepted in the European sphere where there is a stronger tradition for skepticism. Although apparently subscribing to the valid- ity of the inevitability of the spread of liberal democracy, the American political establishment did not relinquish voluntarism in its foreign relations. Aware of the superiority of US power and the uniqueness of American hegemony after the collapse of the USSR and implicitly based on the assumption of the course of history as formulated by Fukuyama, President George Bush, following the repul- sion of the Iraqi invasion of Kuwait, launched the slogan of a "New World Order." In this new international system, America was the superpower—the strongest liberal capitalist democracy—which would exert its strength to make other countries and regimes conform to its course of history as well as satisfying US interests, these being two objectives that were considered to be in harmony with each other.

Although the short war against Saddam Hussein and his bid to access the oil supplies of the Persian Gulf was repulsed under the formal leadership of the United Nations, it was purely an American intervention in an inter-Arab conflict whose roots go back to the division of the Middle East by the European imperial powers.

On the one hand, the US action revealed Washington's ability to control the Security Council of the United Nations while on the other, it revealed US military prowess. But at the same time, it also showed the economic debility of the United States. Not only were Saudi Arabia and Kuwait made to pay, but the allies (especially Japan and Germany) were likewise forced to accord financial support directly to the United States and not to the United Nations! Thus while there was no longer any alternative to "real existing capitalism," the United

States followed a course of disciplining a former strategic Third World ally whom Washington had supported in the war with Iran. Also with regard to its allies and competitors (Japan and Europe), Washington showed that US military might was essential to preserve core capitalism's interests in the periphery.

Contrary to the Fukuyama thesis, the lesson here was that history was in fact not finished. It is not uninteresting to point out that the concept of a "New World Order"—not to be confused with the demand, by the non-aligned movement, for a New International Economic Order in the early 1970s—did have some appeal among a number of strategists and specialists of international affairs. However shortly thereafter, the eruption of civil war in Somalia where the United States—under the UN flag—confronted an impossible situation, together with the dismembering and bloodshed of Yugoslavia, the fear of potential local wars in the former Soviet Union, and the bloodbath in Rwanda, made US think-tanks realize that resources to implement an American-directed "New World Order" were limited. It was realized that the United States would have to be selective in its interventions, not only because of the financial costs but also because of the sentiments of the American public. The Vietnam syndrome is still a factor in US politics. By the time of the 1992 election, President Bush had placed the United States at center stage on the international scene, but the vote for Bill Clinton as well as Ross Perot reflected a refocusing of public opinion on internal problems. Since then, President Clinton has followed on the one hand an aggressive unilateralist course toward economic competitors and allies to protect US interests and moderate interventionism in conflicts in the periphery on the other.

Closely related to the "New World Order" perspective was the thesis of the "coming anarchy," developed by Robert D. Kaplan in an article in *The Atlantic Monthly* (1994). According to the envisaged scenario, the world is facing a general breakdown of political authority as a result of massive population movements, environmental crises, and epidemics. A warning is raised according to which an intermingling of non-compatible people with different experiences of social existence will lead to a collapse of the norms of sociability and governance. Mafias, drug cartels, and warlords are seen as exploiting the legacy of Cold War arms and technology. This scenario paints a picture of a threatened Western world. As Robert W. Cox (1995) formulates it, "Fukuyama's 'post-historical' people, a privileged minority of the world's population, would be living a defensive garrison existence surrounded by this anarchic threat."

A third interpretation of the chaotic era that has followed the end of the Cold War is found in the thesis by Samuel Huntington (Huntington 1993) which can be seen as a battle-cry for the mobilization of "the West against the rest." The main ideas of this essay are further developed in his book *The Clash of Civilizations and the Remaking of the World Order* (Huntington 1996) in which he rejects the idea of the homogenization of non-Western societies on the Western model while at the same time pushing for a strengthening of the Atlantic Alliance. In other words, Western civilization is not universal and therefore harmonization should not be expected. On the contrary, he warns of potential conflicts.

Trade conflicts (wars?)
(Triad)

Religious conflicts
(Afghanistan, Algeria,
Ireland, Israel–Palestine)   **Clash of civilizations**

Ethnic conflicts
(Bosnia, Russia, Rwanda)

New Cold Wars
(China, Russia)

Figure 11.1 The clash of civilizations

This new paradigm represents a rebuttal to the thesis of the end of history. Implicitly its frame of reference is based on the search for a US-dominated world order. With regard to its conceptualization it tries to locate potential conflicts and contradictions in the world system. It is not a thesis without consequences for policy-making at the politico-military level and thus should not be understood as an innocent academic exercise.

To evaluate the notion espoused by Huntington it is necessary to be aware of the forces at work in the international system. What then are the main components of problem areas in the world which Huntington tries to categorize under the heading of "Clash of Civilizations" (Kurth 1994: 4)? The world can be characterized by clusters of potential conflicts as shown in Figure 11.1.

The aim here is to find a new and easily classified determinant to the present-day quasi-chaotic behavior between and within nations. Simultaneously, the thesis strives to influence policy-making and consciously or not plays on the socio-psychological fears of Americans and West Europeans who have difficulty adapting to the fallouts of globalization and no longer have the former frame of reference provided by the hostile images of the Cold War.

Huntington's approach, based on the culturalist level of analysis, shows similarities to the tradition which originally tried to explain the superiority of European society on the basis of quasi-racist portrayals of the "others." In the past, this conceptualization legitimated the colonialism of European nations in Africa, Latin America and Asia.

In fact, the return to the thesis of the incompatibility of civilizations exemplifies an interesting evolution. Within the field of conventional international political science, this is reminiscent of an old controversy between two interpretations of world affairs.[1]

1   *Microcosmic approach*: The proponents of this paradigm look at the state as the basic unit that determines the *yins* and *yangs* of world politics. The Realist school of international politics owes much of its conceptualization to political scientists such as Hans J. Morgenthau, John H. Herz and Raymond

Aron. This approach claims to be the classical exponent of "pure" political science. Its level of analysis is the state system and its frame of reference is the anarchy model of international relations.

The Realist approach which considers the nation-state as the main actor of international politics has been challenged by scholars within the field of international political economy. According to the latter perspective, globalization brings forth other actors such as multinational corporations and other social forces which have to be taken into consideration.

2 *Macrocosmic approach*: The adherents of this school belong to an older tradition. Here, world affairs are viewed from the level of civilizational interaction to which the nation-state belongs but with an added culturalist dimension which can determine behavior. This school was somewhat more philosophical, with scholars like the philosopher Oswald Spengler, historian Arnold Toynbee, the international jurist Quincy Wright, and F. N. Parkinson.

These two schools debated vigorously in the 1950s and we know that the Realists succeeded in shaping US foreign policy during the Cold War. The resurrection of the controversy by Huntington, who wishes to turn the clock back to the civilizational approach, tells us something about the shortcomings of globalism. It should also be mentioned that the civilizationist position was residual in mainstream US modernization theory within development studies in the 1950s. According to this development paradigm, modernization entailed the transformation of traditional societies and cultures along the lines of the Western model.

Huntington's classification differs in a number of ways from that of his predecessors in the macrocosmic tradition. But because he too tries to identify determinants on a grand scale by looking at differences among civilizations, his methodology is similar. Toynbee, in the 1940s, distinguished between what he called primary, secondary and tertiary civilizations according to their historical appearance on the world scene. He contended that their attributes or characteristics influenced contemporary events. Quincy Wright, likewise applying an historical method used a normative classification of civilizations: "bellicose" (including Japanese, Mexican, Syrian); "moderately bellicose" (Germanic Western, Russian, Scandinavian, etc.) and "most peaceful" (e.g. Irish, Indian and Chinese).

In other words civilizational differences were a given and were inherent in the culture and past of these societies. This is of course a problematic proposition. It can be argued that politics, regimes and ideologies are to a certain extent culturally and "civilizationally" determined. But in the interaction of international politics (day-to-day, crisis-to-crisis, war-to-war decision-making), the nation-states remain the most identifiable determinants of events in the international arena. This notwithstanding, Huntington offers the civilization level as the basic unit of analysis. The clash between them will dominate global politics: "The fault lines between civilizations will be the battlelines of the future."

Six reasons are given for what Huntington considers to be inevitable sources of friction:

1   Differences among civilizations are basic. Civilizations are differentiated from each other by history, language, culture traditions and, most importantly, religion. Different views exist on relations between God and man, the individual and the group, the citizen and the state, parents and children, husband and wife, on the importance of rights, responsibilities, liberty and authority, equality and hierarchy.
2   The world is becoming a smaller place. Interaction between civilizations is intensifying consciousness and awareness of differences between civilizations and commonalities within civilizations.
3   Processes of economic modernization and social change throughout the world are separating people from longstanding local identities, as well as weakening the nation-state as a source of identity. Religion has moved in to fill the gap ("fundamentalism" in Western Christianity, Judaism, Buddhism and Hinduism, as well as Islam). This is in fact a general phenomenon which seems to affect all societies at the end of the twentieth century (Kopel 1991).
4   The growth of civilization. Cultural consciousness is enhanced in the non-Western world by the impact of the apparently unlimited power of the West; this often translates in a return to the roots phenomenon in the attempt to preserve identity. The projection of the West gives rise to the following paradox: the de-Westernization and indigenization of elites in some countries, while Western (US) culture, styles and habits—although not easily accessible—become popular among the masses.
5   Cultural characteristics and differences are less mutable, hence less easily compromised and resolved than political and economic ones.
6   Economic regionalism is increasing. Successful economic regionalism will reinforce civilization-consciousness. On the other hand, economic regionalism may succeed only when it is rooted in a common civilization. A case in point is the difficulty Japan has had in attaining regional integration because it is a society and civilization unique in itself, whereas the common Sino cultural roots in East Asia can bring forth a bloc centered on China.

According to the culturalist position as exemplified by Huntington, the main source of concern for the Western world is related to a potential alliance between Confucian civilization (strong in industrial power and population) and Islamic civilization (strong in oil revenue and geographic proximity to the West). This scheme plays on two major areas of Western anxiety. One is the vitality of Confucian-style guided capitalism which has achieved significant results in economic and industrial growth. How is this region to be absorbed in a world economy which is already under stress because of the difficulties facing global capitalism? Will the West be involved in the wealth creation of East Asia or will the region compete with the West? Concerning the Arab countries, the question is how to keep their economies integrated in the world system while the majority of the people are marginalized?

It is interesting to consider a basic shortcoming of the culturalist approach, namely its *elasticity*. While Confucian culture and statecraft are now seen as determinants in the successful East Asian experience with capitalist development, the same oriental cultural traits and administrative capabilities were considered to be obstacles to capitalism by Max Weber. They simply didn't have anything near the Protestant ethic! This was the dominant Western view until the 1970s. But as the political sociologist Peter A. Gourevitch (1989: 12) puts it, such inconsistency is not appropriate in scientific analysis: "If Confucianism explained the absence of growth, how can it be used as a variable to explain growth just a few years later? If culture has explanatory power, it must be relatively constant. If economic change occurs rapidly, the constant cannot account for the change."

As far as Islamic civilization is concerned the problematic is reversed. In the words of Samir Amin (1996: 5): "The Islamic world of the tenth century appeared to many historians as not only more brilliant, but also as containing more potential for progress than Christian Europe during the same period." For various reasons, the shortcomings of modernization (in the sense of Westernization) have now released a fundamentalist discourse and movement in the Arab nations. But this is mostly an internal affair, though not unrelated to Western responsibility. It is in fact an irony of history that when nationalism and socialist pan-Arabism represented strong secular currents in the post-colonial Arab world, the West encouraged Islam as a counter-weight by giving support to Saudi Arabia which engaged in the financing of Islamist movements and organizations in the Muslim world. In Afghanistan, the American CIA contributed directly to the creation of militant international fundamentalism by recruiting "freedom fighters" in various Middle East countries against the Soviet invasion. Israel itself encouraged the creation of Hamas in order to weaken the PLO leadership of the occupied territories of Palestine. On the other hand, Arab nationalists—regardless of their secularism—were all along in the paradoxical situation of acknowledging adhesion to Islam in their confrontation with the West as well as with Israel in order to retain the support of their people (Aguirre 1994). Religion has thus been a political arena of contention between various internal and external forces in Muslim societies.

In the past few decades a general revival of cultural and religious intolerance at the popular level has made its appearance in the West—related to some degree to the role played by sensationalism in the media. Furthermore, the fear of *Homo-Islamicus* in the West has been accentuated by demographical movements. Because of socio-political problems, there has been a flow of refugees and immigrants to Europe from this region. However, it should be remembered that many of these had been welcome as guest workers in many countries during the "Golden Thirties." Absorption of non-European immigrants and refugees at a time of economic crisis has released a xenophobic backlash and ultra-nationalist movements in Europe. While this trend has been fueled by populist movements, even at higher institutional levels preparations are under way to confront the unrest in societies of North Africa and the Middle East. The North Atlantic Treaty Organization (NATO) is accordingly planning strategies that treat this region as a potential area for intervention.

What the civilizationist thesis fails to mention in the search for a new enemy image is that interaction between civilizations has, historically, also been a constructive and creative relationship. This has been more of a constant and perennial feature of civilizational interaction than conflict *per se*. Throughout history, civilizations have adapted and adjusted to one another. However, identity was often manipulated to camouflage the pursuit of power or wealth at the expense of the *other*. This in fact has been the real reason for hostilities and clashes between communities (Muzaffar 1993).

In the present era, it is questionable whether the culturalist approach indicates the appropriate level of analysis in understanding actual and potential instability. A fundamental weakness is related to the Western tendency to analyze the world from a Eurocentric standpoint. Seen from that perspective it is not the Euro-American civilization that is part of the problem. It is only part of the solution! Diversity is not encouraged while at the same time a pronounced cultural relativism and determinism is emphasized as the cause of disorder. Thus the systemic sources for conflicts are overlooked.

This affects the discourse on civilizations. To his credit Huntington does however recognize the limitation of this civilizational paradigm. This is implicit in the awareness of the non-cultural elements behind the confrontational issue of the "West and the rest" in the context of Western dominance and resistance to it. This is an aspect to which critics of the thesis of "Clash of Civilizations" have not paid sufficient attention but which is central to the state of the world and will be more so in the future.

Thus, at the beginning of the essay Huntington states: "In the politics of civilizations, the peoples and governments of non-Western civilization no longer remain the objects of history as targets of Western colonization but join the West as movers and shapers of history." Later, toward the end he concludes: "The West in effect is using international institutions, military power and economic resources to run the world in ways that will maintain Western predominance, protect Western interests and promote Western political and economic values."

What does this mean? The explanation demands an entirely different perspective. It means that more than conflicts of civilizations, we are faced with classic contradictions of international capitalism. This is a system with an uneven division of labor and unequal accessibility to the fruits of its mode of functioning. The resulting polarization on the international plan cannot but release tensions and frustrations. As put in a thoughtful analysis by Fuller (1995: 153–4): "Thus 'civilizational clash' is not so much over Jesus Christ, Confucius, or the Prophet Muhammad as it is over the unequal distribution of world power, wealth and influence, and the perceived historical lack of respect accorded to small states and peoples by larger ones. Culture is the vehicle for expression of conflict, not its cause." Indeed, at the philosophical level most world religions and cultural systems share common perspectives on essential aspects of life such as the relationship between humans and nature, the integrity of the community, the role of the family and clan, the importance of moral leadership and last but not least the meaning and purpose of life itself (Muzaffar 1993: 18).

However, the present material disparity and inequalities on the world scale cannot but bring about a polarization which is the main source of instability and insecurity. What we see is the West, with 800 million people, trying to hold on to a dominant position which subjects the rest, approximately 4.7 billion, to subjugation and inferior status.

The problem is that the globalization of capitalism—which originates in North America and Europe—involves a projection of the Western mode of production and consumption pattern as the only viable model to be imitated. But can this be duplicated? If we look at the resource question we see that a generalization of the "American Way of Life" is an impossibility. Seen from that angle, the last stage of Walt Rostow's modernization model, which foresees mass consumption as the end station for a developed society, reveals itself as an illusion.

Under the present system, as Rufin (1992) points out, a quarter of the world's population appropriates 83 percent of world income, a quarter of the world's population consumes 75 percent of the planet's metals, 85 percent of the planet's wood, 60 percent of the earth's foodstuffs; while three-quarters of the world's population has to do with the rest." In addition, the functioning of the financial system is lopsided. Although we have heard much about the debt crisis of the Third World, it is actually the United States who has been the largest debtor nation. America mobilized and attracted (through high interest rates) a great deal of financial resources from Japan and Western Europe. This was used to service the debt and the discrepancy created by the budget and trade deficits of the American economy. Access to foreign financial resources thus allowed Americans to misuse the international system by living above their means. The resources were thus used to alleviate the contradictions of American society while developing countries and Eastern Europe were starved of capital and affected by the high international interest rates on capital, which furthermore punished the debt-ridden countries.

The gist of the argument of this chapter is that the forces that are responsible for the discrepancies and the malfunctioning of the world political economy are the very same ones that assume a leadership role in the management of the resulting chaos and the struggle to re-establish order—through military expenditures and sale of weapons and interventions. This is a paradox of enormous dimension. According to the dominant discourse, disorder is not caused by the normal functioning of the system, but by elements within the world system which threaten this normalcy.

Thus, East Asia, and especially China, is achieving growth which in the longer run will demand greater access to world resources and markets—and this is seen as menacing. Similarly, in Islamic society where the modernization project has not succeeded in reducing internal contradictions but on the contrary has sharpened them, fundamentalism is also seen as a potential danger. But in fact it can be argued that it is the Western world that is fundamentalistic to the extent that it refuses to accept different societal models by interfering economically, culturally, politically and at times militarily. "Crackpot realists" raise the banner of Western solidarity and warn against a reduction of the West's military capability.

When we discuss the clash of civilizations it could be interesting to ask who has better reasons to fear whom. Seen in this light, Western civilization (or "highly developed capitalism" as it might better be called) represents both a challenge to non-European societies (culturally speaking, but also militarily, politically, and economically) while also being the model of modernization. The outcome of this dichotomy represents an element of instability in the non-Western world. In other words, there is fear and awe which express themselves in political processes mixing both tradition with modernization.

The discussion of the problems created by the apparent dichotomy between globalization and a "clash of civilizations" needs to be put into a processual context related to the evolution of the capitalist system from its European point of origin. From the start, capitalism was a dynamic and international system. This was acknowledged by Marx and Engels who recognized the revolutionary and global impact of this mode of production:

> The need of a constantly expanding market for its products chases the bourgeoisie over the whole surface of the globe. It must nestle everywhere, establish connexions everywhere. The bourgeoisie has through its exploitation of the world market given a cosmopolitan character to production and consumption.
>
> (Marx and Engels [1848] 1958: 37)

However, while capitalism did conquer and unify the world and create a unique economic system, it did not homogenize the different societies and the different classes during this process. As Samir Amin has pointed out, this aspect has had a tendency to be overlooked even by traditional Marxism:

> On the contrary, universalized capitalism was deployed through polarizing the planet and creating a deep contrast between its centres and peripheries. This fact is the root of our cultural problem. Socialism, including historical Marxism, has underestimated this dimension of polarizing capitalism, by virtue of its own nature.
>
> (Amin, n.d.: 4)

Because of the way globalization functions, there is no chance of escaping the needs and moods of the hegemonic power and the system. During the 1960s, when self-centered development was predominant during the Mao-period in China, John K. Fairbanks, an American expert on East Asia, argued that because of historical circumstances China was victimizing itself by not joining in the spread of civilization dispensed from Europe and the United States. China was the last remaining separate, distinct, isolated country: "And this is the background, therefore of real cultural conflict" (quoted by Peck 1975: 73). In this line of thinking the Opium War could be seen as a non consequential event. In other words, China—isolated as it was after the Chinese revolution—was considered a source of disfunctioning. But in fact this isolation was a function of US strategy which contributed to the imposition of the self-centered model on China. Today, China is again seen as a potential menace precisely because of its involvement in the world system!

Before concluding, awareness of new tendencies can contribute to a better understanding of the cultural dichotomies which now appear to be disturbing. As I see it, we are entering a new phase of world capitalism. Western ideological hegemony is becoming unstable in the world although its economic and political power is still predominant in world politics. New developments have challenged the structure of values and understandings of the world order.

But the sources of the challenges to Western societies are also to be found internally—cultures not being static. If we look at the changes taking place in the transition to so-called post-industrialism, we see the societal and political importance which women have acquired. This is affecting family patterns especially of future generations: "The splitting of the family's nucleus, like the splitting of the atom's nucleus, will release an enormous amount of energy (which feminists see as liberating and conservatives see as simply destructive)" (Kurth 1994: 11). In the United States, where multiculturalism is strong, the demands of minorities supported by feminism are having an important influence in universities and are affecting the stability of the ideology of the intellectual elite as a bastion for the status quo.

This sociological evolution has led the American political scientist, James Kurth, to write that the real clash of civilizations, the one with most salience, will be internal within the West itself, especially within the United States (Kurth 1994: 11ff.). Although Huntington (as well as the dominating discourse in Western societies) focuses on political and ideological values inherited from the Enlightenment, the tendencies toward disintegration are discernible. As Hans Magnus Enzensberger sees it, youths in gangs, uprooted from their sense of self in communities characterized by disintegration, wage "molecular civil war." These youths, indifferent to either their future or past, turn their aggressiveness on others (Enzensberger 1995: 25–6).

The appeal to Western values and defense of Western civilization in the face of the challenges coming from the non-European cultural sphere seems hollow. On another level, globalization is seen as threatening the class which has been the backbone of the capitalist nation-state. As an outcome of a process whereby new technologies, as well as economic policies, favor the financialization of economies, jobs and status are threatened allowing few prospects for people's future or that of their children. The imagery of a borderless world imposed from above through a process of global integration breaks old bonds of obligations including loyalty and the sense of belonging to a community. In their endeavor to reduce the significance of national boundaries, global elites are betraying the expectations of the middle classes on which democracy was based. As Christopher Lasch puts it, Western elites cannot at the same time implement globalization while appealing to the defense of their civilization and identity:

> Today it is the elites, however—those who control the international flow of money and information, preside over philanthropic foundations and institutions of higher learning, manage the instruments of cultural production and thus set the terms of public debate—that have lost faith in the values, or what remains of them, of the West.
>
> (Lasch 1995: 25–6)

The middle classes of Western societies, being subjected to the pushes and pulls of the technological revolution and global trade, as well as the insensibility of their political system, are prone to transform their patriotism into xenophobic retrenchment and fear of the future. The distress of this "anxious class" (Reich 1995: 28–30), which can no longer depend on the national community to provide economic or cultural security, opens up political possibilities for all kinds of Western fundamentalisms.

Consequently, the clash at the fault line of Western and post-Western civilization may perhaps be closer to home than that of Western/non-Western civilizations projected by Samuel Huntington.

Bibliography

Aguirre, M. (1994) "Guerres de civilisations," *Le Monde Diplomatique*, December.

Amin, S. (1996) "Imperialism and Culturalism Complement Each Other," *Monthly Review*, June.

—— (n.d) "Culture and Ideology in the Contemporary Arab World," (unpublished paper).

Cox, R. W. (1995a) "Civilizations: Encounters and Transformations," *Studies in Political Economy*, 47, Summer.

—— (1995b) "Critical Political Economy," in B. Hettne (ed.) *International Political Economy: Understanding Global Disorder*, London and New Jersey: Zed Books.

Enzensberger, H. M. (1995) "Molecular Civil War," *New Perspectives Quarterly* 12 (1), Winter.

Fukuyama, F. (1989) "The End of History," *The National Interest*, Summer.

Fuller, G. (1995) "The Next Ideology," *Foreign Policy* 98, Spring.

Gourevitch, P. A. (1989) "The Pacific Rim: Current Debates," *The Annals*, AAPSS 505, September.

Hall, S. (1992) "The West and the Rest: Discourse and Power," in S. Hall and B. Gieben (eds) *Formations of Modernity*, Oxford: Oxford Polity Press.

Huntington, S. (1993) "The Clash of Civilizations," *Foreign Affairs* 72 (3) Summer.

—— (1996) *The Clash of Civilizations and the Remaking of the World Order*, New York: Simon and Schuster.

Kaplan, R. D. (1994) "The Coming Anarchy," *The Atlantic Monthly*, February.

Kopel, G. (1991) *La revanche de Dieu*, Paris: Editions du Seuil.

Kurth, J. (1994) "The Real Clash," *The National Interest*, Fall.

Lasch, C. (1995) *The Revolt of the Elites and the Betrayal of Democracy*, New York/London: W. W. Norton Company Inc.

Marx, K. and Engels, F. [1848] (1958) "The Communist Manifesto," in K. Marx and F. Engels *Selected Works*, vol. 1, Moscow: Foreign Language Publishing House.

Muzaffar, C. (1993) "'Clash of Civilisations' Serves West's Interests," *Third World Resurgence* 39, November.

Peck, J. (1975) "Revolution Versus Modernization and Revisionism: A Two-Front Struggle," in V. Nee and J. Peck (eds) *China's Uninterrupted Revolution*, New York: Random House.

Reich, P. (1995) "America's Anxious Class," *New Perspectives Quarterly* 12 (1), Winter.

Rufin, C. J. (1992) "The New Divide," *Choices (The Human Development Magazine)* 1 (3), November.

Sinclair, T. J. (1996) "Beyond International Relations Theory: R. W. Cox and Approaches to World Order," in R. Cox and T. Sinclair (eds) *Approaches to World Order*, Cambridge: Cambridge University Press.

Smith, A. ([1776] 1937) *The Wealth of Nations*, New York: Random House.

Weeks, A. L. (1993) "Do Civilizations Hold?" *Foreign Affairs*, September/October.

12 From the rubble of modernism, the rise of global civilization?

Mark Juergensmeyer

Almost before the ink had dried on Samuel P. Huntington's arresting essay, "The Clash of Civilizations?," the debate had begun over whether its prophecy was possible, whether labels for civilizations like "Western" or "Confucian" are apt, and whether hegemonic cultural constructions such as "civilizations" exist at all.[1] My position is that civilizations do exist though the labels for them, including "Western" and "Confucian," are highly debatable. I think that the current social and political unrest around the globe, however, is caused less by a clash of civilizations than by a widespread dissatisfaction with all of them. What may emerge out of this discord is either a global cultural anarchy or a global cultural consensus over a new worldwide civilization, or both.

The heart of this thesis is that one civilization which I prefer to call "Modernism" rather than "Western civilization" has been perceived within recent years as a European and American construct forced upon the rest of the world. For this reason it has been rejected not only in formerly colonialized countries (the so-called Third World) but also in certain quarters of the industrialized West. As I have argued earlier (Juergensmeyer 1993), the rise of religious politics is in part a cultural rebellion against the ideology of Enlightenment values. An emerging global civilization, therefore, will have to move beyond the limitations of Modernism and be founded on a multicultural base.

The limits of modernism

What was historically distinctive about Modernism—the ideas and values associated with the European Enlightenment—was not its heritage of open-mindedness and critical thought (traits that religious traditions also shared, at least in their better moments), but its insistence that public order be based on rationality and the will of individuals rather than on cultural identity and divine mandate. Central to the thinking of Enlightenment philosophers was the notion that individuals create a political compact with other people in their geographical region, forming a secular nation. It was an idea that was thought to be not only natural but also universally applicable and morally right. Although it was regarded almost as a natural law, secular nationalism was ultimately viewed as an expression of neither God nor nature but of the will of its citizens.[2]

The leading thinkers of the Enlightenment made clear that public institutions were legitimized solely by secular consent. According to John Locke, humans are "equal and independent" before God, and for that reason have the sole right to execute the power of the Law of Nature. Hence the only way an individual can protect his or her liberty is "by agreeing with other Men to join and unite into a community, for their comfortable, safe, and peaceable living one amongst another" (Locke 1960: 375). According to Jean Jacques Rousseau, the "social contract" that people tacitly form with one another in a geographical area is an admission that they need to be ruled, and an expression of their willingness to relinquish some of their rights and freedoms to the state in exchange for its administrative protection. It is an exchange of what Rousseau calls one's "natural liberty" for the security and justice provided through "civil liberty."

What is implied is that the state does not need the Church to grant it moral legitimacy: the people grant it on their own through a divine right that is directly invested to them as a part of the God-given natural order (Rousseau 1967: 23). Although Locke and Rousseau allowed for a divine order that made the rights of humans possible, their ideas did not directly buttress the power of the Church and its priestly administrators, and they had the effect of taking religion—at least Church religion—out of public life.

Yet to believe in Modernism required having faith in the natural order. Even though this belief was not couched in the rhetoric of traditional religion, the terms in which it was presented were the grandly visionary ones that are associated with spiritual values. Secular nationalism—the political form of Modernism—embraces what one scholar calls "a doctrine of destiny" in much the same way that religion does (Hoover 1986: 3). One can take this way of looking a step further and state flatly, as did one author writing in 1960, that Modernism and its secular nationalism is "a religion" (Hayes, 1960). A few years later the historian, Crane Brinton, described "a new religion, certainly related to, descended from, and by many reconciled with, Christianity," which he called "Enlightenment, with a capital 'E'" (Brinton 1963–4: 315) and which I call Modernism with a capital "M."

Brinton's point that some of the central tenets of Modernism came from Christianity have been eloquently argued by a Christian theologian, Arend Theodor van Leeuwen. In *Christianity in World History*, van Leeuwen argues that the idea of separating out the things of God from the things of man in such a way as to deny the divine nature of kingship was first formulated in ancient Israel, and then became a major motif of Christianity (Leeuwen 1964: 331). As Christianity spread across Europe, it brought the message of secularization with it: "Christianization and secularization are involved together in a dialectical relation," van Leeuwen claimed (Leeuwen 1964: 332). In his view, the great liaison between the medieval church and state was something of a mistake, and the Enlightenment brought Christianity's secularizing mission back on track.

Whether or not one agrees with van Leeuwen's paradox, that the secularism of the Enlightenment had Christian roots, one has to admit that Modernism as a civilization has at times taken on a religious character. The French Revolution, the model for much of the nationalist fervor in Europe in the nineteenth century, infused a religious zeal into revolutionary democracy, taking on the trappings of Church religion in the priestly power meted out to its demagogic leaders, and in the slavish devotion to what it called "the temple of reason." According to Alexis de Tocqueville, the French Revolution "assumed many of the aspects of a religious revolution" (Tocqueville 1955: 11; see also McManners 1969).

As in France, American nationalism developed its own religious characteristics. Not only were the early founders Deists but also over time the ideals of secular nationalism and the symbols of Christianity were blended into what has been called a "civil religion." As Robert Bellah has described, this civil religion is abundantly apparent in the pronouncements of politicians, especially on the occasions of their inaugurations (Bellah 1967, 96: 1–21). The 1993 inaugural address of Bill Clinton, for example, contained 29 direct or indirect references to the Bible, and his acceptance speech in the Democrat Party's convention the year before was organized around the biblical theme of "the new covenant." A civil religion, by coopting elements of religion into nationalism, gives nationalism a religious aura, provides religious legitimacy for the state, and helps to keep religion from building its own anti-national power base.

The civil religion of America indicates some distinctive characteristics of the American form of Modernism. Like European Modernism, the American variety values rational thought and regards democratic consensus as the basis of government. What American Modernism and its civil religion highlight is individualism: the creativity and moral autonomy of individual persons. Linked with American individualism is a certain kind of grassroots popularism that has always been suspicious of any form of centralized power, including big business and big government. For that reason Americans, more than Europeans, have been wary of the state socialism linked with Marxism, which itself can be regarded as a variant of European Modernism. This American obsession with individual identity and expression has been recently analyzed by a team of American sociologists in a trenchant and influential study, *Habits of the Heart* (Bellah et al. 1985).

Enlightenment imperialism and cultural colonialism

Modernism, like Christendom, has had its imperialistic side. The nineteenth century fulfilled de Tocqueville's prophecy that the "strange religion" of Modernism and its secular nationalism would, "like Islam, overrun the whole world with its apostles, militants, and martyrs" (Tocqueville 1955: 13). It was spread throughout the world with an almost missionary zeal, and was shipped to the newly colonized areas of Asia, Africa, and Latin America as part of the ideological freight of colonialism. It became the ideological partner of what came to be known as "nation-building." As the colonial governments provided their colonies with the political and economic infrastructures to turn territories into nation-states, the ideology of secular nationalism emerged as a by-product of the colonial nation-building experience. As it had in the West, secular nationalism in the colonized countries in the nineteenth and twentieth centuries came to represent one side of a great encounter between two vastly different ways of perceiving the socio-political order and the relationship of the individual to the state: one legitimized by culture, the other by the notion of a secular compact.

When Europeans colonized the rest of the world, they were often sustained by a desire to make the rest of the world like themselves. Liberal politicians within the colonial governments were especially insistent on imparting notions of Western political order. In England, Whigs such as Gladstone, for example, regarded the presence of the British in India and elsewhere as necessary "to promote the political training of our fellow-subjects [of the King]."[3] Even when empires became economically burdensome, the cultural mission seemed to justify the effort. The commitment of colonial administrators to the modern values of the Enlightenment explains why they were often hostile to the Christian missionaries who tagged along behind the colonial governments: the missionaries were the liberal colonizers' ideological competitors. The Church's old religious culture was an insult to the new secular ideology that most colonial rulers wished to present as characteristic of the West.

In the mid-twentieth century, when the colonial powers retreated, they left behind the geographical boundaries they had drawn and the political institutions they had fashioned. Created as administrative units of the Ottoman, Hapsburg, French and British empires, the borders of most Third World nations continued after independence, even if they failed to follow the natural divisions between ethnic and linguistic communities. By the second half of the twentieth century, it seemed as if the cultural goals of the colonial era had been reached: although the political ties were severed, the new nations retained all the accoutrements of Westernized countries.

The only Western empire that remained substantially intact in the last half of the twentieth century was the Soviet Union. It was based on a different vision of political order, of course, one in which international socialism was supposed to replace a network of capitalist nations. Yet the perception of many members of the Soviet states was that their nations were not so much integral units in a new internationalism as they were colonies in a secular Russian version of imperialism. This became dramatically clear after the break-up of the Soviet Union and its sphere of influence in the early 1990s, when old ethnic and national loyalties sprang to the fore.

The idea that the colonialized countries of Asia and Africa should be converted to a modern form of Western civilization was held not only by Westerners but also by a good number of new leaders in the emerging nations created out of former colonial empires. The concept of secular nationalism gave them an ideological justification for being, and the electorate that ascribed to it provided them power bases from which they could vault into positions of leadership ahead of more traditional ethnic and religious leaders. But secularism was more than just a political issue, it was also a matter of personal identity. A new kind of person had come into existence—the "Indian nationalist" or "Ceylonese nationalist"— who possessed an abiding faith in both Western values and a secular nationalism identified with his or her homeland. Perhaps none exemplified this new spirit more than Gamal Abdul Nasser of Egypt and Jawaharlal Nehru of India. According to Nehru, "there is no going back" to a past full of religious identities, for the modern, secular "spirit of the age" will inevitably triumph throughout the world (Nehru 1946: 531–2). The new nationalists' attempts to give their ideologies an anti-religious or a supra-religious force were encouraged, perhaps unwittingly, by their Western mentors. Scholars such as Kohn boldly asserted that Modernism's secular nationalism "appears as fundamental today as an understanding of religion would have been for thirteenth century Christendom" (Kohn 1965: 4). Rupert Emerson's influential *From Empire to Nation* shared the same exciting vision of a secular nationalism that "sweeps out [from Europe] to embrace the whole wide world" (Emerson 1960: 158). Emerson acknowledged that in some parts of the globe, such as Asia, as secular nationalism "moved on" and enveloped them, "the religious issue pressed more clearly to the fore," but he expected that eventually the "religious issue" could never impede the progress of secular nationalism, which Emerson saw as the West's gift to the world (Emerson 1960: 158). The fact that in some instances this gift had been forced on the new nations without their asking was noted by Emerson, who acknowledged that "the rise of nationalism among non-European peoples" was a consequence of "the imperial spread of Western European civilization over the face of the earth." The outcome, in his view, was nonetheless laudable, for as he colorfully put it, "the global impact of the West has . . . run common threads through the variegated social fabrics of mankind . . . [and it] has scored an extraordinary triumph" (Emerson 1960: vii).

The Cold War era, which lasted from 1947, when the term was first coined by the American journalist, Herbert Bayard Swope, until the collapse of the Soviet Union in 1990, may be seen as a competition between the United States and the USSR over which version of Modernism would prevail: American or Soviet. Karl Marx was a major figure in the nineteenth-century European Enlightenment tradition, and to this day is carefully studied in the social science departments of American and European universities—perhaps more so than he currently is in universities in the former Soviet bloc. It was not so much the ideas of Marx but of Lenin, and the terrible example set by Stalin, that triggered America's anti-Communist paranoia during the heyday of the Cold War years. The war against Communism, then, was not only a competition between two great superpowers, but also an ideological defense of democratic Modernism against what was perceived as dictatorial Modernism.

Nowhere did this ideological defense of American Modernism have greater foreign policy impact than in Vietnam. With only the most fragmentary of military and economic reasons for entering into what was essentially a Vietnamese civil war, America was able to become militarily mired down in the Indochina peninsula for more than a decade at the cost of tens of thousands of American lives and hundreds of thousands of Vietnamese. Ultimately this military crusade on behalf of democratic Modernism failed, and the United States lost a war for the only time in its history. It was a failure that helped to trigger within American society a growing loss of confidence in its political values.

In the last decades of the twentieth century the most visible form of international Modernism was economic and cultural: the ubiquitous consumer franchises and entertainment media. On the one hand are the multinational and transnational corporate networks symbolized by such fast-food restaurants as McDonald's and Kentucky Fried Chicken; and on the other hand are the movies, videos, and music compact discs which portray the saucier side of American culture, from Madonna to "Santa Barbara" (the television series not the real city, which I can testify is much tamer in real life than on television). These two aspects of contemporary Modernist culture exported around the world are dubbed "McWorld" by one American author who fears that their assault on public consciousness in various parts of the world has triggered the "Jihad" of militant tribalism (Barber 1995).[4]

The response to "McWorld" is a serious matter. In many areas of Asia and the Middle East, the movies and fast-food outlets of "McWorld" are considered forms of cultural colonialism, and have helped to fuel movements of religious nationalism in opposition to them. In Iran, for example, one of the things that most troubled the Ayatollah Khomeini about the urban society in Tehran before the Islamic revolution was what he and others referred to as "West-toxification" or "Westomania."[5] Although Islamic peoples have been infatuated with Westomania to some extent since the eighth century, the Ayatollah maintained that this infatuation had been encouraged and exploited by Western businessmen. The goal of the Islamic revolution in Iran, then, was not only to free Iranians politically from the Shah but also to liberate them conceptually from Western ways of thinking. Another Iranian leader, Abolhassan Banisadr, agreed, claiming that the West assumed that in economic and cultural matters it had "prior rights to the rest of the world" (Banisadr 1981: 40).

The reaction against cultural colonialism has led to a rise of religious nationalism in various parts of the world, which in turn has created a new competition between Western Modernism and religious civilizations such as Islam. Although some writers, such as Francis Fukuyama, have asserted that the ending of the old Cold War has led to an "end of history" and a worldwide consensus in favor of the secular liberal democracy of Modernism, the virulence of new religious and ethnic nationalism belies that assertion (Fukuyama 1989: 12–13; 1992: xi–xxiii). As I argued in my book on religious nationalism, the confrontation between these civilizations has some of the characteristics of the Cold War: it is virtually global in scope, binary in its opposition, occasionally violent, and essentially a difference of ideologies. And like the old Cold War, each side tends to stereotype the other (Juergensmeyer 1993: 2).

Post-modern civilization

The greatest threat to Modernism as a civilization, however, is not from outside but from within. To a large extent the features of Modernist cultures have been criticized and sometimes rejected not only in formerly colonized countries but also in the heartland of Western countries. In America, for instance, there are abundant signs of discomfort over the alienation of individualistic society, the coldness of rationalistic institutions, and the moral relativity of secular culture. This discomfort has led to a resurgent interest in spirituality and a revived interest in an American religious nationalism, represented in its most extreme forms by the Christian militia and the Christian Identity movement, groups that feed on what I have described elsewhere as a widespread "loss of faith" in the secularism of modern civilization (Juergensmeyer 1993: 11).

This loss of faith has been linked to a perception that secular institutions have failed to perform. In many parts of the world the secular state has not lived up to its own promises of political freedom, economic prosperity, and social justice. The government scandals, persistent social inequities, and devastating economic difficulties of the United States and the USSR in the 1980s and early 1990s, for example, made both capitalist and socialist forms of society less appealing than they had been in those more innocent decades, the 1940s and 1950s. The global mass media have brought to everyone's attention the malaise in America caused by the social failures of unwed mothers, divorce, racism, and drug addiction; the political failures of Watergate, Irangate, and the Vietnam War; and the economic failures of the Savings and Loan crisis and the mounting deficit. The political scandals of England, Japan, and other modern societies have been equally widely publicized.

Although the news media have greatly exaggerated these problems in American and other industrial societies, these dismal reports have led some people to a disappointment that has deepened into a lack of trust in public institutions. They experience what Jurgen Habermas has dubbed a modern "crisis of legitimation," in which the public's respect for political and social institutions has been deflated throughout the world (Habermas 1975). Religious leaders have been able to capitalize on this disenchantment. Perhaps many of them never did believe in the validity of secular Modernist values, but now they were able to convince masses of people within their societies, in part because great numbers of them no longer saw modern civilization as an expression of their own values, nor did they see it improving their social and economic situations. More importantly, they failed to see how the Western versions of secular nationalism could provide a vision of what they would like themselves and their nation to become.

The legitimation crisis of modern societies has led some writers to observe that Modernism as a civilization may be on the rocks. History may be entering into a period of post-modernism, where not everyone subscribes to the same view of history, and such values as individualism, equality and a respect for secular civil law are not held equally by all (here I am using "post-modern" to describe actual social phenomena, and not, as the term is sometimes used, a genre of literary and social analysis).[6]

Part of the reason why Modernism as a civilization is in trouble is that its main political artifact, the nation-state, is in trouble. Earlier in this century the nation-state was deemed to be the essential building block for the "world-system" as envisaged both by businessmen and political strategists as well as by critical thinkers such as Immanuel Wallerstein.[7] It was not only the ultimate locus of authority within a territory, but consisted of a relatively self-contained population, economic system, environmental habitat, social identity, and set of cultural values.

Increasingly, however, the old nation-state is no longer self-contained in any of these familiar ways. Its economy is integrated into world markets, and sections of it are purchased outright by corporations that are either foreign, multicultural, or transnational—i.e. not beholden to the location or laws of any single country. Its population is fluid: Los Angeles, for example, has become a major center for Mexico, the Philippines, Vietnam, and Korea, not only because so many people from these countries live in LA, but also because their economies and cultures are intertwined. Environmental problems in one country affect not only its neighbors but, in the case of deforestation and global warming, the whole world. And as the author of *Jihad vs. McWorld* has observed, the youth of major urban centers throughout the world dance to the same music and watch the same videos.

At one time it could be said that the nation-state would remain intact as long as it had its own military and currency. But in the contemporary world, the cost of sophisticated military technology leaves America, NATO and a few other forces virtually alone as the world's policemen. And the viability of the Japanese yen, the German mark, and the American dollar makes these currencies more valued than local currencies in many parts of the world. Moreover, the increased use of credit cards and other forms of electronic monetary transfer will, in time, make paper and metal currency symbolic rather than real expressions of economic self-sufficiency.

But just when the nation-state appears to be irrelevant, the idea of the nation-state in some areas of the world has been rescued by what a few years ago would have been an unlikely ally: movements for religious nationalism. In countries controlled by the former Soviet Union, for example, local religious and cultural traditions have provided identities that were deprived from them when they were simply one more unit in a vast Soviet bloc. Movements of cultural nationalism are successful in part because the old nation-state is not needed for any other reason, including economic or military ones. Hence in an area such as the Balkans, the economies of such small and oddly-shaped nations as Slovakia and Croatia can survive insofar as they participate in a larger world economy; the entity of Yugoslavia is no longer helpful or necessary for their economic existence. For this reason, movements for cultural nationalism—even those that yearn to create the tiniest of nations—are viable in a world where the economic and military reasons for a nation-state no longer exist. Hence new nationalisms can emerge precisely because the nation-state is weak.

The weakening of the nation-state in various parts of the world, however, has consequences for Modernism as a civilization. Insofar as the loss of economic and military reasons for a nation-state gives an impetus to new religious nationalisms, Modernism is challenged on a local level. But it is also challenged globally, for multinational businesses and entertainment media are moving beyond the Modernist ambit to a transnational urban culture that is not tied, as Modernism was, to traditional national societies. This means that on both local and international levels, Modernism as a civilization is about to undergo a global transformation. Or perhaps it will be replaced.

The emerging civilization of globalism

The world appears to be poised on the brink of an enormous cultural change. But if Modernism is finished as a civilization, what will take its place? The pessimistic assessment is that nothing will. Some statesmen, such as Zbigniew Brzezinski, have claimed that the world is already "out of control" (Brzezinski 1993). Others, like Daniel P. Moynihan, have warned of the cultural anarchy and "pandaemonium" that may result if tribalism runs amok and Modernism as a set of civilized values is allowed to collapse (Moynihan 1993). These writers advocate that Modern civilization be protected and preserved before it is too late.

But perhaps it already is too late. If it is true that the forces that cause the erosion of Modern values are largely the result of technological and demographic changes on virtually a global scale, they are not easily dismissed. In this emerging world society, the great question is not whether Modernism will triumph in the coming clash of civilizations, but whether any civilization will survive at all.

I see several options for world order in the near future:

1   Fortress Modernica: An attempt by the formerly Modern societies of Europe and America to shore up their common identities, and say "to hell with the rest of the world." This is the direction I see Huntington leading when he says that "the survival of the West depends on Americans reaffirming their Western identity" (Huntington 1996: 20–1).
2   The North vs. the South: A growing chasm between the McWorld society of transnational corporate capitalism and satellite television culture, and the tribal, Jihad-oriented societies described by Benjamin R. Barber (Barber 1995).
3   Regionalism or Global Balkanization: An expansion of the economic and cultural ties currently being forged by NAFTA (among Canada, Mexico and the United States), East Asian financial liaisons, the European partners of the European Union, and the Islamic trade alliance that extends from Central Asia to North Africa and the Middle East. In this scenario a "clash of civilizations" or at least of regional economic partnerships is indeed a real possibility.
4   Global civilization: A new consensus over fundamental social values, similar to that enjoyed by Modernism in the West in the past two centuries, but now supported by a variety of cultural traditions, not just the Enlightenment. This scenario could co-exist with one or more of the previous ones, as a stratum of global civilization develops over time, and in addition to the particularistic values of individual societies.

The last is clearly the most intriguing. Signs of such an emerging civilization are appearing in areas of the world where the cultural mix of the population puts them on the front lines of intercultural encounter and global demographic change. The picture, however, is not altogether pretty.

In California, for example, the pessimistic view of America's multicultural future is symbolized by the 1992 unrest in Los Angeles involving Hispanics, African Americans and Koreans, which was less an orchestrated riot than it was a sheer collapse of civil order. When poor Black neighborhoods of South-Central Los Angeles erupted in anger over the jury's non-guilty verdict in the trial of police officers accused of beating a Black man, Rodney King, they were joined by large numbers of Hispanics, and their targets were often Korean-owned grocery stores, liquor stores, and convenience stores. The rampage killed scores, caused an estimated $735 million damage, and was televised live throughout the United States.

But there is also an optimistic scenario regarding multiculturalism, and it is symbolized by what has happened in Los Angeles in the years since 1992. The rebuilding of South-Central Los Angeles has been a slow affair, and it is far from being a perfect society. But it is one that has created a modicum of civic pride and a growing respect for the diversity of Los Angeles' common cultural heritages. As one Hispanic leader put it, "the riots created the opportunity for bringing communities together" (Vaquerano 1992). Post-modern multicultural societies like Los Angeles, therefore, may be the incubators for an emerging polyglot civilization, which, for want of a better term, might be called Global Civilization, or simply Globalism.

Like Modernism, Globalism has more than domestic significance, and it may or may not be imperialistic in its encounter with other traditions. The question is whether its various cultural elements—the European, Hispanic, African, Korean, Chinese, Japanese, and other cultural heritages of Los Angeles, for instance—can retain their integrity in a Global culture or whether they are transformed into a homogeneous stew with little specific integrity. The results are too early to be definitive.

The most harmonious outcome of the current cultural encounter is one where values from traditional civilizations such as a respect for the past, communal identities, and the demand for morality in public life can be joined with the more salutary aspects of Modernism, including a respect for rational decisions, equal treatment before the law, a toleration of differences, and the protection of the rights of minorities and individuals. And from both kinds of civilizations, this optimistic outcome of Globalism would retain a spirit of progress about the future.

But even the most optimistic vision of a single, shared Global civilization is not necessarily a formula for peace. Throughout history some of the most vicious wars have been within civilizations—family quarrels, like the one between two great Modernist powers, the United States and USSR. Yet the global sharing of basic values can be a basis for at least a modicum of cooperation between various parts of the world, and allow for a more or less orderly transition to new patterns of economic, social, and political association that will transform and in some cases replace the nation-state. An expansion of the United Nations' role in peacekeeping, human rights, economic regulation, and environmental protection, for example, would be the logical extension of shared global values.

It is not an unlikely outcome, but this scenario will have to contend with the others for primacy in the coming decades. If it is possible to forge a common denominator among the various cultural traditions, to bridle the moralism and naive optimism of religious civilizations and temper them with the rationality of Modernism, and to level the Modernist illusions about the invincibility of human knowledge with a religious sense of the limitations of the human condition, then it is possible to imagine the emerging multicultural civilization of the twenty-first century, Globalism, providing a cultural basis for both social identity and political order. The anarchic alternatives, to my mind, are dismal ones. And since the societies of the world are already forced together increasingly by a technological and communications intimacy, it is not too difficult a leap of imagination to think of a sharing of values on a global scale as well.

Bibliography

Banisadr, A. (1981) *The Fundamental Principles and Precepts of Islamic Government* (trans. by M. R. Ghanoonparvar), Lexington KY: Mazda Publishers.

Barber, B. R. (1995) *Jihad vs. McWorld*, New York: Times Books.

Bellah, R. (1967) "Civil Religion in America," *Daedalus* 96; reprinted in R. Bellah, *Beyond Belief*, New York: Harper and Row.

Bellah, R., Madsen, R., Sullivan, W., Swidler, A., and Tipton, S. (1985) *Habits of the Heart: Individualism and Commitment in American Society*, Berkeley: University of California Press.

Brinton, C. (1963–4) "Many Mansions," *American Historical Review* 49.

Brzezinski, Z. (1993) *Out of Control Global Turmoil on the Eve of the Twenty-first Century*, New York: Scribners.

Emerson, R. (1960) *From Empire to Nation: The Rise to Self-Assertion of Asian and African Peoples*, Boston: Beacon Press.

Fukuyama, F. (1989) "The End of History," *The National Interest* 16, Summer.

—— (1992) *The End of History and the Last Man*, New York: Free Press.

Habermas, J. (1975) *Legitimation Crisis* (trans. by Thomas McCarthy), Boston: Beacon Press.

Hayes, C. J. H. (1960) *Nationalism: A Religion*, New York: Macmillan.

Hillmann, M. C. (1974) "Introduction" to Jalal Al-e Ahmad, *The School Principal* (trans. by J. K. Newton), Minneapolis: Bibliotheca Islamica.

Hoover, A. J. (1986) *The Gospel of Nationalism: German Patriotic Preaching from Napoleon to Versailles*, Stuttgart: Franz Steiner Verlag.

Huntington, S. P. (1993) "The Clash of Civilizations," *Foreign Affairs* 72 (3), Summer.

—— (1993) "If Not Civilizations, What? Paradigms of the Post-Cold War World," *Foreign Affairs* 72 (5), November/December.

—— (1996) *The Clash of Civilizations and the Remaking of World Order*, New York: Simon and Schuster.

Juergensmeyer, M. (1993) *The New Cold War? Religious Nationalism Confronts the Secular State*, Berkeley: University of California Press.

Kohn, H. (1965) *Nationalism: Its Meaning and History*, New York/London: D. Van Nostrand.

Leeuwen, A. T. van (1964) *Christianity in World History: The Meeting of the Faiths of East and West*, New York: Charles Scribner's Sons.

Locke, J. (1960) "Chapter VIII: Of the Beginnings of Political Societies," *The Second Treatise on Government*, New York: Cambridge University Press.

Lyon, D. (1994) *Postmodernity*, Minneapolis: University of Minnesota Press.

Matthew, H. C. G. (1986) *Gladstone, 1809–1874*, vol. 1, Oxford: Clarendon Press.

McManners, J. (1969) *The French Revolution and the Church*, Westport CT: Greenwood Press.

Molnar, T. (1985) "The Medieval Beginnings of Political Secularization," in G. W. Carey and J. V. Schall (eds) *Essays on Christianity and Political Philosophy*, Landham, Maryland: University Press of America.

Monypenny, W. and Buckle, G. (1929) *The Life of Disraeli*, vol. 1, *1804–1859*, London: John Murton.

Moynihan, D. P. (1993) *Pandaemonium: Ethnicity in International Politics*, New York: Oxford University Press.

Nehru, J. (1946) *The Discovery of India*, New York: The John Day Company.

Packard, S. R. (1973) *12th Century Europe: An Interpretive Essay*, Amherst: University of Massachusetts Press.

Rousseau, J. J. (1967) "Chapter VIII: On the Civil State," *Social Contract*, New York: Pocket Books.

Tocqueville, A. de (1955) *The Old Regime and the French Revolution* (trans. by S. Gilbert), New York: Doubleday Anchor Books.

Vaquerano, C. (1992) quoted in M. Corwin, "Understanding the Riots: Six Months Later," *Los Angeles Times*, November 16.

Wallerstein, I. (1991) *Geopolitics and Geoculture, Essays on the Changing World-System*, New York: Cambridge University Press.

Part V

Globalization and forms of resistances

13 Overturning globalization

Rethinking the politics of resistance

Barry K. Gills

Introduction

The ongoing debate on "globalization" is certainly a strategic debate of central importance to the present era. Therefore much depends on its outcome. The first step in changing the terms of this debate, and thus altering its intellectual and then political direction, is to reassert the necessity of placing political analysis and political action at the forefront. We can reclaim the terrain of the political, which has been too often obscured under a new economic determinism, by insisting that concrete strategies and concepts of "resistance" be central to our analyses of globalization.

It is not enough simply to describe the trends of global capitalism or to "document transnational neoliberalism" (Drainville 1994). We must go beyond the limitations of the "technicism" of much of the globalization debate, for example the question of whether globalization exists or not (versus regionalizations, rival national capitalisms, etc.). There is a profound need for serious and sustained (re-)thinking of what practices constitute viable political strategies in the world economy. This can only be done in conscious alignment with dissenting social forces; that is, those constituting the potential counter-hegemonic coalition to the reigning power configuration of global and local elites.

"Resistance" to neoliberal globalization should not be understood as something merely reactive, as the word might at first suggest to some. A "politics of resistance" draws upon analogy with the actions of resistance organizations during World War II.[1] That is, while the world may seem dominated by a very strong entrenched ideology and power structure, there is yet the necessity and the possibility of resistance to it. This resistance is not merely defensive, or representing a tiny minority interest, but rather is a form of struggle with the potential to transform the situation and which does in fact represent a general societal interest. Before turning directly to the problems of political strategy and organization, let us first briefly discuss what we mean by "globalization."

Globalization as the political and economic project of global capital

"Globalization" is an extremely broad concept that can encompass everything. This broad usage renders the general term either meaningless or confusing. However, when "globalization" is rephrased as "neoliberal economic globalization" its meaning becomes much clearer. I would contend that neoliberal economic globalization has four defining characteristics:

1   To protect the interests of capital and expand the process of capital accumulation. (If this is viewed as occurring within and because of a structural crisis in capitalism or a long-term economic stagnation, then neoliberal economic globalization is essentially a strategy of crisis management or "global stabilization.")
2   The tendency toward homogenization of state policies and even of state forms, in the direction of protecting capital and expanding the process of capital accumulation via a new economic orthodoxy, i.e. "market ideology" (wherein even the state itself becomes subject to marketization while simultaneously being deployed instrumentally on behalf of capital).
3   The addition and expansion of a layer of transnationalized institutional authority above the states (which has the aim and purpose of penetrating states and re-articulating them to the purposes of global capital accumulation).
4   The exclusion of dissident social forces from the arena of state policy-making (in order to insulate the new neoliberal state forms against the societies over which they preside and in order to facilitate the socialization of risk on behalf of the interests of capital) (Amoore et al. 1997; Gills 2000).

In summary, the main thrust of neoliberal economic globalization is to bring about a situation in which private capital and the market alone determine the restructuring of economic, political and cultural life, making all other alternative values or institutions increasingly redundant or subservient. In effect, "the economy" becomes the master of society and of all within it. Rather than the economy, and capital, being embedded in society and existing to serve socially defined needs, the relationship is inverted, and society exists to serve the needs of capital and its self-expansion. It is a necessary and not merely contingent aspect of this process that "politics" should become more and more a formalistic set of practices, increasingly stripped of content of a radical or reformist kind which might challenge the hegemony of capital over society. Rather than a triumph of democracy, global capitalism enters the era of a "historic malaise" accompanied by the lingering death of democracy, while new or "low intensity democracies" are characterized more by their limitations than by their transformative power.[2] The claims of social justice are subordinated to the claims of "natural" justice via the market. In short, the impetus of neoliberal economic globalization is socially and politically retrogressive. The more this impetus succeeds the more retrogressive will be the coming era of history. That is why it is imperative to "resist" globalization. The historic retrogression currently underway via neoliberal economic globalization feeds on political cynicism bred by technological and economic determinism. This political cynicism contains the seeds of political defeatism and immobilism. To the degree it succeeds, its aim is the desocialization of the subject and the re-socialization of risk.

Thus, we must begin our analysis of new practices of "resistance" by challenging the "myth" of globalization, i.e. recognizing that neoliberal economic globalization is an idea cast in the mythological mode of thought. That is, "globalization" when wielded as a power concept over society, is an abstraction, deliberately cast in "the ideal" to endow it with emotive powers drawing on a sense of compulsion, fear, and an imperative of speed (Douglas 1997: 165–77; Gills 2000). As such, "globalization" is deployed to invoke a drastic reorganization of social practices, and by being mythological, it is made more powerful. By advocating an inescapable technologically determined necessity for the reorganization of social practices and realignment of social values, globalization (as) discourse devalidates its critics as "unrealistic." When the emperor is exposed as naked, however, we see that this is an ideology and a political project, which seeks to deceive society in the name of economic and "competitive" necessity. It is conservative elites in particular who attempt to use this ideology to cajole society into sacrificing the social gains of the past century (and those not yet established for the future) on the high altar of a "mindless course" (Galbraith 1997: 5–9).

Therefore, we must also begin our critique by challenging the idea that neoliberal economic globalization is either historically obvious or inevitable. Globalization is a contested concept, not a received theory, and we challenge the assumption by its enthusiasts that there is a single determinant economic logic external to society, to the state, or to political processes. We must insist methodologically upon the socially contested and historically open nature of all forms of political economy, "globalization" included. Having made this "historicist" turn, we must operationalize it by putting "people as agents" back into the center of analysis of the processes of globalization, understood as large-scale social and economic change. Globalization, if it is understood as an historically overdetermined "reality," has to be firmly rejected, demystified, and eventually "overturned" via active political "resistance."

Thus, when we say we need to change the terms of the globalization debate and alter its political direction, we mean precisely "rejecting the teleological" and "reclaiming the political" (Amoore et al. 1997). We must come to understand globalization as the non-determinate product of social and political forces, i.e. of conscious human decisions, and not as the inevitable, automatic outcome of a technologically determined market-oriented law of progress. We must likewise reject the errors of definition and over-generalization of neoliberal economic globalization discourse[3] in its quest to assert "the natural law of the market" and an overarching "global logic of capital" above and beyond all other social values or alternatives to the market.

Globalization must not come to mean the "Death of Politics" or the "Death of Social Ideals." On the contrary, we must insist that societies and social forces have the inherent *right* to protect themselves and to choose meaningful ways of politically constituting their actions to this end. This includes the right of society and social forces within it to protection from the destructive vagaries of the unregulated or "self-regulated" market. Other social rights vis-à-vis globalization that could be enumerated would include the right of individuals, families and communities to employment, welfare, social stability and social justice; the right of labor, in both the informal and the formal sectors of the economy, to resist unemployment, austerity measures, reduced life chances, increased insecurity, atomization, alienation, dislocation and immiseration; the right of the poor, dispossessed and marginalized, wherever they exist, to resist the imposition of poverty and the intensification of social polarisation; the right to reclaim and deploy governmental or state power at all levels, from local, regional, national, to international and global, whether through state intervention, a mixed economy, redistribution, reform or radical change; the right to establish social solidarities and autonomous forms of social organization outside the state or the market; and finally the right to imagine "post-globalization" and realize alternative modes of human development.

The neoliberal idea of globalization does indeed represent a teleology of capital, implying a necessary and historically inevitable victory of the market and capital over labor, over the state, and over every aspect of social existence. As such it is ahistorical, but above all it is apolitical, with the objective to inculcate the mythological notion (not an objective truth) that the political process is a mere reflection, a mere "transmission mechanism" from "capital logic" to society.

To begin to resist we must first reject this pernicious logic of inevitabilism inherent in neoliberal globalization and thus recover and mobilize the many political and social alternatives that certainly do exist and are yet to be invented. With Albert Camus, we must assert the right to rebel, as essential as the right to life itself.

Globalization and the new conditions for solidarity and struggle

In this section I will discuss some key issues that must be addressed when we begin to rethink the forms of solidarity and struggle in the context of contemporary national and global economic trends. One of the central issues is the question of "old" versus "new" forms of organization and strategy. It is important to establish at least some basic criteria upon which we can differentiate between different forms of solidarity and struggle. Otherwise, we have no basis to distinguish a reactionary movement from a progressive one, since all forms of "resistance" are not politically or ideologically "equal." Nor would we be able to assess what is useful or not useful about the "new" forms vis-à-vis the "old," nor understand how to critically assess the "old," which is also necessary.

In the current debate there are numerous voices calling for a dizzying variety of alternatives and basing their arguments on sometimes radically different premises. Two elements of this debate will concern us most in what follows: (1) the question of the role of trade unions and their internationalism; and (2) the question of the role of (critical) social movements, and "post-modern" and "post-socialist" strategy and organization. In relation to these concerns, we shall discuss the problem of "fragmentation," based on the "celebration of difference" perspective, versus the call for new "unifying strategies" based on recognition of common material conditions and common progressive goals. A related problem is the debate between those who now call for an outright rejection of "modernity" and "development" along with "Enlightenment" values, versus those who fear the local consequences of the loss of universal values of human progress and call for new forms of internationalism and universalism, sometimes including the call to uphold scientific rationality in the face of assaults by alternative modes of thought such as religion or emotive cultural consciousness.

As a preface to that discussion, I will begin by invoking the need to reassert the values of the broad social and political left, in contrast to conservative and neoliberal values and ideology. The current "market ideology" must be firmly rejected. The benefits of social action and state intervention to control the excesses, flaws, and injustices of the market system must be revalidated and rightfully recognized as a historic necessity. "Wild capitalism" or "savage capitalism" is as unacceptable as the boom and bust cycle and extremes of exploitation and conflict with which it is so clearly historically associated. It therefore follows that we must begin by revalidating certain "old" or "modern" values such as worker solidarity and union rights, the welfare state and its attendant redistributive social policy, state intervention in the economy both for employment and macro-economic stability objectives, and the extension of democratic rights to more and more spheres of social and economic life.

To these traditional values of the broad left we might add "new" or "post-modern" values such as gender equality and, in particular, women's emancipation, protection of the environment, the right of groups in civil society to constitute themselves autonomously from the state or the market, and for social forces more generally to redefine their relationship to the economy and the state in search of new alternative modes of development. This last point does imply a recognition of the validity of the general post-modern claim that the Eurocentric imperialism of the past sought to impose a single mode of development upon all peoples and cultures, thus denying and distorting their genuine historical "difference" and that this project of homogenization should be rejected. However, how far we go in deploying that recognition when reassessing forms of solidarity and struggle in the contemporary period requires caution.

First, I will briefly attempt to sketch how certain trends in the economy have established new material conditions for solidarity and struggle. The general political and economic effects of neoliberal economic globalization on production and finance, or at least the policies enacted with these as a justification, have set a trend for norms in advanced capitalist states to move slowly back to those resembling pre-unionized, pre-welfare-state capitalism. In societies undergoing or aspiring to a transition toward democratic and welfare state capitalism, the effect is generally an intensification of social conflict and a retarding of the prospects of meaningful socio-economic reform.

The overall context of recent economic changes might be described as a period of global economic restructuring. This restructuring is in part a product of the change in social relations in the advanced capitalist states as a result of the post-war compromise with labor, the extension of the role of the state and of social protection and the enhanced position of unions in the economic structure. This, combined with other macroeconomic structural features of the post-war world economy located in the international monetary system and the distribution of productive capacity, brought about the onset of a "crisis" by the end of the 1960s, a process that is generally well understood and about which much has been written.

The response of capital to these macro trends has taken two primary forms, partly to be understood in sequential fashion, but actually simultaneous and still continuing to deepen at present. The "first" of these responses was "de-industrialization" in the core, actually a diffusion of the manufacturing production process from the core to new locations in the "periphery" or developing countries. In Europe this was also accompanied by high levels of structural unemployment, and in both Europe and the United States by an increasing "internationalization" of the workforce via immigration.

The relocation of production "outward" from the core facilitated industrialization in a number of countries, later described via analyses of the "new international division of labor" and the rise of "newly industrializing countries," especially in Latin America and East Asia. Such industrialization in the Third World was obviously accompanied by the rise of new industrial working classes and the struggle for unionization and other rights of labor. As competition between mobile transnational firms of both core countries and NICs intensified throughout the 1980s and 1990s, the spatial dispersal of production sites shifted, with East Asia becoming a particularly favored site, including Southeast Asia and China, but including new tiers of *maquiladora* sites in Mexico, Central America, and the Caribbean.

In this era of intensifying global corporate competition, as global over-capacity in established industries weeds out weaker firms and causes restructuring among the survivors, pressure mounts for further concessions to capital. These concessions include greater capital mobility, greater flexibilization of the workforce on the labor market, lower social burdens for corporate structures, and the freedom to pursue greater concentration in corporate structure. These pressures are felt in both old industrial and new industrial countries.

The flexibilization of labor has in part been accompanied by decreasing size as well as greater dispersal of work sites. Global over-production in sector after sector perpetuates intense price competition. The "down-sizing" program of many corporations was related to their inexorable search for lower costs, greater efficiency and the imperative of recouping a profit in such market conditions.

While individual firms may have found solutions via mass lay-offs, relocation of production and flexibilization of labor, the global trend toward industrial over-capacity was only exacerbated via these solutions. In addition, a global trend toward an under-consumption crisis was also exacerbated. As real wages fall in the core and low(est) wages are sought in the periphery, the income basis for mass production and mass consumption deteriorates. The effect of this is again to dampen prospects for further economic growth via investment in expanded production. One key and well-known element of the processes just described above has been the *feminization* of the workforce, both in the core and in NICs and *maquiladora* (Silver 1998).[4] Flexibilization of labor is often particularly targeted at women workers, who are placed on short-term or irregular contracts. Therefore flexibilization and *feminization* of labor may be seen to be mutually related. Both processes contribute to a growing polarization within the labor force between relatively secure full-time workers and those on part-time or insecure contracts.

The pressure to flexibilize labor, in particular, threatens to further undermine the political position of the traditional union organizations and exacerbates the trend to higher structural unemployment. Firms seeking to relocate production in the new global factory normally pursue a preference not only for ever cheaper labor, but also for weaker or non-existent unions. Theoretically, this should make cross-border union solidarity even more difficult than in the past.

Secondly, the response of capital to the onset of the "crisis" in the 1970s was to "escape" from production via *disinvestment* from the industrial sector of the economy. This movement into finance and "speculation" as a source of profit was at the very least facilitated by, and quite possibly actually brought about, the concomitant trend to financial deregulation so characteristic of many countries in the 1980s and the 1990s. One way of understanding this process is by thinking about "over-accumulation" of capital. A gigantic and ever-growing financial pool of capital came into existence, but due to the competitive conditions prevailing in saturated global industrial sectors could not all be reproduced or expand via industrial investments. As a consequence, capital sought new means of reproducing itself on a global scale. This involved a multi-pronged assault, taking the form of pressure to find new commodities and markets, open new areas to trade and production, privatize and liberalize markets, reduce state expenditure and lower taxation (especially corporate taxation), and defeat the recent gains of organized labor, thus redistributing resources from labor to capital. Thus, as Beverley Silver says, "The growing financialization of capital has gone hand-in-hand with a rapid and unseemly polarization of wealth, both intra-nationally and internationally" (Silver 1998).

Global (haute) finance, whether coupled or de-coupled from the globalized production system, can increasingly disengage from centralized national domestic political processes and re-engage directly with various local or regional actors more freely than in the tighter state-regulated environment of the past. As has been demonstrated repeatedly in recent years, both old and new industrialized countries can be economically de-stabilized by the sudden movements of mobile and speculative capital. Indeed, all governments feel the threat to their macro-economic stability as the power of financial capital increases.

According to the very well-known scenario of transnationally mobile capital, if unions, taxes, or environmental regulations threaten profits in one country, production sites can be relocated to another with lower costs and weaker or non-existent unions. The upshot is a potentially global increase in the rate of exploitation of labor, as politically weakened labor and politically weakened states engage in the "race to the bottom" by competing for the favors of multinational firms. To the extent to which this process deepens, then, globalization of the production, finance, and marketing systems comes at the expense of the national welfare systems of the participating states. The ascendance of "socially barren trade policy" (Galbraith 1997) in international affairs at the level of high diplomacy is a conspicuous aspect of the elite politics of neoliberal economic globalization. The political will for an alternative diplomacy, which would be some form of coordination of social welfare standards, employment targets, fiscal and monetary·policies, international labor standards, corporate "codes of conduct," and controls on cross-border capital movements is presently weak by comparison, though not entirely absent. Elitist neoliberal "globalization from above" must be challenged by "globalization from below" (Falk 1997: 17–24; Brecher and Costello 1994; Gills 2000). The global under-consumption effects of neoliberal policies are yet to be fully accounted for but threaten the long-term stability of the economy or the presumed (national) equilibrium of the self-regulating market. Moreover, as social polarization increases, the central economic legitimating idea of post-war capitalism (and of US hegemony), i.e. mass consumption, comes under greater scrutiny and social doubt. It is no longer possible (if indeed it ever was) to imagine an unproblematic maintenance of mass consumption patterns in the core nor their universal extension to all other societies.

A historical period characterized by greater social polarization, increasing inequality, growing concentration of wealth, intensifying industrial over-capacity and competition for market shares, crippling debt service payments for weaker economies, and an unstable political order and international balance of power will be a period of history in which general popular prosperity (as opposed to the wealth of a privileged few) slowly ebbs away as exploitation increases and redistributive alternatives are dubbed or defeated. The façade of the extension of formal democratic practices masks the gradual reduction of substantive democratic content. The most telling aspect of the new economic liberalization (or "globalization") and its parallel process of formal democratization is the relatively limited nature of the progressive reform these processes and institutions now allow. The overriding goal of capital accumulation drowns out the voice of reform—crying "wealth creation first, reform later!" which is the slogan of the ascendant market and capital over moribund society, politics, and the state. The democratic gains of the past and those potentially in the future are reinterpreted as fetters on the capital accumulation process, which therefore cannot be afforded by society any longer.

It is already abundantly clear that the new era of globalization is far from utopian. As the old banes of economics and of humanity, namely poverty, unemployment, debt, and insecurity return to haunt us we must recall what Alfred Marshall noted, i.e. that there is "no moral justification for extreme poverty side by side with extreme wealth." History also teaches us that social movements will resist these tendencies, and that the outcome of the struggle will be decided politically and not by any presumed economic historical inevitability. In the words of Manfred Bienefeld:

> The alleged irreversibility of globalization will be increasingly challenged as more people experience its costs and recognise that these are not due to minor temporary disturbances affecting a small minority, but are part of an open ended and long-term challenge to the majority's quality of life. Once that majority also understands that the obstacles standing in the way of a reversal of these trends are not immutable historical laws or technological inevitabilities, but political choices imposed on them by a venal and short-sighted minority, the time will be ripe for change.
>
> (Bienefeld 1995: 103)

Concepts and strategies of resistance

This brings me to the question of *rethinking the politics of resistance*. I began by referring to the imperative to address seriously questions of political strategy in the world economy and to define a political practice adapted to the global social formation—to focus on concrete concepts and strategies of resistance. We must imagine and invent the forms of the "post-globalization" era.

Some call for a "new ideology" to provide a method for different groups to develop "unifying strategies," and to prepare new ways to socially control economic activity in response to the instability of markets and the desire for economic stability (Boyer and Drache 1996). In the past, the workers' movement and unions had a special relationship to radical internationalism. Can a new union-based internationalism be the foundation of a new "unifying strategy?" While we should challenge the anti-labor and anti-state ideology of neoliberalism and hold them politically suspect, we must also take care to avoid merely repeating uncritically the labor strategies of the past. We must re-scrutinize the validity and applicability to current conditions of the traditional concepts and strategies of resistance emanating from the labor or trade union movement, as well as other types of dissident social movements. As Dimitris Stevis points out, "Activists would like to know whether labor organizations are basically sound but need to be reformed, or fundamentally unsuitable for a vital international labor politics" (Stevis and Boswell 1997: 93–104; Stevis 1998; Gills 2000).

We would be wise to avoid a "Manichean attitude" toward society and the state, that always locates emancipation in society and oppression in the state (Stevis 1998). It depends on what kind of society and what kind of state. However, given that the state has in recent history increasingly acted as the institutional enabler of neoliberal economic globalization, promoting capital's interest over that of labor, there is clearly a need to reassess "state-society relations" in response to globalization and the new role of organized labor within them. Likewise, organized labor has not always played a progressive national or international role. One strand of radical critique has criticized unions for operating within the confines of the capitalist system in such a way as to be an integral support of that system and limited by its constraints. The foremost example of organizational and ideological conservatism in the post-war era on the part of the trade union movement is probably the AFL-CIO, which has been widely regarded by its critics as having acted as the handmaiden of imperialism around the world—so much so that even one of its new leadership has referred to the past as the era of the "AFL-CIA." The promotion of conservative "business unions" and anti-Communist ideology by the AFL-CIO in the developing countries did much to undermine the building of a strong militant labor movement allied to forces of radical change. This history, combined with the prevalence of repressive/corporatist state-labor relations and bureaucratic hierarchical union organizations has done much to render the "higher tier" labor organizations at national and international level suspect in the eyes of rank and file activists. The tendency for local militants to view "higher tier" union organizations as "inherently autocratic and imperialistic" means that they are "deemed to have little value for efforts at fostering global labor solidarity" (Nash 1998a, 1998b). This results in a union version of localism which focuses on community-level struggle and linkages, while cross-regional and international linkages are viewed somewhat more passively. A more proactive version of this is the advocacy of a "bottom up" construction of national, regional and international solidarity, produced and led organically by grassroots leadership rather than bureaucratic union elites.

Due to precisely these sorts of problems and issues, some advocate that the central question in reformulating labor politics should be organizational as opposed to tactical (Stevis 1998). So what are the prospects for a new labor internationalism in prevailing global economic conditions? According to the optimists, "the present juncture is clearly quite amenable to, and perhaps even demands the establishment of a global labor movement" though the same analyst also admits that "such an outcome is neither historically inevitable or even highly probable" (Nash 1998a, 1998b). Others call for a new universalism via labor, uniting workers worldwide in harmonizing labor standards in order "to protect the political rights of all, so that capital cannot pit one group against another in a race to the bottom" (Bonacich 1998).

It may be possible to construct a confluence of the two streams of organizational effort, that is, combining the "bottom up" with a reformist "top down" effort to construct new cross-border and global solidarities. This would involve "higher tier" efforts to implement international labor standards, intensify cross-border organizing by national, regional and international union organizations, and achieve a new form of transnational coordination between various "peak level" labor confederations (Nash 1998a, 1998b). This involves a debate over whether it is better to establish entirely new peak-level organizations to embody the new transnational labor solidarity or whether it is sufficient and possible to reform existing organizations for this purpose. The recent reformist changes inside the AFL-CIO and its shift to a more progressive internationalism, as opposed to its notorious conservatism and imperialism of the past, has given some scope for optimism on the possibilities of reforming existing peak organizations.

However, the union movement has also been hampered by "internal" flaws such as racism, sexism, nationalism, xenophobia, and "protectionism" (e.g. of rich country unions seeking to protect jobs vis-à-vis a perceived threat from poor country workers or their unions). Such an attitudinal legacy needs to be rejected and transcended if a successful new global solidarity is to be constructed either from the "bottom up" or from the "top down" (Clawson 1998). For example, despite NAFTA and the linkages that were made between many social forces north and south of the Rio Grande to organize an opposition to corporate exploitation of workers and the environment, the union of United Auto Workers (UAW) of the United States still has no formal tie to the Ford Democratic Workers' Movement in Mexico (though UAW local 879 and UAW region 1A have done so). Getting workers from more than one continent together, even from within the same company, has proven to be notoriously difficult in some cases, though the Amsterdam-based Transnational Information Exchange (TIE) has increased this kind of internationalism in recent years, particularly among workers in Europe and the NICs of Latin America and East Asia.

Although native prejudice, bureaucratic labor organization, and corporatist union structures still hamper international solidarity efforts, some analysts nevertheless conclude that "the globalization of the world economy has opened up new possibilities for cross-border labor organizing" (Armbruster 1998). Despite theoretical predictions, referred to earlier, that recent global economic trends should make cross-border labor organizing more difficult, there is evidence that this is not necessarily the case. Recent victories in international solidarity actions with workers in the *maquiladora* factories of Nicaragua, Guatemala and the Dominican Republic, which involved UNITE (Union of Needletrader, Industrial and Textile Employees), the AFL-CIO, the campaign for Labor Rights, Workers for Peace, and the US/Guatemala Labor Education Project point to a new model of internationalism. The international solidarity campaign over the rights of garment workers' unions in El Salvador at Phillips Van-Heusen factories is another example of this new internationalism. PVH contracts out garment production, mainly jeans and shirts, to factories in El Salvador using young female workers. The struggle of their union with the company over union recognition was met with repressive tactics including involuntary dismissals, mass firings, death threats, severance payments, and a threat to cut the contract with the suppliers and move the factory elsewhere. After seven years of internationally coordinated struggle, however, PVH finally recognized the garment workers union. Although obstacles such as the effects of globalization of production, repressive/corporatist labor relations, a legacy of weak local unions, and a long history of AFL-CIO undermining of local unions all existed in this case, new strategies of international solidarity produced a positive outcome for labor. This involved coordinated strategies of legal assistance, media publicity, consumer pressure on retailers, and a concerted effort to criticize the company's carefully crafted public image and "code of conduct." A similar campaign against the activities of the company "the Gap" in El Salvador led to a historic independent agreement with labor and human rights groups who oversee the company's contractors in Central America (Armbruster 1998).

However, there is a continued problem that once unions have been recognized in a country and higher wages and better working conditions are negotiated, that capital will simply "run away" or "cut and run," a situation that requires urgent action by international solidarity movements. One example of this is the response by capital to the wave of mass strikes in the mid-1980s in Brazil's famous ABC region outside Sao Paolo. Industrial employment in the ABC region has been cut by half since the mid-1980s. Another example of corporate response to increased worker rights is South Korea, where the giant Chaebol conglomerates were influential in tailoring government legislation at the end of 1996 for flexibilization of labor, in the name of "globalization" and the imperatives of international competitiveness. A national strike by South Korea's trade unions at the beginning of 1997 eventually brought a climb down by government but only a limited "victory" for the unions (see Kwang-Yeong Shin, ch. 8, this volume). However, this was no solution to the increasing tendency of South Korean firms to relocate abroad, particularly to Southeast Asia, China, and Central America, nor any insurance against the subsequent IMF crisis in South Korea in late 1997 and early 1998 and its resultant austerity measures. Even in Blair's Britain, the relationship between a "New" Labor government and the trades unions congress (TUC) leaves much to be desired when considering the future of state-labor relations. In South Africa, despite the fact that the trades union movement certainly played a key role in the democratization process against the former apartheid regime (Mittelman 1996: 177–243) the current state of reform in South Africa, even under an ANC-led government, does not provide much hope for a progressive redefining of state–labor relations.

Notwithstanding all these problems and continuing obstacles, it is necessary to dispel the widespread view that labor movements are now facing some kind of general or terminal crisis and that therefore "the working class is dead" and no longer an important, or even relevant, social force (Silver 1998). The recent militancy of unions in Germany, France and other countries of Western Europe, when confronted by austerity measures flowing from EU integration or monetary union policies (Krishnan 1996: 1–22), though not really "the first revolts against globalization" are nevertheless positive signs of labor's continuing social and political importance and its pivotal role in resisting neoliberal economic globalization. Outside the core, there is even more evidence for the continued vitality and importance of union activism. As mentioned earlier, the past three decades of industrial relocation of production to sites in non-core economies facilitated the rise of new working classes, often of very militant composition. Such dynamic new unionism arose in countries as diverse as South Korea, South

Africa, Brazil and Poland. Such movements may not have been very influential in terms of global solidarity in the past, but they were certainly pivotal to national democratization movements. It is in the context of such larger social coalitions with a wide range of other social forces that organized labor has perhaps its most promising potential to continue to be an agent of reform and progressive social, economic and political change.

The labor movement, despite its great historic importance, has never been the sole social base of progressive change, so there is no need to falsely accuse it now if it cannot fulfil such an unrealistic role. However, just as organized labor has developed and adapted over the past century and more to changing national and international conditions, so likewise it both must and will do so in the present era of "globalization." Organized labor is an indispensable social actor in any large-scale movement for progressive change. Though obstacles exist, both internally and externally, to its ability to realize new forms of effective global solidarity, the movement to do so is already underway and is absolutely necessary. The issue of its eventual success or failure is a matter for the future and at present cannot be predicted. What is most important is to learn from past experiences and to take every advantage offered by current conditions to enhance and accelerate international solidarity efforts. By doing so, organized labor will increasingly play a rejuvenated part in emerging social movements that combine it with many other social groupings in pursuit of common goals. This certainly requires reform of labor organizations both internally and at "higher tier" or peak level. It also requires the realization of new strategies of solidarity work with broader civil society, both nationally, and especially internationally, as some of the examples cited above attest. The logical response by labor to the globalization of the world's production system should be a parallel "globalization" of labor from both below and above, leading to new effective forms of "global solidarity." Thus organized labor will also play its part in the emergence of "world politics" and "global civil society." In this sense therefore, we may speak realistically of emergent "unifying strategies." Globalization offers both challenges and opportunities to organized labor, and there is no clear pattern as yet between the tendencies to increase divisions or to transcend them. Everything depends on action and organization. There are indeed signs to suggest the emergence of "a global labor agenda that responds to both union and broader social problems" but the success of these movements depends ultimately on their capacity for "channeling local, regional or intercontinental mobilizations toward an inclusive labor politics and away from nativism and sectoralism" (Stevis and Boswell 1997: 93–104).

The role of critical, social, and post-modern movements

As Richard Gott put it in *The Guardian* in late 1996, "there is no future for rebels trapped in the past." The debate over political responses to globalization has occupied many thinkers on the left over the past several years, searching for a reformulating of radical and progressive politics under new conditions of struggle.

Whereas the socialist movement and communism (and their implicit alliance with and reliance upon workers' movements) provided an ideological and practical antipode to capitalist development for most of the present century, recent events of the post-Cold War era have brought old strategies into question.

Given the historic failure and collapse of Soviet communism and the communist systems of Eastern Europe, and the difficulties of building socialism by emulating them in the developing world, some radical thinkers have turned their scrutiny to imagine "post-modern socialism." For example, Burbach, Nuñez and Kagarlitsky (1997) speak of the rise of "post-modern socialism" which attempts to go beyond the traditional left's analysis of state power and revolution, but retains a central emancipatory orientation. There is a relation to be defined between such post-modern socialism as a new project of emancipation, and new post-modern social movements, which may presumably be central agents in the new strategies of change.

Post-modern social movements are defined by the fact that they aim not at the goals of the politics of "modernity," i.e. to seize state power in the name of revolution and pursue a grand strategy via a rigid formal model of (socialist) change. Rather, the new movements are characterized by their new objective of activating mass movements, via civil society, and to articulate new national popular movements, but via inclusive approaches when it comes to strategy and models of change. Therefore, they reject the centralized (Leninist) leadership structures favored by past revolutionary and radical movements, in favor of decentralized community-based decision-making. Their "inclusiveness" is marked particularly by their attention to the empowerment of women and previously "voiceless" groups or minorities. It is this combination of the politics of inclusion, egalitarian organizational structure, new gender empowerment, and a willingness to explore alternative strategies that makes these movements different from traditional movements of resistance or liberation. In terms of organization and strategy, they often use approaches that collapse space and time via use of telecommunications, and which link the local, national, and global within their struggle. One primary example of this new type of post-modern movement is the Zapatista Front for National Liberation (EZLN) in Mexico (see Burbach 1996: 34–41; Morten 2000) which not only convened a Democratic National Convention of some 6,000 delegates from all over Mexico in its local region of Chiapas, but via internet and other telecommunications solidarity links was instrumental in convening two global solidarity meetings against neoliberal globalization, one in Mexico and the other in Spain.

"Critical" social movements, as discussed by Walker (1994) for example, are defined by their self-consciousness about how prevailing social practices emerge and what forces may change or transform such practices; they look beyond the immediacy of the struggle, to try to understand the wider connection and possibilities between local and global structures and thus discover new spaces in which to act, and even to reconstruct social practices; they express skepticism about the possibility or desirability of taking over the state as the primary objective of political activity, and instead focus on consciousness-raising as a form of emancipatory politics, and to overcome the previous "politics of closure" (which can be read as an implied criticism of the exclusiveness of workers and socialist movements in the past).

Their new agenda includes newly formulated developmental, ecological, gender and cultural themes as well as new levels of democratic decision-making in participation processes. Their character engenders a reflective attitude toward the creative capacity of people to learn about their experience via their own struggles. Thus, such critical social movements and the critical social theorists engage in reconceptualizing and re-articulating emancipatory concepts and practices.

All this has the effect, in Gramsci's terminology, of undermining the cooptive strategy of elites, which he called *transformismo*, and of expanding and enhancing the political centrality of the alternative to it, that is *reformismo*. It may be argued that *reformismo* must be central to any genuine counter-hegemonic project which shifts the balance of forces more in favor of popular and democratic movements, whether in societies of the North or the South. Radical resistance, via *reformismo*, rejects the hegemony of the ruling elite and their use of the state as a conduit or "transmission belt" of the interests and agenda of transnational capital onto and into society. *Transformismo*, on the other hand, is characterized by the convergence of "alternative" programs until there ceases to be any substantive difference between them and the elite conservative position. We might see Tony Blair's engineering of the British Labour Party's move to the center-right and adoption of many formerly conservative policies as an example of this type of program of "globalization with a human face." A previous process occurred earlier in the Labor party and government of New Zealand.

However, there is considerable disagreement and skepticism about the potential of such new critical or post-modern social movements. For example, Andre Drainville concludes that "the new internationalism . . . seems to involve little beyond a vague humanism, a concern for the victims of the world economy" and furthermore "the new internationalism of social movements . . . is a mutable and ever-changing collection of narrowly focused social movements that are continually reminded of their transitory nature by the unrelenting restructuring of production in the world-economy" (Drainville 1995: 226–30). Warren Wagar echoes this sentiment and is particularly scornful of the capacity of new movements to mount an effective challenge to globalization. Wagar cautions against placing too much faith in the "nominally or apparently anti-systemic movements visible in today's world" referring to them as "a slender and wobbly reed, and at all odds little inclined to collaborate" (Wagar 1996: 1–16). Indeed, not all putative "anti-systemic" movements are anti-capitalist movements and many such movements are (easily) coopted by the reigning power structure of the capitalist market system. This is a recurring problem of resistance, past and present, and a criticism which is often leveled against the heterogeneous ranks of "nongovernmental organizations" (NGOs).

Others are more specific in their criticism of the limits of new movements to resist and challenge neoliberal globalization. Sklair (1995: 495–512) and Walker

(1994: 669–700) both accept that local level challenges to globalization can achieve successes; however, both appear to reject the idea that new social movements, or even "old" movements like labor, can actually mount an effective global level challenge to neoliberal globalization. Walker's interpretation rests on his argument that social movements are restricted to the "inner realms of society, in particular civil society." On the other hand, there is evidence of new global social movements, such as the women's health movement (Dodgson 1996), and the continuance of old ones such as the global environmental movements, and even the international peace movement. Nevertheless, Sklair's skepticism is based on the view that social movements lack the capability to reach the levels of international cooperation and coordination necessary to resist globalization beyond the local or national level. Other observers are less skeptical. Peter Waterman, who has devoted most of his career to studying international labor politics, has recently investigated the prospects of "social movement unionism" as a new strategy and organizational model (Waterman 1988: 289–328, 1993: 245–78; for further discussion see Scipes 1992: 81–101) and the relationship between social movements, local places, and global solidarity (Waterman 1998, 2000). Waterman understands the condition of globality as providing an increasingly central terrain for social movements, but he goes beyond traditional social movement experience and theory which suggest that locality is a privileged site for movements, and what flows upwards or outwards from here is "resistance" and/or "reform." David Harvey, for example, has argued that most social movements "command place better than space" which accordingly strengthens the tie between place and social identity. Thus social and working class and other oppositional movements, in the face of globalizing capital, "In clinging, often of necessity, to a place-bound identity become a part of the very fragmentation which a mobile capitalism and flexible accumulation can feed upon" (Harvey 1989: 302–3). Waterman argues that theoretically critical and socially committed understandings of globalization suggest that the local and the global are increasingly and inextricably interpenetrated. However, the new necessity of this condition is the bridging of local and global levels of organization and strategy by popular forces and social movements. Success requires a new worldview (in both senses of this term) and new understandings of "global citizenship" and "global solidarity" mediated by the emergent global communication/culture. There is a necessary connection between the emergence of these new practices and the emergence of new theoretical understandings, from which may flow an alternative global civilizational project. (For more discussion of the implications of "global citizenship" for a new civilizational project, see Steenbergen 1993: 37–61; Falk 1995; Held 1995; Waterman 1996). Waterman goes so far as to suggest that "Globalization . . . makes it possible, for the first time in human history, for emancipatory forces to at least begin to see the world both whole and holistically, to understand the interlocking of civilization/barbarism and to propose understandings and strategies aimed directly at the civilizing of global society" (Waterman 1993). According to Waterman, much of the practice to date by social forces in response to globalization, has been "globalization from the middle." The goal is to articulate this with "globalization from below," which must be continually strived for. In this process, traditional inter-nationalism (etymologically and historically a relation between nations, nationals, and nation-alities) must be transformed into global solidarity. "This means replacing the rhetorical internationalism of the nation-state period (when mass real-life experience was not universal and the universal was therefore unreal to masses) by one addressable and addressed to a world increasingly experienced by such masses of people—though differentially and unevenly—as both real and universal" (Waterman 1993).

The invoking of a new universalism flows from this argument but raises an inevitable question of historical tensions. The first tension is between rejection of the homogenizing imperialist universalism and modernism of the past and the grand strategies based on this way of thinking (including "socialism"), and the "post-modern question" of how to preserve and nurture "difference" which is fundamentally social, cultural, and historical, and thus autonomy from global capital. The second, and much more problematic tension, is that of how to reconcile the desire to transcend the "place-bound" localism of fragmented resistance movements with the "objective" requirement of our times in the "condition of post-modernity," which is precisely the "new universalism" which bridges the local and the global and thus establishes a basis for "global solidarity" among social movements, working classes, and other oppositional social forces. Waterman's formulation of this bears repeating:

A new universalism, both recognising and promoting plurality, must be based on a relational ontology, in which universalistic principles dominate procedures—requires surpassing with a dialogic ethic, in which procedures allow for the possibility of developing a common discourse between different and unequal partners.

(Waterman 1993)

This mode of communication and networking (for an alternative view of the idea of the network and its implications see Castells 1996) must transcend the earlier prototypes of the religious universalist, the liberal cosmopolitan, or even the socialist internationalist. Perhaps for the first time however, the contrast with the "global capitalist" is clear and openly expressed, including magazine advertisements with the banner "revolutionary" headline: "Capitalists of the world unite!"[5] Many regard it as a danger to limit the rethinking of alternatives simply to a new "global reformist utopianism" or to the revival of the liberal (or Keynesian) democratic national welfare state or the socialist-nationalist state. Both models have been criticized from the perspective of social movement theory for having disarmed social movements and civil society, thus preparing the way for the onset of national and global neoliberal economics. The debate on the new responses has to be much more radical, in the true sense of that word (i.e. "going to the root") and more bold and imaginative (Pieterse 1997: 367–82). It also has to overcome a certain "lack of efficiency" of past solutions offered by intellectuals of the critical persuasion to overcome North–South conflicts (Murphy 1994: 273). Simply pointing out that forming a new counter-hegemony at global civil society level by the promotion of transnational intersubjectivities is not enough (Morten 2000).[6] It is necessary to analyze and propose, from a meeting of practice and theory, concrete concepts and strategies of an alternative to neoliberalism within the current historical conjuncture.

To be successful, resistance to neoliberal globalization must be conducted in a coordinated manner on a local, national, regional and global level. Global re-structuring is occurring on all levels, which means that resistance movements cannot defeat global capital by concentrating on one level alone; capital can usually find ways to side-step such opposition. Although the local is the site of much resistance and a source of great strength to resistance movements, primary or exclusive emphasis on the local can lead to becoming colloquial and blinkered to other forces of resistance, leaving a movement exposed to defeat or even destruction in the absence of sufficient social alliances. The tragedy of the Ogoni people in Nigeria is an example of what can happen when a resistance move-ment is too preoccupied with local issues and the local scale of organization, yet operates against a national state allied to global economic actors (Obi 1997). History has shown that once a resistance movement becomes marginalized it will fail. Whereas the Ogoni were all too easily isolated and destroyed, due in large part to their failure to make sufficient social alliances in their own country and region (whereas their leadership was quite good at making international link-ages), the EZLN and the Zapatista movement in Mexico have so far survived (armed) attempts at suppression, aided by their attention to national coalition building, their linkages of this to regional and global solidarity networks with other social movements, and it must be said, ultimately to their own capacity for self-defense.

We must understand that there is a necessary (and perhaps inevitable) linkage between local, national, regional, and global resistance to transnational neoliberal hegemony and globalization (For a discussion of the need to link local and global reform movements see Pieterse 1997: 79–92.) Some authors are optimistic about the future of resistance movements to globalization precisely on the basis of the broad popular appeal of these resistance movements and to the struggles won by grassroots resistance movements against neoliberal economic restructuring in countries as diverse as India, Mexico, Nepal, and Costa Rica (Bond and Mayekiso 1996: 1–10). The issues on which these resistance groups campaign may seem diverse, ranging from regional and national land reform and social justice, resistance to structural adjustment campaigns, or the struggle for national and international labor rights, but all are a product of the same phenomenon—market-driven economic globalization and its destabilizing effects on society. Analysts such as Robert Cox invoke the historical inevitability of the process whereby "the counter force to capitalist globalization will also be global" (Cox 1996: 310). Richard Falk suggests that emergent global social forces are indeed challenging neoliberal globalization (Falk 1996: 13–27, 1997: 17–24; see also Lipshutz 1992: 389–420; Shaw 1994: 647–76; Spegele 1997: 211–41).

Workers and NGOs in the North have much to learn from their counterpart organizations in the South. Indeed, one of the most important points about the new global social movements, such as the women's health movement, is the positive empowering and energizing effects of a leadership role by people from the South (and in particular women) in a global solidarity movement. In the past, imperialist and Eurocentric attitudes were all too often present in international solidarity work, and it was deemed "natural" that Northern leadership asserted itself, though not always with very good results. Unions in the North can and should learn from those of the industrializing countries such as South Korea, Brazil, and South Africa (Boyd et al. 1987; Scipes 1992: 81–101; Rodrigues 1995: 30–4; Stevis and Boswell 1997: 13–104) while all social movements, including women's resistance movements need to pay increasing attention to regional and global solidarity (see Marchand 1994: 127–44). A key aspect of this process of rethinking resistance is for all these movements to recognize the close relationship between the state and economic restructuring, and not to run away from or default on state-level political processes. Resistance to globalization will continue to come predominantly from within national civil society and national social movements and union movements and confederations. The future success of resistance movements to neoliberal globalization will be enhanced if these organizations seek to break down the myth of the helpless state, often propagated by governments seeking to implement neoliberalism, a myth incidentally which even *The Economist* finds difficult to swallow in the face of evidence of the continued strength and importance to the economy of "the visible hand" (*The Economist* September 20, 1997: 19–20).

The emergence of global sites for resistance to neoliberal globalization is primarily a matter of organization and coordination. There are a growing number of organizations whose expressed purpose is to coordinate resistance on a wider scale than national movements. For example, the Maquila Solidarity Network (MSN) works to promote solidarity between labor and social movements between Mexico, Canada, and Central America and to develop organizing strategies that connect community and workplace issues, address health and environmental issues and problems of women workers in the *maquiladora;* Women Working Worldwide (WWW) supports women workers through international networking and public education and studies the impact of liberalization on women workers in many countries; the International Center for Trade Union Rights (ICTUR) works to defend and extend the rights of trade unions and workers worldwide; and the International Restructuring Education Network (IRENE) works to develop strategies and campaigns to protect workers' rights worldwide and to develop a code of conduct for transnational corporations. Such movements and the new practices of global solidarity will form new sources of democratic and progressive change at both national and global scales, as well as constituting new sources of knowledge and epistemology for "global civilization."

Resistance from within civil society and from the base of organized labor and new social movements working in combination in popular coalitions will be an indispensable part of the new resistance to neoliberal globalization. Through such action and consciousness, an incipient global civil society is emerging and may develop further capacity to bring about change. The process of "reflexive modernization" as developed by Giddens (Giddens 1990) implies an increasing ability by agents to reflect on structure. Ulrich Beck's "paradox of modernization" proposes that although increasing reflexivity should lead to positive political action and change, increasing individualization makes this more difficult to achieve via collective organization (Beck 1992). This "paradox," though more likely to apply in flexibilized post-Fordist workplaces, is certainly "uneven" in terms of the experience of workers in the North and those of the South, among sectors of the economy, and in many instances between women and men. Whatever the salience of Beck's concept and the realities of "risk" in the new conditions, the creation of new collectivities is an absolute necessity if we are ever to realize a post-neoliberal world economy.

In closing, the necessity of a "guiding ideology" need not entail creation of new grand narratives and new grand strategies. It can consist of a small core of values. I would suggest the following credo: There is no social progress without reform, and the reduction of poverty and inequality are yardsticks of human progress, not the unbridled accumulation of private wealth. Historically, capitalism thrives on an increase in exploitation only at its own peril, for it is an *unsustainable* strategy. Let us not forget why the state's social compromise with labor was so central to post-war solutions to poverty, unemployment, and structural crisis. The wealth and prosperity of "the people" are social products, not individual acquisitions, and are achieved through distribution of social product. They are thus about the realization of greater equality and social justice in social existence. Neither the market nor capital logic ever create equality or social justice automatically. The creation of a just prosperity always requires conscious normatively committed human action.

Therefore, it is by acts of resistance that we will establish our solidarities and our identities in the "era of globalization." As Camus (1984: 27) said, "rebellion is one of man's essential dimensions. It is our historical reality. Unless we ignore reality, we must find our values in it . . . Man's solidarity is founded upon rebellion, and rebellion can only be justified by this solidarity . . . In order to exist, man must rebel . . . Rebellion is the common ground on which every man bases his first values. I *rebel*—therefore we *exist*."

It is time to *overturn* neoliberal globalization, and by doing so to create a new world.

Bibliography

Adler, G. (1996) "Global Restructuring and Labour: The Case of the South African Trade Union Movement," in J. Mittleman (ed.) *Globalization: Critical Reflections* (International Political Economy Yearbook, vol. 9).

Amoore, L., Dodgson, R., Gills, B. K., Langley, P., Marshall, D., and Watson, I. (1997) "Overturning 'Globalization': Resisting the Teleological, Reclaiming the 'Political,'" *New Political Economy*, 2 (1), March; in B. K. Gills (ed.) (2000) *Globalization and the Politics of Resistance*, Basingstoke: Macmillan.

Armbruster, R. (1998) "Globalization and Cross-Border Labor Organizing," *Journal of World System Research* 4 (1), Winter.

Beck, U. (1992) *Risk Society*, London: Sage.

Bienefeld, M. (1995) "Capitalism and the Nation State in the Dog Days of the Twentieth Century," in R. Miliband and I. Panitch (eds) *The Socialist Register*, London: Merlin Press.

Bonacich, E. (1998) "The Problem and the Prospects," in "Forum: Prospects for a Global Labor Movement," *Journal of World System Research* 4 (1), Winter.

Bond, P. and Mayekiso, M. (1996) "Toward the Integration of Urban Social Movements at the World Scale," *Journal of World System Research* 2 (2).

Boyd, R. et al. (eds) (1987) *International Labour and the Third World: The Making of a New Working Class*, Aldershot: Avebury.

Boyer, R. and Drache, D. (eds) (1996) *States against Markets: The Limits of Globalization*, London and New York: Routledge.

Brecher, J. and Costello, T. (1994) *Global Village or Global Pillage? Economic Reconstruction from the Bottom Up*, Boyer: South End Press.

Burbach, R. (1996) "For a Zapatista Style Postmodern Perspective," *Monthly Review* 47 (10), March.

Burbach, R., Núñez, O. and Kagarlitsky, B. (1997) *Globalization and its Discontents: The Rise of Postmodern Socialisms*, London: Pluto.

Camus, A. (1984) *The Rebel*, Harmondsworth: Penguin.

Castells, M. (1996) *The Rise of the Network Society*, Cambridge MA: Blackwell.

Clawson, D. (1998) "Contradictions of Labor Solidarity," *Journal of World System Research* 4 (1), Winter.

Cox, R. W. (1996) "Global Perestroika," in R. W. Cox and T. J. Sinclair, *Approaches to World Order*, Cambridge: Cambridge University Press.

Dodgson, R. (1996) "Global Social Movements," paper presented at the Colloquium on Political and Economic Restructuring in a Post-modern Era, Department of Politics, University of Newcastle upon Tyne, May 27.

Douglas, I. (1997) "Globalization and the End of the State," *New Political Economy* 2 (1), March; in B. K. Gills (ed.) (2000) *Globalization and the Politics of Resistance*, Basingstoke: Macmillan.

Drainville, A. C. (1994) "International Political Economy in the Age of Open Marxism," *Review of International Political Economy* 1 (1).

—— (1995) "Left Internationalism and the Politics of Resistance in the New World Order," in D. A. Smith and J. Borocz (eds) *A New World Order? Global Transformations in the Late Twentieth Century*, Westpart: Praeger.

Falk, R. (1995) *On Humane Governance: Toward a New Global Politics*, Cambridge: Polity Press.

—— (1996) "An Inquiry into the Political Economy of World Order," *New Political Economy* 1 (1).

—— (1997) "Resisting 'Globalization-from-above' Through 'Globalization-from-below,'" *New Political Economy* 2 (1), March; in B. K. Gills (ed.) (2000) *Globalization and the Politics of Resistance*, Basingstoke: Macmillan.

Galbraith, J. K. (1997) "Preface," *New Political Economy* 2 (1), March; Special issue: "Globalization and the Politics of Resistance."

Giddens, A. (1990) *The Consequences of Modernity*, Cambridge: Polity Press.

Gills, B. (1996) "Whither Democracy? Globalization and the 'New Hellenism,'" in C. Thomas and P. Wilkin (eds) *Globalization and the South*, Basingstoke: Macmillan.

Gills, B., Rocamora, J., and Wilson, R. (eds) (1993) *Low Intensity Democracy: Political Power in the New World Order*, London: Pluto.

—— (eds) (2000) *Globalization and the Politics of Resistance*, Basingstoke: Macmillan.

Harvey, D. (1989) *The Condition of Postmodernity*, Oxford: Basil Blackwell.

Held, D. (1995) *Democracy and the Global Order: From the Modern State to Cosmopolitan Governance*, Cambridge: Polity Press.

Hirst, P. and Thompson, G. (1996) *Globalization in Question*, Cambridge: Polity Press.

http://csf.colorado.edu/wsystems/jwsr.html Special Issue on "Global Labor Movements," edited by B. Nash.

Jones, R. J. B. (1995) *Globalization and Interdependence in the International Political Economy: Rhetoric and Reality*, London: Pinter.

Krishnan, R. (1996) "December 1995: The First Revolt Against Globalization," *Monthly Review* 48 (1).

Lipshutz, R. D. (1992) "Reconstructing World Politics: The Emergence of Global Civil Society," *Millennium: Journal of International Studies* 21 (3).

Marchand, M. H. (1994) "Latin American Voices of Resistance: Women's Movements and Development Debates," in S. J. Rosow, N. Inayatullah, and M. Rupert (eds) *The Global Economy as Political Space*, Boulder CO: Lynne Reinner.

Mittleman, J. H. (ed.) (1996) *Globalization: Critical Reflections*, Boulder CO: Lynne Reinner.

Morten, A. D. (2000) "The Postmodern Resistance of Critical Social Movements?" in B. Gills (ed.) *Globalization and the Politics of Resistance*, Basingstoke: Macmillan.

Murphy, C. N. (1994) *International Organization and Industrial Change: Global Governance since 1850*, Cambridge: Polity Press.

Nash Jr., B. (1998a) "Globalizing Solidarity: Praxis and the International Labor Movement," *Journal of World System Research* 4 (1), Winter; special issue: "Global Labor Movements" (ed. N. Bradley, Jr.).

—— (1998b) "Organizing a Global Labor Movement from Top and Bottom," *Journal of World System Research* 4 (1), Winter.

Obi, C. I. (1997) "Globalization and Local Resistance: The Case of the Ogoni versus Shell," *New Political Economy* 2 (1), March; in B. Gills (ed.) (2000) *Globalization and the Politics of Resistance*, Basingstoke: Macmillan.

Pieterse, J. N. (1997) "Globalization and Emancipation: From Local Empowerment to Global Reform," *New Political Economy* 2 (1), March.

—— (1997) "Going Global: Futures of Capitalism (A Review Article)," *Development and Change* 28 (2).

Robinson, W. I. (1996) *Promoting Polyarchy: Globalization, US Intervention and Hegemony*, Cambridge: Cambridge University Press.

Rodrigues, I. J. (1995) "The CUT (United Workers Central of Brazil): New Unionism at a Crossroads," *NACLA Report on the Americas* 28 (6).

Ruigrok, W. and Tulder, R. V. (1995) *The Logic of International Restructuring: The Management of Dependencies in Rival Industrial Complexes*, London: Routledge.

Scipes, K. (1992) "Understanding the New Labor Movements in the 'Third World': The Emergence of Social Movement Unionism," *Critical Sociology* 19 (2).

Shaw, M. (1994) "Civil Society and Global Politics: Beyond a Social Movement Approach," *Millennium: Journal of International Studies* 23 (3).

Silver, B. (1998) "The Global Restructuring of Labor Movements," *Journal of World System Research* 4 (1), Winter.

Sklair, L. (1995) "Social Movements and Global Capitalism," *Sociology* 29 (3); special issue: "Global Labor Movements" (ed. N. Bradley, Jr.).

Spegele, R. (1997) "Is Robust Globalism a Mistake?" *Review of International Studies* 23 (2), April.

Steenbergen, B. V. (1993) "Towards a Global Ecological Citizen," in B. Van Steenbergen (ed.) *The Condition of Citizenship*, London: Sage.

Stevis, D. (1998) "International Labor Organizations, 1864–1997: The Weight of History and the Challenges of the Present," *Journal of World Systems Research* 4 (1), Winter; special issue: "Global Labor Movements."

Stevis, D. and Boswell, T. (1997) "Labour: From National Resistance to International Politics," *New Political Economy* 2 (1), March; in B. Gills (ed.) (2000) *Globalization and the Politics of Resistance*, Basingstoke: Macmillan.

The Commission on Global Governance (1995) *Our Global Neighbourhood: The Report of the Commission on Global Governance*, Oxford: Oxford University Press.

"The Globalization Debate" (1997) *Foreign Policy*, Summer.

"The Visible Hand" (1997) *The Economist*, September 20; Special issue: "World Economy and the Future of the State."

Wagar, W. W. (1996) "Towards a Praxis of World Integration," *Journal of World System Research* 2 (2).

Walker, R. B. J. (1994) "Social Movements/World Politics," *Millennium: Journal of International Studies* 23 (3).

Waterman, P. (1988) "The New Internationalisms: A More Real Thing than Big Big Coke?" *Review* 11 (3).

—— (1993) "Social Movement Unionism: A New Model for a New World Order?" *Review* 16 (3).

—— (1996) "A New World View: Globalization, Civil Society, and Solidarity," in S. Branan and A. Sreberny-Mohammadi (eds) *Globalization, Communication and Transnational Civil Society*, Cresskill: Hampton Press.

—— (1998) *Globalization, Social Movements and the New Internationalisms*, Mansell/Cassell: London/Washington.

—— (2000) "Social Movements, Local Places, Global Solidarity: Towards a New Internationalism," in B. Gills (ed.) *Globalization and the Politics of Resistance*, Basingstoke: Macmillan.

14 Lessons from Ladakh?

Local responses to globalization and social change

Martijn van Beek

Ladakh, a trans-Himalayan region in the Indian state of Jammu and Kashmir, is frequently held up as an example of a place where the negative impact of development and globalization can be observed particularly clearly (Crook 1980, 1991, 1994; Norberg-Hodge 1991).[1] The argument, in brief, is that this region was until recently isolated from the rest of the world, and was characterized by a way of life based on harmony with nature and strong community ties.[2] This Shangri-La is now rapidly being destroyed by ill-conceived, if not ill-willed development, modernization, or "Western industrial monoculture" (Norberg-Hodge 1991, 1997a, 1997b). The emergence in 1989 of a movement for regional autonomy spearheaded by the Ladakh Buddhist Association (LBA) is commonly explained as a natural defensive response of the local community, who seek to restore or maintain their traditional self-reliance (Crook 1994; Emmer 1996; Norberg-Hodge 1997a).

A growing literature concerned with "new social movements" readily appropriates agitations like the one in Ladakh and fits them into an overall interpretative scheme. Local communities, it is argued, are resisting the universal recipes of progress and Western-style development, which are regarded as the cause of social, economic, and cultural dislocations. These movements, it is suggested, share a comprehensive critique of what Sachs (1993: 5) calls "the Occidental worldview." They do not seek to take over the institutional forms of the nation-state and capitalism, but to replace them with something entirely new (Esteva 1987; Shiva 1987; Escobar 1992; S. Kothari 1993).

I will discuss some of the shared assumptions of this disparate literature and will examine the case of Ladakh. While there is no doubt that the agitation for regional autonomy was largely a response to profound changes to local livelihoods and decision-making processes, this chapter wishes to look more closely at what local movements such as these are actually demanding. Whether the movement constitutes indeed a community's *resistance*, or rather a more nuanced *response* and engagement with locally experienced realities of "development" and "globalization" is one part of this question. Paralleling Rangan's observations regarding the Chipko/Utarranchal movement in Uttar Pradesh (Rangan 1996), I will suggest that the Ladakhi autonomy movement is a call for a strengthening of the development project and state involvement, albeit planned and implemented through a Ladakhi local administration.[3] This disparity between the anti-development discourse about Ladakh and anti-development discourse in Ladakh suggests that it might be too soon to celebrate the emergence of popular alliances of radical forces.

Globalization, states, and communities

The anthropologist Sherry Ortner has taken a critical look at studies of resistance and accuses their authors of "ethnographic refusal," a lack of attention for what Geertz called "thickness," "producing understanding through richness, texture, detail, rather than parsimony, refinement, and (in the mathematical sense) elegance" (Ortner 1995: 174). She goes on to deplore the lack of politics in studies of resistance, as analyses tend to be reduced to a monolithic "dominant" and an equally monolithic "oppressed" or "subaltern." The problem that Ortner identifies here is indeed a common one. Generally, these "local" studies do not escape Ortner's complaint about a lack of "thickness," for example in that they already conceive their object of study, local movements, community predominantly through the lens of the global, erasing local politics, contradictions, voices and projects.[4]

The interest in local responses and resistance to development and globalization, of course, is not new, but has always been characterized by a multiplicity of foci, such as environmentalism, indigenous rights, feminist, and other forms of critique, which, however, often failed to "connect." In recent years, a new convergence on a shared frame of understanding has been emerging. With roots in the debates and critiques surrounding the sustainability debates popularized through the Brundlandt Commission report, this "post-developmentalism" literature broadly shares the characteristics attributed to the "new social movements."[5]

As Rahnema writes in the introduction to *The Post-Development Reader*, postdevelopment critiques are subversive, human-centered, and radical (Rahnema and Bawtree 1997: xi–xii). Similarly, new social movements, by definition, are grassroots, democratic movements that offer an anti-development critique. More than a mere failure of economic policies and the project of the welfarist/developmentalist state, Escobar (1992, 1995a, 1995b) and others see a "crisis of paradigms" beyond the strictly economic, a refusal to accept the *cultural* project of modernity: a eurocentric, rationalist and individualist post-enlightenment worldview (Watts 1995: 45). Escobar (1992: 402) for example, notes a "crisis of modernity" which he attributes to the "failure of the policies and strategies of development pursued during the past forty years." Drawing on Touraine (1988), Escobar asserts that new social movement actors "recognize the stakes in terms of a cultural project." Resistance, then, is not aimed merely at the dislocation of local (relative) economic and political autonomy by commodification and bureaucratization, but at the entire project of modernity, and especially its cultural forms. Resistance, in this reading, is a natural and necessary expression of local identity. The locus of that identity is called the "community," a wonderfully vague and generally undefined term that can cover everything from "gender" through "tribe" and "caste" to "race" (or its contemporary code word: culture).

The prevalence of local identity politics thus has become understandable because, at last, communities are finding avenues for self-expression through, for example, NGOs, global fora, and "movements." Thus the local agitation of "'peasants', 'urban marginals', 'those belonging to the informal sector', 'women bypassed by development', the 'illiterate', and 'indigenous people who do not modernize'" (Escobar 1992: 407) becomes meaningful and understandable through reference to a common, hegemonic enemy: development/globalization/ the West. In a move reminiscent of structuralist domestications of diversity, new social movements theorists and many of the movement activists who provide the "data" for the theorists can see resistance wherever there is agitation, community where there is a claim of representation, and cultural identity and counter-development as its driving force wherever identity is called upon in justification of demands.[6]

Movements, including "ecological" ones such as Chipko and the Narmada movements in India, "indigenous" ones such as the Chiapas rebellion, it is said "are not merely utilizing democracy with a critical edge, they are redefining it" (Kothari and Parajuli 1993: 224). The movements, then, are looked upon as not merely a possibility for challenges or resistance to globalization and developmentalism, but are already practicing it, it is argued. In a recent article Smitu Kothari lists a number of examples of "innovative endeavor" in the Third World that illustrate the "vast outpouring of democratic activity in the civil society" (S. Kothari 1996: 13). Among his many examples he lists assertions of democratic rights by "subjugated communities" and "minorities;" struggles of women; the numerous efforts to "nurture folk and indigenous traditions of song and theatre;" cooperatives movements; campaigns against destructive tourism and for human rights, against corruption and for local control over natural resources. Where Rajni Kothari (R. Kothari 1993) calls for a mobilization of the peoples of the South and of the excluded globally as a project to be accomplished, the post-development and new social movements theorists see such movements all around in full bloom: the critique is already available, appropriated, and put into practice.[7] All that remains to be done now is to create the alliances between these movements to set things right and achieve justice in the world.[8]

Indeed, there are signs of hope (but for what?) and perhaps they even constitute a trend (but leading where?). Upon closer examination of such movements, important questions arise about the goals of "the people" who are being mobilized or represented, and more specifically about the convergence between activists' ideas and popular ideas of what the movement stands for. The common enemy is generally seen to be failed government policies or a lack of government intervention. But are these movements offering radical democratic alternatives? Are they indeed rooted in ancient traditions, harmony with nature, and egalitarian conceptions of community as is the shared assumption of so many of those writing about the dawning of a new post-development era? The problem, it seems to me, is less with the diagnosis of why movements, resistances, or responses emanate from "civil society." But are these resistances? If so, to what? And do their objectives reflect broad popular sentiment?

In the rest of this chapter, I will use the case of Ladakh to discuss the question of resistance (i.e. goals and demands of the movement) and convergence between leadership and "popular" notions about development and the state. First, I will briefly summarize some of the dominant ideas about "traditional Ladakh" as a model for "sustainable development."[9] These include an assumed egalitarian, Buddhist economy and society, where people lived happily and harmoniously with nature. Then, I will look at some of the changes in Ladakhi society and economy in the years since independence and the inception of what McMichael (1996a) has called the "development project." These changes have caused serious disruptions in "traditional" ways of living. Even if we do not accept the romantic vision of an original affluent society (Sahlins 1972) as presented by some observers, there is no doubt that the development project and state interventions in general have profoundly, and often negatively, affected livelihoods in Ladakh.[10] But do people in Ladakh regard these as negative? And do they attribute them to development *per se*?

Finally, I will turn to the movement for regional autonomy in Ladakh which began in 1989 and ended with the institution of the Ladakh Autonomous Hill Development Council, Leh, in September 1995. Specifically, I will focus on the Ladakhi grievances, demands, and the kinds of policies they expect from their new self-governing body. Basically, as I have already indicated, most Ladakhis wanted *more* and *faster* development along a conventional development path.[11]

Traditional Shangri-La

In Ladakh I have known a society in which there is neither waste nor pollution, a society in which crime is virtually nonexistent, communities are healthy and strong, and a teenage boy is never embarrassed to be gentle and affectionate with his mother or grandmother. As that society begins to break down under the pressures of modernization, the lessons are of relevance far beyond Ladakh itself.

(Norberg-Hodge 1991: 4)

Helena Norberg-Hodge wrote her book *Ancient Futures: Learning from Ladakh* with the specific aim to show her Western audience that an alternative to "industrial monoculture" not only is possible, but already exists.[12] The book, based on her prolonged annual summer stays in Ladakh since 1975 and her "counterdevelopment" work, as she herself calls it, has sold very well. It "has struck a powerful chord with non-Western peoples and has been translated into 28 languages, including Navajo, Czech, Burmese, and Korean."[13]

Norberg-Hodge's depiction of Ladakh as a primordial Shangri-La is not original, but hers has been particularly influential in shaping the image of Ladakh around the world as well as in Ladakh itself among NGOs such as her own Ladakh Project and Ladakh Ecological Development Group (now a formally independent organization). *Ancient Futures* fits well in the genre of utopian novels, such as James Hilton's *Lost Horizon*, which offers a similar vision of a blissful society beyond the Himalayas.[14] Quoted widely, used in colleges throughout the United States and Europe, and recommended and excerpted in textbooks on (post-) development, the case of Ladakh, in Norberg-Hodge's interpretation, has indeed become a prominent one.[15] The film of the same title, completed in 1993, has also had considerable success both in terms of broadcasting and video sales, and is available in 13 languages.

Yet, while the book and film's attraction, also for educational purposes, lies primarily in its unambiguous, black-and-white depiction of a blissful traditional society ravaged by the evils of development, there are few Ladakhis who share Norberg-Hodge's rosy view of traditional Ladakh.[16] In a review of *Ancient Futures*, Ladakhi Buddhist scholar Nawang Tsering writes:

> Old Ladakh is painted as a Shangri-La par excellence. The contrasts between Western and Ladakhi cultures are striking. A picture of a self-sustaining and interdependent society in which the people have equanimity, contentedness, tolerance, humanism, balance and frugality is drawn. A Ladakhi reader may even get an inflated ego from the author's description of the wonderful qualities that she attributes to our people.

He goes on to offer a polite critique and reminder of some historical facts as he sees them:

> No doubt the faces of Ladakhis were brighter, and their songs and joys louder in the 1970s, when their celebration from the *beggar* system of forced labour was newer. But if one asks the older generation to comment on whether they were happier and better off in the 1940s or the 1990s, they would unhesitatingly say that as far as the comfort of their lives is concerned there is no comparison—in that respect they are better off now. Don't the people feel themselves masters of their own patches of land and don't they find their harvests sweeter as nobody now dares to lay a hand on them?
>
> (Tsering 1994: 46)

Nawang Tsering's critique of overly positive depictions of "traditional" Ladakhi society is corroborated by many oral testimonies I have collected over the years, as well as by written historical records, including those produced by Ladakhis themselves.[17] In general, older Ladakhis relate stories of life in pre-Independence Ladakh as characterized by widespread poverty and indebtedness. This is in line with contemporary accounts such as that of tehsildar A. N. Sapru, who wrote in 1941:

> It would be difficult to imagine a country more ground down by the burden of debts than Ladakh, and the extraordinary feature is that in one of the poorest countries on the face of the earth, the rate of interest is the highest

... The rate of interest is 25, and the more astute the creditor is the more interest does he contrive to compound.

(Sapru 1941: 13)

In addition, heavy tax burdens imposed by the Dogra state, landlords, and monasteries are documented in several surviving written submissions to the Maharaja, grievances and complaints submitted to the Glancy Commission of Enquiry in Kashmir in 1931, and accounts of travelers, researchers, and administrators.[18] Ladakhi historian Tashi Rabgias wrote of the Dogra period that "At that time, with respect to secular government the Ladakhis had been made powerless, poor, and without direction, with respect to religion the bases of offerings and power of monasteries declined and taxes were abandoned" (Rabgias 1984: 488, my translation M.B.).

Assessing development

Norberg-Hodge, Crook, and others contrast their harmonious, happy "traditional" Ladakh with a terribly depressing picture of the results of development interventions: the "development hoax," as Norberg-Hodge calls it (1991: 141). "Modernisation is undermining the very foundations of the traditional culture and giving rise to a familiar pattern of devastation, environmental and social problems . . . many Ladakhis are abandoning their farms . . . Children . . . are left 'educated' but unemployed . . . Soulless concrete housing colonies sprawl . . . the thin air is choked by diesel fumes . . . rubbish piles up . . . women are increasingly marginalised." With respect to "ethnic" violence in Bhutan and Ladakh, she writes: "Just fifteen years of exposure to outside economic pressures resulted in violence that left many people dead" (Norberg-Hodge 1997a).

Neither Norberg-Hodge nor Crook deny that "development" has brought benefits. Crook writes: "The historic shift in the economic base of Ladakhi culture is undoubtedly of great material benefit to the Ladakhi people" (Crook 1980: 159). Both stress that these benefits come at the price of increased dependence on India, through imports of commodities, including food and fuel. The most serious effect according to these assessments is the detrimental impact of development on the traditional culture and "psychological well-being" through "a subversion of values that allows only corrosive social change" (Crook 1994: 811). Emmer (1996: 43) speaks of "einem radikalen Bruch mit traditionellen Werten [a radical break with traditional values]." In general, Crook and Norberg-Hodge acknowledge the superficially positive effects of "development," but both rate the overall and especially long-term environmental, social and cultural changes as simply negative. "By almost any meaningful measure, the quality of life is declining" (Norberg-Hodge 1997b: 196). They are bound to come to this conclusion, given their uncritical assessment of "traditional" Ladakhi culture and social relations.

Many Ladakhis have a less negative view of the effects of development. Tashi Rabgias, a respected historian and Buddhist scholar and one of Norberg-Hodge's longstanding associates, writes about the experiences of the past four decades and comments approvingly on the progress made in vegetable farming, construction of roads and bridges, modern education, radio, and electricity supplies. Results, according to Rabgias, have been mixed, and he specifically mentions the introduction of pesticides and chemical fertilizers in agriculture. Regarding Ladakhi culture he notes that "religious affairs in the monasteries have continued as before, . . . statues and frescoes of a high artistic standard have been created in the many new temples . . . Dances continue to be performed on all happy occasions . . . music and songs remain as popular as ever, new songs continue to be composed, and books written" (Rabgias 1994: 19). Reverend Elijah Gergan, the highly regarded pastor of the small Christian community at Leh, in a piece on "Globalization of Ladakh" writes:

> Two good roads and regular air links with important cities of the north-west Indian region has meant that people from all parts of India and the world come to Ladakh for trade, jobs, research, humanitarian works, mountaineering, leisure and sight-seeing . . . No, Ladakh is not a hermit kingdom. A cricket match played in South Africa is transmitted in Ladakh simultaneously. Fresh vegetables from Punjab can reach Leh within an hour. Globalization . . . has taken Ladakh into its fold. The effects of this have been both good and bad. We pick up new ideas in agriculture, education, ecology, health care, business, technology and living . . . However, we often forget that this globalization often has many bad effects on our society.
>
> (Gergan 1993)

The view of Tashi Rabgias, Ngawang Tsering, and Elijah Gergan is widely shared among the urban elite. They have mixed feelings about the blessings of development, refuse to romanticize the past, and wish to see Ladakhis take control of development planning and implementation, to develop "a Middle Path," as Rabgias calls it (1994: 19).

It is practically impossible to find a Ladakhi, rural or urban, old or young, who will judge social change in Ladakh since 1947 entirely negatively, and generally people will deem change to have been positive. Especially in the rural areas, the government's interventions (irrigation canals, roads, schools, health care) are seen as almost entirely beneficial.[19] Many older as well as young Ladakhis will blame development for also having caused negative social and cultural change, such as increased individualization and greed, and declining respect for older people. Yet, it is patronizing to see this ambivalence as a sign of "confusion," as Norberg-Hodge does. Rather, it bears witness to the serious reflection that Ladakhis already give to the range of possible effects of development, quite contrary to assumptions of blind and wholesale celebration or rejection of "development."

Given their different and complex assessments of "traditional" society, the effects of development, and possible or desired future trajectories, a simple "response to negative change" explanation cannot suffice for the movement for regional autonomy. What then, in the eyes of the Ladakhi people, was the movement *against*, what was it *for*, and to what extent can it be said to represent a *popular* demand and project?

Development and social change in Ladakh

In July 1949, while on his first visit to Ladakh, Prime Minister Jawaharlal Nehru put it bluntly: "In Ladakh you are backward and unless you learn and train yourselves you cannot run the affairs of your country" (Amrita Bazaar Patrika 8/7/1949). Characterizations such as this have become normalized and permeate many if not all discussions regarding development and politics in Ladakh. Ladakh's marginality and backwardness are both justifiers for state intervention and for the *demand for* state intervention, and for the demand for greater local control.[20] Ladakh's "backwardness" is not denied by Ladakhis. Previously the elite, now a broader public recognizes it, at least economically and politically, and has been striving for "development" at least since the 1930s: education, infrastructural development, as well as "social reforms" have been pursued by Ladakhis (Beek 1996, 1997). It has not been merely an exogenous, imposed process, as many contemporary Western observers argue. The success of various political leaders in securing such conventional development goods, their ability to deliver the development project to the doors of Ladakhi farmers and entrepreneurs, was the principal subject of political campaigns, and still largely determines people's assessment of past and present political leaders.[21]

Ladakh's perceived marginality, in economic and social terms, is itself a product of the developmentalist view of the world, with its implicit and explicit assumptions of a global (and national) process of economic and socio-cultural development toward a "modern," literate, industrialized or at least monetized, largely urbanized society. From such a perspective, whether expressed in Nehru's statements in 1947, with Delhi as the leading light and glowing example for Ladakh to follow, or in the broader global sphere where India is now applauded for abandoning its policies for national development through self-sufficiency and is adopting the standard package of neoliberal economic wisdom, Ladakh must be seen as backward, poor, and marginal. After all, the region has no industry, and no real potential for any; literacy rates are low; cash incomes are low; most villages are not electrified; etc., etc.[22] The official perception of Ladakhi backwardness is illustrated by the general descriptions of and prescriptions for the area in official and academic writings. For example, the Leh District Annual Plan for 1994–5 stresses that

> the key for development of any place is the development of a basic infrastructure . . . The thrust areas in this District are the development of an effective and efficient system of communication like roads, bridges, air services, telecommunications, etc. Education, health, and medical services, optimum development and utilization of the energy potential, poverty alleviation and income generation by developing appropriate linkages with agriculture

and its allied activities particularly livestock development, tourism sector and handicrafts sector. Apart from this, there is a great need to preserve and promote the culture of the people by encouraging its handicrafts and other folk-art forms.

(Jammu and Kashmir 1994: 2)

Their "backwardness" established (and gladly accepted by many in Ladakh), the State was ready to step in and help Ladakh develop. Indeed, this developmentalist vision constituted what Jessop (1990) calls a state project, and is enshrined in the Constitution of Jammu and Kashmir:[23]

The State shall promote the welfare of the people by publishing and preserving a socialist order and that it shall develop in a planned manner the productive forces of the country with a view to enriching the material and cultural life of the people and foster and protect:

(a) The public sector where the means of production are owned by the State;

(b) The cooperative sector whose means of production are cooperatively owned by individuals, and;

(c) The private sector where the means of production are owned by an individual or corporation employing labour provided that the operation of this sector is not allowed to result in concentration of wealth or of the means of production to common detriment.

(Quoted in Jammu and Kashmir 1986)

Beginning around 1950 with abolition of labor obligations/taxes (*beggar* or *res*), the cancellation and settlement of debts, and a land reform with limited impact in Ladakh, state and central agencies took on a central role in promoting the national project of development. A rapid build-up of state bureaucracy and agencies, plans, and schemes followed. The main targets of the development strategies, apart from infrastructural projects such as construction of roads and airports, were agriculture and animal husbandry. Agricultural change has been characterized by a shift toward cash cropping of vegetables (catering to the army and seasonal tourist populations) to the detriment of "traditional" staples such as barley. In addition, both districts of Ladakh, but especially Leh District have seen a dramatic increase in population which has almost doubled since 1971, and quadrupled since independence. Not surprisingly, there has been an increase in imports of "essential commodities" by the government through the Food and Supplies Department, Cooperatives, and private traders.[24] Imports of rice have increased from 13,859 quintals in 1980 to 37,849 quintals in 1994; flour has seen a comparable increase, while kerosene imports have gone from 324,000 liters to 1,414,000 liters.[25]

The result of these processes, in addition to the general move toward urban, nuclear, wage-dependent households, is an increased dependence on the market and especially the government, which is responsible for much of the coordination and transport of "essential commodities" for the basic food needs of an ever-increasing share of the population. The precarious dependence on the daily convoys from Srinagar to Leh during the short summer when the mountain routes are passable, and upon which winter survival truly depends for many urban dwellers, is an important concern and topic of discussion among Ladakhis. People are very much aware of where the food is coming from, and who is supposed to organize its arrival in sufficient quantities at affordable rates: the government.[26]

As noted also by Crook, Norberg-Hodge, and Singh (1997), in recent decades trends have been toward increased dependence on the outside and the expansion of the role of government in Ladakhi lives and livelihoods. Mutual aid systems, nuclear families, and the agricultural and trade-based economies have been gradually broken down. Combined with the self-proclaimed responsibility of the government for "upliftment" of the "backward" population, this has made the (state) government the primary target of complaints, grievances, and demands.

Demanding more and faster development

The sector of the population most immediately affected by the changes of the past decades are the young people. Ever since the 1930s, and especially after independence "modern" education has been promoted by local leaders as a key to a better life, one that was wage-based and increasingly urban. However, as it was "geared towards the tertiary sector, non-agricultural, non-industrial" employment, this emphasis on modern education has produced a whole generation of people with at best a decent education in a labor market without jobs.[27] There is a limit to how many engineers the District can use. In most cases, however, the education system itself is so poor that most students (almost 100 percent in 1995) fail the matriculation exam which offers a chance to go to college. Even more so than the college-educated students, these young people "find themselves caught between two worlds," as Sonam Wangchuk, the founder of the Students' Educational and Cultural Movement of Ladakh (SECMOL) puts it: "They cannot work on the farms to produce their own food or even eat the food so produced by others, in that they cannot work with the animals to produce their own clothing, that they cannot build their own house" (Sonam 1995: 12). Moreover, they have been imbibing from an early age the promises of the modern life—money, fashion, consumption—and find that this avenue is closed to them. It is these young Ladakhis—Muslims, Buddhists, and Christians alike—who truly wonder what to do with their lives and who is to blame for their bleak future.

The second group of people who have a significant stake in "development" and resource allocation in Ladakh are those who *have* become directly involved in the money economy as entrepreneurs: tourism operators, contractors, and professionals. Some depend on infrastructural development to expand their market and business opportunities, others depend on the government's hiring for their career. And it is in this group of often very well-educated, younger people that the leadership and skills, as well as the energy and force, can be found to organize a campaign of resistance.[28] It is these younger leaders, well versed in the idioms and practices of Indian political strategy, who in cooperation with some members of the old aristocracy and religious leaders organized the agitation for regional autonomy.

In July 1989, the Ladakh Buddhist Association (LBA) launched an agitation for regional autonomy for Ladakh. A resolution adopted at the time states:

> Realising that Ladakh has always been treated as a colony and Ladakhis as third-rate citizens of JandK State and accordingly, Ladakh having been neglected in every sphere of life Socially, Politically and economically. We firmly resolve to launch a movement for an alternative administrative setup wherein the ethnic, cultural and traditional identity of Ladakhis is safe-guarded and that alternative is in declaring Ladakh as a Union Territory.[29]

In a pamphlet published later that summer, the demands and complaints are listed in more detail. Here, it is stated that "the traditional mainstay" of the economy, agriculture, has received scant attention, with the result that "farmers are still using the anachronistic cropping method with no new crops being introduced." Moreover, "the department has failed to produce a single hybrid seed" ("Ladakh Peoples Movement for Union Territory Status" 1989: 7). Other problems listed include the lack of development of irrigation facilities; the 25-year saga of the construction of the Stakna Hydroelectric Project; road construction; and the slow and insufficient flow of funds for development.

> Ladakh's tragedy is two pronged with both the Government and the bu-reaucracy singling it out for batterings. When projects get clearance from the Ministerial level, there is the bureaucracy, with its deeply entrenched anti-Ladakh attitude, firmly putting its foot down. Excepting the I.A.S. lobby, which in any case does not carry much weight in the state, the entire bureaucratic establishment has a kind of xenophobia of Ladakh: a patho-logical hatred.
> ("Ladakh People's Movement for Union Territory Status" 1989: 9–10)

The problem, according to the pamphlet (p. 6), is "misplaced priorities, faulty planning and a pale green attitude to implementation of schemes." The authors do not challenge the need or desirability of development but the marginalization and neglect of the region, the slow pace of development.[30]

The complaint of insufficient government support for development of the region and blaming this on the discriminatory attitude of the Kashmir govern-ment has been a consistent theme of Ladakhi political statements at least for the past 50 years. In 1952, the Ladakhi member of the Kashmir Assembly, Kushok Bakula Rinpoche, attacked Sheikh Abdullah's government for its neglect of Ladakh's economic needs—an act that received wide media coverage. Similar demands and complaints figure in the reports of the Gajendragadkar (1969) and

Sikri (1979) Commissions. They were raised in agitations in 1969 and in 1981–2. In the course of the latter, a series of negotiations with representatives of the State government led to an agreement in which the following issues were specifically mentioned: the allocation of Plan funds; speeding up of the Stakna Hydro-electric Scheme; opening of the Leh–Manali road; investigation of possibilities for improvement of transport links with Srinagar; establishment of a central school at Leh; proper maintenance of a seniority list for state employees; promotion of small-scale industries; subsidies for hotel construction; additional buses for the District; and speeding up of the Igoo-Phey irrigation canal construction.[31] These are the type of demands that are made again and again in memoranda, speeches, and letters to the Center and State governments. Clearly, Ladakhi demands for regional autonomy have been characterized by complaints about a *lack* of development, rather than a *critique* or *rejection* of it. The blame for present problems is placed on the Kashmir Government, not development, and as we shall see, solutions are sought in terms of planning, administration, and decision-making powers.

New administration, old development project

As posters in Leh bazaar proclaimed in 1989, there is "one cause for Ladakh's problems: the Kashmir Government; One Solution: Union Territory status."[32] As we have seen, complaints from Ladakh have focused on the alleged inability and unwillingness of the State Government to foster development in Ladakh. Government's communal, anti-Buddhist bias, it is alleged, interferes with the "objective" assessment and addressing of Ladakh's "unique needs." Hence, the necessity to "Free Ladakh from Kashmir."

Documents and minutes produced at the negotiations with the central and state government in 1992 show that what was demanded was for all practical purposes statehood, which as a long-term goal very clearly remains on the agenda of the LBA.[33] The Hill Council, logically, was to be as close as possible to full statehood. Among the powers sought by the Leh leadership were: control over all State lands in the district; supervision and control over panchayats (local councils); power to delimit constituencies for the Council; control over all plan funds as well as non-plan funds; power to raise land and other taxes; drafting of budgets and plans for the district; all state employees should become Council employees; and in general the supervision of health, food and supplies, rural development, animal husbandry and sheep husbandry departments.[34] In short: the Council was to replace the State government in practically all matters except law and order and the judiciary. With some limitations, this has in fact become the reality.[35]

The "Reasons for Enactment" accompanying the Hill Council Act state that the council can serve as a means "to promote and accelerate the pace of development and equitable all-round growth and development having regard to its peculiar geoclimatic and locational conditions." Neither the Act, nor the Ladakhi memoranda, pamphlets, internal documents or any other agitation-related statements ever suggest that Ladakh's future development should be radically different.[36] That concern is expressed at times, as mentioned before, but it is hardly a dominant theme in the events that we have been discussing. Ladakhis have not fought development or Western hegemony. If anything, they have fought their own exclusion from development as they saw it in Delhi, Jammu and Srinagar. They have fought the dominance of Srinagar, as they perceived it. In the understanding of some Ladakhis, they have been fighting an anti-colonial struggle against Kashmiri rule that began with the Dogra invasion in 1834. That was when "traditional" Ladakh and its ways of life began to decline, according to these people.[37]

Conclusion

Generally, in spite of the rhetoric of democracy and grassroots emanating from local politicians, NGOs, and many a foreign "friend of Ladakh," the opinions and formulations that are heard in memoranda, pamphlets, magazines, and political programs, are those of a small urban elite, both in the case of "development" and "ecology" advocacy. There is no single person or organization who can be said to represent a unified Ladakhi voice. By focusing on the grievances, demands, and notions about development as contained in the writings of politicians and other members of the urban "intelligentsia," the present discussion does not seek to replace the dominant (Western?) black-and-white readings of Ladakh as a Shangri-la under threat from Western/global monoculture with an equally simplistic "Ladakhi" one that simply demands development. Rather, I have tried to show that across different sections of the Ladakhi elite, including "traditional leaders" such as members of the nobility (*sku drag*), religious leaders, the "new" entrepreneurs, as well as the educated youth (and these categories overlap to a considerable extent), there is little disagreement on what is needed ("development"), why it has been absent or too slow (a discriminatory, "colonial" government), and what to do about it (autonomy). With regard to "traditional" society, again there is general disagreement with the idealized picture painted by many Western observers.

This significant measure of agreement among the urban elite, which to a considerable extent is also shared in the villages, does not lead to a wholesale embrace of "modernity" or "Westernization," as some observers have suggested, but rather to a careful consideration of both "tradition" and "development." Reform of "traditional" practices has been high on the agenda of Ladakhi activists, including principal religious authorities such as Kushog Bakula Rinpoche, as expressed in campaigns against hunting, excessive drinking, and animal sacrifice. Also, the efforts of an emergent modern educated elite in the 1930s and 1940s to reduce the power of the nobility, in part inspired by their exposure to socialist ideas during their schooling in Kashmir and other parts of India, are well-documented (Kaul and Kaul 1992; Beek 1996). The political process in Ladakh, as elsewhere, is characterized by shifting coalitions. The "traditional elite" does not form a monolithic bloc against development. Young people do not uniformly embrace development. There are differences in emphasis, disagreements over certain aspects of social and economic change, and there are differences of opinion on how to proceed. To ignore those different voices, desires, hopes and fears, as development bureaucrats *and* "counter-development" activists often do, can only be detrimental to one's project.

For those who desire ecological, sustainable development (and who doesn't?), there are indeed critical voices of "fellow travelers" to be heard and lessons to be learnt in Ladakh. In some respects the Ladakh Ecological Development Group, SECMOL, LEHO, Tilonia, LNP, and others do adopt more critical stances toward some aspects of "conventional" development, and interesting, creative solutions to certain local issues have been devised. Many if not all of these organizations were and are inspired by the efforts and ideas introduced by Helena Norberg-Hodge. With varying success, these organizations have involved villagers in the formulation of problems and the evolution and implementation of solutions. At the same time, even among the staff of some of these organizations there is little evidence or even awareness of the kind of comprehensive "civilizational" critique that post-development and new social movement theorists would impute. Moreover, most of them are heavily dependent on outside funding, draw heavily on Western ideas and practices, and are remarkably hierarchical and bureaucratic, which has given rise to negative perceptions and suspicions among the urban and rural population, which in turn has proven to be a serious impediment to the organizations' work.

As I have tried to show in this discussion, easy generalizations may not be possible. For a critical approach to globalization and development, in order to warn of the dangers and to develop alternatives, it is important that we do not jump to conclusions, that we take those who are living in places like Ladakh seriously, and that we do not dismiss their voices simply because they *look* like they have "lost their culture." For most Ladakhis the choice is not whether or not to "develop," whether or not "globalization" will affect their lives and livelihoods; for them, the issue is *how* to tackle the challenges of the present and the future, starting with basic issues such as food security, roofs that can withstand rain, and basic health care. What is necessary is a real dialogue, not merely an ecological vanguard leading the way. The serious engagement of those who disagree, including the angry young men in Leh bazaar, is a prerequisite for any movement of post-development, new social, or liberation ecology persuasion. At the very least, the voices of those who are supposed to be constituting these movements should not be silenced, ignored, or deemed mere expressions of false consciousness.

Bibliography

Bakula, K. G. (1955) "Ladakh Today," *Kashmir*.
—— (1958) "Ladakh Today," *Kashmir Today* 2.
Baviskar, A. (1995) *In the Belly of the River: Tribal Conflict over Development in the Narmada Valley*, Delhi: Oxford University Press.

Beek, M. van (1996) "Identity Fetishism and the Art of Representation: The Long Struggle for Regional Autonomy in Ladakh," Ph.D. dissertation, Cornell University.
—— (1997) "The Importance of Being Tribal, or: The Impossibility of Being Ladakhis," in T. Dodin and H. Räther (eds) *Recent Research on Ladakh* 7, Proceedings of the Seventh Colloquium of the International Association for Ladakh Studies, Bonn/St. Augustin, June 12–15, 1995. UKAS: Ulmer Kulturanthropologische Schriften, Band 9. Ulm: Universität Ulm.
Beek, M. van and Bertelsen, K. B. (1997) "No Present Without Past: The 1989 Agitation in Ladakh," in T. Dodin and H. Räther (eds) *Ladakh Studies* 7, Proceedings of the Seventh Colloquium of the International Association for Ladakh Studies, Bonn/St. Augustin, June 12–15, 1995. UKAS: Ulmer Kulturanthropologische Schriften, Band 9. Ulm: Universität Ulm.
Bertelsen, K. B. (1997) "Our Communalised Future: Sustainable Development, Social Identification and Politics of Representation in Ladakh," Ph.D. thesis, Aarhus University.
Bhasin, M. K. (1992) "Cold Desert: Ladakh," *Ecology and Development*, Delhi: Kamla-Raj Enterprises.
Brass, T. (1991) "Moral Economists, Subalterns, New Social Movements, and the (Re-) Emergence of a (Post-) Modernised (Middle) Peasant," *Journal of Peasant Studies* 18 (2).
Chohan, A. S. (1984) *Historical Study of Society and Culture in Dardistan and Ladakh*, New Delhi: Atlantic Publishers.
Crook, J. H. (1980) "Social Change in Indian Tibet," *Social Science Information* 19 (1).
—— (1991) "Buddhist Ethics and the Problem of Ethnic Minorities: The Case of Ladakh," in C. Wei-Hsun Fu and S. A. Wawrytko (eds) *Buddhist Ethics and Modern Society*, New York: Greenwood Press.
—— (1994) "Tradition, Development, and Conservation in Ladakh," in J. H. Crook and H. Osmaston (eds) *Himalayan Buddhist Villages*, Delhi: Motilal Banarsidass.
Cunningham, A. (1973) *Ladak, Physical, Statistical and Historical*, Delhi: Sagar Publications.
Dodin, T. and Räther, H. (eds) (1997) *Mythos Tibet*, Köln: Dumont.
Ekins, P. (1992) *A New World Order: Grassroots Movements for Global Change*, London: Routledge.
Emmer, G. (1996) "Ladakh, eine Kultur gerät unter Druck," in G. Emmer and H. Mückler (eds) *Alltagskulturen in Indien. Aktuelle Entwicklungen in der indischen Gesellschaft*, Frankfurt: IKO-Verlag für Interkulturelle Kommunikation.
Escobar, A. (1992) "Culture, Practice and Politics: Anthropology and the Study of Social Movements," *Critique of Anthropology* 12.
—— (1995a) "Imagining a Post-Development Era," in J. Crush (ed.) *Power of Development*, London: Routledge.
—— (1995b) *Encountering Development. The Making and Unmaking of the Third World*, Princeton: Princeton University Press.
Esteva, G. (1987) "Regenerating People's Space," *Alternatives* 12: 125–52.
Ganhar, J. N. and Ganhar, P. N. (1956) *Buddhism in Ladakh*, New Delhi.
Gardner, K. and Lewis, D. (1996) *Anthropology, Development and the Post-Modern Challenge*, London: Pluto Press.
Gergan, E. (1993) "Globalisation of Ladakh," *Ladags Melong* 1 (34).
Gielen, U. (1995) "Traditional Buddhist Ladakh: A Society at Peace," in L. L. Adler and F. L. Denmark (eds) *Violence and the Prevention of Violence*, London: Praeger.
Gompertz, M. M. L. A. (1928) *Magic Ladakh*, London: Seeley, Service and Co.
Gregory, D. (1994) *Geographical Imaginations*, Oxford: Basil Blackwell.
Harvey, A. (1983) *A Journey in Ladakh*, London: Cape.
INTACH (1988) "Leh Development Plan 1989–2009," New Delhi: Indian National Trust for Art and Cultural Heritage.

Jammu and Kashmir [Government of] (1986) "Government of Jammu and Kashmir State: Ladakh Region," *Srinagar.*

Jammu and Kashmir [Government of] (1994) *8th Five Year Plan (1992–1997) and Annual Plan 1994–1995, Leh District,* Leh: Office of the District Development Commissioner.

Jessop, B. (1990) *State Theory,* University Park: University of Pennsylvania Press.

Kaul, S. and Kaul, H. N. (1992) *Ladakh Through the Ages: Towards a New Identity,* New Delhi: Indus Publishing Co.

Kothari, R. (1993) "Towards a Politics of the South," in T. S. Centre (ed.) *Facing the Challenge: Responses to the Report of the South Commission,* London and New Jersey: Zed Books.

Kothari, S. (1993) *Social Movements, Ecology and Justice,* Cornell University: Conference on Global Environmental Change and Social Justice.

—— (1996) "Rising from the Margins: The Awakening of Civil Society in the Third World," *Development* 3.

Kothari, S. and Parajuli, P. (1993) "No Nature Without Social Justice: A Plea for Cultural and Ecological Pluralism in India," in W. Sachs (ed.) *Global Ecology: A New Arena of Political Conflict,* London: Zed Books.

KRBMS (1935) *Triennial Report of the Kashmir Raj Bodhi Maha Sabha,* Srinagar: Kashmir Raj Bodhi Maha Sabha.

Laclau, E. and Mouffe, C. (1985) *Hegemony and Socialist Strategy; Towards a Radical Democratic Politics,* London: Verso.

"Ladakh Peoples Movement for Union Territory Status" (1989), information booklet, Leh.

Lamb, A. (1993) *Kashmir: A Disputed Legacy. 1846–1990,* Lahore: Oxford University Press.

McMichael, P. D. (1996a) *Development and Social Change: A Global Perspective,* Thousand Oaks CA: Pine Forge Press.

—— (1996b) "Globalization: Myths and Realities," *Rural Sociology* 61 (1).

Mehra, P. (1992) *An "Agreed" Frontier: Ladakh and India's Northernmost Borders, 1846–1947,* New Delhi: Oxford University Press.

Moorcroft, W. and Trebeck, G. (1837) *Travels in the Himalayan Provinces of Hindustan and the Panjab, in Ladakh and Kashmir, in Peshawar, Kabul, Kunduz and Bokhara,* 2 vols, London: John Murray.

Norberg-Hodge, H. (1991) *Ancient Futures: Learning from Ladakh,* San Francisco: Sierra Club Books.

—— (1997a) "Buddhism in the Global Economy," *Resurgence* 181.

—— (1997b) "The Social and Environmental Costs of the Global Economy: Lessons from Ladakh," in H. Osmaston and N. Tsering (eds) *Recent Research on Ladakh 6,* Proceedings of the Sixth Colloquium of the International Association for Ladakh Studies, Leh, August 1993. Bristol: Bristol University Press.

O'Hanlon, R. and Washbrook, D. (1992) "After Orientalism: Culture, Criticism and Politics in the Third World," *Comparative Studies in Society and History* 34 (1).

Ortner, S. B. (1995) "Resistance and the Problem of Ethnographic Refusal," *Comparative Studies in Society and History* 37 (1): 173–93.

Paljor T. (1987) "The Economics of Tibetan Monastic Estates in Ladakh," Ph.D. thesis, University of Wisconsin.

Peet, R. and Watts, M. (eds) (1996a) *Liberation Ecologies: Environment, Development, Social Movements,* London: Routledge.

—— (eds) (1996b) "Liberation Ecology: Development, Sustainability, and Environment in an Age of Market Triumphalism," in R. Peet and M. Watts (eds) *Liberation Ecologies: Environment, Development, and Social Movements,* London: Routledge.

Prakash, G. (1992) "Can the 'Subaltern' Ride? A Reply to O'Hanlon and Washbrook," *Contemporary Studies in Society and History* 34 (1).

Rabgias, T. (1984) *Mar yul la dvags kyi sngon rabs kun gsal me long*, Leh: C. Namgyal and Tsewang Taru.

—— (1994) "Where Do We Stand Today?" *Ladags Melong*.

Radhu, A. W. (1981) *Caravane Tibétaine* (trans. R. Du Pasquier), Paris: Fayard.

Rahnema, M. and Bawtree, V. (eds) (1997) *The Post-Development Reader*, London and New Jersey: Zed Books.

Rangan, H. (1996) "From Chipko to Uttaranchal: Development, Environment and Social Protest in the Garhwal Himalayas, India," in R. Peet and M. Watts (eds) *Liberation Ecologies: Environment, Development, Social Movements*, London: Routledge.

Sachs, W. (ed.) (1993) *Global Ecology: A New Arena of Political Conflict*, London: Zed Books.

Sahlins, M. (1972) *Stone Age Economics*, Ann Arbor: University of Michigan Press.

Sapru, A. N. (1941) *Note on the Economic Condition of the Ladakh Tehsil*, Leh: Tehsildar.

Shiva, V. (1987) "People's Ecology: The Chipko Movement," in S. H. Medlovitz and R. B. J. Walker (eds) *Towards a Just World Peace: Perspectives from Social Movements*, London: Butterworths.

Singh, H. (1997) "Ecology and Development in High Altitude Ladakh," in H. Osmaston and N. Tsering (eds) *Recent Research on Ladakh* 6. Proceedings of the Sixth Colloquium of the International Association for Ladakh Studies, Leh, August 1993. Bristol: Bristol University Press.

Sonam, W. (1995) "In the Name of Education," *Ladags Melong* 1.

Spivak, G. C. (1988) "Can the Subaltern Speak?" in C. Nelson and L. Grossberg (eds) *Marxism and the Interpretation of Culture*, Basingstoke: Macmillan Education.

Touraine, A. (1988) *The Return of the Actor*, Minneapolis: University of Minnesota Press.

Tsering, N. (1994) "Book Review of *Ancient Futures*," *Ladags Melong* 1: 46–7.

Tsering S. and Crook, J. (1994) "Monastic Economics in Zangskar in 1980," in J. H. Crook and H. Osmaston (eds) *Himalayan Buddhist Villages*, Delhi: Motilal Banarsidass.

Watts, M. (1995) "A New Deal in Emotions," in J. Crush (ed.) *Power of Development*, London: Routledge.

15 Conceptualizing a new social contract

Ellen Brun

Premises and assumptions

Realistic concepts of alternative change require an understanding of the interaction between internal social relations and the international environment.

The transnationalization of the world economy has been changing all the rules of the political game! All along, the process has been accompanied by an almost unchallenged praise of free trade and free competition. In reality, however, increasing parts of global capital movements, production, distribution, and trade operate outside the sphere of free competition. They are internal transactions of a restricted number of actors, who operate independently of borders and are accountable to no one except their often anonymous shareholders. The situation has been exacerbated by the deregulation of capital movements paving the way for a delinking of financial capital from the productive sphere. The outcome has been "Casino Capitalism," a system of speculation on a global scale at the expense of often defenseless populations. As a result, an enormous sphere of non-accountability has emerged. Moreover, according to the Egyptian economist, Samir Amin, new forms of control have been produced. Five radical monopolies (those of finance, technology, resource-management, the medias, and the means of mass destruction) have been globally established and today seem to operate as one. One of the effects is a new historical phase of worldwide social polarization (Amin 1994: 17). Moreover, urged on by competition, an international division of labor at the level of production is rapidly replacing the former set-up based on the nation-state. This process has conferred to the capitalist class a new bargaining power which is fundamentally changing the balance of class forces (Ross and Trachte 1990: 25). Its lever of control is capital movement: the threat or reality of capital flight.

As a result, the restructuring power of the global accumulation process today constitutes a concrete and increasing menace to human survival in various ways and degrees. No corner of the world or level of existence is safe. Another important result is the division of the world into powerful, competing blocs. Many perceive this global power structure as a megamachine, in the face of which human beings are reduced to helplessness.

This contribution, however, is based on the assumption that it is the present internal societal organization which explains the prevailing political impotence.

In other words: If we could find a framework able to free our hands and minds so as to create a more intelligent way of consuming and producing in the highly industrial societies, *our* more sensible behavior might remove important obstacles to the efforts of reform in the Third World. Eventually this could make it easier to solve international problems as well. In this chapter, the attempt is made to formulate such a framework. In the context of globalization, the absence of an alternative vision or project is crippling or paralyzing initiative, as well as diverting social movements in dangerous directions. In order not to be accused of being overly abstract, the focus here will be North European, specifically Denmark. Internationally known as one of the most accomplished examples of a Social Democratic welfare state, the choice of Denmark should dramatize the effect of my argumentation.

Social change is always a function of relations of power.[1] Unable to legitimate itself through positive self-images, the ruling discourse presents the existing regime as unavoidable and eternal. In order to break this ideological hegemony, a mobilizing counter-project is needed. The implementation of effective change furthermore depends on the ability to create a political force or agency based on political alliances. For historical reasons, earlier examples have usually been alliances formulated by and for men. This has restricted political imagination. During the latest decades capitalist production relations have penetrated deeply into the sphere of close human relations—the "life world." This means that the ongoing crisis can no longer be understood exclusively in terms of struggle and cooperation between capital and wage labor (itself part of capital). Included in the dialectical relationship is the increasingly acute contradiction between wage labor and the whole human being (Lebowitz 1992). In varying degrees, globalization is giving rise to a life and death struggle between the world system as such and the whole human being, including the natural conditions for human reproduction. By choosing an ideal-type woman's perspective and seeing society "from below" power relations become more transparent and new forms of resistance visible.

People in the "North" usually pretend to know what is best for the rest of the world. The fact is that we don't! It is argued here that people in the "North" in their efforts to come to terms with their own problems under the conditions of globalization will be forced to become part of the solution rather than remaining part of the problem. Potentially this would create a basis for international solidarity not just as a splendid idea, but as a reality.

In the following I shall look at some of the real-life implications of the processes described in the introduction.

The social contract under attack

As already suggested, we are living through a global crisis. The environmental crisis is well-known. Very briefly the problem could be summed up as follows: The present Scandinavian way of life is based on global inequality. Danes, for example, belong to the privileged 20 percent of the world's population which consumes between two-thirds and three-quarters of the world's resources and produces about 90 percent of the industrial waste. This implies that our ways of producing and consuming are neither sustainable nor can they be generalized. This not withstanding, the international medias, our development experts, and the financial advisors insist on making *our* way an international model to be emulated by the rest of the world. This fact in itself makes our style of life a threat to humanity's means of existence not in a distant future, but today. The issue is not exclusively a moral one. It is recognized—although the consequences are ignored—that energy and other crucial non-renewable resources are rapidly being depleted.[2] Some believe that we are reaching the objective limits to growth. At any rate political, economic and social reorientations are certainly required, for which our societies are entirely unprepared.

The problems of the environment and the coming scarcity of resources are calling into question the whole historical concept of society in our part of the world. The key problem is that if human beings are to survive on Earth, this generation of Finns, Germans and Danes will have to change their way of life. On the other hand, private individuals (the electorate) in our societies depend on jobs based on a particular pattern of production and consumption for their livelihood. This is the political problem which has to be solved. But it is not the only one!

The aforementioned state of affairs is combined with an economic crisis. Both crises are undermining the basis of the social contract under which we have lived until now.

Since World War II, the social contract has been based on a compromise between the state, the labor movement, and private enterprise. The state and the labor movement cooperated to create a business-friendly atmosphere. In return private business was expected to invest and deliver the jobs providing people with a livelihood. Most men and women believed in this arrangement. They behaved and cooperated accordingly. Today however, this social trade-off no longer works. And labor is reluctantly being forced to adapt to the so-called "new realities" of a transnational world. In fact, there is ample reason to question the basic assumption even of the former arrangement.

In Denmark, statistics show that during the entire post-war period, employment was created not by private business, but by the public sector. Figure 15.1 shows that while total economic growth during the post-war period increased by 253 percent, total employment grew by only 32 percent, while the net employment in the private sector decreased by 1 percent (*Ugebrevet Mandag Morgen* 1992).

As we all know, the post-war period included the longest period of uninterrupted economic expansion in the history of capitalism, i.e. its "Golden Age." In fact, the economy was kept going and relative full employment created by large-scale expansion of the public sector. This was also the period when women entered the labor market in great numbers. Thousands of new jobs were created in the public sector to provide the (social and health) services to make this possible. In the process, Danish women became less economically dependent on their husbands. Instead, a new dependence was created: reliance on a patriarchal

Index: 1948 = 0

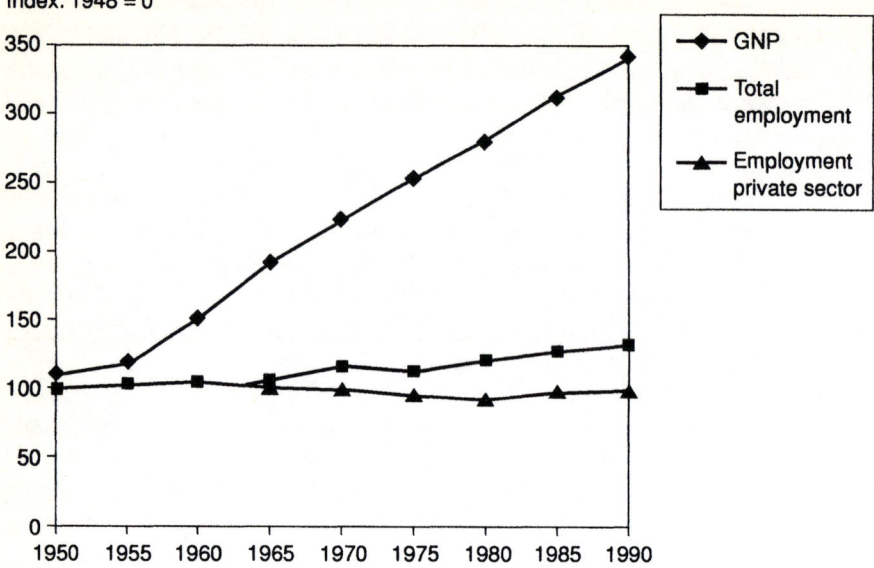

Figure 15.1 Employment and economic growth, Denmark, 1948–1991
Source: adapted from ADAMs databank, Danmarks Statistik

state for both social services and jobs. The traditional housewife almost disappeared to make room for the commodification of the private sphere and the rise of consumerism.

Today the party is over. Society is facing a situation of ill-disguised mass unemployment, while the state is paying the price of former expansion in the form of a fiscal crisis—the problem of financing the public debt. In other words it is not very likely that the private sector (the Market) can increase the number of jobs, with the state increasingly also incapable of doing so. There are of course great differences among the individual European welfare states. But the structural problem is almost universal.

All over Europe (both East and West) the preconditions of the social contract which operated and created relative harmony since World War II are evaporating. Unemployment is increasing while financial insecurity is reaching unprecedented proportions. In Denmark, the labor market participation of women is among the highest in the OECD countries. Families have come to depend upon this income. High mobility related to job possibilities has contributed to the breaking up of family and neighborhood networks. The dependence on childcare, health and welfare services is complete. Now cuts in social spending by the state are creating problems at all levels. The subsistence culture that formerly guaranteed the reproduction of the whole human being is disappearing.

The issue also concerns democracy. During the post-war period, market forces penetrated deeply into civil society. Unlike the situation in the 1930s when households could economize and be somewhat self-sufficient, people are today entirely dependent on commodity production either in the market or with the state as an intermediary. Mass unemployment combined with our existential need for a livelihood make people an easy prey to political blackmail. To live, we are told, we must be competitive. This translates into competition with East Asia, with Mexico, with low wages in Poland or with American technology! To live, we must not take unilateral initiatives to prevent ecological destruction in connection with our very own way of producing and consuming: rather we have to wait for international agreements, otherwise others will take our jobs. For the same reasons we are incapable of solving the international debt crisis let alone relieve the increasing inequality of the international division of labor— processes that lead to growing polarization between poverty (destitution and insecurity) for the many and historically unprecedented affluence (based on institutional waste) for the few. Thus, in the midst of formal democracy, real democracy and political legitimacy are being eroded.

And it will still go on. Even when we submit to the destructive pattern of competitive austerity, little will change. Unemployment keeps increasing and so does the gap between the rich and the poor in our own country. This creates a climate of social insecurity, a pathological resistance to change while paving the way for new unpleasant trends (xenophobia, break-down of solidarity etc.).

If the entire foundation of the Social Contract is indeed disappearing, we must ask ourselves: What will be the unifying idea of the new social contract? What can be the new platform for political struggles? The new social compromise capable of uniting people across the political spectrum? As we have seen, under the present international conditions neither the market nor the public sector can guarantee people the means of making a living. Still we have to live. The logical answer must be to organize in order to create the means of survival independently of the labor market and preferably of the state as well.

In fact, the ecological crisis and the socio-economic crisis converge in the sense that the obstacle to a solution of both is related to people's need for jobs in order to live.

The dilemma is exemplified in the report on global environmental problems, *Our Common Future* (the so-called Brundtland report) which sees economic growth as a precondition for sustainability. The idea being that growth creates employment and that jobs are needed for people to be free and responsible. But what if growth does not create jobs and does not liberate? Basic material security is the precondition for responsible action and the creation of sustainability.

This, I believe, is the new political project.

Practical implications of the new project

In the 1970s there was an international debate on a so-called "basic needs strategy" for Third World countries. What I am suggesting is a "basic needs strategy" for industrial societies. As an "ideal-type" model, one might call it a new form of mixed economy. We have today a societal organization consisting of the public sector (the state) and the private sector (the market). A third sector needs to be created, one of *subsistence* (or necessity sector), *as financially independent as possible of the two others*.

The creation of a sector of subsistence or "necessity" (a survival sector?) means establishing a new social space based on the logic of civil society. Its rationality would resemble that of the family or the household, where activities are needs-oriented, independent of market considerations. When I call the model an "ideal type" construction it means that in practical politics some compromise must be made at least initially and that its implementation may vary according to local conditions.

One can imagine different paths to the creation of universally guaranteed basic security independent of the labor market.

Conventional thinking conceives of change as the outcome of *politics from above*. In the context of the financial crisis, re-establishing control of capital movements is, indeed, a minimum political requirement for implementing almost any type of socially or ecologically responsible policy from above.

An obvious method of saving and consolidating the welfare state would be the redefinition of the role of the state, but not in the direction of an all-comprising, centrally planned economy based on hierarchy and control which very few people want. As we know, such a structure doesn't guarantee social and environmental responsibility, and leaves ordinary people little influence on their basic life conditions. But this doesn't mean that the public sector couldn't undertake selective income generating activities (to cover the deficit and the costs of necessary services). The concept of public infrastructure favored by classical economics could be enlarged to include for instance what neoliberalism adamantly refuses, namely public ownership and control of financial institutions (for economic and social reasons) or the energy sector (for environmental reasons) as well as the sectors recently privatized: telecommunications, public transportation, the health sector (including the production of medicine).

Given a sufficient political consensus, the aforementioned new "necessity sector" (parallel to and coexisting with the market) might be publicly promoted or organized. The Swedish economist Gunnar Adler-Karlsson years ago suggested a system where, as an alternative to income tax, all citizens would contribute a restricted amount of flexibly organized labor in the course of their lifetime to collectively produce the minimum necessary, in exchange for receiving a purchasing card giving lifelong access to the minimum goods and services to guarantee basic material security. This "Necessity" sector would coexist with what he calls the sector of "affluence," i.e. the sphere of free initiative and enterprise (Adler-Karlsson 1977).[3]

Another important (but at the moment hardly realistic) step would be a financial reform abolishing interest on money. For many, this would spell instant relief from a situation which is becoming unbearable (most home owners, farmers, fishermen, small business, students etc. are in debt). Interest rates constitute an enormous obstacle to necessary initiatives on almost every level, including the welfare sector. In Denmark, old people's homes, hospitals, all public buildings, and institutions pay large amounts every year on debt servicing. Since interest payments are tax-deductable, the financial system contributes to the state's fiscal crisis both directly and indirectly. Such a reform would abolish money in the commodity form, while retaining money as means of circulation.[4] However practical and reasonable the suggested reforms would be (and more could be added), they are not (yet?) part of the political agenda.[5]

Moreover, politics aiming at social and environmental sustainability will hardly succeed unless combined with a mass movement and a clear vision. Under the conditions of globalization the space for national politics, exclusively from above, is limited. Nevertheless, "for better or for worse," the situation is bound to change . . .

In contrast to conventional political thinking, most grassroots movements perceive change as something that grows from below. Deliberately choosing such an approach implies a strategy of transformation based on the step-by-step creation of basic material and social security from below, namely solidarity.[6] On every turn, for every choice of options the measuring rod must be: What would be the consequences for the most exposed groups? The immediate objective of universally guaranteed basic security is to remove the fear of loosing one's job, one's means of livelihood. Nobody should legitimately fear that any proposed change would be at his or her expense. The method involves creating a very thinly meshed security net, starting from below. As an "ideal-type" vision on this basis, the sector of subsistence (necessity sector) should, to the largest possible extent, be self-organized, economically independent and rooted in everyday practice. Its existence could, as a long-term perspective, lead to a shrinking of the state. The strategic question becomes: How Do We Move From Here to There? In a less complex society (or in a situation of social collapse and general upheaval) the policy might consist of promoting (from above and from below) the voluntary formation of cooperation and redistribution covering basic needs, independent of, but coexisting with, the market. An organized survival network would need to guarantee all participants a lifetime provision of basic necessities. In some societies, a land reform and the collectively organized provision of funds would be required. In Denmark, the relatively self-sufficient household of the 1930s belongs to the past. The majority is entirely dependent on income-generating activities or welfare, the availability of which can no longer be taken for granted. Life in society is complicated, housing and rents are high, and most people have private debts. The private car has expropriated the "commons," i.e. the public space, where civil society should ideally unfold. There is a serious problem of social disintegration and atomization. This background indicates a different road to universally guaranteed subsistence.

The movement

Most academics and scholars of the social sciences working with theoretical constructions are reluctant to venture into the territory of everyday life.[7] The same applies to anti-systemic Marxists who fail to look beyond the capital—labor nexus. As a consequence, they see the present period as characterized by a poverty of political movements. In reality, however, in Denmark (and I believe the same is true for several European countries) the social activities to carry out the forementioned project already exist. It may be described as a movement on three levels.

The roots . . . on which everything else depends

Here I am referring to the everyday practice of individuals, small local groups, basis groups, initiative groups or networks, but mainly mutually independent activities. The "model" is based on the premise of starting from where you are: removing the obstacles that can be removed. There is a caring for the environment and for each other: the sorting of waste, environmental activism, promotion of health, recycling, mutual aid (social, psychological, practical), organizing get-together parties in the department building, spring celebration between neighbors on the street, setting up non-profit cafes or clubs in the specific neighborhood. There is the common cultivation of gardens (allotments), the exchange of clothes, furniture, services, food, the produce of the garden. There is communal living (small and big collectives), the sharing of habitations and production collectives. Some do it because they are in financial difficulties, others for practical reasons, and still others simply as a way of socializing. Some are anti-consumers. There is a strong element of rebellion against the ruling logic (the market forces, wage labor, the tax authorities, social control). Many activities are characterized by a popular, profusive and exuberant cultural life on all levels: songs, music, dancing, performance, decorations, dressing up and making of masks, political dialogues, street theatre, caravans, clowns, etc.

A significant informal sector (green, "black" or red) has emerged which constitutes people's way of surviving and establishing control over part of their life conditions. It is characterized by a needs-oriented perseverance, relatively independent of exchange value. As little money as possible is involved. Of course there is a considerable amount of moonshining. But that is only part of the phenomenon. Things are exchanged, given away, fished out of garbage containers. The gift principle is widespread. There is an implicit feeling that human relations and things tend to lose their value when you ask to be paid for them. There is a considerable amount of social tolerance: What is taking place is not a matter of "free and equal exchange," but the unfolding of variety and living together.

Out of this confusion, controlled and surveyed by nobody, a new political culture is emerging. A cooperation for survival and for the unfolding of potentials. The approach is concrete and practical. In the midst of contradictions everyone does his or her best. Some people constantly lose courage, and constantly new beginnings are made. Not just socially and culturally. Protection of the environment and resource management constitute a growing community of interest. What is at issue is the conquest of areas of social self-determination: control over basic life conditions independent of wage labor and the market.[8]

Experimentation and innovation

There are two processes operating here. The first is the *practical* process of innovation which goes on from the grassroots to the higher specialized level—a movement of experimentation, learning from each other and assigning each other new tasks, etc. For example, developing ecological farming, forms of cohabitation, trading and artisanal cooperatives, new forms of technology friendly to the environment and appropriate for the user's purpose and purchasing power; experimentation with new forms of recycling, renewable energy, muld-closets, houses built from mud or recycled waste, creative cooking based on home-grown products, holistic health, artistic creativity and play as new pedagogical forms. Several groups are working on alternative banking systems, which operate practically without interest and invest in environmentally or socially "sound" activities. Some areas have developed their own means of exchange, some experiment with new exchange networks such as LETS.[9]

The other part of the process is *theoretical* and involves the attempt to solve concrete problems in connection with the organization of a different society. What does an environmentally sustainable form of transportation, health services, educational system, farming, fishing, housing, etc. look like? How do we, step by step, change the physical structure of urbanization in the direction of sustainability? City-ecology, energy problems, control of poisonous waste, the protection of drinking water—all of this is accompanied by ethical, scientific, theoretical or philosophical re-evaluations.

Busy as beavers this work is being pursued, but with scarce attention from research institutions and with little public support. It is hardly exaggerated to claim that the solution to many of the most serious problems are theoretically available if not already practiced in the free space people have managed to create.

The political level

Here the experience gained from the other two levels should ideally be translated into political action. Instead we see a great deal of confusion and impotence.

Because of the lack of alternative thinking, the past 20 years have seen the emergence of a multitude of one-issue movements: the greens, peace, and anti-war movements, women's movements. We have the "Revolt from the Center" movement with its demand for a citizen wage, solidarity movements with the Third World or with oppressed minorities, anti-racism, the so-called "autonomous" movement, social solidarity, etc; and in more recent years the rebellion from the marginalized (in a Danish context the so-called C-Team) and the fast expanding ecological network. Nearly all of these operate on the basis of voluntary contributions and unpaid labor. On top of this, ordinary, upright Danish citizens every year anonymously donate vast sums of their hard-earned money for humanitarian purposes. They constitute the antithesis to the claim of conventional economics that human beings are born with a mercenary, calculating mind!

These activities are separate, non-coordinated. A closer look, however, reveals a community of attitudes: solidarity with oppressed people or people in need, care for the environment, resistance to tyranny, inhuman structures and behavior such as militarism and racism, and positively, the fight for democracy, liberation and solidarity. These currents spring out of a natural ethical consciousness related to what the Danish philosopher K. E. Loegstrup calls "sovereign life expressions"—instincts and ideals about the relationship between people which lend direction to our actions (Loegstrup 1956). Similar trends have existed earlier in history, but seldom so quietly and on a comparable scale.

The political problem consists in creating a space for these potentials to unfold and turning them into an agency of real political change. The most logical answer which is being discussed in Denmark, would be the introduction of a citizen wage.[10] The citizen wage (or guaranteed basic income) is conceived in anti-systemic circles not as a goal in itself but as a *method*: a first step to remove social obstacles to sustainability and create a more flexible situation, or a setting free of the potentials of civil society.

The concept of the citizen wage

The basic idea is to provide every individual with a minimum material security *independent of participation in the labor market*. This could be achieved in the form of collectively guaranteeing all citizens free access during their lifetime to certain basic goods and services. It could also be in the form of monetary entitlements. In Denmark, the simplest way would be for the State to guarantee every person above the age of 18 a fixed sum of, say, DKK 5,000 a month. The amount should be tax-free and no public or private creditor should be able to lay claim upon it (the insecurity of many Danes is linked to private debt). The entitlement could be supplemented through unemployment insurance so that people who unintentionally lose their job (and remain at the disposal of the labor market) receive the same compensation as today. The citizen wage is conceived as a somewhat lower amount than what is left after tax deduction in the highest unemployment rate. It corresponds approximately to the Danish old age pension.)

Financing the citizen wage

The most mundane argument against the project rests on the financial crisis of the Danish state, where income tax has reached a record high. A common question is: won't the introduction of a universal citizen wage be too expensive? The strategy as outlined above implies that it cannot be financed at the expense of the welfare state. It does not substitute special arrangements and care for the handicapped, the elderly, the children or other exposed groups. Rather the opposite is the case. The whole idea behind the citizen wage implies a strengthening of the social safety-net. Apart from human considerations, the envisaged reorganization of society, imposed by environmental imperatives and the growth of unemployment, can only be harmoniously achieved if it is based on solidarity.[11]

Nevertheless, in a country like Denmark—and the same goes for other countries with large state budgets—the project need not impose an additional financial burden as long as we keep in mind its strategic purpose. The citizen wage should *not* be understood as an extra income everybody receives every month, i.e. as a kind of general wage increase. This would cause inflation, apart from being absurd. The intention is not to make the rich even wealthier, but to make everybody more socially secure and free.

For those employed in the public sector, the citizen wage could be that part of the wage which is retained, whether you have a job or not. It would be identical with the tax-free lowest income. To cover the difference (from the point of view of the state) caused by the higher level of tax deduction, the wage itself could be lowered proportionally, following the rule that *the personal net income after tax should remain unchanged.* For the majority this would make the difference between the citizen wage and the full wage rather small and the temptation to take time off to live on a citizen wage correspondingly greater. Assuming that the lower salaries in the public sector spill over to the private sector, business would suddenly be able to employ people at a lower cost, since they are now receiving a "subsidy" in the form of a guaranteed basic income. As the company owner also gets a citizen wage, this would be a bit too much of a good thing! Keeping in mind that the intention is not to make well-to-do people even richer, the State would have to cover the difference by means of some particular tax or employer contribution.[12]

Of Denmark's population of 5.1 million, only about 300,000–400,000 adults need to be accounted for, namely, those engaged in the free enterprise sector, farmers, businessmen, etc. Here, the citizen wage might replace some of the present proliferation of state subsidies or tax privileges which are very unequally distributed among private entrepreneurs. In Denmark, private enterprise receives a large amount of direct and indirect state support so that in many branches the ability to fill out questionnaires and write applications is more decisive for financial success than production itself. The new system would imply that money follows the person rather than things.[13] The latter part of the reform would perhaps have to be implemented as a gradual process based on negotiations and adaptation to specific sectoral needs. Once established, such a system would be much more democratic, creating new life conditions for activities in less populated areas, etc. It would simplify private bureaucracy for the individual as well as public administration. The introduction of the citizen wage in itself would save a lot of administrative expense. Being universal, it requires no control, and once established, it could be distributed by means of a computer and the post office!

The citizen wage is only the first step

The citizen wage, thus conceived, initially has to be paid for through a redistribution of public expenditures. At present the latter are financed by the tax system. This situation is far from ideal. What happens, for instance, if the citizen wage succeeds? If a lot of people use the opportunity to engage in an independent lifestyle, if thousands of citizen initiatives and civil societies flourish independently of the market, who will then pay the taxes to finance the citizen wage and the welfare state? The crisis in state finances might in itself undermine the citizen wage from within in the form of privatizations, deregulation, public savings, higher prices for public transportation, medicine, etc. All this implies that the citizen wage is to be seen not as an objective, in and of itself, but as a method or a strategy. Through citizens' initiative the citizen wage (defined as universally guaranteed basic security) should, as soon as possible, become self-reliant and gradually self-financed as well—not in the absolute sense, of course, but understood as an ever-present priority, lending direction to our practice.

With a guaranteed basic income, people would to an increasing extent be free to create their own mutual aid networks and mutual subsistence networks so that basic material security could gradually take the form of real goods and services collectively produced and distributed. In the Danish context, the idea is not historically new. In the 1930s, unemployed workers established a number of successful cooperative enterprises. Today, such initiatives could be supported through interest-free loans either from new alternative banks, or from existing pension savings and other employed peoples' savings (though whether or not an individual contributes would be a matter of free choice).

In other words, for practical reasons, the citizen wage will, in the first instance, have to be an unconditional universal right financed through the tax system. As a gradual process, however, minimum basic security could be redefined as the reward everybody receives in exchange for socially useful labor. A universal right to basic material security which citizens mutually guarantee each other through the universal obligation to take part in flexibly organized production, the extent and content of which are democratically decided by the participants themselves (in its "mature" form, such a "sector of necessity" would probably function as a combination of centralized and decentralized organization operating independently of but at the same time coexisting with the market).

The implications of the citizen wage

The citizen wage implies a change in the concept of the welfare state from patriarchal, patronizing welfare from above based on tutelage and social control to a welfare society as a liberating project. It would guarantee universal material security independent of the labor market as the precondition for freedom and responsibility (social responsibility in turn becoming the precondition of freedom).

In this new form of mixed economy (state, market, necessity sector) the role of the market would change. It has been said that the market is an excellent servant but a terrifying master. By abolishing the *coercive* part of wage labor, the market would function as the excellent servant of everyone—not as the master of society. In other words, the marketplace would be liberated from the most distorting effects of the "market forces" (Polanyi 1944), creating a type of competition based on voluntary exchange. It would also change attitudes to consumerism.

People would now have a real choice between the amount of wage labor they want to invest, and the material standard of living to which they aspire. Some would realize that letting out a room or giving up the car could make the difference between full-time labor and a freer, more flexible style of life.

The concept of labor would change

The present social contract makes it virtually impossible for people on the dole or on welfare to engage in voluntary non-paid activities which might threaten the job of somebody else. With a citizen wage the role of organized labor would change. The atmosphere on the labor market would become more relaxed, competition for jobs less acute, and the relationship between buyers and sellers of labor power more equal. This implies a potential for organized labor to play a more active and positive role in the reorientation of production inside and outside the formal sector. The citizen wage creates the preconditions to overcome economism within the labor movement: a capitalist legacy which the socialist tradition has had difficulty overcoming.

In Denmark, the majority of people would probably still want a job. Not only because wage labor has become part of a person's identity (this would change) but because modern living is expensive. Modern adults have become socialized to expect others to organize their time and feel correspondingly insecure at the prospect of almost unlimited disposable time—not least in the light of present conditions where the private sphere has become depopulated and devoid of meaning. The citizen wage conceived in the above manner does not in itself create more jobs. There would, however, be more job-rotation, more part-time or flexible employment, greater mobility in and out of the labor market according to needs in the different stages of one's life. Experience in Denmark indicates that the universal possibility to take leaves of absence (full time or part time) would create a turnover on the labor market that would render terms such as "unemployment or "exclusion" obsolete. Also the material basis for inequality between the sexes would be removed possibly implying a fundamental change in the relationship between old and young, children and adults, men and women.

After the introduction of the citizen wage

It is always difficult to predict the future. The freedom which would be released by removing the constraints of wage labor would be channeled in directions which are viewed as "uneconomical" under a market economy. Not only real needs, but imagination would be in command. First of all many would probably start spontaneous activities to guarantee their purchasing power implying an explosion in recycling activities: clothes, furniture, spectacles, tools, bicycles etc. and an expanded exchange of services, the sharing of living space,[14] transportation.

Moreover, if people can move in and out of the labor market according to their needs it opens up the possibility of their engaging in really meaningful activities together with others on a lifetime basis. This used to be a positive part of collective workers' culture. Fragmentation, individualism, and the stress of modern jobs have undermined employed people's feeling of fellowship and community. Lots of people are presently frustrated because too little is done to solve the many problems of our society. Some would start organizing nationwide preventive health campaigns, others would start reorganizing public transportation in such a manner that private cars would become less indispensable. Some would organize work-teams to establish a list of priorities to save the environment, while voluntary groups would organize their implementation (one of the initial obstacles to ecological farming is the present price of labor power). Within the sphere of care and nursing (children, the sick, and elderly) one might foresee a reorganization to make these services more humane. Empirical evidence from existing movements seems to indicate that many people are so eager to start solving our most urgent environmental and social problems that they would be willing to work without extra pay if they and their loved ones were guaranteed lifetime basic material security.

In this contribution, the idea of a citizen wage has been elaborated as a first step to facilitate essential changes. Indeed, one of the obstacles to political struggle has been the lack of perception of how to move from "here" to "there." The concept is simple and, provided it is carried forth by a strong political mass movement, easy to implement. It is, moreover, an ideal platform for the creation of broad political alliances across the political spectrum: judging from debates in Denmark, hard core opponents so far are a minority of the people in power, including some labor union bosses, and those addicted to the control of their fellowmen. The most serious objection to such a reform is the fact that it may paint an altogether too rosy picture of what can be achieved under our present democratic system. Nevertheless, short of civil war, the necessary social change can only be achieved through strong alliances. As an idea, the citizen wage combines the realization of the liberal dream and the socialist vision!

The fact that a case can be made for a citizen wage in Denmark does not imply that one might not conceive of other ways and means to universally guaranteed basic material security, which must, I believe, be considered a precondition for sustainability. Inspired by the Swedish economist Gunnar Adler-Karlsson, I have described a new type of "mixed economy" where the market and the state are supplemented by a "necessity sector" preferably independent of the two others. Such a structure might be created from above through state intervention, or, as illustrated, through collective initiatives from below. Better still would be a combination of both. The presently existing world order makes the movement from below the more realistic. In this connection, the question of power is of course essential. For the time being, however, power is first of all relative and relational. Nevertheless, removing the coercive part of wage labor constitutes an attack on the core element of capitalist power. This will not go unchallenged.

Experience from the debates in Denmark reveals that raising these issues works as a catalyst for political awareness. At the moment, "Casino capitalism" has taken the nation-state hostage, limiting its room for political manoeuvre. This means that successful implementation of the citizen wage would probably require cooperation among peoples of several countries (for instance, those in the Nordic countries) or, even better, its simultaneous introduction across the whole of Europe (East and West)! Working in such a direction would undoubtedly enrich the concept by enlarging the basis of social experience.

As we know, a general articulation of a new vision is not really useful unless it suggests a framework which can guide political interventions. Such a framework has been suggested in the above. It will, in all events, be influenced by forthcoming changes brought about by the crisis of capitalism. In the coming period we may have to experience various degrees of environmental collapse combined with social disintegration, and perhaps conflict. The process is fraught with dangers, which may at any time create entirely new situations. Under such circumstances, what is feasible today may not be feasible tomorrow. *It is essential to start preparing for the transition to a different form of social organization.* For each passing day, the stakes are increased.

Taking the present crisis into consideration, I see the platform of struggles in Europe in the coming years being based on the need for a new social contract where the former struggle for full employment and equal rights in the formal sense is transcended and redefined in a liberating vision based on universally guaranteed subsistence. A "basic needs strategy" from below for industrial countries is a precondition for achieving the difficult transition to sustainability on a world scale.

APPENDIX: Outline of a utopian society based on guaranteed basic material security (translated and abridged by E. Brun from G. Adler-Karlsson 1977)

In the utopian society, here described, we find four large sectors: two economic ones, one political sector and one for all the rest. We could call them the Sector of Necessity, the Sector of Affluence, the Power Sector and the Freedom Sector . . .

The Necessity Sector should be public. It takes care of people's basic material needs. Its size is determined by the sum of those needs which the State has to cover, as well as by the amount of labor required at any given technical stage to produce the essential material goods. This necessary amount of labor should be equally distributed as the citizen's right and duty. In return, the citizen receives a purchasing card, which can neither be sold nor pawned, and which guarantees the individual basic material security on a lifetime basis.

For those individuals who desire a higher economic standard than the one implied by basic security, the Sector of Affluence exists. Here individuals should be able to freely buy and sell, invest and produce, save or waste, to the extent that nobody else is harmed by the activity. In this sector all sorts of enterprise-forms could exist, except the public one. The State should essentially stay outside of this sector which should be regulated through general laws. Within the Affluence Sector, private, cooperative, worker-owned, etc. enterprises should be able to compete freely.

For those who are not primarily interested in making money to achieve a higher living standard than the one provided by the basic needs' sector, there would be the third sector—the Freedom Sector for culture, sports, cohabitation or whatever else human beings like to spend their life doing. In this sector a need for extra income may arise because it may be costly to realize some of the dreams people have. Such money can be earned through temporary employment in the Sector of Affluence. But, provided it does no harm to others, the Freedom Sector should try to grant people the utmost degree of freedom from material anxiety in order to realize whatever dreams their imagination may conceive.

The fourth sector, the Power Sector, should look approximately as it does today. Through open and free elections the people should appoint the representatives who ultimately will have to decide those conflicts and contradictions which naturally arise in any social system. Besides, there would probably be a need for a special constitution, drawing the borderline between the three other sectors in such a manner that they remain stable and prevent, for instance, the Sector of Affluence expanding at the expense of those of Necessity and Freedom.

The Power Sector, moreover, should be the owner of the means of production in the Necessity Sector. But to maintain the balance of power, the people in political power should only under exceptional circumstances have leading positions in the public enterprises.

Through this combination the individuals would be guaranteed not only a good, albeit modest economic standard, but considerably more freedom than they have at present to live a many-sided and harmonious life in a less onesidedly materialistic society.

Bibliography

Adler-Karlsson, G. (1977) *Nej til fuld beskaeftelse—Ja til materiel grundtryghed*, Copenhagen: Erling Olsens Forlag.

Amin, S. (1994) "The Future of Global Polarization," working paper from Aalborg University.

Gesell, S. (1919) *Die natürlich Wirtschaftsordnung durch Freiland und Freigeld*, Arnstadt in Thürbingen: R. Gesell.

Lebowitz, M. A. (1992) *Beyond Capital. Marx's Political Economy of the Working Class*, Basingstoke: Macmillan.

Loegstrup, K. E. (1956) *Den etiske fordring*, Copenhagen: Scandanavian University Press and Gyldendal.

Mills, C. W. (1959) *The Power Elite*, New York: Oxford University Press.

Nord (1991) The Research Group for the New Everyday Life and Nordic Council of Ministers, Copenhagen, no. 19.

Polanyi, K. ([1944] 1957) *The Great Transformation*, Boston: Beacon Press.

Ross, R. J. S. and Trachte, K. C. (1990) *Global Capitalism—The New Leviathan*, State University of New York.

Ugebrevet Mandag Morgen (1992) no. 42, November 30.

White Paper from the European Commission (1993) "Competitivity, Growth and Employment," December, Brussels.

Notes

Introduction: globalization or the coming-of-age of capitalism

1 This concept is to be understood as the complex of institutions supporting the process of capital accumulation including industrial relations, work process, the role of money and banking, the role of the state, etc. (Kotz et al. 1994: Introduction).
2 This denotes the ideology, policy prescriptions and hegemony of the World Bank, the International Monetary Fund, and the US Treasury.
3 Although the IMF and the World Bank are engaged in some window-dressing created by spin doctors to establish another public image, the policies remain basically the same.
4 For a discussion of the role played by the CIA and the AFL-CIO (US labor union) in the neutralization of European labor unions, see Julien 1968: ch. 9.
5 See also Greider 1997: 45–53 for a compelling discussion about surplus production or what he terms the supply problem.
6 See various Human Development Indexes, *Human Development Report 1990–1999*, New York: Oxford University Press.
7 This was envisaged in the *Manifesto* by Marx and Engels more than a century ago.

3 Globalization and social change

1 This phrase was repeatedly used by a Wall Street analyst (Weinstock) who appeared with Sylvia Ostry and me on a panel in September 1993 to discuss the "economic issues underlying the up-coming Canadian election" with the journalists of the Canadian Broadcasting Corporation.
2 In a remarkable series of papers, Joseph Stiglitz (1998a, 1998b, 1999), writing as the World Bank's chief economist, has argued that these policies have often been misguided and destructive and has variously referred to the "Washington Consensus" as a "misguided," "dogmatic," and "fundamentalist" approach to policy-making.
3 See my article in Southall et al.
4 This is the term used by Deepak Lal to describe the new fundamentalist belief that the laws of economics apply universally across space and time, thereby rejecting the more pragmatic approach of "development economics," which had sought to modify its policy prescriptions for the developing world in ways that took account of its institutional, cultural and geopolitical specificities (Lal 1983).
5 Amazingly, in its 1988 report entitled *Structural Adjustment: Ten Years of Experience*, the World Bank actually referred disparagingly to its earlier policy advice as "text book policy," and welcomed the fact that it was learning to "go beyond" such naive and misguided advice, by taking more adequate account of the particular circumstances of low income countries like those in SSA.

6 This phrase was used by Ronald Reagan in a speech commending the IMF for its militant promotion of market oriented policies around the world.

7 After 15 years of intransigence—and only when the disastrous consequences of the demand for "full repayment" had become overwhelmingly evident.

8 This has to do both with the scale and the timing of outcomes. Neoliberal "adjustment" requires countries to take on new debts, new obligations, new risks. The hope is that these will enhance efficiency, investment, and growth on a sufficient scale to service those debts, fulfil those obligations and, manage those risks. And, as every businessman knows, if they fail to do so in time, they will fail; they will further deepen the economic, social, and political crisis.

9 This is precisely the way—i.e. via the accumulation of anomalies—in which Thomas Kuhn described the demise of any scientific paradigm, creating the need for an alternative paradigm to take its place (Kuhn [1962] 1970).

10 "The alternative paradigm of the social market became acceptable in light of the experience in several donor countries [i.e. the Nordic countries, Germany and Holland]" (Agarwala and Schwartz 1994).

11 The Bank's efforts to ensure "consistency" between its policy prescriptions and its "research results" have often led to unseemly conflicts as researchers have sought to protect their findings from dilution, or worse. See Robert Wade's article describing the horse-trading that preceded the Bank's "Miracle Report", and especially the Bank's efforts to suppress a report issued by its own Operations Evaluation Division because it disagreed with the Bank's standard policy prescriptions. A senior member of staff was quoted as saying that the Bank did not want to publish this report, because "people might think that it was changing its policies, if it were to do so. So much for the idea, that the policy should be based on the research results. It seems in this Alice in Wonderland world, the research results have to be brought into line with the policy (Wade 1994).

12 Given the latent tensions created by the period of repression and torture, the arrival of democracy occurred in a context where governments had to be seen to be addressing the welfare issue. And because Chile's administrative capacity was relatively well developed, and because its communities and its civil society organizations were relatively strong, it was able to achieve a lot, with a little. However, these conditions will be eroded over time, as neoliberalism undermines civil service capabilities through downsizing and fiscal cuts, and as the organizing capacity of communities and of civil society organizations is eroded by the cynicism and conflict that is engendered by these divisive, inequitable policies. Moreover, the government's commitment to dealing with the welfare issue does also have to be balanced against pressures emanating from other sources, and especially from the financial markets, both national and international. And, over time, their demands for cost reduction and for fiscal restraint will tend to become dominant, especially in the periods of crisis that are an inevitable feature of the unstable world associated with deregulated global finance.

13 It is important to remember that Chile's first attempt at economic liberalization ended in disaster in the early 1980s. And that experience meant that the "second attempt" was much more cautious, especially as regards financial liberalization.

14 ILO press release: "Despite decade-long reforms, social progress risks stalling in Latin America, Caribbean, warns new ILO report," simultaneously released in Lima (Peru) and Geneva (Switzerland), ILO/99/26, August 23.

15 Caio Koch-Weser, managing operations director at the Bank as cited in R. Colitt "Latin American reforms 'fail to cut income disparities,'" *Financial Times*, November 13, 1997: 7.

16 John Gray "Not for the First Time, World Sours on Free Markets," *The Nation*, October 19, 1998: 17–18. This article summarizes the argument developed in his book *False Dawn: The Delusions of Global Capitalism*, Granta Books: London, 1998.

8 Globalization and class politics in South Korea

1 The concept of globalization itself is a contested concept. While some argue that national boundaries are dissolving and the states are weakened due to the process of economic globalization (Ohmae 1990, 1993), others insist that globalization is extremely exaggerated by wishful thinkers and the world economy is not yet really global (Hirst and Thompson 1996). Others see globalization as a reality revealing the intensification of the international division of labor and economic interconnectedness beyond the scope of the nation-state (see Axford 1995; Kofman and Youngs 1996; Mittelman 1997). Ideologically neoliberalists appraise the dominance of liberalism as a core principle of globalization. But some Marxists like Cox (1987) also foresee the possible development of new international solidarity that will provide the basis for a global resistance to neoliberal globalization.

2 In 1972, President Park Jung He (1963–79) declared the Yushin constitution which literally meant the restoration of old virtues. In reality, it was a declaration of martial law.

3 The United States suffered from the "twin deficits," the trade deficit and budget deficit. These contributed to the revival of the conservative political forces in the late 1970s and 1980s.

4 Japan forcefully opened the Korean harbors with the help of gun boats in 1878, as the United States had done to Japan in 1854.

5 The labor law does not permit unions to participate in politics and only allows one single all-encompassing confederation controlled by the state.

6 In 1990 the Ministry of Labor suggested a reduction in the number of national holidays and, in 1991, an extension of standard working hours from 44 to 46 a week.

7 KDI, *Major Indicators in Economic Trends*, May 1995 (in Korean).

8 The minister of labor declared that the revision of the labor law had not succeeded in October 1994 and that he would prepare a draft of the revised labor bill in late 1995.

9 National competitiveness is a controversial term because it can only be proved in the market. Thus national competitiveness is a contradictory term because nations do not compete in the market. They only fight in wars. See Krugman 1994 and Burton 1994 for the debates on this issue.

10 The Korean state ratified only four ILO conventions—the smallest number of ratifications among the East Asian and Pacific countries (World Bank 1995: 150). The ILO has demanded the revision of the authoritarian labor law three times since 1991. The Human Rights Code Committee of the United Nations also recommended the revision of the labor law. The TUAC of the OECD insisted in 1995 on the revision of the labor law as a necessary condition for membership of the OECD.

11 Before its establishment, the reform-oriented presidential advisor negotiated the possibility for the abolition of the oppressive labor codes, which was the demand of labor, and the introduction of new labor codes permitting flexible manpower management, which was the demand of capital, simultaneously.

12 The version of the Confederation of Employers insisted on the maintenance of prohibition of plural unionism and unions' political activity, free replacement of the workers on strike by new workers, abolition of discharge payment, etc. The representatives from the Confederation of Employers argued that in order to improve competitiveness, the revised labor law should restrict union activity as before and enhance the discretion of managers with respect to employment.

13 The working hours per week were reduced from 46 hours to 44 hours in 1987. The costs of the Korean capitalists increased because they had to pay the overtime work. The average working hours per week is still around 50 hours. This is the longest working time among OECD members.

14 Upon discharge, the worker received a retirement payment proportional to the length of one's employment.

15 Disputes among ministers were conspicuous according to pending issues. For example, the Minister of Finance and Economy did not accept the demand of the revision of the plural unionism that was suggested by the Labor Minister. The Minister of Education did not support the legalization of the teachers' union, while the Labor Minister accepted it.

16 The flexible working hours system permits employers to reduce working hours during the slack season and to increase working hours during the peak season. In reality, employers can save the overtime payments when they utilize this code. In contrast, it means that a worker's wage decreases.

17 In 1993 the national security law was revised to abolish the code which was used to oppress political opponents. The old law allowed the state to prosecute those who did not report North Korean spies when they recognized them. However, the code was frequently used to prosecute political dissidents by the security agency.

18 In order to get support from the people, the striking automobile workers opened up 27 car check-up points throughout the country to provide free service.

19 According to a nationwide opinion poll, 75.0 percent of the respondents supported the general strike and 84.6 percent agreed to the demand for the revision of the new labor law (*Hangyerae* 21, January 30, 1997: 26).

20 Announcing full support for the general strike in Korea, the international secretary of the CFDT in France and TUC in Britain, for example, criticized the revised labor law in Korea as a brutal and primitive way to enhance flexibility of production (*Hangyerae* 21, February 6, 1997: 71–2).

21 The general secretary of the OECD officially announced that the revised labor law in South Korea did not fully meet the international standard of workers' rights (*Hangyerae*, January 23, 1997).

22 The People's Congress for New Politics, the largest opposition party established in 1987, was led by the opposition leader, Kim Dae Joong, whereas the Democratic Republican Party, the second largest opposition formation established in 1992, was led by the conservative political leader, Kim Jong Pil, who was a key member of the military junta and served as the prime minister during the military dictatorship.

23 Until 1995, the Korean government had ratified only five codes out of the 170 codes provided by the ILO.

24 The term "neoliberalism" may be a misnomer in the sense that it only refers to the full freedom of capital from state regulations rather than the freedom of labor from capital or of the state in the case of the authoritarian state.

9 Globalization, democratization, and labor social welfare in Thailand

1 Parts of this chapter were previously published as Briefing paper BP 99/02 by the European Institute for Asian Studies, Brussels, 1999.

2 The classic example being Nike, the American sports shoe supplier, which uses about 40 factories; 20 have closed in the past five years (1992) or so and another 35 have opened. The basic reason why Nike has made substantial investment in Indonesia is because of the extremely repressive labor regime. For details, see William Seaman, "The Current Crisis in Indonesia. Interview with Benedict Anderson," *ZMagazine* December 1996.

3 Note that 12 countries are included in the sample (Kowalewski 1989: 73).

4 This and the following are cited in Chomsky 1991: 238–9, 250. See also Gray 1990a and 1990b.

5 For this and parts of the following, see Lambert and Caspersz 1995: 572 and 580 and 583.

6 See, for instance, two studies of my own: Schmidt 1993a: 98–144, 1993b: 71–111.
7 This statement is a matter of great dispute whereas a new body of literature in a neo-institutionalist perspective points to concepts as *liberal corporatism* and *inclusionary institutionalism* to illuminate a growing influence of business coalitions and associations challenging the autonomy of the state. For the most prominent, see Doner 1991; Dhiravegin 1992; and Laothamas 1992a, 1992b. See also Pongchaipit in MacIntyre and Jayasuryia (eds) 1992. And from a statist point of view, see Wade 1990, 1996. For an example of an integrated synthesis, see Cotton 1991, and for a critique of the neo-institutionalist perspective in the Thai context, see Schmidt 1996.
8 For a parallel discussion in the Latin American context, see Nun 1968: 145–85.
9 See also the discussion in Schmidt 1993a: 98–144.
10 Quoted from the excellent discussion about the artificial creation of a myth (the middle class as the defender of democracy) in Callahan 1994: 366.
11 This and the following is based on Richardson, *International Herald Tribune*, September 16, 1997.
12 Ibid.
13 For the following information about Thai labor unions and the Social Security Bill, see Sivaraman, *Asia Times*, May 1, 1997.
14 Ibid.

10 States and governance in the era of "globalization"

1 By weakening of the nation-state, I refer to the erosion of the institutions associated with citizenship and social rights, including full employment policies. This does not mean the state itself is weakened, rather it is transformed, and becomes, in my judgement, increasingly a "global state."
2 Drainville (1995: 60) argues that the globalization project depends directly on the strengthening of the national ties of citizenship in order to pre-empt a global (and potentially politicized) citizenry and thereby sustain global capital accumulation. I would emphasize that this necessitates an emptying of the socio-historical content of the term, and elevating (reifying) its liberal premise of the juridical individual.

11 Civilizational conflicts and globalization: a critique

1 Albert L. Weeks reminds us of this dichotomy in his comment on Samuel Huntington's thesis. See "Do Civilizations Hold?" in *Foreign Affairs*, September/October 1993.

12 From the rubble of modernism, the rise of global civilization?

1 Huntington's essay was originally published in *Foreign Affairs*, Summer 1993, 72 (3): 2–11, and reconsidered in Huntington 1993, 72 (3), November/December. An expanded, revised, and much more moderate thesis is presented in the book-length version (Huntington 1996: 186–94).
2 Although the Enlightenment firmly established the idea of the secular basis for government, challenges to the divine right to rule in Europe reach back at least to the twelfth century, when John of Salisbury held that rulers could be overthrown—violently if necessary—if they violated public trust, and in the fourteenth century when William of Ockham argued that "secular rulers need not submit to spiritual power" (quoted in Molnar 1985: 43; see also Packard 1973: 201).
3 Quoted in H. C. G. Matthew, *Gladstone, 1809–1874*, vol. 1 (Oxford: Clarendon Press, 1986), p. 188. Conservatives such as Disraeli, however, felt that the British should "respect and maintain" the traditional practices of the colonies, including "the laws and customs, the property and religion" (from Disraeli's speech delivered after the

Sepoy Rebellion in India in 1857, quoted in William Monypenny and George Buckle, *The Life of Disraeli*, vol. 1, *1804–1859*, London: John Murton, 1929, pp. 1488–9).
4 The book is based on the author's widely discussed essay published in 1993 in *The Atlantic*.
5 The terms "Westomania" and "West-toxification" are translations of the Farsi word, *gharbzadegi*, coined by Jalal Al-e Ahmad. It is discussed in Hillmann 1974.
6 For the distinction between post-modernity as a social phenomenon and as a mode of analysis, see Lyon 1994.
7 Immanuel Wallerstein's classic statement on the role of nation-states in world politics has been updated in his *Geopolitics and Geoculture: Essays on the Changing World-System* (1991).

13 Overturning globalization: rethinking the politics of resistance

1 I am indebted to Susan George for this analogy, made at a Fellow's meeting of the Transnational Institute, Amsterdam.
2 For a fuller elaboration of this argument on the relation between neoliberal globalization and democracy see Gills et al. 1993; Gills 1996.
3 For example, Ruigrok and Tulder 1995 empirically test claims for the "global firm;" Paul Hirst and Graham Thompson investigate the distinction between multinational and transnational corporations in Hirst and Thompson 1996; and R. J. Barry Jones examines the claims of globalization versus those of interdependence in Jones 1995. Initial counter-attacks against globalization can be found in Mittleman 1996 and Boyer and Drache 1996.
4 http://csf.colorado.edu/wsystems/jwsr.html Special Issue on "Global Labor Movements" edited by B. Nash. See also the special issue of *Monthly Review* (July–August 1997) and that of *Work and Occupations* (August 1997) on globalized labour solidarity; the World Labour Group's special issue of *Review*, vol. 18, no. 1 (1995); and the Special Section on International Labour Standards of *New Political Economy*, vol. 1, no. 2 (1996).
5 For examples of the new triumphalism, see Special Issue "The Globalization Debate," *Foreign Policy* Summer, 1997.
6 Following Drainville, Morten criticizes neo-Gramscians, including W. I. Robinson *Promoting Polyarchy: Globalization, US Intervention and Hegemony*, Cambridge CUP, for over-emphasis on "concepts of control" and failing to concentrate on "concrete strategies of resistance."

14 Lessons from Ladakh? Local responses to globalization and social change

1 This chapter is based on research and development work in Ladakh since 1985. Research in 1994–5 was funded through a Peace Scholar Award from the United States Institute of Peace, with supplemental support from the Peace Studies Program, International Political Economy Program, and South Asia Program at Cornell University. Research would have been impossible without the generous help of many people in Ladakh, including Abdul Ghani Sheikh, Tsewang Rigzin Kalon, Rigzin Jora, Thupstan Chhewang, Tsering Samphel, P. Namgyal, the late Mohd. Akbar Ladakhi, and many others. I thank Kristoffer Brix Bertelsen and Michael Khoo for valuable comments on an earlier draft. Responsibility for opinions expressed in this chapter rests with the author.
2 Ladakh, with a population of about 175,000, comprises an area of approximately 60,000 km^2 in India's northernmost state, Jammu and Kashmir. (The official size is 97,782 km^2, but this includes large areas claimed by India now effectively under

Chinese or Pakistani administration.) Its extremely sparse population reflects the environmental characteristics of the area: a desert of high mountains and deep valleys, with human settlements largely restricted to the valleys of the region's main rivers: Shyok/Nubra, Zangskar, and Indus. Historically, the mainstay of local livelihoods has been subsistence agriculture complemented with animal husbandry (mostly goats, sheep, cows, dzomo and yak), supplemented by intraregional trade (wool, meat, and salt for grain) and international transit trade (wool, carpets, tobacco, spices, etc.) with Tibet, Yarkand, Kashmir, and the Indian plains.

3 A similar problematic is discussed by Baviskar (1995) in her study of resistance against the displacement of populations by the construction of dams in the Narmada valley in Central India.

4 This problem is also common in other studies of resistance, such as some subaltern studies, where the subaltern is constructed against the dominant, but within the same frame of dominant/subaltern: the subaltern, in other words, comes into existence as an agent through conceptualization and objectification. See also O'Hanlon (1992) and Spivak (1988), and the rejoinder by Prakash (1992). A useful summary of the debates surrounding "subaltern studies" can be found in Gregory (1994). A more general critique of resistance studies from a Marxian perspective is offered by Brass (1991).

5 Gardner and Lewis (1996) attribute the term "post-development" to Arturo Escobar (1992, 1995). For a related set of ideas and concepts, see Peet and Watts (1996a). The introductory article by Peet and Watts in this collection (1996b) offers a good discussion of the convergence of theoretical and activist trends that I refer to.

6 For a more detailed discussion of this problem and "identity fetishism" in general, see Beek (1996).

7 See also Paul Ekins (1992).

8 The final goal is often called "radical democracy" (e.g. Escobar 1992, 1995a, 1995b). One of the classical formulations of the project is Laclau and Mouffe (1985).

9 The question of sustainability will not be addressed in this chapter. With reference to Ladakh, Bertelsen (1997) offers a detailed discussion.

10 See, for example, Sahlins (1972), the *locus classicus* of the concept.

11 I will not address the question of mobilization and representation here with regard to who actually participated in this movement, how popular it was. For that issue, see van Beek and Bertelsen (1997).

12 Rather than as a factual account of Ladakh's past, present and future, the book is best read as a kind of parable. This also reflects better the development in Norberg-Hodge's own writing. In 1981, she was still primarily concerned to stop development in Ladakh, warning about what *might* go wrong. By the late 1980s, she had shifted toward using Ladakh as an example of what *did* go wrong and had focused her attention on more global processes and audiences. *Ancient Futures* reflects this past–present dichotomization which is less prominent in her earlier writings. In the process of this shift, Norberg-Hodge's Ladakh has become more abstracted, floating free from time and space, to the point where it has become a Utopia in terms of both past and present. In part, this shift may also be attributed to the objectification of certain events in Norberg-Hodge's experiences in Ladakh which she sees as paradigmatic and re-cycles in an iconic manner to make her points about globalization, community, and tradition. A fuller analysis of the development of Norberg-Hodge's writing is beyond the scope of this chapter.

13 The quote is from a brochure published by the International Society for Ecology and Culture (ISEC), the organization founded by Norberg-Hodge as a global supplement to The Ladakh Project. Originally published in Danish and Swedish in 1988, *Ancient Futures* was not available in Ladakhi until 1995.

14 For one general discussion of the Shangri-La imagery in Western travel writing about the Himalayas, see Bishop 1989. See also the new collection *Mythos Tibet* edited by

Dodin and Räther (1997). For an early idyllic image of Ladakh, see, for example, Gompertz (1928). An important difference between Hilton's novel and Norberg-Hodge's account is that, of course, the latter claims authenticity and facticity. Positioning herself in the deep ecology movement inspired by Arne Naess and contemporary (Euro-American) Buddhism, Norberg-Hodge rejects science and technology, and makes her *experience* the measure of authenticity. Her representation of Ladakh also gets support from psychologists such as Crook (e.g. 1980, 1991) and Gielen (e.g. 1995), novelists such as Harvey (1983), and numerous journalists and travel writers, and is replicated on many sites of the worldwide web.

15 A short excerpt from one of the chapters is included in *The Post-Development Reader* (Rahnema 1997), but very prominently: it is the second paper in the first section entitled "The vernacular world." The book is recommended as supplementary reading by McMichael (1996a). I cite these examples to illustrate the attractiveness of the text and its wide influence. Both books are among the very best recent works on development.

16 Rahnema (1997: xiii) calls *Ancient Futures* "unbiased testimony." This assumption and attribution of authenticity of the account is, of course, another important factor in its success. Regarding the film, the *Times Education Supplement* wrote: "Narrated with deceptive simplicity, the clear, bright images of the Ladakhi people linger in the mind" (quoted in advertising brochure for the video).

17 A Ladakhi account that concurs with much of the romantic vision of traditional society is Radhu (1981).

18 Some of the strongest advocates of Ladakhi interests shared this bleak assessment of Ladakhi lives. Sapru wrote: "The pigtails, the chortens, the maniwalls, the monasteries, the lamas, the dances, and the altitudes that are the lure of the land all conspire to produce the misery in which the people live, the misery from which it does not even occur to them that they may get out." (Sapru 1941: 1). His contemporary Shridhar Kaul's (KRBMS 1935) report referred to the Ladakhis as "dumb-driven cattle," while Ganhar and Ganhar (1956: 190) refer to Ladakhis on the eve of Independence as "one of the most backward people, steeped in ignorance, superstition, squalor and poverty." These reports of poverty are also supported by the accounts of e.g. Moorcroft (1837), Cunningham (1973), and many others. Chohan (1984: 213), extensively citing archival sources from the nineteenth and early twentieth century, concludes that "Ladakh was definitely grubby, backward, ignorant, poor and superstitious." See also van Beek (1996) for more detail.

19 As acknowledged by several of them, this was a source of some frustration for the agitation leaders who wished to mobilize the population in the late 1980s. Since they argued that the Kashmir government was discriminating against Ladakh, "people needed to be educated" that this was indeed the case, as one leader put it. Teams of "workers" toured villages in 1988–9, preceding the agitation, to ensure that people were aware of their miserable plight at the hands of the Kashmir government.

20 The demand for greater Ladakhi participation in planning and decision-making regarding development activities is justified locally by emphasizing Ladakh's "unique conditions," which outsiders could not possibly understand. Of course, this uniqueness in this claim is in part a product of the very process of marginalization and classification as backward and quaint which the claim is a response to.

21 For examples of these political assessments, see e.g. Bakula's writings in the 1950s and 1960s (Bakula 1955, 1958). These celebrations (or criticisms) of development accomplishments are still common. Recently, for example, Khanpo Rinpoche of Thikse monastery threatened to launch another agitation, among other reasons citing the continued "indifference" of the Kashmir government to Ladakh's developmental needs. In general, it is considered a fact of political life that in order to secure villagers' votes, one goes around and lists ones achievements in terms of roads, schools, irrigation

canals, electricity, or whatever other development "goods" one has managed to secure for the village/constituency concerned. The tactics of the opposing candidates, of course, is to promise to do even better. "Culture" or "identity" plays little part in campaign rhetorics.

22 The annual *District Statistical Handbook* of 1992–3 has a table of "indicators of development" which include the following: cultivators as percentage of workforce (58.48%); workers engaged in manufacturing and processing (2.35%); road length per 100 sq. km; workers in registered factories (0); rural drinking water facilities, etc. Of course, the "indicators" were devised for India proper, as illustrated by the use of irrigation as a measure of development. Ladakh has one of the highest scores on this indicator, but that is hardly surprising in an area where without irrigation nothing will grow.

23 Jammu and Kashmir, due to the historical circumstances of its accession to India in 1947, is the only Indian state with a separate constitution and continues to enjoy a special status within the Indian federation. There is a vast literature on the Kashmir issue. Two competent historical studies are Lamb (1993) and Mehra (1992).

24 Cooperatives in Leh district include the following: wholesale stores; primary consumer stores; cooperative marketing society; cooperative employees' credit society; industrial cooperative society; transport cooperative society; meat dealer cooperative society; labor cooperative society; primary agricultural credit cooperative society; dairy cooperative society; handicraft society. See Bhasin (1992) and INTACH (1988).

25 These quantities refer only to the commodities imported through the Food and Supplies department, not those imported by private traders and co-ops. This department, through the Public Distribution System, makes these commodities available at heavily subsidized rates. The cost of transport is subsidized to the extent that rice in Leh costs about the same as it does in the plains where it is grown, more than 1,000 kilometres and four or five days' drive away. I have no reliable figures on private and cooperative imports.

26 The Ladakh Hill Council, which was sworn in *after* the snows closed the roads to Srinagar in September 1995, was blamed for the lack of adequate supplies during the following winter. Ironically, not only did the problem originate before they took office, but import of essential commodities is one of the areas that do *not* fall within their competence. Still, popular resentment against the former heroes of the agitation rose very rapidly.

27 The quote is from a report of a seminar on education held in Leh in April 1990.

28 This is not to say that leadership could not be found elsewhere, but it is what happens in practice.

29 LBA, Resolution dated July 19, 1989.

30 It is worth noting that the leadership of the agitation included the President of the Ladakh Ecological Development Group, Thupstan Chhewang. The director, Sonam Dawa also played a central role, albeit from backstage. Some of the younger staff were active in the earlier stages as vigilantes of the Youth Wing of the LBA.

31 This is based on the "Record note of the discussion between the Cabinet Committee and the Ladakh Action Committee held on 12th, 14th and 15th January 1981 at Leh" written by S. S. Blowria and D. C. Leh.

32 Union Territory would mean that the area would be administered directly from New Delhi. In the course of negotiations, Ladakh's political leadership, Buddhists, Muslims and Christians, agreed on a scaled-down, but shared demand for an autonomous Hill Development Council within the framework of Jammu and Kashmir. This has been in place in Leh District since 1995. On October 4, 1997, the Kashmir Assembly passed a bill consistent with the Presidential Act of 1995 that had created the Council, but Jammu and Kashmir Chief Minister Farooq Abdullah stated that the Council is only temporary while a statewide regional autonomy solution is being formulated.

There have been considerable tensions between the Leh Council and Farooq Abdullah's government, in part also because the Leh Council is dominated by members of the Congress (I) which is in opposition to Abdullah's National Conference.

33 At least until the summer of 1996, the map on the wall behind the desk of the President of the LBA bore the title "Union Territory of Ladakh," comprising the tehsils of Leh and Kargil, as well as the areas occupied by China or Pakistan and claimed by India.

34 This is based on an anonymous "Annexure," dated September 27, 1992, which was produced for the negotiations with the Government. This 18-page document has three columns with headings: "Demand of Leh," "Pattern of Darjeeling Council," and "Views of the State Government."

35 See the full text of the Ladakh Autonomous Hill Development Councils Act 1995, published in *The Gazette of India*, May 9, 1995.

36 Among the Council's policies that clearly differ is a new educational policy broadly reflecting the priorities and critique of SECMOL. This includes greater emphasis on Ladakhi language, culture and ways of living. Another important innovation introduced by the Council is that new land allocations are made in the name of both husband and wife, rather in that of the male alone. This reflects the more immediate influence of women in the policy- and decision-making process.

37 Perhaps ironically, they turned to the British in India for support. On the eve of India's independence and Kashmir's accession Ladakhi political leaders Kushok Bakula and Tsewang Rigzin Kalon appealed to the universal right to self-determination to justify Ladakh's independent right to choose not to accede to Pakistan, whatever the outcome of the Kashmir dispute.

15 Conceptualizing a new social contract

1 Power, according to C. Wright Mills, is the ability to realize one's will although others resist (*The Power Elite*, 1956: 9). Power, however, is not only the visible interaction between actors, but also the ability of some actors to prevent certain issues from becoming part of the political agenda, or even arising. An example is the crisis of the welfare state, where neither the role of the financial sectors nor the possibility for the State to engage in income-generating activities enters into the discussion. According to Gramsci's idea of ideological hegemony, if capitalist ideas are sufficiently dominant in a given political culture, even challenging forces will formulate their interests within the confines of concepts that assume the continuity and natural right of current arrangements (Ross and Trachte 1990: 9). Thus, challenging the dominant discourse may be the first step to change the relations of power. For Marx, power under capitalism is essentially capital itself, defined by him as a social relation based on the control of other's labor power. Capital accumulation is thus an accumulation of power! In the French edition of *Capital* (corrected by Marx personally) he defines capital accumulation as a never-ending process of expropriation of people's means of subsistence. This concept is more comprehensive and stimulating in its implications than his original formulation (expropriation of means of production). In such a perspective, capitalist power rests on the ongoing expropriation of people's means of reproducing themselves culturally, materially, socially.

2 Cf. White Paper from the European Commission: "Competitivity, Growth and Employment," Bruxelles December 1993. Since then, the depletion accelerated as an effect of the crisis.

3 Gunnar Adler-Karlsson (1977). Originally written at the request of the Swedish Institute of Future Research, it draws for inspiration on historical Dutch and German "models." In the 1970s the Danish Social Democratic party organized study groups on it. Adler-Karlsson's argumentation has inspired important aspects of my own work. It also inspired Andre Gorz (see Appendix).

4 Earlier this century, the economist Silvio Gesell (1919) in his work developed such a system. His ideas influenced Keynes and other later economists. A simple description of the system is found in Margrit Kennedy "Inflation- and Interest-free Money," *Salt* 3 (May 1995) carried a translation of Silvio Gesell's main argument. It would be appropriate if experts from the financial sector form groups to study the possibility of implementing a better financial system. Reforming the national financial system could be a first step toward an overhaul of international finance.

5 Denmark is part of the European Union. At present most member countries have chosen to cut social security and health services in their effort to curb budget deficits and meet the criteria of the European Monetary Union (EMU). The result has been social polarization and conflict (cf. *The European* November 16–22, 1995). Nationalization and social control of the entire European financial sector could have made the EMU less socially costly and easier to implement. But this would have been counter to the Union's unwritten political agenda.

6 The concept of solidarity needs elaboration. The word is derived from the Latin *in solidum* meaning joint responsibility. In common parlance it means "making common cause with." In the labor movement the concept is political implying a mutual relationship between people with the same interests. It is symmetrical: "Today I am in trouble. If you don't help me now, what do you expect will happen tomorrow, when you are in need of support?" "Together we are strong."

Defining solidarity as a universal, abstract political concept based on community of interest and symmetrical relationships makes it negotiable, subject to rational, utilitarian considerations. This turns the concept into a caricature, a disguise for particular interests opposed to real solidarity.

For women, solidarity is by definition asymmetrical: it is a sovereign life expression deeply rooted in human being—an existential imperative. To leave helpless people, sick or exposed individuals or groups to their destiny without care or efforts to help is contrary to the idea of being human. Asymmetrical relations are basic to human survival: children would not survive without it. It is non-negotiable! In my text the word is used in the latter meaning.

7 An important exception is the Nordic Network of women researchers: *The New Everyday Life—Ways and Means* (Nord 1991: 19).

8 This asserts the fact that real "economics" cannot be understood exclusively in terms of market-economic rationality. After all the transition to industrial capitalism implied the violent expropriation of people's means of (material, social and cultural) reproduction. As economic anthropology has shown, market-based exchange is only one of three historical forms of economic transaction. The other two: "reciprocity" and "redistribution" always played a major role. Of the three, market exchange was historically marginal. What made the transition to the market society possible was the violent commodification of land, labor, and money (Polanyi [1944] 1957).

In fact, today, within family or close social relations, the concept of "free and equal exchange" hardly operates. Here the stronger members contribute according to ability and the children receive according to needs. Otherwise the human species would hardly have survived.

9 LETS (Local Exchange Trading System) is a local exchange network, which originated in Canada. It is widespread in England and Denmark.

10 The Danish debate on citizen wage was launched in the 1970s by the movement "Revolt from the Center." It caught the imagination of many. At that time the concept was insufficiently defined and the fathers of the movement saw full employment as a precondition for its practical implementation. Later the Greens took it over as part of their programme. In the 1990s, the debate spread to most Danish newspapers and political parties. Among the rank and file the interest is keen across the entire political spectrum. The political establishment is rather hesitant or directly opposed to the idea. Several political parties have established committees to study the

idea, and a few of them are officially in favor of it. The youth movement of several liberal and Christian parties favor the citizen wage proposal.

11 Denmark introduced so-called "green" taxes in contempt of social considerations. As a result the enterprises and the rich continue their wasteful practices, while people on welfare or the elderly have to apply for additional support whenever the weather gets cold. The principle of solidarity would have implied a low fee for fixed installations and minimum consumption (of water, electricity, heating) and high taxes on excess consumption: punish wastefulness and reward responsibility. As everybody pays according to consumption, this would have involved no practical problem. As it is, "green" taxes have become yet another disguise for balancing the state budget by undermining social security.

12 The latter type of tax already exists and is widespread in the rest of Europe. This means that it could easily be adapted to the new situation.

13 In European agricultural policy, this way of thinking has been advanced as a method of preserving rural communities at a time of crisis. It is implemented in various forms in the new agricultural policy to prevent the sector's inherent tendency to over-produce.

14 Close to half the adult population in Denmark live alone. Many have excess space. At the same time, there is a shortage in apartments or houses. Indirectly the citizen wage might serve to relieve the housing question. Ultimately, a financial reform is called for.

Index